The Wolf by the Ears

Thomas Jefferson by Rembrandt Peale. (White House Historical Association.)

The Wolf by the Ears

Thomas Jefferson and Slavery

❧

John Chester Miller

THE FREE PRESS
A Division of Macmillan Publishing Co., Inc.
New York

Collier Macmillan Publishers
London

The substance of this book was delivered in the form of public lectures at the Virginia Military Institute under the auspices of the Mary Mood Northen Chair in the Arts and Social Sciences.

The Free Press
A Division of Macmillan Publishing Co., Inc.
866 Third Avenue, New York, N.Y. 10022

Collier Macmillan Canada, Ltd.

Library of Congress Catalog Card Number: 76-51590

Printed in the United States of America

printing number

1 2 3 4 5 6 7 8 9 10

Library of Congress Cataloging in Publication Data

Miller, John Chester
   The wolf by the ears.

   Includes bibliographical references and index.
   1. Jefferson, Thomas, Pres. U. S., 1743-1826--
Views on Slavery. 2. Jefferson, Thomas, Pres.
U. S., 1743-1826--Relations with Afro-Americans.
3. Presidents--United States--Biography.
4. Slavery in the United States. I. Title.
E332.2.M54   301.44'93'0924   76-51590
ISBN 0-02-921500-5

We are grateful to the following institutions and libraries for permission to reprint the photographs in this book:
White House Historical Association: *Thomas Jefferson* by Rembrandt Peale
Virginia Historical Society: *Edmund Pendleton* by Thomas Sully
Virginia State Library: *George Wythe* by J. B. Longacre
Library of Congress: Title page of Jefferson's pamphlet, *A Summary View* (1774), and Paragraph concerning slavery in Jefferson's "original rough draft" of the Declaration of Independence
Maryland Historical Society: *Benjamin Banneker*, woodcut from his almanac (1795)
Rare Book Collection of the University of North Carolina Library: *Phillis Wheatley*, frontispiece from her *Poems* (1773)
Tracy W. McGregor Library, University of Virginia: *Isaac Jefferson*, a Monticello slave
Henry E. Huntington Library and Art Gallery: *Maria Cosway*, miniature painted on ivory
Collection of Washington and Lee University, Virginia: *John Marshall* by Chester Harding
Massachusetts Historical Society: Design for Remodeling Monticello, drawn by Robert Mills in 1803
Musée de la Nation Haitienne: *Toussaint Louverture*

To the memory of my late friend Pieter Geyl, the eminent Dutch historian, who said that history is an endless debate, and who delighted in "Debates with Historians" as the spice of historical writing.

"*We have the wolf by the ears; and we can neither hold him, nor safely let him go. Justice is in one scale, and self-preservation in the other.*"

Thomas Jefferson, 1820

Contents

—◆—

Preface

INEVITABLY, A BOOK DEALING with Thomas Jefferson and slavery must address itself to certain questions which do not admit of an easy, simple, or final answer. In view of Jefferson's abhorrence of slavery, which he called a "blot" and a "stain" upon America, why did he remain a slave-owner all his life and fail to direct that his slaves be freed after his death? Why did Jefferson not play a more forceful role in the antislavery movement inspired by the Enlightenment and the American Revolution? To what extent was the Declaration of Independence intended to serve as a charter of freedom to the slaves? What induced him to couple the emancipation of the slaves (a development which, he said, he wished above all else) with the removal of the black population from the United States "beyond the reach of mixture"? Why did he insist upon measuring the intelligence of illiterate, hopelessly disadvantaged black slaves by criteria applicable to free white Americans? Why, in 1819–1821, during the Missouri controversy, did Jefferson advocate the diffusion of slavery over the entire national domain under the guise of a positive good for both the slaves and for white Americans?

With the publication in 1974 of Fawn Brodie's *Thomas Jefferson: An Intimate History,* a further question has been imposed upon his biographer: did Jefferson, in defiance of his professed principles and precepts, make the mulatto slave girl Sally Hemings his paramour, and did she conceive by him children who were reared at Monticello as slaves under the promise that they would be freed when they reached adulthood? Jefferson himself denied this sensational allegation, and the "Sally Hemings story" had, in fact, long been dismissed as a mere political canard until it was revived, refurbished, and given the gloss of verisimilitude by Ms. Brodie.

To answer these and other questions raised by Jefferson's career, it has been necessary to explore the workings of his mind and the cast of his character, insofar as that is possible at the distance of almost two hundred years, and to examine critically his political philosophy; for Jefferson was

a scientist and a philosopher as well as a politician and a man of action—
a combination of diverse talents supported by a fund of knowledge that
has rarely graced the presidency of the United States. In this general
scrutiny, Jefferson's personality could not be left out of account. For
example, his confidence in a benign futurity—which sustained his conviction that slavery, along with other social evils, would ultimately yield
to the combined power of right reason and a divinely implanted moral
sense—colored his views of all the great events of his lifetime. Yet
Jefferson was also given to brief moments of pessimism in which the
darker side of human nature—especially greed and avarice, which at an
early age he singled out as the great enemies of his particular version of
the American Dream—seemed to him to be gaining ascendancy. His
countrymen, he feared, might delay the work of emancipation until the
slaves, despairing of attaining freedom by waiting for the philanthropic
impulses of their masters to overcome the baser side of human nature,
would strike incontinently for freedom. Jefferson's single most significant
contribution as an opponent of slavery was the repeated warning to his
countrymen of the catastrophic consequences certain to follow upon a
failure to put slavery in the course of extinguishment.

This analysis of Jefferson's antislavery views and the actions to which
they gave rise, the subject matter of *The Wolf by the Ears,* is necessarily
episodic; while chronology has been generally observed, it was not possible to weld this disparate material into the form of a biographical narrative. Deliberately, I have dealt only with such aspects of Jefferson's
personality, conduct, and ideas which impinge upon the subject of slavery;
I have reserved for a later book a more comprehensive and well-rounded
portrait of Jefferson and a more definitive assessment of his contributions
to American democracy. The present volume is presented as an addendum
to the endless debate which revolves around the paradox that the author
of the Declaration of Independence was one of the largest slaveholders
of his time.

The Wolf by the Ears

～ 1 ～
Slavery and the
Declaration of Independence

THOMAS JEFFERSON WAS INTIMATELY associated with slavery from the cradle to the grave. His first memory was of being carried on a pillow by a slave; and a slave carpenter made the coffin in which he was buried at Monticello. The labor of black slaves made possible Jefferson's cultivation of the arts; the building of Monticello and the Virginia State Capitol, his principal architectural monuments; the acquisition of the books which made his library one of the largest private libraries in the United States (and which eventually formed the nucleus of the Library of Congress); the accumulation of choice wines and the fine food prepared by a French chef, both of which made dinner at the President's House a notable event in the lives of congressmen; and the leisure which he devoted to science, philosophy, and politics. Even Jefferson's salaries as Secretary of State, Vice-President and President were indirectly paid in large part by slaves: their labor provided the tobacco, cotton, and sugar, the export of which stimulated Northern shipping, manufacture, banking, and insurance and enabled the United States to make remittances for imported manufactured goods and to attract the foreign investment capital vital to the agricultural, industrial, and commercial development of the Republic. Next to land, slaves constituted the largest property interest in the country, far larger than manufacturing and shipping combined. Truly, one of the main pillars of the world of Thomas Jefferson was black slavery.

This pillar Jefferson was resolved to destroy. As he saw it, the eradication of slavery was to be the crowning achievement of the American Revolution; that revolution could not be considered complete, he insisted, until this ugly scar, a vestige of the colonial period, had been removed. Compared with many of his fellow patriots, Jefferson was a radical revolutionary: revolutions, he said, were not made with rose water, and the purpose of a revolution was not to dispense sweetness and light but to effect needed changes in the existing social, political, and economic structure. He never supposed that the American Revolution consisted merely of the severance of the political ties that united the colonies to Great Britain or that it was an effort to maintain liberties already enjoyed in full plenitude by Americans. Among other things, Jefferson proposed to destroy in Virginia the last vestiges of "artificial aristocracy" based upon wealth and family connections and to bring to the fore the talents and virtues that lay submerged and fallow in the lower strata of society. Even though he was born into the aristocracy, Jefferson put his hope of a new order in "the plebeian interest." Without the abolition of slavery, Jefferson realized that the attainment of a society based upon freedom and equality of opportunity would forever elude the American people.

Although nineteen "Negars" had been brought to Virginia as early as 1619 by Dutch traders, the black population had increased slowly during the seventeenth century. By 1700, there were only between six thousand and ten thousand black slaves in the Old Dominion; but thereafter, partly as a result of the curtailment of the flow of white immigrants, most of whom came as indentured servants, and also because the Indians, despite the best efforts of the whites, failed to make satisfactory slaves, large numbers of Africans were imported to work the plantations of Tidewater Virginia and, later, of the Piedmont. By 1776, Virginia contained more than two hundred thousand blacks, over half the entire colored population of the United States.[1]

As a result, slaves were ubiquitous in the society in which Jefferson was reared and in which he came to his majority. Especially in the privileged circles of society in which Jefferson moved, it was difficult to find anyone who did not own slaves. His father was a slaveowner from whom Thomas inherited both land and slaves; all the Randolphs, to whom he was related through his mother, held slaves; and when he went to Williamsburg in 1760 to attend the College of William and Mary he took with him a personal slave, "Jupiter," whom he later made his coachman. Jefferson's wife's dowry consisted of 132 slaves and many thousands of acres of land. Like other Virginia patricians, he reckoned his wealth principally in slaves and land. By the time he wrote the Declaration of Independence he had become, by inheritance, purchase, and marriage, one of the principal slaveowners and one of the wealthiest men in Virginia.

Jefferson's perception of slavery was determined by several ambivalent circumstances: he was a planter-slaveowner, a Virginian whose strongest allegiance, when the test came, was to his state and section, and withal a man of the eighteenth century Enlightenment. This circumstance created in Jefferson's mind an ambiguity and a dissonance which he never succeeded in resolving to his own satisfaction. While Jefferson regarded

slavery as a "hideous evil," the bane of American society, and wholly
irreconcilable with his ideal of "republican virtue," he was never able
wholly to cast aside the prejudices and the fears which he had absorbed
from his surroundings toward people of color; he did not free himself from
dependence upon slave labor; and, in the end, he made the expansion of
slavery into the territories a constitutional right, and a *conditio sine qua
non* of the South's adherence to the Union.

If Jefferson as a Virginia planter was caught inextricably in the toils of
slavery, as a man of the Enlightenment he knew the institution to be
antithetical to the ideals by which he lived. The Enlightenment of the
eighteenth century has been well characterized by Sir Isaiah Berlin, the
English philosopher and historian of ideas, as the best and most hopeful
episode in the history of mankind. To the men of the Enlightenment,
their age was like the dawn of a new day of humanism, rationality,
scientific methodology, and religious toleration after a long night of
superstition, intolerance, and misery. During the preceding century,
Europe had fallen prey to visionaries, rabid dogmatists, and religious
"enthusiasts," with the result that it had been devastated by religious
wars. From the havoc wrought by unbridled religious zeal, European
thinkers turned their attention in the eighteenth century to the problems
confronting man upon this earth rather than in the next world and to
utilitarianism rather than metaphysical speculation. Man—his psychology
his physical characteristics, his political and social institutions, and his
place in the universe—became the principal theme of the age. The
eighteenth century discovered a new world in which man figured as a
free, independent individual and in which his worth and dignity, rather
than his depravity and proneness to sin, were regarded as his dominant
characteristics. From the idea of a rational benevolent Creator, the men
of the eighteenth century Enlightenment proceeded to the idea of rational, benevolent man, the finest work of the author Nature and the
center of all created things.[2]

It was assumed by these eighteenth century minds—and they made some
very bold assumptions based upon their faith in an orderly, rational, and
comprehensible universe—that the creative intelligence of man, working
in harmony with the designs of Nature, was capable of creating a social
order in which oppression, want, and misery would be replaced by
freedom, happiness, and contentment. If man's potential was assumed to
be without limit, then all things were possible once the restraints he had
himself imposed upon his nature—and, above all, upon his reasoning
powers—had been removed. Then, for the first time since man left the
state of Nature, he would be free to function according to his ability and
thereby to attain the stature intended for him by a benevolent Creator.
The quintessence of wisdom, as the men of the Enlightenment conceived
it, was to bring the existing social, political, and economic order into

conformity with the plans of a benign Creator who wished well to mankind.

Without exception, the men of the Enlightenment condemned slavery as a vestige of barbarism, an offense against the moral law, and a flagrant violation of the rights of man derived from the Creator. It was agreed that all men received from Nature, by virtue of their common humanity, an absolute right to the fruit of their labor and to the freedom of their persons of which they could not lawfully be deprived. Where human rights were concerned, the Enlightenment studiously ignored skin coloration.

As a student at the College of William and Mary, Jefferson was introduced to Enlightenment ideas by his mentors: Dr. William Small, a professor at the college; Edmund Pendleton and George Wythe, two of the leading lawyers of the province; and Lord Francis Fauquier, the Royal Governor of Virginia. The direction given Jefferson's thinking by these men was reinforced by his wide reading in history, philosophy, and the classics; he found in Stoic philosophy and in Cicero and Seneca conclusive evidence that many Enlightenment ideas had pedigrees that could be traced to classical Greece and Rome. At a relatively early age (when he wrote the Declaration of Independence he was thirty-three) Jefferson became one of the principal exponents of the ideals and attitudes of the Enlightenment in the American colonies and subsequently in the new American Republic. But Jefferson was never content merely to expound ideas: he conceived of the United States as the proving ground where Enlightenment ideas were to demonstrate that they could serve as the basis for a rational and morally perfected political and social order.

Among those ideas, Jefferson always included the Enlightenment's uncompromising rejection of slavery. Even while asserting the rights of white colonists against the British government, he did not forget the rights of the slaves—a position which set him apart from most of his contemporaries. When he was elected to the Virginia House of Burgesses in 1769, one of his first acts was to attempt to make the manumission of slaves easier for owners. For half a century, manumission had been permitted only with the consent of the governor and council; Jefferson sought to give every slaveowner the right to free his slaves if he so desired.

Characteristically, Jefferson chose to work through others to effect this reform. One of the more revealing stories told of his boyhood is the account of how, when a pupil at a plantation school taught by the Reverend Mr. Douglas, Jefferson decided that some changes in the curriculum were needed. Instead of going directly to Mr. Douglas, young Thomas persuaded one of his fellow students to go in his place. For his temerity, the hapless accomplice was roundly rebuked by the clergyman-pedagogue while Jefferson himself remained undetected and unscathed.

Jefferson, one of the great managers of men, began his career as a manager of children.

In 1769, his boyhood aversion to personal confrontations having hardened into a settled habit, he induced his cousin Richard Bland, a longtime member of the House of Burgesses, to introduce a bill facilitating manumission—Jefferson's role being confined to that of seconding the motion. Bland, a respected defender of colonial rights against Great Britain, found himself "treated with the grossest indecorum" and denounced as an enemy of the province. Because of his youth and inexperience (he was twenty-six years old) Jefferson escaped most of the censure so liberally bestowed upon Richard Bland.[3]

As a lawyer (he was admitted to the Virginia bar in 1769), Jefferson took several cases dealing with slavery. In 1770, he drew up without charge a brief in support of the claim of the grandson of a mulatto woman and a black slave who was suing for his freedom. Jefferson had a weak case; for while the law was specific in providing that the child of a white woman and a black slave father was to go free after serving until the age of thirty years as a slave, it made no exception in the case of the children or grandchildren of a mulatto woman. In contrast to Latin America, no mulatto class existed in Virginia or, indeed, in any British colony: a mulatto was a "black" or a "Negro" and, unless his or her mother were white, a slave for life. No one was free in colonial Virginia merely by virtue of the possession of white genes: to be valid they had to be derived specifically from the maternal side. The law declared that any person with one-eighth African "blood" was a mulatto; it was not possible to "pass" into the white community until all obvious physical traces of African ancestry had disappeared.[4]

In 1770, with the facts against his client, Jefferson had no choice but to try to move the case beyond the law of Virginia which, in these matters, was usually strictly interpreted. He did so by asserting that "under the law of nature, all men are born free, and every one comes into the world with a right to his own person, which includes the liberty of moving and using it at his own will." Unless this natural right to freedom were recognized, Jefferson declared, the status of the mulatto grandmother would be transmitted not merely to her grandchild but to her latest posterity.[5]

Among Jefferson's friends, the idea of the natural equality and freedom of man occasioned no sense of shock; in this particular, both Christians and Enlightenment rationalists agreed in holding that all men had been created free and equal. Edmund Pendleton, George Wythe (although he served as counsel for the defendant in this case), and George Mason did not take exception to the proposition boldly advanced by Jefferson. But as Jefferson was quickly given to understand, the idea of the natural equality and freedom of man was not to be applied to blacks or mulattoes in a Virginia courtroom. The judge dismissed the case not, however, because Jefferson had appealed to a higher law but because he had failed to prove that his client was the descendant of a free woman and was therefore entitled to freedom.

In 1770, Jefferson had not contended that the slaves held in Virginia had the right to instant, unqualified freedom because they had been born free. The law of Virginia described slaves as chattel property; as such, they could be bought, sold, mortgaged, seized for debt, and devised by will. Jefferson recognized that the emancipation of the slaves waited upon the voluntary act of their owners or upon the will of the majority as expressed in statute law. Until and unless either of these conditions was fulfilled, the legal status of slaves could not be changed—as Jefferson himself implicitly recognized when in 1769 he advertised for the return of a slave who had stolen a horse and run away.[6]

Abortive as this case of 1770 proved to be, it revealed Jefferson's propensity for relating human rights to the laws of nature. In the struggle for American freedom against Great Britain, Jefferson habitually rationalized American rights by reference to the laws of nature which, his English adversaries complained, always worked in favor of Americans—leaving the only possible conclusion that the Great Lawgiver himself must be an American.

In 1772, Jefferson was appointed by the court as counsel to a mulatto suing for freedom, an assignment which suggests that he was acquiring a reputation as a defender of the rights of mulattoes. But his client died before judgment could be rendered, and two years later Jefferson abandoned the practice of law in order to devote himself to the management of his estate and to the cause of American freedom. Only on one occasion thereafter did he briefly espouse the cause of mulattoes and of free blacks. The American Revolution, while it enhanced his determination to abolish slavery, marked the end of his efforts to advance the cause of black freedom without simultaneously providing for the removal of the blacks themselves from the territory of the United States.

☙

Jefferson delivered his first attack in print upon slavery in 1774, when he published a pamphlet entitled *A Summary View of the Rights of British America*. Intended to serve as a policy guide to the Virginia House of Burgesses in its controversy with the British government, *A Summary View* took the radical ground that Americans owed no allegiance whatever to the British Parliament, a position not assumed by the Continental Congress until 1775. Although Jefferson's handiwork was rejected by the House of Burgesses, it helped create a favorable opinion of his literary ability and called attention to his advanced views in the matter of colonial rights. Had it not been for the publication of *A Summary View,* it is unlikely that Jefferson would have been designated in June 1776 to write the Declaration of Independence.

In the *Summary View,* Jefferson assailed slavery where it was most vulnerable: the traffic in human beings by which slaves were transported from Africa to the slave barracoons of the New World. Perhaps nowhere in the world were the rights of man by which the Enlightenment set inestimable store more flagrantly violated than on the Middle Passage between Africa and the western hemisphere. Since 1671, when the Royal African Company was founded with King Charles II and James, Duke of York, among the principal stockholders, British and American slave-traders had carried over a million black Africans across the Atlantic.

Yet Jefferson was not content merely to deplore this evil: he converted it into an indictment of the British government and, specifically, of King George III. Jefferson declared that the abolition of slavery was "the great object of desire in these colonies" and that the American people had been thwarted in this objective by the king, thereby proving the existence not only of a "deliberate, systematical plan of reducing us to slavery" but of an equally sinister plan of compelling Americans who asked to be free of the "detestable" institution of slavery to keep in servitude men, women, and children of another race.

Jefferson based this arraignment of the British monarch upon the fact that many colonial assemblies had imposed duties—in some instances virtually prohibitive—upon the importation of African slaves. Most of these acts of the colonial legislatures, especially those which seriously impeded the traffic in slaves, had been disallowed by the Royal Privy Council on the ground that they interfered with the free flow of "a considerable article of British commerce." On the strength of these abortive attempts by the colonial legislatures to tax the importation of slaves, Jefferson laid it down as an incontestable truth that the American people had set their hearts upon abolishing slavery and that they had been prevented from accomplishing that objective by the malice, greed, and inhumanity of George III.

In his draft of the Declaration of Independence, Jefferson amplified the charge that the King was responsible for the perpetuation of slavery and the slave trade. Among the twenty-seven crimes and misdemeanors of which the Declaration accused the British monarch, none was more important in Jefferson's opinion than George III's complicity in foisting slavery upon the American people. And he deliberately presented this charge as the concluding article of his indictment of George III, obviously intending that it should serve as the capstone of his catalogue of royal misdeeds. On the subject of slavery, Jefferson could not restrain his righteous indignation against his late sovereign. By negating the salutary laws against the slave trade enacted by the colonial assemblies, Jefferson declared, George III had "waged cruel war against human nature itself, violating the most sacred right of life and liberty in the persons of a distant people who never offended him, captivating and carrying them into slavery in another hemisphere, or to incur miserable death in their transportation thither"—and this crime against humanity was committed merely in order to enrich a few African corsairs by keeping open the markets "where Men should be bought and sold."

There was a compelling reason for Jefferson's efforts to fix the responsibility for the perpetuation of slavery upon the British monarch. Jefferson and other American patriots had repeatedly accused the British government of trying to reduce them to "slavery." If it could be shown that white Americans—the very citizenry who had taken up arms in defense of freedom—had, for their own profit, reduced hundreds of thousands of Africans to a real state of slavery, the appeal to a candid world might fall very flat indeed. Already, Dr. Samuel Johnson had, in fact, raised the embarrassing question: "How is it," he asked, "that we hear the loudest yelps for liberty from the drivers of Negroes?"* Therefore, by placing the burden of guilt wholly upon George III, Jefferson rhetorically relieved the American people of any culpability for the existence of an institution so utterly abhorrent, as he saw it, to their humanitarian instincts and to the ideals of the Enlightenment. If it could be made to appear that the slave trade and slavery itself had been forced upon a virtuous, virginal, and moral people who yearned to be free of this detestable institution, Jefferson would succeed in exalting his fellow countrymen into champions of freedom at the same time that he held up George III to the execration of his subjects and of the world.[7]

To Jefferson's mortification, the Continental Congress struck out this climactic passage from the Declaration of Independence, thereby putting Jefferson in the position of a prosecuting attorney who finds the culprit in the dock held not guilty on the main charge. Jefferson attributed the "mutilation" of his original draft (Congress made many more deletions, emendations, and additions) to the influence of Northern slavetraders who, having profited from the slave trade, did not wish to see it condemned and to the "avarice" of some Southerners, especially South Carolinians and Georgians, whose demand for slaves remained unsatisfied. Even though John Adams considered the arraignment of the king on the charge of

---

* In his *Observations Concerning the Distinction of Ranks in Society* (1771), John Millar, the Scottish philosopher and sociologist, remarked that "it offers a curious spectacle to observe, that the same people who talk in so high a strain of political liberty, and who consider the privilege of imposing their own taxes as one of the inalienable rights of mankind, should make no scruple of reducing a great proportion of the inhabitants into circumstances by which they are not only deprived of property, but almost of every right whatsoever." Jefferson was familiar with Millar's work. See Harris 1968, pp. 51–52.

collusion with slave traders to be the best part of the Declaration, Congress was, however, well advised to eliminate it. More aware than was Jefferson—who was obviously carried away by his zeal for pillorying the king—of the dangers of propagandistic overkill, Congress wisely took the position that the monarch, already burdened by Jefferson with culpability for "murder," "piratical warfare," and inflicting "miserable death," could not be held accountable for all the evil extant in the British Empire.* Moreover, the inclusion of Jefferson's strictures on slavery and the slave trade would have committed the United States to the abolition of slavery once the tyrannical yoke of George III had been thrown off—a commitment few Southerners were willing to undertake at this time. Finally, in presenting facts to a candid world, Congress felt that these facts had to be historically verifiable. In the case of the laws enacted by the colonial assemblies levying duties upon the importation of African slaves adduced in *A Summary View* as irrefutable proof of Americans' abhorrence of slavery and their desire to rid themselves of the institution, the facts were clearly at variance with his postulate. These acts were designed to raise revenue, enhance the price of slaves, prevent the glutting of the slave market, and, especially in the case of Virginia, to keep the slave population within manageable bounds—everything, in short, except to prepare the way for the abolition of slavery. At least in this regard, Jefferson had obviously thought too well of his countrymen, especially those who had a financial stake in slavery and who were dependent upon it for their labor supply.[8]

Similarly, the Royal Privy Council, in disallowing the acts of colonial legislatures imposing high duties upon the importation of African slaves, was acting less out of solicitude for slavery itself than in consequence of the fact that the slave trade had become "big business" and was too powerful and too important to the British economy to be successfully challenged by the government. About two thousand British and American ships were regularly engaged in transporting forty to fifty thousand Africans annually to the western hemisphere; of these slave ships, over a hundred were based in Liverpool, the British seaport most heavily involved in this traffic. The slavetraders, allied with the mercantile, shipping, and manufacturing interests, constituted a powerful lobby in

* Even John Adams who, as Jefferson said, fought "fearlessly for every word" of the Declaration as written by Jefferson and who especially approved of holding George III responsible for the slave trade, privately felt that Jefferson had gone too far in his arraignment of the British monarch. In Adams's opinion, George III was not a born tyrant: "I always believed him to be deceived by his courtiers on both sides of the Atlantic and in his official capacity, only, cruel. . . . I thought the expression (as it came from Jefferson's pen) too passionate and too much like scolding, for so grave and solemn a document." See Lipscomb and Berg 15 (1903), p. 463 and the *Virginia Magazine* 31, p. 299.

Parliament, and the British government was inclined to proceed upon the assumption that what was good for the slave trade was good for the empire.[9]

But Jefferson had not done with George III; indeed, he never tired of inveighing against the iniquities of his one-time sovereign. Ten years after writing the Declaration of Independence, Jefferson met George III face to face in London. That brief encounter did not persuade Jefferson that he had done His Britannic Majesty an injustice: "the ulcerations in the narrow mind of that mulish being" indicated to Jefferson that the warmest feeling of the monarch's heart was his undying hatred of the United States and of the freedom for which it stood.

Under the firm conviction that there was nothing to which George III would not stoop to crush the American revolt, Jefferson, in his draft of the Declaration of Independence, sought to compound the numerous crimes of which the king already stood accused by charging him with attempting to foment a slave insurrection and thereby inflict the horrors of racial war upon Americans; which people were already exposed, by the express orders of the sovereign, to the incursions of merciless, bloodthirsty Indians in whose massacres and scalpings he presumably took a vicarious delight.

In November 1775, Lord Dunmore, the Royal Governor of Virginia, issued from the British man-of-war on which he had taken refuge from the patriots a proclamation promising freedom to all slaves belonging to rebels who joined "His Majesty's Troops . . . for the more speedily reducing the Colony to a proper sense of their duty to His Majesty's Crown and dignity." On the strength of this promise of freedom, about a thousand slaves rallied to the British standard; some of them wore the emblem "Liberty to Slaves." But Dunmore had little force at his command and he and his black allies were easily routed by the Virginia militia, whereupon the governor and the British fleet left Virginia waters carrying with them the "property" of the patriots.[10]

Even though the slave uprising had been crushed, Jefferson used the event to blacken further the reputation of His Britannic Majesty. He pictured the king, from the security of Whitehall, engaged in "exciting these very people to rise up in arms among us, and to purchase that liberty of which *he* deprived them, by murdering the people upon whom he also intruded them; thus paying off former crimes committed against the *liberties* of one people, which crimes he urges them to commit against the *lives* of another." Here again Jefferson rehearsed the familiar litany: Americans wished to abolish slavery; they were prevented from doing so by the intervention of the Crown; and now the king was inciting *his* slaves to murder freedom-loving white Americans who, had they been free of royal control, would have abolished slavery of their own accord.[11]

Jefferson made Lord Dunmore's proclamation the final, damning proof that a conspiracy against American freedom existed at the highest levels of the British government. Only men bent upon establishing despotism, Jefferson argued, would seek to foment a racial, servile war. The Declaration of Independence, as revised by the Continental Congress, did not go that far: although the members adopted the view that the king himself was behind the effort to use black slaves to impose "slavery" upon white Americans, they did not see fit to mention in the Declaration that a slave insurrection had occurred in Virginia—and, indeed, *that* might have been difficult to explain to a candid world. Instead, the Declaration merely accuses the king of "exciting insurrections against us." In 1776, "insurrections" signified to the American people the Loyalist uprising in North Carolina and, above all, Lord Dunmore's efforts to stir up racial war in Virginia.[12]

Thus, the Declaration of Independence, in sum, while it asserts the right of white Americans to rebel against attempts to reduce them to "slavery," denies inferentially, in the context of the events of 1775–1776, the right of black slaves to rebel against their masters in order to attain freedom. It is accounted a major crime against American freedom for the king to have incited an insurrection among a people whose experience of the tyranny of slavery was real and palpable against those whites who, in the words of Edmund Burke, merely "snuffed tyranny in every tainted breeze" and who rebelled even before they actually felt the lash.

～ 2 ～
Slavery and the
Rights of Man

———◆———

BY EXCISING ALL REFERENCE to the slave trade and slavery and by watering down Jefferson's impassioned tirade against George III, the Continental Congress considerably weakened the impact of the Declaration of Independence as an antislavery manifesto. It left American revolutionaries in the ambiguous position of asserting human rights without unequivocally branding the enslavement of blacks as a violation of those rights. Still, despite their refusal to find George III guilty of all the "assemblage of horrors" depicted by Jefferson, the members of the Continental Congress, by adopting the first paragraph of the Declaration of Independence, seemed to set the seal of their approval upon principles which precluded the perpetuation of slavery in the new American Republic.[1]

In this momentous preamble, Jefferson asserted that the right to life, liberty, and the pursuit of happiness was inalienable and self-evident. He understood "inalienable" in the sense that no man could be lawfully deprived of this right and no man was privileged to divest himself of it. "Self-evident" in Jefferson's vocabulary meant that this postulate carried the force of an axiom when presented to the reason and moral sense of man. Since all men were sensible of this truth from the beginning of time, "self-evident" truths must be regarded as irrefutable and eternal. To establish the validity of such *a priori* truths, no proof was necessary; they were not equations to be tested by mathematical formulae; rather they were verities from which there could be no dissent. Men knew intuitively, and reason confirmed, that Nature had ordained that all men were created equal in the sense that they were endowed equally with a common humanity and therefore endowed equally with those rights appertaining to members of the human race. In the Declaration of Independence Jefferson did not assert the legal and constitutional rights of Englishmen and Americans; he asserted the natural, imprescribable and "self-evident" rights of all men everywhere.

But a more urgent question in the American context was whether these "universal" human rights applied equally to black slaves (who were, after all, "property") and to free white men. Were black slaves to be debarred from participating in the enjoyment of equal rights by their servile status and, perhaps, by their skin color? Unfortunately for the slaves, even before the adoption of the Declaration of Independence this question had been answered in the negative. In the Virginia Convention held in May–June 1776, Robert Carter Nicholas, one of the delegates, had expressed the fear that the insertion of a clause in the Virginia Declaration of Rights drawn up by George Mason in favor of human equality and inalienable rights would prove to be "the forerunner or pretext of civil commotions" on the part of black slaves inflamed by the hope of freedom and the promise of racial equality. But the apprehensions of Nicholas and those who shared them were allayed by the assurance that slaves, not being constituent members of society, "could never pretend to any benefit from such a maxim." [2]

The rights of man, it appeared, while theoretically and ideally the birthright of every human being, applied in practice in the United States only to white men: the black slaves were excluded from consideration because, while admittedly human beings, they were also property, and where the rights of man conflicted with the rights of property, property took precedence. Being property, they could not participate in the compact by which government was brought into being. They were no more than spectators of the transactions of free men taking place in Philadelphia and in the several states.

In this manner, the theory that government was created by a compact agreed to by free, rational, independent men—postulated by John Locke and confirmed by American experience in the Mayflower Compact and the colonial charters—served to exclude the black slaves from sharing in the benefits of independence. By this doctrine they were consigned to the status of a special category of noncitizens to whom bills of rights and declarations of the rights of man had no relevance whatever.

With this tacit qualification the Declaration of Rights adopted by the Virginia Convention in June 1776 asserted, as did Jefferson's draft of the Declaration of Independence, that all men are created equal and that they are endowed by virtue of their common humanity with certain inalienable rights. One third of the signers of the Declaration of Independence were slaveowners, most of whom had no intention of sacrificing their right to hold human beings in servitude upon the altar of American freedom simply because the Declaration asserted the ideal equality and universal rights of abstract Man. This restrictive interpretation tended to deprive the Declaration of the universalism with which Jefferson had sought to endow it. As Anthony Benezet, a Philadelphia Quaker, observed, "When men talk of liberty, they mean their own liberty, and seldom suffer their thoughts on that part to stray to their neighbor."

And so the doctrine that all men are created equal was reconciled comfortably with the sociological reality of slavery. To have been created equal was, it appeared, no guarantee of actual equality in the social order of the new American Republic. The slaveowners who signed the Declaration of Independence seemed to be saying that, while there could be no doubt that all men were created equal, they differed greatly in the sequel. For the slaves, it was the sequel—that is, the actual condition to which they had been reduced—rather than the original event which determined their status and their rights in society.

Even though the doctrine of human equality and participation in the creation of the social compact was restricted in practice to white men, it was peculiarly fitting that this principle should have been proclaimed in the United States. As compared with Great Britain and Europe, there existed in the thirteen revolted colonies a remarkable degree of actual social equality within the white community: there was no nobility; no rigid, exclusionary class lines; and no privileged class at the apex of the social pyramid. The United States, the first nation to make the doctrine of human equality an integral part of its official ideology, had in some respects attained a closer approximation to this ideal than had any other nation, but where racial distinctions were involved, few nations had farther to go.

Moreover, although Jefferson never admitted it publicly, in Virginia and other states which contained large slave populations, slavery helped to foster among whites the kind of equality he prized. The white man— any white man—could feel superior to the black slaves; and a white skin conferred a certain feeling of equality among those fortunate enough to possess it. Racial prejudice and the fear of a servile uprising were powerful forces in the Southern states, generating and sustaining the conviction that all men free of African genes were not only created equal but, more importantly, remained so in the Southern social milieu.

Except in the Northern states where slavery had not struck deep roots, the Declaration of Independence, in its immediate bearing upon blacks (as well as upon Indians and women), consisted largely of "glittering and sounding generalities" without meaning or substance. The tyranny envisaged by the Declaration is exercised by governments rather than by individuals, classes, or social groups. It emphasized the necessity of bringing governments into conformity with the laws of nature and requiring them to respect and foster the rights of man, but it is less heedful of other more subtle and less easily identifiable forms of oppression.[3]

Yet the possibility remains that Jefferson sought to accomplish by stealth what he could not hope to do openly—namely, to make the Declaration of Independence a charter of freedom for slaves. By omitting the word "property" from his enumeration of the rights of man—life, liberty, and the pursuit of happiness—Jefferson seemed to place human rights above property rights, thereby removing one of the principal obstacles to the emancipation of the slaves. The Declaration of Independence can, in fact, be interpreted to assert the absolute primacy of human rights precisely because it fails to take explicate cognizance of property rights.

Significantly, Jefferson himself never put forward this explanation of his failure to include the right to property among the inalienable rights of man. He may have chosen to leave it to inference as a right too self-evident to require mention. In the Declaration of Independence, Jefferson did not pretend to enumerate all the rights of man: the right to life, liberty, and the pursuit of happiness are listed under the heading, "among which are." The view that he did not exclude property from those unformulated additional rights is supported by the many statements in his writings attesting to the high regard in which he held property rights. He left no doubt that under peacetime conditions he followed John Locke in believing that every individual had a natural right to appropriate property for his own use from the great storehouse of Nature and that the genesis of government itself lay in the necessity of providing security for life, liberty, and property of the individual.

A devotee of limited government and an agrarian who thought that the ownership of land was essential to the moral development of the individual, Jefferson was not prepared under ordinary conditions to give the state sweeping powers over property. Like other leaders of the American Revolution, he believed that any government that could take real estate and chattel property from its citizens without their consent could likewise divest them of every other right at its pleasure; the rights of property were the first line of defense of civil and all other rights. Viewed in this light, there was no valid distinction between the rights of property and the rights of man: they were indissolubly joined by "the benevolent design of nature." [4]

Yet at the time Jefferson wrote the Declaration of Independence, the conditions of peace and social concord upon the existence of which he predicated his theory of the sanctity of property and civil rights did not prevail. On the contrary, the United States was engaged in a desperate struggle for its existence. As a result, a new set of rules came into effect, and property ownership and civil rights became a casualty of war and revolution. When the existence of the government was at stake, Jefferson acknowledged that "the unwritten laws of necessity, or self-preservation, and of the public safety control the written laws of *meum* and *teum*."

If Jefferson excluded property from the inalienable rights of men in the Declaration of Independence for any ulterior purpose, he did not do so in order to weaken the tenure of slaveholders, but to facilitate the confiscation by the new state governments of property belonging to Loyalists and other British subjects. Even before he wrote the Declaration of Independence, Jefferson had proposed an invasion of property rights: in August 1774, he and Patrick Henry had recommended that all payments on British debts be suspended for the duration of the dispute with the British government. Instruments of debt, properly secured and attested, were a form of property as legally valid as title to land. In *Common Sense,* published in January 1776, Tom Paine predicted that the money derived from the confiscation and sale of Loyalist property would sustain the war effort for at least two years. By this pragmatic logic a revolution undertaken ostensibly to protect American property from taxation by the British Parliament acquired, as a result of the exigencies created by the war with Great Britain, an ambivalent attitude toward the sanctity of property which was perhaps reflected in the omission of the word "property" from the Declaration of Independence.* 5

Had Jefferson been a doctrinaire defender of property rights to whom even Loyalist and British property was sacrosanct, he would have forfeited much of his effectiveness as a revolutionary, for it is one of the functions of revolution to transfer the ownership of property to the revolutionaries—as, in fact, the American Revolution did. Because Jefferson never exalted the right to property above the public good, he was in a strong position to advocate during the War of Independence the sequestration of Loyalist and British property, including real estate, under the wartime powers of the commonwealth of Virginia. In January 1778, the bill introduced by Jefferson in the House of Delegates confiscating enemy property for the benefit of the state became law.

Yet Jefferson's concept of property rights and, more importantly, his convictions regarding the absolute rights of man, led him to regard the possession of human beings as an illegitimate form of property. No man had a natural right to enslave another man and to take from him the fruits of his labor. "A right of property," he said, "is founded in our natural wants, in the means with which we were endowed to satisfy these wants, and that right to what we acquire by those means without violating the similar rights of sensisble beings." No dialectical ingenuity can reconcile chattel slavery with such a definition of property.6

No doubt Jefferson was aware, at the time he wrote the Declaration of Independence, that by admitting "property" into his roster of the inalienable and imprescriptible rights of man, he would have endowed the tenure of slaves with a sanctity to which slaveowners could appeal in defense of their right to hold slaves. Nor can he have been unaware that

---

* The concept of the sanctity of property did not always work in favor of the American patriots. The destruction of the tea belonging to the East India Company, for example, was condemned by conservative Americans such as Robert Beverly of Virginia as an attack upon private property by "mobbish Bostonians." See Ammerman 1974, pp. 36–37.

any effort to abolish slavery would have been denounced as an invasion of an inviolable right of free white Americans. Jefferson certainly did not write the Declaration with slavery primarily in mind; his assignment was rather to justify the act by which the thirteen colonies separated themselves from the mother country. Even so, by omitting the word "property," he made it possible for the opponents of slavery to cite the Declaration of Independence in support of human freedom.

In 1776, however, Jefferson gave no overt aid or encouragement to those who put this construction upon the Declaration of Independence; he did not assert that it was intended to be a charter of freedom for the slaves or that the omission of the word "property" had any significance whatever. While the Continental Congress scrutinized and amended his draft of the Declaration, Jefferson sat silent: no exegesis of the Declaration was forthcoming from the author. By his silence, Jefferson seemed to acquiesce in the solution arrived at by slaveowners who joined in proclaiming liberty and equality for the white portion of the community, while totally denying it to black slaves. Yet it is clear that Jefferson was convinced that the self-evident truths he had enunciated precluded the continued existence of slavery in the United States. Shortly after the adoption of the Declaration of Independence he drafted a constitution for the state of Virginia in which he provided for the gradual abolition of slavery. He did not insist upon the immediate and absolute emancipation of the slaves; he would have been content—and, indeed, none of his proposals ever went further—if slavery were placed in the course of ultimate extinction. Nor did he then or at any later time claim for blacks the same measure of freedom in the United States that he demanded for white Americans. Jefferson never ceased to believe that an indelible color line had been drawn by Nature between the two races and that this line determined the rights and liberties to which they were entitled in America.

Even hedged with these qualifications, the plan for the gradual abolition of slavery and the democratization of the government he proposed for Virginia in 1776 was rejected. The delegates to the Virginia Convention liked neither his scheme of government nor his prescription for the ultimate abolition of slavery. They were content, as Jefferson later observed, with a constitution which established a "legislative despotism" and which left the institution of slavery intact.

During the War of Independence, Jefferson made no further public overtures toward the abolition of slavery. By the summer of 1776, he had become convinced that slavery was far too solidly entrenched in Virginia to be easily vanquished by the idealism generated by the American Revolution. Victory over slavery, when it came, would not be the result of a summer's campaign but of a long, hard-fought war. Thus far, his efforts to further the dismantling of the institution had proved unavailing: as a lawyer, legislator, author of the Declaration of Independence, and finally as a constitution-maker for the state of Virginia, he had suffered a succession of rebuffs. He had learned that, while many Virginians deplored slavery and professed to wish nothing so much as to be delivered from its hateful embrace, when a plan for eliminating slavery was proposed they became strangely immobilized.

Accordingly, Jefferson adopted the unheroic but eminently prudent and pragmatic policy of biding his time, awaiting the "ripening" of public opinion. During the War of Independence he carefully avoided sounding a clarion call for what he regarded as the climactic event of the Revolution; instead, during the war of national liberation, Jefferson deliberately contented himself with a policy of palliation and delay, determined to keep the divisive issue of emancipation out of view and to prevent at all costs a slave insurrection which, while it might conceivably win freedom for the blacks, would almost certainly cost white Americans *their* hard-won freedom. To Jefferson, as to most Southern patriots of the revolutionary generation, "slavery" was primarily an evil which George III and his ministers had imposed upon the American people rather than an indigenous institution which held almost half a million blacks on American soil in bondage.

~ 3 ~

Slavery and the
Revolution in Virginia

◆

IN SEPTEMBER 1776, during an intermission in the debate on the Articles of Confederation, Jefferson abruptly left the Continental Congress and returned to Virginia. He was anxious to be with his wife who, as usual, was ill and pregnant, but he also had compelling political reasons for leaving Philadelphia. Jefferson believed that the most important scene of action of the American Revolution was in the states. Here, he felt sure, the fundamental question raised by the revolution—whether free men were capable of governing themselves—would be decided. Unless the new state governments were thoroughly republican, he was convinced that the American Revolution would end in failure. As he saw it, upon Virginia, the largest and most populous of the states, devolved a special responsibility: it was incumbent upon the Old Dominion to demonstrate the capacity of man to establish a political and social order based upon freedom, order, and justice. By leaving Philadelphia in September 1776, Jefferson hoped to put himself in a position to play a major role in this epochal struggle.

During the next eight years, Jefferson remained in Virginia; at no time during the War of Independence did he leave his native state to participate in the national councils. As a result of his voluntary withdrawal from the national stage, his public stature was reduced to that of a state leader. To George Washington's pleas that he take his place in the Continental Congress, Jefferson replied that his first duty was to see the revolution brought to a successful conclusion in Virginia.[1]

The task upon which Jefferson expended the most effort during the war years was the revision of the laws of Virginia. In 1776, Jefferson, George Wythe, and Edmund Pendleton were named by the House of Delegates members of a committee charged with responsibility for making the statute and common law commensurate with Virginia's new position as a sovereign commonwealth. James Madison maintained that Jefferson's work on this committee was the most arduous and time-consuming that he undertook during his entire career.

In Jefferson's opinion, it was time and effort well spent, for he regarded legal reform as one of the paramount tasks of the Revolution. In the interests of clarity and order—the dominant characteristics of his mind— he sought to accommodate the existing body of common and local law to the new republican form of government by omitting "everything obsolete or improper, insert what was wanting, and reduce the whole within as moderate a compass as it will bear." Even more important, in the longer perspective, his position on the committee gave him an opportunity to introduce his bills for religious freedom, abolition of primogeniture and entail, and for the establishment of a state-supported system of education for Virginia.[2]

Especially with regard to the criminal law, Jefferson's objective was to incorporate into the jurisprudence of Virginia the ideas of the Enlightenment upon crime and punishment as expounded by Cesare Bonesana di Beccaria (1738–1794). In 1764, Beccaria published *On Crimes and Punishments,* an English translation of which appeared in 1768. Beccaria maintained that the purpose of punishment should be to effect a reformation of the criminal rather than to exact retributive justice; humanity and rationality, he argued, should supplant vindictive killing; and punishment ought to be proportioned to the flagitiousness of the offense.

For the benefit of the white citizens of the commonwealth of Virginia, Jefferson liberally applied Beccaria's principles to his revision of the laws. In 1769, clearly under the influence of the European Enlightenment, Virginia had abolished the *lex talionis*—the Old Testament injunction to exact an eye for an eye and a tooth for a tooth, on the ground that it was "revolting to the humanized feelings of modern times." The committee headed by Jefferson not only retained this juridical innovation which could only work to the benefit of the white citizenry, but reduced the number of capital crimes to two. The infliction of the death penalty, Jefferson said, ought to be "the last melancholy resource of society." By the same token, he recommended the abolition of the practice of leaving the bodies of executed criminals "to rot like scare-crows on gibbets": instead of deterring crime, this barbaric practice tended, he believed, by familiarizing people to such horrors, to "blunt the sentiments and destroy the benevolent prejudices of people."

Except for the privilege of knowing that their corpses would not rot on gibbets, the slaves profited little from the enlightened humanitarianism of Cesare Bonesana di Beccaria as it manifested itself in the laws of Virginia. Jefferson and his colleagues actually tightened the slave code in their revision and codification of the laws. This, after all, was a time of war, and the slaves were being tempted by the offer of freedom to leave the plantations and escape to the British lines. Recognizing that a continuation of the labor of slaves was necessary to the winning of freedom by white Americans, Jefferson tried to ensure that this indispensable labor force remained intact and that the danger of servile revolts stirred up by the enemy be countered by increased vigilance on the part of white revolutionaries.

Jefferson and his colleagues were well aware that a simple intensification of the rigors of the slave code, however justified by the exigencies of war, was not a satisfactory answer to the dilemma created by the continued existence of slavery in a country fighting for independence under the banner of liberty and equality. They therefore planned to submit in their final report to the legislature a plan intended for implementation after the war, providing for the gradual abolition of slavery and the evacuation of the blacks from the state. In this, as in all of Jefferson's plans of emancipation, emphasis was placed upon the word "gradual." Had the committee's ideas been enacted into law, slavery would have existed in Virginia for at least three generations. But upon one point Jefferson, Wythe, and Randolph were adamant: the freed blacks must leave the commonwealth forthwith. They had the right to be free, but not the right to remain in Virginia.

But even this embryonic overture toward eventual emancipation was stillborn. On the ground that public opinion was not yet sufficiently "refined" to permit the adoption of any plan providing for the emancipation of the slaves, the committee decided to hold their handiwork in abeyance, awaiting a more propitious moment which, unfortunately, never came.[3]

Like the slaves, the free blacks actually lost ground as a result of the Jefferson committee's revision of the laws of Virginia. No effort was made to accord them the rights of citizens or equality before the law. During 1770–1772, Jefferson had sought to further the rights of mulattoes; now, during the War of Independence, he found the presence of free blacks and mulattoes undesirable. True, they were believed to constitute a kind of fifth column working with the British to incite the slaves to rebellion, but Jefferson had an even more persuasive reason for advocating their expatriation: since 1773 he had conceived an overmastering loathing for and fear of "racial mixture."

Nevertheless, Jefferson had lost none of his ardor for emancipating the slaves as a first step toward their eventual removal from Virginia soil. In 1782, largely in consequence of the work of Quakers, Methodists, Baptists, and other denominations opposed to slavery on religious grounds, the Virginia legislature enacted a law facilitating private manumission. During the colonial period, no slave could be freed except with the permission of the governor and council and then only for meritorious service. By the law of 1782 which, in effect, enacted the bill Jefferson

himself, acting through Richard Bland, had introduced in the House of
Burgesses in 1769 (which was defeated at that time), individual slaveowners were permitted to manumit those of their slaves under forty-five
years of age who were not likely to become public charges, by will or
affidavit at the owner's discretion. A few years later, Maryland and
Delaware followed Virginia's lead in liberalizing the process of manumission.

According to the law of 1782, free blacks were permitted to remain in
Virginia—a provision which, in Jefferson's opinion, served to exacerbate
the racial problem by enhancing the opportunity for miscegenation.
Therefore, in a draft of a constitution for Virginia which he drew up in
1783 when a convention to revise the constitution of 1776 seemed imminent, he included in his plan for the gradual abolition of slavery (all
children born of slave parents after 1800 were to be free after attaining
adulthood) the stipulation that these children, after being trained as
apprentices, should be deported from the state upon reaching maturity.
But this plan was shelved when the contemplated constitutional convention failed to materialize. Unlike Jefferson's other plans for the
abolition of slavery and the expatriation of freed blacks, this one did
appear in print: the proposed constitution for Virginia, including the
provisions on slavery, was printed in 1785 as an appendix to Jefferson's
Notes on Virginia. It is the only concrete evidence published in his lifetime
revealing that he had actually formulated a scheme for eliminating not
only the "hideous evil" of slavery, but the blacks themselves.[4]

The acts of 1778 abolishing the slave trade, a measure for which
Jefferson was in part responsible, and of 1782 liberalizing manumission
were the only concrete legislative achievements of the war years with a
direct bearing upon slavery. For Jefferson, it was a disappointing performance: he had hoped that Virginia would take the lead among the
states in providing for the eventual abolition of slavery and in arranging
for the resettlement of the freed blacks outside the United States after
peace had been restored. Still, he took heart from the fact that Virginia
was among the first states to make the abolition of the slave trade a part
of the revolutionary program of reform. Yet in assuming, as he did, that
the termination of the slave trade was the beginning of the end of slavery
itself, Jefferson presumed too much: as they had already demonstrated
during the colonial period, Virginians had reasons for taking action
against the slave trade which bore little relevance to the question of the
continued existence of slavery itself.[5]

4

Slavery and the Ordinance of 1784

◆

IN 1779 JEFFERSON was elected governor of Virginia. In this, the fourth year of the war, the military situation did not permit him to use the modest authority and influence of his executive office to further the work of social and governmental reform: the British army under Sir George Clinton and Lord Cornwallis opened up a new, and for the Americans, initially disastrous, theater of war in the Southern states. In 1780, with the fall of Charleston, South Carolina, and the capture of over five thousand of the city's defenders, most of them troops of the Continental army, the war entered upon a critical phase that did not end until Cornwallis's surrender at Yorktown in October 1781.

As a result of the military strategy adopted by Governor Jefferson and his predecessor, Patrick Henry, Virginia was in a poor position to aid its beleaguered neighbor states to the South. In 1778, with George Rogers Clark in command, Virginia forces embarked upon the conquest of the British outposts in the region north of the Ohio River—an enterprise which absorbed most of the state's military resources. With heavy demands placed upon its manpower and supplies both in the western and southern theaters of war, coupled with an Indian war inadvertently provoked by Governor Jefferson, the Old Dominion was stripped of its Continental troops and compelled to draft militiamen for service both in and outside the state.

Because of the critical shortage of manpower not only in Virginia but throughout the United States, some Americans began to advocate the enlistment of blacks, slave as well as free, for the armed forces. In 1778–1779, Colonels Alexander Hamilton and John Laurens, with the approval of General Washington, tried to induce the legislatures of South Carolina and Georgia, the states where the British military threat was most acute, to raise several battalions of slaves. Hamilton argued that slaves, being accustomed to subordination and discipline, would make excellent soldiers; and, he predicted, if offered their freedom with their swords, they would fight bravely for the American cause. No one need fear that the blacks were unintelligent, Hamilton said: "Their natural faculties are as good as ours. . . . The contempt we have been taught to entertain for the blacks, makes us fancy many things that are founded neither in reason nor in experience." "The interests of humanity, and true policy," he concluded, "equally interest in favor of this unfortunate class of men." Hamilton's good opinion of the potential of black slaves as soldiers and citizens was borne out by the experience of General Nathaniel Greene, who reported that "there is a spirit of enterprise among the black people; and those that come out as volunteers are not a little formidable to the enemy." [1]

Jefferson, by contrast, did not welcome blacks as soldiers. While admitting that they sometimes displayed courage, he attributed their valor to their inability fully to appreciate the peril in which their actions placed them. Nor did he believe that they were conditioned by slavery to make good soldiers: they were too conscious of the degradation they had suffered at the hands of whites, he said, to fight zealously for the freedom of their masters. Finally, he stood in far too much dread of slave insurrections to approve of the idea of putting guns—together with the intoxicating slogans promising liberty and equality to all men—in the hands of blacks. Instead of regarding the black population as a potential reservoir of fighting men, Jefferson, throughout the war, acted on the assumption that neither free blacks nor black slaves could be safely trusted with arms.

In consequence, despite the fact that comparatively few white Virginians were willing to enlist in the armed forces of the continent or the state, Jefferson played no part in the effort to mobilize the blacks in Virginia. He seemed more inclined to appease than to challenge the "triple-headed monster, that shed the baneful influence of avarice, prejudice, and pusillanimity" which Colonel John Laurens said he encountered in all the state assemblies, including that of Virginia. It was not in response to Jefferson's urgings but out of sheer necessity that free blacks and mulattoes were permitted in Virginia after 1777 to enlist in the Virginia militia; that the state later authorized the purchase of slaves for service as laborers with the militia; and that white slaveowners were allowed to send slaves as substitutes in the militia on condition that on the expiration of their term of service they would be made freemen. More in conformity with his views was the state legislature's refusal to permit slaves to enlist in the Continental Line, the state navy, or the militia. Indeed, during his term as governor, slaves were used as a bonus to persuade whites to enlist in the army. In October 1780, Jefferson approved a bill by which the Virginia legislature voted to give every white male recruit who enlisted for the duration of the war "300 acres of land plus a healthy sound Negro between 20 and 30 years of age or 60 pounds in gold or silver." [2]

As governor of Virginia, Jefferson was too acutely conscious of the fact that he was dealing with a community of free white men resentful of every infringement put upon their liberty—were they not engaged in a struggle for liberty?—to be entirely effective as a wartime leader. Unwilling to make government appear oppressive, he deferred to the people's sensibilities, especially their high notions of freedom; and, on occasion, he actually placed the rights of individual citizens above the exigencies of war. Since the people were averse to draft and impressment, he was slow to call out the militia and quick to discharge them. In March 1781, for instance, Governor Jefferson refused to order the militia to work on river fortification on the ground that "a militia of freemen cannot easily be induced to labor in works of that kind." This was proper work for slaves and he accordingly recommended that they be used in place of white militiamen. In one of his less well remembered assertions of the rights of man, he declared that the executive "had no power to call a freeman to labor even for the public without his consent, nor a slave without that of his master." Every individual, including slaveowners, he insisted, had a right "to an explanation of the circumstances which give rise to the necessities under which they suffer."

This solicitude for the rights of property even when applied to slaves could not be maintained in the face of the military reverses suffered by the American army in the spring of 1781. In May 1781, while Lord Cornwallis was striking terror in Virginia—Colonel Tarleton's dragoons almost succeeded in capturing Governor Jefferson himself at Monticello—Jefferson called upon the legislature, citing the indubitable fact that "Money will not procure Labourers," to authorize the government to impress slaves to work as laborers with the state militia. Under the spur of necessity (prior to Cornwallis's surrender at Yorktown) Virginia—admittedly less by choice than under duress—utilized more slave labor in the cause of freedom than did any other state. But only a small proportion of the slaves received their freedom as a result of their war service, and those who did achieve the status of freemen soon discovered that they were not as free as they had supposed: in 1784, the Virginia legislature declared that only free white persons could be citizens.[3]

As a land- and slaveowner, Jefferson suffered heavy losses during the War of Independence. In one of his forays, Cornwallis made Jefferson's Elk Island estate his headquarters for ten days; when he evacuated the plantation, he left behind burned tobacco houses, crops wasted in the fields, and the carcasses of domestic animals wantonly slaughtered. Among the movable property carried off by Cornwallis were thirty of Jefferson's slaves. At the time, Jefferson seems to have been conscious only of his financial loss, but eight years after the event he remarked that had the British general freed the slaves he carried off, "he would have done right." As it happened, however, twenty-seven of the blacks died from camp fever, smallpox, and other diseases. Only three of the abducted slaves were eventually returned to Jefferson.

Because of these and other atrocities—burning towns, pillaging, treating prisoners inhumanely, inciting the slaves to rebellion, and unleashing the Indians against the American frontier—Jefferson declared that the British were guilty of waging war in a manner "savage and unprecedented among civilized nations," and unexampled in the history of warfare. "History," he said, "will never relate the horrors committed by the British army in the Southern states of America"—a circumstance which fully justified, in his opinion, "an irresistible hatred against so detestable a nation." [4]

Jefferson estimated that during the war Virginia lost about thirty thousand slaves, twenty seven thousand of whom died of disease behind the British lines—a wastage of Virginia's labor force that he later cited against the efforts of British merchants to recover the interest on prewar debts owing by Virginia citizens. His own losses he reckoned to be larger than the debt he owed British merchants—which meant that the British army had doubled his debt at the same time that it had seriously impaired the means of paying it. [5]

The death of his wife in 1782 marked a decisive turning point in Jefferson's career. Hitherto, he had remained resolutely in Virginia, content to watch the unfolding of events from that vantage point. On several occasions he had refused election to the Continental Congress: he could not bear the thought of leaving his ill wife and his children at Monticello. In 1783, however, disillusioned with the petty animosities and intrigues of Virginia politics—he was forced to defend himself in the legislature against an abortive attempt at his impeachment—and seeking refuge from the sorrow that had overwhelmed him when he lost his wife, he accepted election to the Continental Congress.

The situation Jefferson found in 1784 in Annapolis, Maryland, the temporary meeting place of Congress—during the period of the Articles of Confederation all its meeting places were provisional—was far more favorable for moving decisively against slavery than that which he had left behind in Virginia. The definitive Treaty of Peace with Great Britain had been ratified in January 1784, leaving the Congress free to direct its attention to the manifold and increasingly urgent problems of peace. Paramount among these was the specific manner in which the West should be opened to settlement—whether land should be sold directly in small parcels to settlers or to large land companies bent upon speculative profits from the sale of land; and how, in the process, the financially hard-pressed federal government could gain a dependable source of revenue.

Virginia's cession in 1783–1784 of its claim to territory north and west of the Ohio River made the Continental Congress the custodian of millions of acres of arable land which, once the Indians were removed, promised to relieve the immediate financial needs of the Congress and to add new states to the Union. It was therefore incumbent upon Congress in 1784 to formulate a definitive policy toward the territories that had unexpectedly come under its jurisdiction. As chairman of a committee to draw up an ordinance specifying the kind of government and land policy that should be established for the governance and economic development of the territories and the method of admitting new states to the union, Jefferson was in a strategic position to influence the future course of American history.[6]

If this "western world" were to be preserved as a part of the union, it must, Jefferson was convinced, be made into a stronghold of self-sufficient yeomen farmers, the breed of men he regarded as the mainstay of republicanism. To turn this developing region over to land companies and to encourage the introduction of the plantation system of agriculture would, in his opinion, not only put the Union in jeopardy but weaken the springs of republicanism in the West, the region upon which he relied to save republicanism after the virtue of the seaboard had been sapped by corruption, luxury, the growth and proliferation of urban centers, and by creeping "monarchism."

Accordingly, in the ordinance which Jefferson and his fellow committeemen presented to the Congress in 1784, land ownership was placed within the reach of most citizens. Furthermore, settlers in the territories were given full civil rights, including manhood suffrage and the prospect of speedy admission of the territories to statehood on terms of complete equality with the original thirteen states.

In order to make the West more attractive to yeomen farmers, Jefferson and his colleagues specified in the Ordinance of 1784 that the region be closed to slavery and all other forms of involuntary servitude after 1800. Clearly, Jefferson envisaged the West not as a projection of Tidewater Virginia—where the plantation system with its major reliance upon slave labor had driven out the yeoman farmers—but as an inviolable refuge for those who wished to have no contact with an institution hostile to their social, economic, and political welfare.*

In Jefferson's draft of the Ordinance of 1784, this prohibition of slavery and involuntary servitude applied to all the territories of the United States, south as well as north of the Ohio. Although none of the

---

* Perhaps too much credit has been given Jefferson's initiative in incorporating the exclusion of slavery from the territories in the Ordinance of 1784. The idea was first put forward by Timothy Pickering, later John Adams's Secretary of State, and by David Howell of Rhode Island, a member of the committee, whose commitment to the antislavery cause was at least as great as Jefferson's. See *William and Mary Quarterly* 29, pp. 231–232.

territory south of the Ohio had yet passed under the control of the Continental Congress—North Carolina, South Carolina, and Georgia did not surrender their claims to their prerevolutionary western boundaries until after the adoption of the Federal Constitution—Jefferson chose to treat this area as though it were already part of the national domain. (Actually, North Carolina had made a tentative grant to the general government which it rescinded after the adoption of the Ordinance of 1784). Had Jefferson's plans been realized, and had they stood the test of time, slavery would have been excluded from the present states of Tennessee, Alabama, and Mississippi. Kentucky would not have been affected; it remained a part of Virginia until 1792.[7]

But as Jefferson well knew, the Articles of Confederation did not authorize the Continental Congress to govern and administer, much less to prohibit slavery in the territories of the United States. Attempting to further the national welfare, as he saw it, Jefferson gave the same kind of broad interpretation to the powers of the Continental Congress under the Articles of Confederation that Alexander Hamilton later gave to the powers of the federal government under the Constitution of 1787 in order to further the interests of commerce and manufacturing. Jefferson was accordingly responsible for one of the first invocations of the doctrine of inherent power—the power residing in Congress "resulting from the union of the whole"—in order to accomplish ends he believed essential to the national welfare. Slavery was considered to be a matter of state concern, yet Jefferson based the Ordinance of 1784 upon the premise that Congress had the power to exclude slavery and involuntary servitude from the territories because it was not a matter of local option but of national concern.

The real issue raised by Jefferson's draft of the Ordinance of 1784 was whether, in order to achieve an objective he deemed vital to the national welfare, he had not deprived American citizens of an inviolable right. If the territories were an extension of the Union, as Jefferson said they were, they were equally open to all citizens *and their property*. In his draft of the Ordinance of 1784, however, Jefferson took the position that slaves were a special kind of property, the possession of which was not necessarily guaranteed by the general government and which, in fact, the government could withhold from citizens at will.

To Jefferson's mortification, the plan to abolish slavery and involuntary servitude in the territories failed of passage in Congress by a margin of one vote. Because one individual, a delegate from New Jersey, was too ill to attend the meetings of the Congress and to cast his ballot in favor of the prohibition upon slavery, the vote of New Jersey was lost. "Thus," Jefferson later wrote in his autobiography, "we see the fate of millions unborn hanging on the tongue of one man, and heaven was silent in that awful moment."[8]

But Virginia was not silent. Except for Jefferson, every delegate to the Congress from the Old Dominion voted against the antislavery clause of the Ordinance of 1784. In fact, only one Southern delegate—Williamson of North Carolina—voted "aye" with Jefferson.

Manifestly, Jefferson had temporarily lost touch with public opinion in his own state and the South, insofar as that opinion was registered by the members of Congress. The Southern representatives were unwilling to see slavery excluded from the territories of the United States in order to attach the region west of the Appalachians more firmly to the Union and to make it a refuge for small farmers. In their opinion, a prohibition upon slavery in the national domain was an unconstitutional violation of their rights as citizens and property owners—a position with which Jefferson, paradoxically, was to find himself in full agreement many years later.[9]

Because of passions aroused by this issue, it is improbable that if the Ordinance of 1784 had been enacted in its entirety, it would have remained in perpetuity, as Jefferson imagined, a barrier to the expansion of slavery in all the territories of the United States. The prohibition upon slavery contained in the ordinance, since it was not an integral part of the fundamental law, could have been changed at any subsequent time by a vote of the Congress. It is unlikely that Southerners would have tolerated after 1793 the exclusion of slavery from the rich cotton lands of Mississippi and Alabama by mere governmental fiat; and had the Northern states then attempted to hold the line drawn by Jefferson in 1784 they would have put the Union itself to hazard.

In 1787, a sectional compromise, the Northwest Ordinance, banned slavery and involuntary servitude after 1800 from the region north of the Ohio and east of the Mississippi Rivers while permitting it in the area south of the Ohio. Jefferson and other proponents of the exclusion of slavery from all of "the western world" had to be content with half a loaf.

As a result of this experience in the Congress at Annapolis in 1784, it was again brought home to Jefferson that his "countrymen" (long after the War of Independence, he continued to refer to Virginia as his "country" and to Virginians as his "countrymen") were not ready to abolish slavery. If they were unwilling to take action in the territories of the United States toward removing this "blot" upon American republicanism, how much less disposed were they voluntarily to dispossess themselves of the benefit of slave labor? In rejecting the antislavery provisions of the Ordinance of 1784, Virginians actually acted contrary to their own economic interests in order to uphold slavery, for, as James Madison pointed out, the exclusion of slaves from the West was certain to prevent a ruinous competition in the production of tobacco between Virginia and the newer sections of the Union.

Despite the defeat of the antislavery provision of the Ordinance of 1784, Jefferson detected signs that the conjugation of revolutionary idealism with opposition to slavery—in his opinion, essential to the completion of the American Revolution—was moving toward its consummation: the purgation of slavery from the United States. He detected signs of this process at work in both the moral, spiritual, and economic spheres—a change of attitude on the part of masters toward their slaves and the declining profitability of slavery as a result of the postwar depression. The Marquis de Chastellux, who visited Virginia soon after the ending of the war, reported that the planters were "constantly talking of abolishing slavery, and of contriving some other means of cultivating their estates. . . .The philosophers and the young men regard nothing but justice, and the rights of humanity." [10]

Certainly this marriage of Enlightenment idealism with indigenous antislavery sentiment was already manifesting itself in the North where, especially in those states where slaves composed a relatively small part of the labor force, emancipation was making large strides. In 1777, Vermont abolished slavery by its state constitution, and in 1781–1782, the Massachusetts Superior Court held that slavery was incompatible with the state constitution which ratified the doctrine that all men were created free and equal. Although no reference was made in this decision to the Declaration of Independence—the state constitution alone was subject to adjudication—the action of the Massachusetts judiciary served notice upon slaveholders that the argument that slaves were not constituent members of society and therefore not entitled to the rights of man would not pass unchallenged. Pennsylvania, Connecticut, Rhode Island, and New Hampshire adopted schemes of gradual abolition; only in New York and New Jersey, where slaves were relatively numerous, did slaveowners succeed in mounting an effective delaying action. As Virginians noted, the abolition of slavery had little adverse financial, social, or economic effect upon those Northern states that held aloft the torch of revolutionary idealism. In those states, on the other hand, such as New York and New Jersey, where the eradication of slavery threatened important material interests, the victory of morality and idealism was long delayed.

❦ 5 ❧

Slavery and the
Decline of "Republican Virtue"

◆

IN 1784, JEFFERSON was appointed by the Continental Congress one of the American ministers charged with negotiating treaties of commerce with European governments, and in 1785 he succeeded Benjamin Franklin as American minister to France. For the next five years he surveyed the American scene from Paris. During this period he was wholly dependent upon his correspondents in America for news from the antislavery front in Virginia, and his advice to his countrymen on tactics and strategy in that continuing struggle was conveyed in his letters to his friends at home, chief among whom was James Madison.

It was while Jefferson was in France that he learned of the emergence of a wholly unexpected threat to the manners and morals which, he supposed, had been created by the American Revolution and consolidated by the establishment of a republican system of government. Anything which adversely affected the manners and morals of Virginians could not, in Jefferson's opinion, fail to have an equally pernicious effect upon the antislavery cause. For he had always believed that the abolition of slavery required a unique intellectual and sociological environment.

During the War of Independence, Americans had been sustained by the conviction that they were the most moral, virtuous, frugal, and self-denying people in the world and that they were engaged in separating themselves forever from an effete, corrupt, and inveterately degenerate Old World. No patriot leader had been more firmly persuaded than Jefferson of the moral superiority of Americans; and none was more astonished and chagrined when they revealed during the postwar period that they were not the paragons of patriotism, spartanism, and rectitude he had supposed them to be.

When he left Virginia in 1783 to attend the meeting of the Continental Congress, Jefferson had flattered himself that republican virtue was firmly established in his "country." Now, two years later, he was informed that the plain living which Virginians had practiced during the war years was no more than a concession to wartime necessity which, as soon as peace had been restored, was replaced by the ostentation and self-indulgence he had deplored prior to the Revolution and which he confidently assumed would not survive the severing of political ties with the mother country.

It is true that Jefferson had frequently complained even during the war years that Virginians lacked a work ethic; his "countrymen," he lamented, were prone to laziness, improvidence, and carelessness about paying their debts—all of which he traced to the demoralizing influence of monarchical government and chattel slavery.

He condemned most of the sports and recreations popular in Virginia: cardplaying ("cards are for blackguards"), cockfighting, and gaming ("which corrupts our dispositions and teaches us a habit of hostility against all mankind"). But he always enjoyed a good horse race; characteristically, he justified the sport on the utilitarian ground that it improved the breed of horses. Nevertheless, nothing had prepared him for the excesses in which many well-to-do Virginians began to indulge after independence had been won. He was told that Americans in general and Virginians in particular were engaging in extravagance of every kind and devoting themselves recklessly to the pursuit of pleasure, regardless of cost, upon the credit advanced them by British merchants. These profligates were the very people upon whom Jefferson had depended to set an example to their countrymen of "republican austerity," revolutionary idealism, and devotion to the public good. By virtue of their superior moral substance, weight of character, and influence, these enlightened *aristoi,* in Jefferson's vision of future felicity, would compel the unenlightened majority who condoned slavery because it contributed to their material well-being to follow the dictates of their torpid and hitherto ignored consciences. Thus the forces of morality, right, and justice would vanquish the "greed and avarice" from which the institution of slavery drew its principal sustenance.

To Jefferson, the abandon with which Americans, including the virtuous, dedicated few, rushed into debt and squandered borrowed money upon British "gew-gaws" and "trumpery" vitiated the blessings of peace. Extravagance seemed to him to be "a more baneful evil than toryism was during the war"; and, worst of all, the example was set by "the best and most amiable characters among us." From Paris—an unlikely podium from which to sermonize—Jefferson preached frugality, temperance, and the simple life of the American farmer. Buy nothing whatever on credit, he exhorted his countrymen, and buy only what was essential. "The maxim of buying nothing without money in our pocket to pay for it," he averred, "would make of our country (Virginia) one of the happiest upon earth." Pay as you go, he insisted, was the maxim which, above all others, would "lay the foundation for happiness." Every man who wished well to his country ought to set an example of simple living, pure morals, and high thinking.[1]

As Jefferson saw it, the most pernicious aspect of the postwar preoccupation with pleasure, luxury, and the ostentatious display of wealth was the irremediable damage it did to "republican virtue." At this time in American history it was commonly believed that the republican form of government could not exist without "virtue"—which signified, in the vocabulary of the eighteenth century Enlightenment, love of country, an austere style of living, probity, strict observance of the moral code, and willingness to sacrifice private profit for the public good. If "virtue" ceased to be the animating force in the United States, Jefferson was inclined to despair of the Republic; the people would then be ready, by his reckoning, for the advent of unbridled self-seeking, corruption, and, finally, monarchism; and, to crown this catalog of abominations, slavery itself would be rendered impregnable to the forces of conscience.

In the agitation of spirit engendered by the spectacle of the decay of republican virtue, Jefferson prayed for the coming of a missionary who would scour the land, excoriating extravagance, easy credit, vice, and corruption and preaching temperance, austerity, and pay-as-you-go as the way to salvation. If such an American Savonarola appeared, Jefferson said that he would be the first to join the crusade.[2]

To account for this backsliding on the part of American patriots, Jefferson, as was his settled habit, blamed the British. It was the credit advanced by British merchants, eager to regain their prewar markets, on insidiously easy terms which encouraged Americans to plunge deeply into debt for imported merchandise they did not really need. Here, he exclaimed, was the serpent in the American paradise, tempting the people to sell their freedom, independence, and rectitude for British "baubles."

From Paris, Jefferson reminded his errant countrymen that unbridled luxury had been the cause of the downfall of the Roman Republic. He looked back nostalgically to the war years when Virginians had perforce lived frugally. During this period of enforced austerity, Jefferson observed, Virginia farmers had depended on their own land for food and clothing and had been content with a small surplus which permitted them to buy salt, sugar, coffee, a little finery for their wives and daughters, and to entertain and visit friends. The secret of this felicity, Jefferson believed, was that no one tempted Americans to buy on credit. This was the true American idyll: people had been content with simple pleasures and rejoiced in the "pleasing and healthy occupation" that kept them close to Nature. "I know no condition happier than that of a Virginia farmer might be, conducting himself as he did during the war," Jefferson declared; at that time every man "slept sounder and awakened happier than he can do now." [3]

To bring back the halcyon days when men practiced "republican virtue" and women dressed simply, Jefferson was prepared to take strong measures. For a people seemingly bent upon self-ruin, Jefferson saw no remedy "but an open course of law." "Harsh as it may seem," he said, "it would relieve the very patriots who dread it, by stopping the course of their extravagance because it renders their affairs entirely desperate." Specifically, he proposed to require by law the wearing of a state-designed costume for women—plain, austere, and truly republican. (Shades of Chairman Mao!) Constrained by wholesome sumptuary laws from indulging their love of European finery, American women hopefully would no longer endanger by their luxury, dissipation, and extravagance the foundations of the American republic.[4]

Nor was Jefferson content to confine the government's discretionary powers to this invasion by the lawmakers of the world of *haute couture* —an extension of the authority of government so audacious and so dubious in its results that even Alexander Hamilton would have quailed before it. In order to prevent Americans from giving free rein to their passion for foreign superfluities, he recommended that the government prohibit the purchase of British goods on credit—an idea approved by George Washington and John Jay but not, significantly, by Alexander Hamilton. Aware of the almost insuperable difficulties standing in the way of the implementation of this policy—after all, the United States was officially dedicated to furthering freedom of trade between nations and the freedom of the individual—Jefferson took comfort in the hope that the British themselves, discouraged by the difficulties they experienced in collecting debts in the United States, would cease to sell merchandise to Americans on credit.[5]

In deploring the propensity of his countrymen to conspicuous consumption, Jefferson was, in fact, arguing *contra* David Hume and Adam Smith. These two philosophers, products of the Scottish Enlightenment, defended expenditures on luxury goods on utilitarian grounds. They argued that the desire to possess and display finery, when not carried to excess, tended to keep men industrious and productive beyond the level of energy output required for bare subsistence, thereby stimulating the arts and sciences and fostering the exercise of benevolence, and generosity. These philosophers contrasted the "bleak and barren poverty of savage life" with the amenities affordable in a "refined age," and concluded that the love of the embellishments of life was natural to man and that it enhanced human happiness, freedom, and comfort.[6]

John Adams found it easier than did Jefferson to accommodate himself to the unexpected fall of his countrymen from their wartime condition of republican virtue. "Our Countrymen," he remarked, "had never merited the Character of very exalted Virtue"; far from being Spartans in their contempt of wealth and luxury, they were a money-making people who relished the amenities of life. And rightly so, Adams argued, for without this powerful incentive to industry, it was doubtful if the agriculture, commerce, and manufacture of the country would prosper. According to John Adams, the national character was not degenerating as a result of the new opportunities for money-making created by national independence; Americans had never been, and presumably never would be, any different from what they revealed themselves to be in the postwar years.[7]

But Jefferson had a peculiarly cogent reason, by which Adam Smith, David Hume, and John Adams were unaffected, for decrying the corruptive consequence of luxury. Jefferson had always taken comfort from the fact that Virginia gentlemen did not live off each other by buying and selling, by overcharging the common people for merchandise, and by hounding their debtors: they left that demeaning business to British merchants. He had found solace in the reflection that greed and avarice were vices peculiar to businessmen and that farmers and country gentlemen were immune to the debasing passion for inordinate wealth, luxury, and power. Yet he now beheld this same pernicious spirit unexpectedly rising like a specter among the Virginia planters to whom he had assigned the task of exorcising with the talisman of republican virtue the familiar demons who ruled the marketplace.

In the Jeffersonian scheme of things, materialistic values were the eternal enemy of the epochal republican experiment upon which the United States had embarked. If the American people became infected with the passion of getting rich quickly, regardless of the social cost, they would, he predicted, "forget themselves, but in the sole faculty of making money, and will never think of uniting to effect a due respect for their rights." In that event, he feared that "the jealous spirit of liberty which shaped every operation of our revolution" would be submerged. "The natural progress of things is for liberty to yield and government to gain ground," he said, and liberty never stood in greater danger of succumbing to the encroachments of government than when a people had been corrupted by the spirit of money-making.

While Jefferson never denied the compelling force of the acquisitive instinct—no American could entirely ignore that reality—he relied upon the good sense of the American people to practice self-restraint in the pursuit of wealth. Important as it was to acquire property, it was equally important to know when to stop. This point was reached, Jefferson said, when one attained comfortable circumstances, a sufficiency of the necessities of life, and a modicum of the conveniences and embellishments. He expected the American people, situated as they were in the midst of incalculable riches, to observe a civilized and enlightened restraint in their pursuit of material well-being, to recognize the metes and bounds dictated by social responsibility, and to accord higher respect to talent, integrity, and moral excellence than to the ability to amass wealth regardless of the means and of the consequences that might be visited upon the social environment.

In Jefferson's way of thinking, the preservation of republican virtue, and the frugality and plain living by which it was sustained, against the passion for money-making and the profligacy, luxury, and ostentation to which it gave rise, had proximate relevance to slavery and its eradication. Not only did a people vitiated by a fixation upon wealth lose their love of liberty; such a people, Jefferson believed, also lost their zeal to do justice to their fellow men. A people whose scale of values was determined by dollars and cents were not likely to free their slaves: to them, slaves figured only as a source of the profit which made possible the conspicuous consumption to which they had become inextricably attached. One of Jefferson's predicates was that only a people who practiced self-denial and who put justice above material gain would be willing to renounce a right to the ownership and exploitation of human beings sactioned by tradition and enshrined by economic advantage.

Yet, if Jefferson's correspondents could be believed, this spirit seemed to be sadly wanting in postwar Virginia. "Our experience here teaches us," James Madison told Jefferson, "that our people will extend their consumption as far as credit can be obtained"; not until they had borrowed the last farthing that British merchants were willing to lend would they voluntarily abandon their prodigal ways. Even those few enlightened planter-aristocrats upon whom Jefferson depended to spearhead the campaign to extirpate slavery "at some period of time not very far distant" seemed to be in no hurry to get on with the work of liberating their own slaves. While expressing their abhorrence of slavery, they were content to appropriate the usufruct of their "servants' " labors in order to regale themselves with the luxuries which they and their wives seemed to consider essential to their social position.

It thus came as no surprise to Jefferson that the proslavery forces in Virginia began to mobilize in earnest in 1785. While some slaveowners took advantage of the Act of 1782 by freeing their slaves without prior permission from the governor and council, the proponents of slavery denounced the law and petitioned the legislature for its repeal. Over fifteen hundred signatures, mostly from people living south of the James River, were fixed to a single petition. These citizens did not bother to assert the inferiority of the blacks: they assumed that such inferiority was as self-evident as any of the truths enunciated in the Declaration of Independence. The thrust of their complaint was directed against the increasing number of blacks freed under the Act of 1782 who, they complained, had proved to be destructive of the happiness, peace, safety, and good order of the commonwealth. And, the petitioners declared, the more slaves that were freed, the worse "the Horrors of all the Rapes, Murders and Outrages" would ensue when a "vast Multitude of unprincipled, unpropertied, revengeful and remorseless Banditti" was unleashed upon the hapless white citizenry. It was precisely to prevent such havoc and death, they asserted, that the Bible permitted God's people to hold bondsmen and bondswomen. Slavery, in short, was a divinely instituted institution and blacks were slaves by divine decree.[8]

Although a bill to repeal the Act of 1782 was defeated in the Virginia House of Delegates in 1785 by a vote of 52 to 35, the members gave no hope that the abolition of slavery was likely in the foreseeable future: a bill sponsored by the Quakers calling for a general emancipation was unanimously rejected by the House of Delegates.

Clearly, revolutionary idealism had collided head-on in Virginia with the racial prejudice and the economic viability which endowed the institution of slavery with the extraordinary resilience and powers of endurance it displayed during its long life. As the Virginia petitioners opposed to manumission implied, slavery was an effective means of maintaining control over a restive black population compelled to labor against its will and of extracting profits from their labor. Viewed from this perspective, slavery was eminently justifiable on utilitarian grounds. And in the United States, institutions have historically risen or fallen on precisely these grounds.[9]

❧ 6 ❧

Slavery and the
Notes on Virginia

◆

In 1785, while Jefferson was deploring the inroads of the money-making spirit upon republican virtue and antislavery sentiment, he published in Paris an impassioned indictment of slavery, the *Notes on Virginia*. Although only a small part of this book dealt specifically with slavery, here, for the first and last time he unburdened himself fully in print upon the subject. Yet in writing the *Notes on Virginia*, Jefferson had no intention of laying his sentiments before the world. Originally written in 1781–82 at the request of the Duc de Barbé-Marbois, the French chargé d'affaires in Philadelphia, this survey of the government, economy, geography, and sociology of Virginia was intended to be circulated in manuscript among a select group of "estimable characters," primarily French *philosophes*. For an author, Jefferson displayed astonishing reluctance to see his work in print and, indeed, he did not consent to its publication until a pirated, poorly translated French edition forced his hand. Even then, he tried to publish it anonymously and to restrict its circulation to a few European savants, members of Congress and the students at the College of William and Mary.[1]

The reason for Jefferson's singular reticence was that in the *Notes on Virginia*, addressing himself, as he supposed, to European intellectuals, he had outdone himself in expressing his dislike of the Virginia Constitution of 1776, his abhorrence of slavery, and his doubts about the innate intelligence of blacks. On these subjects, Jefferson delivered himself of opinions that he did not intend for public consumption. After all, Virginians could hardly be expected to relish being told that they were living under a form of government that violated some of the basic principles of the American Revolution and that their minds and hearts were being brutalized by the presence of slavery. He especially feared that the views on slavery he expressed in the *Notes on Virginia* would prove counterproductive: instead of furthering the cause of emancipation, they would actually prejudice it by acting as an "irritant." Had Jefferson had his way, the only book he ever wrote would not have been published and his opinions on slavery would not have become public knowledge during his lifetime.[2]

Jefferson was the more indisposed to see the *Notes on Virginia* published because the news from Virginia gave him reason to believe "that the moment of doing it with success was not yet arrived, and that an unsuccessful effort, as too often happens, would only rivet still closer the chains of bondage." This is a familiar theme in Jefferson's antislavery activities: he always assumed that the timing of the assault upon slavery was all-important and that a premature effort would result in an irreversible setback. While it was said of Jefferson that he always preferred to be slightly ahead of public opinion, he was careful not to get so far in advance that he lost his political followers. In the case of slavery he was especially alert to that peril. Here his soundings of public opinion were generally negative. "The public mind would not yet bear the proposition" of emancipation, he said, and this seemed a sufficient reason to postpone positive action. Two weeks before his death, Jefferson defended the policy of palliation and delay he had consistently observed toward slavery: "A good cause is often injured more by ill-timed efforts of its friends than by the arguments of its enemies. Persuasion, perseverence, and patience are the best advocates in questions depending on the will of others. The revolution of public opinion which this cause requires is not to be expected in a day, or perhaps in an age; but time, which outlives all things, will outlive this evil (slavery) also." With respect to slavery, Jefferson did not act upon the maxim *"De l'audace, et encore de l'audace, et toujours de l'audace,"* but upon the very different principle of "prudence, and again prudence, and always prudence." [3]

Similarly, Jefferson expected that the destruction of aristocracy in Virginia—a work he believed had been begun by the abolition of primogeniture and entail—would be a slow and arduous process. But, as in the case of slavery, he was certain of the eventual outcome: that "the plebeian interest will prevail over the old aristocratical interest"—provided, that is, that the leaders of the plebeian interest did not rashly attempt to achieve too much too soon.[4]

Among American leaders, Jefferson was one of the most conspicuously successful practitioners of the gradualist approach to the resolution of social and political problems. Instead of attempting a great leap forward, he was usually content to move slowly, circumspectly, and patiently toward what he called "the reformed order of things." He no more believed in the practicability of instant reform than in instant democracy for a people untrained in political processes. "Truth advances, and error recedes by step only," he observed, "and to do to our fellow men the most good in our power, we must lead where we can, follow where we cannot, and still go with them, watching always the favorable moment for helping them to another step." He insisted that reform, to be effective, must be founded solidly upon public opinion; only the manifest will of the people could legitimatize fundamental changes in the body politic and the social order. To exemplify this dictum he was fond of citing the American Revolution which, he believed, had germinated for generations in the minds and hearts of the American people and had assumed the form of open revolt only after a long course of "intolerable" oppression.

Forty years of practical experience, Jefferson once said, was a better teacher than a century of reading. And he was convinced that his policies and the methods he used to attain them were, in fact, the fruit of experience in the world rather than speculations conceived "in a closet." Chief among the salutary lessons for the guidance of statesmen he derived from experience were a wariness of "visionary principles" and the expectation of miracles, and fortitude in the face of public indifference. In effecting changes in government and society, it was necessary, he observed, first to decide what was to be done and, secondly, to determine how much could be achieved under the existing circumstances. "What is practicable must control what is pure theory"; "we cannot always do what is absolutely best. . . .We see the wisdom of Solon's remark, that no more good can be attempted than the nation can bear"; "it is practise alone which can correct and conform them (the plans of statesmen) to the active current of affairs." [5]

Nor did Jefferson suppose that reforming zeal was always in the ascendant and that it could be summoned up at will by those advocating change. "It is only by a happy concurrence of good characters and good occasions," he said, "that a step can now and then be taken to advance the well-being of nations." This fortuitous conjunction had occurred during the American Revolution, but Jefferson did not recommend that the United States rely upon an indefinite continuation of its good fortune. Great crises did not always produce great men.

This caveat, Jefferson frequently observed, applied with special force to the abolition of slavery: the "blot" could be erased only slowly and with infinite patience. And it required the leadership of a very special order of men who had themselves conquered the demons of greed and avarice and were thereby qualified to exorcise them from the public counsels.

During the American Revolution it had frequently been observed that the enthusiasm for freedom displayed by Southerners was enhanced by the ownership of slaves. Edmund Burke, for example, although he disapproved of slavery, remarked that slaveowners were among the foremost in asserting the rights of man precisely because they were slaveowners. "Where there is a vast multitude of slaves as in Virginia and Carolina," he observed, "those who are free, are by far the most proud and jealous of their freedom. . . .To the masters of slaves, the haughtiness of domination combines with the spirit of freedom, fortifies it, and renders in invincible." With the human degradation and misery produced by slavery manifest on every hand, free men were adamantly resolved that "slavery" should not be forced upon them by the king and Parliament or by any other body of men. When Southerners decried "slavery," "oppression," and "tyranny," they knew whereof they spoke.

Likewise, the necessity of controlling a large servile labor force was credited with creating a habit of command, a consciousness of innate racial superiority, a sense of responsibility to the lower orders and, by extension, the graciousness and civility that characterized the Virginia gentleman. John Randolph of Roanoke went so far as to contend that the possession of slaves was necessary to the creation of a perfect gentleman.[6]

In the *Notes on Virginia* Jefferson challenged this notion that slavery helped promote the love of freedom and the gentlemanly virtues. The ownership of human beings, he declared, fostered only cruelty, false pride, tyranny, and mindless brutality—the most uncivilized behavior of which man was capable except in time of war. Viewing slavery from the moralistic standpoint he usually assumed, Jefferson concluded that the institution served only to degrade the slave and debauch the morals of the master. "The whole commerce between master and slave," he said, "is a perpetual exercise of the most boisterous passions, the most unremitting despotism on the [one] part, and degrading submission on the other." Slavery was, in fact, devoid of redeeming qualities: it robbed the blacks of all incentive to labor; it discouraged the immigration of whites to Virginia; it retarded public improvements; and it created an atmosphere deadly to the kind of public and private virtue without which a republican form of government could not survive.

Although Jefferson did not ignore the effects of slavery upon the slaves themselves, his overriding concern was always with the free white citizenry, their psychology, their institutions, and their morals. He believed that blacks could endure slavery and still emerge with their moral sense intact, whereas whites were utterly demoralized by the intoxicating sense of power it engendered.*[7]

---

* George Mason, who anticipated Jefferson in the expression of many "Jeffersonian" ideas, had analyzed as early as 1774 the baneful effects of slavery upon the white community. His conclusions were remarkably similar to those described by Jefferson in the *Notes on Virginia*. "Every gentleman here is a petty Tyrant," Mason said in 1774. "Practised in the Arts of Despotism and Cruelty, we become callous to the Dictates of Humanity, & all other finer feelings of the Soul. Taught to regard a part of our Species in the most abject & contemptible Degree below us, we lose that Idea of the Dignity of Man, which the Hand of Nature had implanted in us, for great & useful purposes. . . . Habituated from our Infancy to trample upon the Rights of human Nature, every generous, every liberal Sentiment, if not extinguished, is enfeebled in our Mind. And in such an infernal School are to be educated our future Legislators and Rulers." See *Virginia Magazine* 80, p. 151.

While Jefferson took little note of this aspect of the problem, the effect of slavery upon women, in the opinion of some foreign observers, was no less injurious than upon men. Permitted little share in the amusements and no share whatever in politics of males, and surrounded by a small circle of household slaves, women tended to become indolent, self-indulgent, frustrated, and unhappy—and quite as tyrannical to their slaves as were their husbands, brothers, and fathers. The slowdown and the "playing dumb" resorted to by some slaves as a form of passive resistance to slavery exasperated the wife of William Byrd II to such a degree that she lashed the slaves herself and had to be restrained by her husband from doing them serious physical harm.

Worst of all, Jefferson argued, the ownership of human beings brought into play one of the least appealing aspects of human nature—the lust for power which lurked in the heart of every human being. Power tended to corrupt; even a virtuous man who exercised absolute power over other human beings could not resist its corrosive effects. It was comparable, he believed, to the corruptive effect of political power. When a man so much as cast a longing eye on political office, Jefferson observed, a "rottenness" began to set in; thenceforth he had to be watched narrowly, for no politician was above suspicion. Against the passions aroused by the exercise of power, reason was helpless; for power, Jefferson discovered, always believed itself to be right, "that it has a great soul and vast views, beyond the comprehension of the weak; and that is doing God's service, while it is violating all his laws." His reading of history had convinced him that in no country did the rulers, even those duly elected by the people "fail to betray and oppress those for the care of whose affairs they were appointed, by force if they possessed it, or by fraud and delusion it they did not." [8]

Because he took little pleasure in the direct exercise of power over other human beings, Jefferson consistently underestimated the strength and durability of slavery. "Never have I ever been able to conceive how any rational being would propose happiness to himself from the exercise of power over others," he remarked. Yet absolute power over slaves gratified one of the human instincts which Jefferson believed himself to have transcended in his own personality; as a result, he failed to comprehend the mentality of many of his fellow slaveowners, to whom the exercise of power was a source of ineffable satisfaction.

Yet it is clear that Jefferson believed that exceptional individuals escaped the corruptive effects of slavery. He never accused James Madison, George Mason, or James Monroe, all of whom were slaveowners, of being cruel, tyrannical, and morally corrupt; in his eyes they were Virginia gentlemen, models of benevolence, compassion, virtue, and love of liberty. The case of George Wythe, however, was less edifying: while he resisted the temptation to cruelty to which slaveowners were exposed, he succumbed to the sexual attractions of a slave woman.

Because of his preoccupation with the effects of slavery upon whites, Jefferson never really put himself vicariously in the position of the blacks: it did not occur to him to say, for example, "There but for the grace of a white skin, go I." Nevertheless, he found no benefits in slavery for the slaves themselves: he rejected as unworthy of discussion the argument that slavery had the benign effect of civilizing and Christianizing a barbarous people who, if they had not been enslaved, would have remained in ignorance, squalor, and degradation. Slavery, he declared, was an unmitigated evil to master and slave alike.

So unmitigatedly evil was slavery, so devastating in its effects upon whites, and so flagrantly was it in violation of the laws of nature that Jefferson declared in the *Notes on Virginia* that if Americans expected Heaven to support their struggle for freedom—and he believed that the aid of Heaven could not be dispensed with—they must lose no time in eradicating it. Indeed, Jefferson went further: he predicted that unless slavery were put in the course of extinguishment, a justly licensed Deity would punish Virginians by a signal act of retribution. "I tremble for my country" (by his "country" Jefferson meant Virginia), he said, "when I reflect that God is just."

Long before the birth of Christ, the historians of China had remarked that disasters inevitably befell the Son of Heaven when he violated the mandate of Heaven. Jefferson invested this mandate in the American people rather than in a Son of Heaven, but the effect was the same: either obey the mandate or suffer the consequences of divine displeasure.

Despite the fact that in the Age of Reason the intervention of the Deity in human affairs was deprecated by the *philosophes,* Jefferson did not himself believe that events were left "to the guidance of a blind fatality." The "Creator and benevolent Governor of the world," he was convinced, suspended the operations of natural law whenever it suited His purposes. Usually those acts were the result of derelictions on the part of nations: "The moral condition of the world," Jefferson asserted, did not permit national crimes to go unpunished and national virtues to go unrewarded. "We are not in a world ungoverned by the laws and power of a superior agent," he observed. "Our efforts are in His hand, and directed by it; and He will give them their effect in His own time." [9]

In his own lifetime Jefferson witnessed many events which seemed to substantiate his view that the affairs of mankind were in the custody of an all-wise, omnipotent Author of Nature. The separation of the American colonies from Great Britain, for example, struck him as the consummation of a process ordained by God and Nature: "It was the will of Heaven that the two countries should be sundered." He saw the workings of the same guiding hand in miraculous victories of the armies of the French Republic over the allied despots of Europe. In 1795, when the French-supported Dutch patriots won a notable victory over the British, Jefferson celebrated the event as proof "that there is a god in heaven, and that he will not slumber without end on the iniquities of tyrants." The downfall of Napoleon afforded additional proof, he said, that the moral nature of the universe did not permit a great crime to pass unpunished. The Creator, it appeared, watched over people struggling to be free at the same time that He administered chastisement to peoples and individuals who violated the divine ordinances.* [10]

By invoking the image of an avenging Lord of Hosts, Jefferson seemed to have attained the state of mind of Jonathan Edwards when he preached his sermon upon the theme of "Sinners in the Hands of an Angry God." But while Jefferson was not free of the humorless self-righteousness of a Puritan, he was wholly lacking in the Puritan's sense of his own sin, guilt, and loathsomeness in the sight of God. Jefferson believed in original goodness, not in original sin: if man had fallen from grace it was not because he had eaten of the forbidden fruit, but because he had submitted his own free will to the oppressive rule of kings, priests, and nobles. He regarded the New England Puritans as obscurantists who, like Calvin, preached false religion derogatory to man and God alike. He found Puritan theology abhorrent: total depravity, original sin, and the salvation of the elect were in his opinion part of that "savage enthusiasm which represents man as a criminal and God as a tyrant"—a dogma which had spawned swarms of fanatics and drenched the earth in blood. Between John Calvin's God—"a demon of malignant spirit"—and the "Creator and benevolent Governor of the world" in whom Jefferson and other Men of the Enlightenment believed [11] there was a deep intellectual gap.

Although he denied any spiritual or intellectual affinity with the New England Puritans, Jefferson's steadfast conviction that the American Republic was under divine guidance established a certain kinship between him and the Puritan clergy. Like the Puritans, he felt that his own destiny was linked to that of a consecrated people set apart from the rest of mankind. He likewise shared their abiding apprehension of divine chastisement. Any apostasy on the part of Americans from the divine plan was certain to catch the attention and provoke the wrath of the Almighty, unrelenting as He was in His scrutiny of their activities. And, where moral deviations were involved, Jefferson's "Author of Nature," like the Puritans' Jehovah, was apt to wreak his wrath on an apocalytic scale upon those who incurred His displeasure.

Other American patriots shared Jefferson's fear that until the "blot"

* Jefferson could have derived from his reading of the classics the idea that the affairs of mankind were under divine superintendence. As Horace said, "God should not intervene unless the matter is worth it."

of slavery had been erased, the United States stood in imminent danger of divine punishment. In New England, for example, slavery was denounced as "a God-provoking and wrath-procuring sin." In 1774, George Mason of Virginia warned that Providence might "avenge upon our Posterity the Injury done a set of Wretches, who our injustice had debased almost to a° Level with the Brute Creation. . . . As nations cannot be rewarded or punished in the next world they must be in this." During the War of Independence, Abigail Adams, John Jay, and many others declared that unless the slaves were freed, Americans' "prayers to Heaven for liberty will be impious" and certain, therefore, to go unanswered.[12]

As he made clear in the *Notes on Virginia*, Jefferson expected that the vengeance of the Almighty, if and when it came, would take the form of a slave revolt. He never deprecated the courage of the blacks and he never doubted that unless they were given the hope of freedom, they would rise in rebellion. In that event, Jefferson said, whites could not expect to find God on their side; more probably, God would be on the side of black freedom. He did not rule out the possibility that "a revolution of the wheel of fortune, an exchange of situation (between masters and slaves) by supernatural interference" might occur as a result of the racial war that would devastate the South. "The Almighty," he declared portentously, "has no attribute which can take sides with us in such a contest."

Fortunately for white Southerners, Jefferson's state of mind was not known to the black slaves. Had they been as certain as he that the Lord of Hosts would be fighting on their side, they might not have been willing to wait while their masters debated the sociological, economic, and moral merits and demerits of slavery. In that event, Jefferson's prediction of a massive slave insurrection might have become self-fulfilling.

At the time he wrote the *Notes on Virginia*, Jefferson did not really expect that his countrymen would provoke the Creator to such cosmic anger. Believing, as he did, that the affairs of mankind were under the superintendence of an "overruling Providence," which had foreordained that the slaves should go free, his confidence in the reason and moral sense of man strongly inclined him to discount the likelihood of divine retribution. He took consolation in the reflection that the Creator had given Americans a clear option: they could wait until the "god of justice," in response to the pleas of the slaves, unleashed his "exterminating thunder," or they could abolish slavery peacefully, gradually, and with a minimum of inconvenience to themselves. Jefferson did not seriously doubt which option Americans, and especially his fellow Virginians, would elect once they clearly understood the alternatives between which fate compelled them to choose.

⌖ 7 ⌖
The Question of
Racial Inferiority

THE EIGHTEENTH CENTURY ENLIGHTENMENT sought to raise the study of man into a science, "the science of human nature." Human conduct was assumed to be based upon ascertainable and predictable laws. David Hume, the Scottish philosopher, summed up the thought of an era when he observed that "it is universally acknowledged that there is a great uniformity among the actions of man, in all nations and ages, and that human nature remains still the same, in its principles and operations. The same motives always produce the same actions." Such differences as existed between the several races of mankind were generally attributed, especially in the late eighteenth century, to climate and other purely environmental conditions.

In the *Notes on Virginia*, Jefferson tried to apply the scientific methodology and the governing ideas of the eighteenth century Enlightenment to a study of Afro-Americans. The question he asked himself and answered, at least tentatively, was: to what extent were the differences between whites and Afro-Americans attributable to environment and to what extent they were due to inherent, biological, and therefore irreversible factors.

In subjecting American blacks to scientific scrutiny, Jefferson sought to observe all the canons of eighteenth century science: to reach no definitive conclusions without factual data to support them and to keep an open, sceptical, and detached mind until all the evidence had been assembled. Jefferson regarded himself as an impartial, wholly objective observer who viewed "the gradations in the races of animals with the eye of philosophy." He prided himself upon his unremitting enmity to irrationalism, superstition, prejudice, and dogmatic authority—none of which, he said, entered in the slightest degree into the comparative study of whites and blacks he undertook in the *Notes on Virginia*.[1]

Jefferson was not dissuaded from making this comparison by the fact that the blacks were for the most part slaves, whereas the whites were free—with all the differences in opportunity and education that these dissimilar situations necessarily implied. He boldly set out to discover not a common denominator between the two races but to determine in what particulars blacks and whites were superior or inferior.

Among the premises upon which Jefferson based his evaluation of the two races was that white was a more pleasing color than black. He admitted that he was repelled by blackness: "The eternal monotony, which reigns in the countenances, (of blacks) that immovable veil of black which covers all the emotions" struck him as markedly inferior to the beauty of a red and white complexion which permitted "the expressions of every passion by greater or less suffusions of colour." Unhappily for them, blacks could not blush. Likewise, the "flowing hair, a more elegant symmetry of form" characteristic of whites seemed to him more attractive than the "woolly hair" and "ungainly" physique of blacks.[2]

Here Jefferson reflected the age-old belief that blackness was somehow a curse. As Henry Home, Lord Kames, an eighteenth century Scottish philosopher whose writings influenced the development of Jefferson's philosophy, said, "the colour of the Negroes . . . affords a strong presumption of their being a different species from the whites"; and his immediate, though not his final, impression was that their skin coloration indicated "inferiority of understanding." Color—"the radical distinction which nature has made"—formed forever, in Jefferson's opinion, an insuperable barrier to the creation of a multiracial society.*

In the *Notes on Virginia*, Jefferson compiled a list of attributes and talents in which he judged the blacks to be superior, equal, or inferior to whites. He emphasized that his opinions were "scientific"—that is, they were based upon empirical observation—and that, where conclusive evidence was wanting, he ventured no more than provisional suggestions which might or might not be confirmed by later, more precise and persuasive data. With this proviso, he advanced tentatively the hypothesis that Afro-Americans were superior to whites in music and equal to them in courage, memory, adventurousness and the moral sense but inferior to Caucasians in reasoning powers, forethought, poetry and imagination.[3]

Jefferson, who loved music and played the violin assiduously, conceded in this sphere the superiority of the blacks: he had frequently heard their singing and had observed how quickly they mastered musical instruments. And, although he was inclined to assume their courage and adventurousness proceeded from an inability fully to comprehend danger, he did not deny them equality with the whites in this regard. As for their moral sense, he was prepared to concede that the deficiencies they revealed

---

* James Madison once told Harriet Martineau "that if he could work a miracle, he knew what it would be. He would make all the blacks white; and then he could do away with slavery in twenty-four hours." See Martineau 1968, p. 208.

were attributable to the degradation they experienced as slaves rather than to a congenital "depravity of the moral sense." He explained their proneness to thievery—much complained of by their masters—on the ground that people who owned no property and who were debarred from ever owning property could hardly be expected to respect the property rights of others. He even raised the question whether the slave might "justifiably take a little from one, who has taken all from him?" [4]

Admitting that the institution of slavery had taken "all" from its victims, the question remained—and it was this question that primarily concerned Jefferson—just how much had the blacks lost by slavery? He rejected the idea that Afro-Americans were white men with black skins: there were, he argued, ascertainable differences which seemed to indicate that Nature had established a hierarchy among the various races of men. Especially on the score of intelligence, imagination, and poetic fancy the evidence seemed to him to point irresistibly to a marked inferiority on the part of blacks which had nothing to do with their condition of servitude in the New World or other environmental circumstances.

In the *Notes on Virginia,* Jefferson marshaled the evidence which seemed to him to support this interpretation of the designs of Nature. Among other symptoms of congenital mental lassitude, he cited their "disposition to sleep when abstracted from their diversions and unemployed in labor" and their laziness and slowness in obeying orders. He deemed it particularly significant that blacks seemed unable to derive any perceptible benefit from contact with the white man's culture. Household servants, he observed, had ample opportunity to listen to their masters' dinner conversation, yet they gave no sign that they profited from exposure to the feast of manners, taste, and polite learning spread before them. Finally, they did not understand mathematics—Jefferson said that he had never heard of a black capable of comprehending Euclid—and they did not write poetry.

A man less intent upon establishing the case for black inferiority might have pointed out that the slaves' disposition to sleep was the result of laboring from sunrise to sunset in the fields. Nor, seemingly, did it ever occur to Jefferson that the slaves' appearance of mental vacuity, backwardness, dilatoriness, and, on occasion, downright childishness, were actually part of a charade—a feigning of ignorance, docility, and subservience in order to survive under the dangerous and difficult conditions of slavery. By simulating stupidity, the slaves acquired a protective coloration; indolence, inefficiency, and stealing were ways of sabotaging the system. The gameplan was to do as little work and to accomplish as much waste and breakage as possible without incurring punishment. [5]

As for the alleged failure of black household servants to absorb the culture of their masters, George Tucker, a Virginia planter and author, observed that the conversation at the dinner tables of the Virginia gentry dealt less with philosophy and literature than with politics, cards, horse-racing, local gossip, and the price of tobacco, wheat, and slaves. Tucker admitted that slaves had not become philosophers but, he said neither had their masters despite their infinitely greater advantages for self-improvement. Other readers of the *Notes on Virginia* suggested that Jefferson might gain a new perspective upon the relative intelligence of the two races if he lived among American frontiersmen; the savagery, barbarity, and immorality prevalent in their settlements would prove to be a salutary corrective to concepts formulated in the sheltered, cultured, and bookish environment of Monticello.

In this same vein, John Davis, an English traveler, reported that in South Carolina the slaveowners had a very mean opinion of the understanding of their slaves. "But it is obvious to a stranger of discernment," Davis remarked, "that the sentiments of black *Cuffy* who waits at table, are often not less just or elevated than those of his white ruler, into whose hand, Fortune, by one of her freaks, has put the whip of power. . . . Indeed, it must occur to every one, that were things to be re-organized in their natural order, the master would in many parts of the globe, exchange with his servant." [6]

Blacks seemed to Jefferson particularly deficient in imaginative powers: here they were "dull, tasteless, and anomalous." What evidences of *joie de vivre* Jefferson expected of slaves he did not say, but their failure to write poetry struck him as proof of a serious congenital shortcoming. "Among the blacks is misery enough, God knows," he exclaimed, "but no poetry."

If blacks were really the equals of whites, Jefferson felt sure that the misery they experienced as slaves and the hope of a better world to which their condition gave rise, would inspire them to write poetry. The theory that hardship, degradation, and back-breaking labor could inspire great poetry was not original with Jefferson, but he was the first to use it to advance the "suspicion" that blacks were genetically inferior to whites in the important areas of intellectual activity. He compared black American slaves with white Roman slaves, and he found that Roman slaves were far superior to Afro-Americans in the arts, philosophy, and literature. Misery had not prevented Roman slaves from equalling and, in some instances, surpassing their masters. Slavery, therefore, did not necessarily condemn its victims to intellectual sterility; it was race, and race alone, which accounted for the differences in intellectual achievement between white Roman slaves and the blacks who toiled on American plantations.

In *The Decline and Fall of the Roman Empire*, the first volume of which was published in 1776, Edward Gibbon had already invalidated Jefferson's comparison of Roman with American slavery. While admitting that slaves were "the most abject part of mankind," Gibbon had observed that "Hope, the best comforter of our imperfect condition, was not denied to the Roman slave"—and that this hope was realized when, having acquired his freedom, he was admitted into the political community of which his former master was a member. Even though the vestiges of a servile origin were sometimes not completely obliterated until the third or fourth generation—especially in the conferring of civil and military honors—the Roman slave could not be compared in that respect to his American counterpart, who forever bore in his race the emblem of his servitude.[7]

Moreover, although the mass of Roman slaves were agricultural workers who made no contribution to the art, science, or literature of their time, Greeks, who were specially prized as slaves, were often educated when they were enslaved and served their masters as tutors, philosophers, and physicians. Cicero kept a Stoic philosopher in his retinue of slaves; his secretary, Tiro (a Greek), was a slave; and he asked his friends to be on the lookout for "cultured slaves." Seneca highly valued slaves who were proficient in quoting Homer. The poet Terence, a Carthaginian, was a slave; Horace was the son of a freedman; and Quintus Annius, the author of annals in the form of poetic history, received his freedom from his patron and became a Roman citizen.[8]

By contrast, American slaves were totally uneducated, and there was not a single slave secretary in the entire South; the only lot most of them knew was hard physical toil which effectively precluded the possibility of any literary accomplishment. "One would have thought," remarked one of Jefferson's critics, "that modern philosophy herself could not have the face to declare that the wretch who is driven out to labor at the dawn of day and who toils till evening with the whip flourishing over his head ought to be a poet." [9] And, as Alexis de Tocqueville said, there was another, more subtle, and far more insidious difference between the position of the slaves in classical antiquity and that of the slaves in the antebellum South. While Americans did not augment the hardships of slavery—on the contrary, Tocqueville admitted, they had improved the physical condition of the slaves—they had added the incalculable element of brainwashing. The ancients had maintained slavery by the use of fetters and other forms of physical constraint, but the Americans, Tocqueville pointed out, "have employed their despotism and their violence against the human mind." Instead of merely taking precautions, as did the ancients, to prevent the slaves from breaking their chains, white Southerners sought to deprive blacks of even the desire for freedom—to bring them to see themselves through the eyes of their masters as a race fit only for servitude and irrevocably condemned to that status by God and Nature. And, although they did not wholly foreclose the hope of manumission—in the antebellum South, a slave's chance of attaining freedom was about one in ten—they were given no prospect of escape from wretchedness and ignominy.[10]

Probably no American of his generation was more familiar with the classical world, its literature, history, and philosophy than was Thomas Jefferson. He needed no instruction from Edward Gibbon regarding the position of slaves in ancient Rome; on the other hand, he could have given Gibbon some illuminating sidelights upon the position of slaves in eighteenth century Virginia. Jefferson drew the analogy between Roman and American slaves in order to prove the point he made repeatedly in his private correspondence: that blacks were, in all probability, congenitally incapable of attaining distinction in the higher ranges of intellectual endeavor—mathematics, science, and literature.

In calling the innate intellectual capacity of blacks into question, Jefferson did not thereby cease to be a man of the Enlightenment of the early eighteenth century. Paradoxically, the eighteenth century, which discovered environmentalism, the natural equality of man, and the imprescriptible rights of human beings, also produced "scientific" evidence of the innate inferiority of black Africans. Although the early Enlightenment relieved the black Africans of the supposed Biblical curse of being the descendants of Ham, Noah's errant son—to most of the men of the Enlightenment this was an idle tale told by barbarous Semite herdsmen— they were put under the equally damning imputation of innate intellectual inferiority almost equivalent to original sin. David Hume, for instance, the most illustrious figure of the Scottish Enlightenment, argued that people living in the tropics were radically inferior to inhabitants of the temperate zones. "There never was a civilized nation of any other complexion than white," Hume pontificated, "or even any individual eminent either in action or speculation." In Jamaica, where there was reputed to be a Negro "of parts and learning," Hume thought it likely that he was "admired for very slender accomplishments, like a parrot, who speaks a few words plainly." Voltaire was a firm believer in polygenesis and in a fixed hierarchy of races determined by relative intelligence; blacks, he said, were so "greatly inferior" that they were incapable of entertaining abstract ideas. While Edward Gibbon welcomed the abolition of the slave trade, he feared the consequences of the dissemination among blacks of "wild ideas of the rights and natural equality of man." [11]

Among British philosophers, Adam Smith expressed a distinctly minority view when he acclaimed Africans and Indians as "nations of heroes" who, he asserted, possessed a more highly developed moral sense than their white masters, whom he described as "the refuse of the jails of Europe." The taunt struck home, for at least thirty thousand convicts had been transported from English and Irish jails to the American colonies. Of these undesirables, Maryland and Virginia had received the largest quota.

In contrast to the English and Scottish philosophers of the first three quarters of the eighteenth century, the French *philosophes* in whose company Jefferson moved in France accepted the natural equality of mankind. D'Holbach, for example, denied the existence of racial and hereditary differences in talent, arguing that all such disparities were owing to differences in education; Helvetius found no evidences of racial inferiority; and Diderot idealized the Polynesians who, he said, could teach even the French something about the art of living—and loving. By suggesting that black Africans were innately inferior to whites, Jefferson placed himself in opposition to a major premise of late eighteenth century Enlightenment thought, namely that all mankind was originally the same, and that the existing diversity of races was the result of accidental, environmental circumstances.[12]

Manifestly, Jefferson was under powerful psychological compulsion to believe that the blacks were innately inferior. Had he thought that he and his fellow Virginians were keeping in subjugation and debasement thousands of potential poets, philosophers, scientists, and men of letters— mute, inglorious Miltons—he could not have endured even temporarily the continued existence of slavery. Supposing—and there could be, from Jefferson's point of view, no more awful supposition—that he and other white Americans were denying all opportunity to a black Sir Isaac Newton, a Sir Francis Bacon, or a John Locke—in Jefferson's opinion the three greatest men who ever lived. In that case the tension produced by his view of slavery as "a hideous evil," together with the fact that he himself was a slaveowner, would have been intolerable. By expressing "suspicions" of the inferiority of blacks, Jefferson succeeded in preserving his inner equilibrium and made it possible to live temporarily with an institution which, he constantly assured himself, was in the course of eventual extinguishment.

Although Jefferson did not advance it as a "suspicion," he raised the possibility in the *Notes on Virginia* that blacks might be a separate creation. He cautioned that he did not wish speculations on this subject to degrade "a whole race of men from the rank in the scale of being which their Creator may perhaps have given them," but this statement implied that the Creator may have consigned them to a lower scale of being.[13] The key word is "perhaps." Jefferson did not accept monogenesis as a self-evident, irrefutable fact: he retained an open mind pending the possible discovery of new scientific evidence which might lend support to the theory of polygenesis or, conversely, effectively explode the notion.*

* The first distinctive school of American anthropology adhered to the doctrine of polygenesis. Yet, despite the obvious attractiveness of a theory which postulated the primal differences among the several species of men, polygenesis was not generally adopted by Southern proponents of slavery. The antebellum South became a bastion of fundamentalist Christian orthodoxy, and the doctrine of polygenesis conflicted with the Old Testament version of the origin of the several races of man. All men, the Bible asserts, were the descendants of Adam and Eve—which meant, of course, that blacks and

Most of the luminaries of eighteenth century science rejected polygenesis in favor of the theory that all mankind were descended from a single prototype; as Hannah Arendt has observed, the Enlightenment "believed in the variety of races but in the unity of the human species." Jefferson's friend Benjamin Rush, the Philadelphia physician, compared mankind to an immense, extended family. And in 1774, George Mason of Virginia specifically condemned the theory of polygenesis as a false and pernicious doctrine.[14]

The idea that blacks had been created separately and were consequently a unique and presumably inferior variety of Homo sapiens received support from Edward Long, an Englishman who in 1774, after long residence in the British West Indies, published his *History of Jamaica*. Long asserted that blacks could claim at best a distant, tenuous relationship with the white race. The *History of Jamaica*, because it reinforced prejudices and sanctioned suspicions already firmly rooted in the British colonies, enjoyed considerable popularity; educated Americans, certainly among them Jefferson, knew that Long had called into question the theory of monogenesis and had presented "evidence" that blacks were set apart by the Creator from the rest of mankind.

Jefferson's scientific views were entirely compatible with a separate creation of the various races of man. He believed that man, together with all Nature, had been brought into being spontaneously in the not very remote past and that all living creatures retained very much the form with which they had been endowed at the moment of genesis. There was no room in Jefferson's cosmology for evolutionary change in Nature or in man: they were essentially static creations of the Author of Nature who provided neither for the extinction of existing species or the introduction of new ones. No species had ever become extinct—upon that point Jefferson was adamant. Although he confessed that he could not be absolutely sure, he inclined to the belief that mankind were created with the same racial characteristics that they evinced in the eighteenth century. He certainly considered it unlikely that black Africans and white Europeans had sprung from an Original Pair; his theory of genesis effectively precluded the acceptance of such a version of events.*

---

whites had a common ancestry. But according to the Old Testament the different races of men emerged in the sons of Noah: Ham, the third and the accursed son, was the progenitor of the black race, a degenerate offshoot of the Original Pair. Southerners preferred to stay with the Bible rather than embrace the more dubious but "scientifically" sanctioned concept of polygenesis. By accepting Biblical monogenesis they did not weaken their position that slavery was the most humane condition for an inferior order of men. See M. Harris 1968, pp. 89–92.

* A major obstacle to the acceptance of monogenesis was the brief span allotted to geological time in the eighteenth century. Pope Clement VIII set the date for genesis at 5199 B.C. and Archbishop James Ussher, a prelate of the Church of England, reduced it to 4004 B.C. Although Buffon in his *Epochs of Nature* contended that geological time extended over seventy-five thousand years he believed that Adam and Eve had

In the *Notes on Virginia,* Jefferson did not merely register without comment the hypothesis that blacks had a distinct place in the scale of being: he cited "evidence" newly discovered by travelers which could be used—although Jefferson did not put it to that purpose—to give scientific validity to the idea of a separate creation. This "evidence" drew a significant parallel between orangutans and black African females on the one hand and that of African males and white women on the other.

Discovered by Europeans in the seventeenth century, the orangutan, one of the four species of nonhuman primates, confronted naturalists with a baffling enigma in the Great Chain of Being. Gentle, docile, intelligent— admittedly not all preeminently human characteristics—these tailless anthropoids, more than any other primates prior to the discovery of the gorilla, seemed to resemble man. (In actuality, as subsequent study has shown, this unclaimed place of biological and evolutionary honor belongs to the chimpanzee).

For a brief period in the eighteenth century, the orangutan was credited with being the principal link between Homo sapiens and so- called brute creation. Indeed, some African travelers and European savants were prepared to accept the orangutan as a prospective member of the human family. In his *Discourses on the Origin and Foundation of Inequality Among Men,* published in 1755, Rousseau, a dedicated believer in the infinite possibilities of education, went so far as to suggest that the orangutan, if properly educated might effect a graceful transition from ape to man. Charles Bonnet (1720–1793), a minor French *philosophe,* believed that the orangutan was capable of being trained to become a polite and creditable *valet de chambre;* and the great naturalist Buffon declared that, except for the soul, the orangutan "lacks nothing we possess." James Burnett, Lord Monboddo, author of *The Origin and Progress of Language* (1774), a book with which Jefferson was familiar, went even further: Orangutans, he declared, were actually uncultivated human beings, men in fur coats, a "barbarous branch of humanity" who, with patient instruction, could be taught to talk.*

According to some travelers, the orangutan needed little urging to transcend the limitations of his species. It was reputed that in their native habitat they exhibited a preference for black women over the females of their own kind. Among other orangutan fanciers, Lord Monboddo

---

existed no more than six thousand years before the Christian era. In such an attenuated time span how was it possible to explain the existence of different skin coloration and other distinctive physical characteristics between whites, blacks, and Orientals? If exposure to the tropical sun occasioned the skin pigmentation of black Africans, the processes of Nature must have been rapid indeed. See M. Harris 1968, pp. 84–86 and Jenness 1972, pp. 90–91.

* Shortly after the Declaration of Independence, a patriot asserted that British policy had been "to suffer us to sink down to so many Ouran-Outangs of the wood, lost to the light of science." See Hindle 1956, p. 250.

asserted that orangutans actually copulated with black women and had offspring by them. For these puissant anthropoids, the attraction of black women was not only that they gratified the simian sexual drive, but they fulfilled by such intercourse their primal urge to ascend in the Great Chain of Being. In the popular anthropology of the eighteenth century, it was believed to be a Law of Nature that inferior species sought to mate with superiors in order to raise the biological level of the lower orders. It followed therefore that the cohabitation of anthropoids and black women was Nature's way of creating a new protohuman species midway between ape and man.[16]

In the *Notes on Virginia*, Jefferson argued not only that black was not beautiful but that the blacks themselves knew it. The black male, said Jefferson, showed a preference for white women "as uniformly as . . . the preference of the Orangutan for the black women over those of his own species." [17]

Even though he based his case wholly upon the superior beauty of white over black women and refrained specifically from suggesting that in pursuing white women blacks were trying to raise themselves in the scale of creation, those familiar with the tales out of Africa knew that the orangutans' preference for black woman had a deeper significance than mere sexual attraction. There were forces at work here that transcended mere physical beauty: the orangutan was fulfilling some mysterious, primal inner law of its being. To Jefferson's eighteenth century readers who were familiar with the popular anthropology of the time, the implication for blacks was unmistakable and devastating.*

Jefferson's comparison between black males and orangutans did not, however, pass unchallenged. St. George Tucker, a professor of law at the College of William and Mary, with as strong an antislavery bias as Jefferson's, pointed out that whatever Jefferson's experience may have been, the eroticism of black males was directed toward women of their own color rather than toward white women. Had Tucker wished to demolish the "aspiring Ape" theory completely, he might have pointed out that there were in the South white men who shared the orangutans' alleged lecherous passion for black women—and with no thought whatever of rising in the biological scale by ascending the Great Chain of Being.[18]

St. George Tucker was not alone in objecting that Jefferson had done less than justice to the blacks. George Tucker, a Virginia essayist, poet,

---

* Jefferson was led to believe that the orangutan was found in Africa. Actually, the habitat of the so-called Man of the Woods was confined to Borneo and Sumatra. The orangutan may have been confused with the gorilla, a native of West Africa from the Congo to the Cameroons. The first English account of the gorilla, the largest living primate, was published in 1613; but as late as 1855 it was known to zoologists only by its skeleton. Another possibility is that the orangutan may have been confused with the chimpanzee. See Clark 1957, pp. 13, 55–56, 98, 101; Coon 1965, p. 21; Howells 1959, pp. 81–82, 85–87; and Jordan 1974, pp. 10, 15–19.

and novelist, observed that Jefferson did not seem to realize that beauty lay in the eye of the beholder: Jefferson's wholly subjective notion of the superior comeliness of whites did not necessarily reflect the views of the Creator. To which Jefferson answered that "we have indeed an innate sense of what we call beautiful" and that sense was based upon objective laws of harmony, symmetry, and proportion established in the minds of men by the Author of Nature. But Tucker would have none of this invocation of Heaven and the Most High: he insisted that Jefferson's theory of black inferiority had actually led masters to mistreat their slaves. "After all," he remarked caustically, "whether the blacks are uglier or handsomer than the whites, can prove nothing as to their inferiority in the endowments of the mind, unless we are to take it for granted that beauty and genius always go together, a proposition for which Mr. J. ought not to contend." [19]

Other critics of the *Notes on Virginia* objected that Jefferson's "suspicions" bore a closer resemblance to dogmatic assertions of fact than to hypotheses awaiting scientific verification. Anthony Benezet, Dr. Benjamin Rush, and Gilbert Imlay, among others, took the position that the proofs of inferiority adduced by Jefferson were the consequences of an environment that debased men's understanding and vitiated their moral faculties. John Davis, an English traveler, said that the whites owed their alleged superiority to their education, not to their biology or skin-coloration: "They [the blacks] would be the equal of their masters in virtue, knowledge and manners had they been born free, and with the same advantages in the scale of society. . . . It is to civilization that even *Europeans* owe their superiority over the savage." [20]

In divulging his "suspicions" of black inferiority, Jefferson took care to leave open a line of retreat: everything, he said, was tentative, inconclusive, subject to qualification, and, above all, modifiable by new evidence. He admitted that the deficiencies in intelligence evinced by the blacks might, like their moral lapses, be attributed to the servile state to which they had been reduced, and that under more favorable conditions they might, within a few generations, demonstrate that they were the equals of whites in every particular. But regardless of where the weight of evidence inclined, it did not follow, he was careful to point out, that blacks could be lawfully enslaved. No title or metaphysical prescription conferred the right upon a superior race to enslave a lesser breed. "Because Sir Isaac Newton was superior to others in understanding," Jefferson observed, "he was not therefore lord of the person or property of others."

Smarting under the charge that he had judged the blacks too harshly on the basis of nonscientific evidence, Jefferson emphasized the tentativeness of the opinions he had expressed regarding their intellectual inferiority. "My doubts," he said, "were the result of personal observation on the limited sphere of my own state, where the opportunities for the development of their genius were not favorable, and those of securing it still less so. I expressed them therefore with great hesitation." Moreover, he insisted, "it was impossible for doubt to have been more tenderly or hesitatingly expressed than it was in the *Notes on Virginia* and nothing was or is farther from my intentions, than to enlist myself as the champion of a fixed opinion." [21]

Jefferson's claim that he had done no more than offer harmless conjectures regarding the putative inferiority of blacks is not supported by a close reading of the *Notes on Virginia*. On two occasions, he declared categorically that this inferiority was innate in origin, and he took the position that affirmations of the blacks' ability in anything except music had "yet to be proved." He could not bring himself to concede that all differences in ability were solely produced by "differences of condition, of education, of conversation." Some differences, he felt sure, could not be explained merely by reference to environment: "It is not their condition, then, but nature, which has produced the distinction." [22]

In his conversation and private correspondence, Jefferson was far less reticent than in the *Notes on Virginia* in ventilating his opinion of black inferiority. In 1807, Jefferson astonished Augustus John Foster, a British diplomat in the United States, by roundly declaring that he considered blacks "to be as far inferior to the rest of mankind as the mule is to the horse, and as made to carry burthens." It is true that the arrogance, condescension, and pretensions to moral superiority of British diplomats— they seemed wholly unimpressed by Americans' claims to preeminence— often succeeded in goading Jefferson to an explosive pitch, and he said things in the heat of indignation which he would not have uttered in calmer, more reflective moments. Yet it is obvious that the idea of the innate racial inferiority of blacks afforded Jefferson some alleviation to the harrowing sense of guilt which beset him. Sir Isaac Newton could lay claim to no right to act as lord of the persons or property of others; neither could Thomas Jefferson. [23]

Nevertheless, the seemingly gratuitous disparagement of blacks which has been imputed to the *Notes on Virginia* appears to be temperate, judicious, and "scientific" compared with the conventional view which pictured them as "brutish, ignorant, idle, crafty, treacherous, thievish, mistrustful and superstitious." If Jefferson had challenged racial prejudice by hazarding the "suspicion" that blacks were the equals of whites—or would prove to be the equals when given equal opportunity to excel—he would have found himself at odds with his fellow Virginians, who regarded the inferiority of blacks as an indubitable fact, and who believed that slavery itself was a "natural," Heaven-ordained institution.

By expressing "suspicions" of the inferiority of blacks, Jefferson considerably weakened the impact of his appeal for freedom for the slaves. The alleged inferiority of blacks served as a justification for slavery; by raising doubts as to the slaves' capacity for freedom, it was possible to regard slavery as the proper condition of the non-Caucasian members of the human race. Slaveowners made it a point to inculcate in the slaves a sense of their unworthiness, their helplessness, and their complete dependence upon the mercy of their masters. By creating a slave mentality, they hoped to instill in the blacks a fear of freedom. Indeed, until the conviction of inferiority had been thoroughly implanted in the slaves, Southern slaveowners could not account themselves secure in either their person or their property. White superiority and black inferiority were psychological imperatives of the system. In the nineteenth century, when slavery was acclaimed as a "positive good" for both races, the biological inferiority of blacks was exalted into "an ordinance of Providence." Thomas Carlyle, the nineteenth century English historian and publicist, asserted with the certitude of one privy to the Divine Plan that blacks had been created inferior in order to serve the whites, and that their status was fixed by a decree of the Almighty for all time. "That," he told people of color, "you may depend on it, my obscure Black friends, is and always was the Law of the World for you and for all men."* 24

To a degree which might have astonished Jefferson himself, the dogma of black inferiority proved to be one of the hardy perennials of American anthropological, sociological, and historical scholarship. As late as 1925, the notion of the innate inferiority of blacks was accepted as axiomatic by most anthropologists and historians. Scripture, science, and history combined to relegate the American blacks to the status of poor, congenitally backward relatives—a relationship sometimes reluctantly acknowledged—of the white population. The seamy side of Reconstruction—the graft, corruption, and sleazy politics—was attributed by historians to "Africanism," a quality utterly alien to the high moral standards and the irreproachable rectitude of conduct habitually displayed by Anglo-Saxons.

Despite the professions of tentativeness and the cautionary annotations with which he hedged his conjectures regarding black inferiority, Jefferson helped to inaugurate the historical tendency in America to invest racial prejudice with the gloss of pseudoscientific verification it acquired in the nineteenth century when, as Marvin Harris says, "no 'truth' had

* Jefferson believed that the questions he raised in the *Notes on Virginia* regarding black inferiority were susceptible of scientific enquiry and that science, in the form of psychological testing, would provide an authoritative answer. Recently, Dr. William Shockley of Stanford University, a recipient of the Nobel Prize in physics, has called upon the scientific community to conduct such an empirical investigation. (Dr. Shockley's own tentative conclusions are that blacks are genetically inferior to whites, but that whites, in turn, are inferior to Chinese and Japanese.) But many scientists have taken the position that present-day techniques do not permit a valid measurement of aptitudes, abilities, personality, interests, and motivation. The University of California at Berkeley has banned academic research that might jeopardize "the reputation or status of a social group or an institution."

become more 'self-evident' than that all men were created *unequal*."
Moreover, by coupling racism with overt professions of belief in the
natural and inalienable rights of men, he set the tone for much of subsequent American liberalism which, throughout a large part of the long
history of its struggle for a more just and economically equitable society,
preserved its unacknowledged but nevertheless pervasive racial prejudices
intact.[25]

⇜ 8 ⇝

Blacks and Indians

———◆———

THE ALLEGED INFERIORITY of blacks to whites in intellectual capacity, while it did nothing to hasten the end of slavery (indeed, as has been seen, it served as an argument in favor of its perpetuation) did tend to strengthen Jefferson's arguments for the removal of the black population from the United States. In the *Notes on Virginia,* he made clear that in his scheme of things the black African always remained an alien, an interloper in a "lovely land" where he could sink no roots. As his draft of the Declaration of Independence indicated, Jefferson attributed the presence of blacks in the United States to a historical accident, the work of unconscionable slavetraders who, abetted by George III, violated a decree of Providence reserving the western hemisphere for Indians and white Europeans. To eject the black population from the United States was therefore to act in obedience to the same "overruling Providence" which had decreed that they should be emancipated. Since it had never been part of the plan of the Author of Nature that black Africans should be brought in the first place to the Garden of the World, white men therefore had a right derived from the Author of Nature himself to require that blacks depart the United States as soon as they received their freedom. In the face of this decree of Providence, it was of no avail for blacks to plead that the Rights of Man entitled them to remain in the United States and to partake of the liberty and the material bounty that that country afforded.

While denying the right of a man to enslave another man, Jefferson did not admit that the individual who had been enslaved had a right to residence in the country to which he had been forcibly transported. Slavery, it is true, violated all the rights of human nature, but the victims could claim only the right of free transportation to their homeland. Jefferson applied this principle of expatriation even to white citizens of the United States who insisted upon pursuing methods of money-making of which the majority disapproved, chief among which were "licentious commerce and gambling speculations." "Every society," Jefferson argued, "has a right to fix the fundamental principles of its association, and to say to all individuals, that, if they contemplate pursuits beyond the limits of these principles, and involving danger which the society chooses to avoid, they must go somewhere else for their exercise." He thought that Americans who loved "licentious commerce and gambling speculations" would feel considerably more at home in England than in the United States.

The strength of conviction and the certitude with which he habitually articulated his ideas was owing to his steadfast belief that he was engaged in executing some higher law, an ordinance of Providence. Jefferson liked to feel that he was acting in concert with cosmic forces. Like other important figures of the eighteenth century Enlightenment, he presumed to have penetrated the designs of the Author of Nature for mankind. He was not in the habit of questioning whether his interpretation of the will of the Creator was based upon subjective experience; he assumed the existence of purely objective Laws of Nature and the capacity of man to comprehend them. This process of reasoning—or rather rationalization—led Jefferson to the conclusion that the diaspora of American blacks was the Will of Heaven.

Jefferson was never under the illusion that the abolition of slavery would resolve the racial problem in the United States as he understood it. He always looked beyond emancipation to the conditions that would inevitably follow upon it. Since the United States was already embarked upon a great experiment to prove that free men could govern themselves, Jefferson believed that it would be folly to undertake another and far more dubious experiment designed to prove that blacks and whites could coexist in amity and concord, sharing equally in rights, privileges, and opportunities.

It was impossible for Jefferson, situated as he was in the heart of a slaveholding community, to believe that in the United States blacks would ever cease to be the victims of racial prejudice regardless of whether they were slave or free. In his imaginative flights—and, as he said, he loved to "peep into the future"—he could not envisage the day when Afro-Americans would become full-fledged citizens of the United States, enjoying the right of freedom and equality which was the birthright of every white American and engaging in the pursuit of happiness as freemen. Jefferson expected much of his fellow white Americans, but he never thought that they would accept blacks as their equals—nor, if Jefferson's "suspicions" of black inferiority were given authentication by science—*ought* they be expected to do so.

Jefferson did not have to look far to find evidence that hatred of slavery was perfectly compatible with hatred of the blacks themselves. Arthur Lee, a Virginia patriot and slaveowner, although he detested slavery, considered blacks to be "a race the most detestable and vile that ever the earth produced" and therefore unfit to mix with the white race. Similarly, Landon Carter, a Virginia planter, held both the institution of slavery and the slaves themselves in abhorrence. "Slaves are devils," he said, "and to make them otherwise than slaves will be to set devils free." Carter's solution was to pack the "devils" off to Africa.

In many instances, the proponents of slavery took a more charitable view of blacks than did the professed enemies of the institution: the former at least intended to keep the blacks with them in the capacity of "servants," and to profit from their labor rather than to evict them as undesirables.[1]

If even Virginians who condemned slavery as a moral wrong could not abide the presence of free blacks, the prospects of a peaceful, orderly, harmonious biracial society seemed dim indeed. But Jefferson was also aware that the difficulties in the way of the creation of such a society were compounded by the attitude of the blacks themselves. He believed that centuries of slavery had created so much hatred and resentment on the part of blacks toward whites that it would never cease to affect racial relations as long as the blacks remained in the United States. Perhaps, after they had returned to Africa, the former slaves might think more kindly of their masters, but as long as they continued to reside in this country they would be constantly reminded of the affronts inflicted upon their dignity, pride, and rights, both as slaves and as free men.

Still it was not out of commiseration for the blacks that Jefferson insisted upon their expulsion; his overriding concern here, as elsewhere, was the effect he feared that the presence of large numbers of colored freedmen would have upon the whites. Jefferson had no doubt of the outcome: if the blacks were permitted to remain, it would be a disaster for the white race and for the republican experiment.[2]

In one field of human activity Jefferson was prepared to concede that blacks were unsurpassed: whites could not compete with them in sexual ardor. But Jefferson doubted that this overcharged sexuality had anything to do with love: it was, he said, almost purely animalistic libidinousness—"more an eager desire than a tender delicate mixture of sentiment and sensation." He put the case against permitting blacks to remain in the United States bluntly and succinctly: if the slaves were freed, the sexual ardor of black freemen would be turned against white women. As he observed in *Notes on Virginia,* black men showed the same preference for white women that orangutans exhibited for black females, and this is the theme that permeates his thinking upon racial relations.

To Jefferson, the prospect opened up by emancipation of widespread miscegenation between the two races provided the most compelling reason for insisting upon the evacuation of the black population from the United States. At least since 1773, he had been convinced that the "dignity and beauty" of whites and the civilization they had created depended upon the preservation of racial purity. Against miscegenation he raised, as was his settled habit when confronted by anything that offended his sense of what was right and just, a Law of Nature: the same eternal laws to which Americans had appealed in their struggle against Great Britain prohibited racial mixture.

Early in Virginia's history, miscegenation had been made a crime. Shortly after the restoration of Charles II, the House of Burgesses had enacted a law penalizing fornication between whites and blacks, and a law of 1691 prohibited interracial marriage. The act of 1691 described the offspring of such unions as "that abominable mixture and spurious issue." [3]

In the eighteenth century, as the population of free blacks proliferated in Virginia, the fear of miscegenation as a consequence of emancipation increased apace. Everywhere he went in the Chesapeake region in the 1790s, the Duc de la Rochefoucauld-Liancourt heard planters express the apprehension that if slaves were emancipated and permitted to remain as free men, the consequences would be disastrous to the white race. " 'In future generations,' they say," reported the French nobleman, " 'there would not be a countenance to be seen without more or less of the black color.' " [4]

Fear of rampant black male sexuality directed against white women rose to fever pitch whenever rumors of a slave conspiracy were rife. It was supposed that the blacks intended to kill all white males, reserving the women as the spoil of victory. It was the Rape of the Sabine Women etched in black and white. In actuality, however, black slave insurgents seemed to have their minds upon attaining freedom rather than upon running amok sexually in the white community. Significantly, there is no record of blacks seizing a white woman during a revolt for the gratification of the lust with which Jefferson endowed black males in the *Notes on Virginia*.[5]

Despite the laws and the popular abhorrence of miscegenation, visible evidence of the practice was widespread in the Old Dominion. The Duc de la Rochefoucauld-Liancourt agreed with his Virginia hosts that it was a real and present threat to racial purity in Virginia (he detected proof of this danger even at Monticello), but he and other observers attributed it not so much to black as to white lubricity. It was not free black women but slave women who were subjected to the lust of white men. Slave women were in no position to resist whites. As a result, as the Duc de la Rochefoucauld-Liancourt observed, a new race was being created in Virginia; the black race was being permeated by white genes.[6]

Even though it was impossible to ignore the evidence that racial taboos did not serve to keep white men out of the slave quarters, Jefferson put the case for the deportation of the free black population almost entirely upon the alleged libidinousness of black males. The direction taken by his thinking is revealed by a bill he proposed to the Virginia legislature requiring a white woman who had given birth to a mulatto child to leave the state forthwith or be placed "out of the protection of the laws."

In sum, from the vantage point of Monticello, it appeared that as long as the blacks remained slaves they would be implacable enemies of their masters and would never cease to try to break their chains, even at the cost of bloodshed. As freedmen, on the other hand, they would take their revenge upon their former masters by "corrupting" white blood. Miscegenation on the scale Jefferson apprehended would have snuffed out the Jeffersonian vision of a republic of independent, virtuous, liberty-loving white farmers.

Basically, Jefferson feared blacks. He had grown up on a Virginia plantation surrounded by black slaves, and as a mature man he lived at Monticello where blacks far outnumbered whites. The sheer force of numbers, coupled with the fact that they were held forcibly in servitude, was calculated to produce fear. A highly impressionable man, Jefferson was particularly sensitive to the emanations of resentment and hatred he felt from the presence of large numbers of restive black slaves. It is unlikely that a small number of blacks would have generated this feeling, but Jefferson lived in the state which contained over half the black population of the United States.

Although many of Jefferson's fellow planters insisted as strenuously as did he upon the removal of free blacks from the commonwealth, few put as much emphasis as he did upon the danger of black male sexuality as the chief reason for putting them "beyond the reach of mixture." Other planters recognized that it was the white man who was culpable in matters of miscegenation and that the real problem was putting black women out of the reach of white men. James Madison did not even mention the sexual relations between the two races as a reason for the removal of the blacks: he put the case wholly on racial prejudice on the part of whites "proceeding principally from the differences of color which must be considered as permanent and insuperable." [7]

Contrary to Jefferson's expectations, emancipation, coupled with the presence of free blacks in the United States, did not produce a saturnalia of miscegenation. There was probably more sexual intercourse between blacks and whites in the United States during the eighteenth century than at any subsequent time. Instead, emancipation had the effect of strengthening racial prejudice—with decisive consequences upon the sexual relation of the two races. [8]

Toward the aborigines of North America, Jefferson entertained feelings and attitudes very different from those he held toward people of

African descent. Indians could not be regarded as intruders upon the Garden of the World: they had been there many centuries before the coming of the white man and they were obviously part of the natural order of the western hemisphere. Deciphering the intentions of the Author of Nature, he decided that it was inconceivable that the New World had been reserved for an inferior order of men: ergo, the natives of America could not be one of the lesser breeds. As Jefferson said, the Creator was not a "pitiful Bungler": there was order, design, and intelligibility in the cosmos, indicating the existence of a master plan of which the American Indians were manifestly an integral part.

Although he inclined to the theory that the Indians were mainly of Asiatic origin (he would not have been surprised to learn that the New World was the birthplace of man and that Asia had been populated from North America, but he would have certainly resisted as utterly incredible the idea that man originated in Africa), he did not, for that reason, distinguish them from Caucasians: in his opinion, Indians and whites were essentially one people, and the differences between them were superficial, the effects of environment rather than of biology.

As a result of his observation of "thousands of Indians" and of "the proofs of genius given by the Indians," Jefferson concluded that they were the equals in intelligence, physical strength, and moral sense to Homo sapiens Europeaneus. He found their skin color—a decisive factor in the case of the blacks—to be only slightly different from that of Europeans living in the Mediterranean basin; and he thought that their stage of civilization compared favorably with that of Europeans living north of the Alps at the time of the Roman Republic. He detected no evidence of genetic inferiority in a people who, like the Indians, possessed "a masculine sound Understanding." [9]

Since the Indian was really a white man in moccasins and a breech-clout and the potential equal in every respect to his white relatives, Jefferson welcomed the mixture of Indian and Caucasian genes. There was no question here of species-climbing. Jefferson consequently addressed the Indians in a way he never could have assumed towards blacks: "Your blood will mix with ours," he assured them, "and will spread with ours over this great land" until the two had become "one people" and "one nation."* Jefferson was not a little proud of the fact that both his daughters had married descendants of Pocahontas and that, in consequence, royal Indian blood flowed in the veins of his grandchildren. On the other hand, he never boasted of the fact that through the Randolph side of his family he was descended from the British aristocracy.[10]

Viewed through Jefferson's eyes, the Indian was truly a Noble Savage: wise in council, brave in battle, loyal to friends and family, honorable,

---

* In 1784, Governor Patrick Henry urged the payment of a bounty by the State of Virginia to persons of European descent who married Indians.

proud, self-reliant, and "breathing an ardent love of liberty and independence." Whatever might be said against the Indian, it could not be
said that he was a born slave; quite as much as white Americans, Indians
had acted upon the motto "Give me liberty or give me death"—but, unfortunately for them, they usually got death. As a classical scholar, Jefferson was eager to discover evidences in American Indians of the qualities of
the noble Greeks and Romans—and he did not fail to find them. He
strongly inclined to the theory that the Creek Indians, one of the most
civilized of the so-called Civilized Tribes, were the descendants of Cartha-
ginians and that the Creeks exhibited many characteristics derived from
their putative Old World progenitors. In the Creeks and other advanced
tribes, Jefferson saw traces of the virtues described by Cicero, Epictetus,
and Marcus Aurelius, especially in their "glowing and elevated imagina-
tions," which produced orations he rated not inferior to the "whole
orations of Demosthenes and Cicero." In his opinion, no orator in the
history of mankind had attained the heights of eloquence and pathos
reached by Logan, the chief of the Mingos, when he lamented the death
of his wife and children at the hands of American frontiersmen.[11]

Next to the Indians' oratorical powers which, he believed, betokened
a higher order of intelligence and imagination than he found in Afro-
Americans, Jefferson was impressed by the stoicism with which they endured torture and even death at the hands of their enemies. An Indian
deemed it beneath the dignity of a warrior to betray the emotions of
pain, fear, or even surprise. Perhaps the supreme test of Indian stoicism
occurred when an Osage chief, sitting in the Visitors' Gallery, "showed
no surprise during the debates of Congress." [12]

Jefferson approached Indians in the spirit, but not with the techniques, of an anthropologist. He laboriously compiled dictionaries and
grammars of the Indian languages known to him, but the fruit of his
research was lost in transit from Washington to Monticello. From his
comparative studies of Indian languages, Jefferson concluded that there
were twenty basic, wholly unrelated, languages (actually there are at least
one hundred and twenty) which indicated to him that the Indians had
been resident in the New World for a far longer period than commonly
supposed.

Filled with trophies from the Lewis and Clark expedition, Monticello
resembled an Indian museum. The entrance hall was decorated—among
portraits and busts, heads of moose, mountain ram, and buffalo—with an
assortment of Indian costumes, war clubs, peace pipes, moccasins, and
other native artifacts. The vestibule contained the painting of a battle
between the Panics and the Osages and a map of the Missouri River, both
executed by Indian women upon buffalo skin.[13]

In the American Indian, Jefferson beheld man in the state of nature described by John Locke: in full possession of his natural liberty and equality, endowed with an innate moral sense and a high order of intelligence, and capable of raising himself out of the state of nature into civil society by the exercise of his reason and will. Living in accord with the Laws of Nature, the Indians seemed to Jefferson to be far happier than the oppressed and degraded peasantry of Europe. From a study of the Indian way of life Jefferson believed that even white Americans could learn some salutary truths. For the Indians had proved that strong government was not necessary to the happiness of mankind; among them the operations of the power of public opinion supplemented by the moral sense moulded the conduct of individuals "as powerfully as laws did anywhere." Moreover, by dividing themselves into small self-governing groups they confirmed Jefferson's conviction that the only place in which real freedom could be enjoyed was in a small community where the authority of those in official position was limited by those who knew them personally and who closely observed their conduct lest they be accused of abusing their power.[14]

Obviously, Jefferson did not fear Indians in the way he feared black slaves. He had not grown up among large numbers of hostile tribesmen; by the eighteenth century, the Virginia Indians had been reduced to a dispirited, debilitated remnant of the once powerful tribes that confronted the early white settlers. Jefferson rarely saw Indians except when delegations of the more westerly tribes passed near his father's house on their way to and from councils at Williamsburg. From these brief encounters he conceived a deep "attachment and commiseration" for Indians; he did not view *them* as an internal enemy that might rise at any time against their oppressors and on whose side the Lord of Hosts would fight. As he said of the Indians, "We presume that our strength and their weakness is now so visible that they must see we have only to shut our hand to crush them, and that all our liberalities to them proceed from motives of pure humanity only." [15]

In actuality, however, the Indians had accounted for the deaths of far more white people than had the black slaves. Especially on the frontier, the mortality rate among whites was high, and, in time of war, settlements near the frontier line were devastated. During the War of Independence, while some powerful tribes had supported the Americans, in general the southern and western tribesmen had taken the British side. Jefferson declared that the Indians had "made war on us without the least provocation or pretense of injury" and that they had wantonly committed "savage cruelties," murdering and scalping defenseless men, women, and children, burning settlements, and committing atrocities which even the British found it difficult to surpass. Despite Jefferson's praise of the courage of black slaves, no one would have known from reading the *Notes on Virginia* that nearly five thousand blacks had served in the American armed forces. In Jefferson's account, they figure mainly as victims of British barbarity, not as "heroes of liberty." [16]

The Indians, no more than the black slaves, Jefferson recognized, had no reason to love the white man, nor did he expect them to forget and forgive centuries of oppression. Yet he believed that if the Indians were shown justice and humanity, "real affection" might yet prevail between them and the whites. As President he said that his policy was to do everything "just and liberal . . . within the bounds of reason" for the Indians. As he told an Indian chief, "We, like you, are Americans, born in the same land, and having the same interests."

&

In the *Notes on Virginia,* Jefferson defended the Indians against the aspersions of a school of European *philosophes* who cited them as examples of the singular degeneracy that afflicted plants, animals, and even human beings in the New World. Once acclaimed as a Noble Savage, the Indian, by the time of the American Revolution was pictured in some European intellectual circles as an ignoble, debauched, enervated, and sexually impotent barbarian, an object of pity or contempt rather than an admirable child of Nature.

Three *philosophes,* in particular, had distinguished themselves by their derogation of all things American. Of these *philosophes* the most important was George Louis Leclerc, Comte de Buffon (1707–1788), Director of the Jardin du Roi, "the Pope of eighteenth century zoologists," one of the forty Immortals of the French Academy, a member of the American Philosophical Society and the American Academy of Arts and Sciences, and the author of the monumental (forty-four volumes) *Système de la Nature.* Buffon advanced the theory that in the New World native plants and animals were smaller than in the Old World and that European plants and animals tended to degenerate in size, producing "cold men and feeble animals." In America, said Buffon, "everything languishes, corrupts and proves abortive"—a circumstance he attributed to an atmosphere "overloaded with humid and noxious vapor." Guillaume Thomas Francis Raynal (1713–1796), a French popularizer of science, author of the *Historie philosophique et politique* (1770), elaborated upon Buffon's theme, observing that among the other evidence of regressive traits in the New World, "America has not produced a good poet, a capable mathematician, or a man of genius in a single art or a single science"—a phenomenon he attributed to the debilitating influence of colonialism. Cornelius de Pauw, a Dutch-born *philosophe,* author of *Recherches philosophiques sur les Americains* (1769), concluded that the deterioration of the human species in the New World had affected European settlers as well as the aborigines, leaving the bleak conclusion that the United States would forever remain sterile in terms of cultural or intellectual accomplishment. Indeed, de Pauw deplored the discovery of America as the most calamitous event in the history of civilization; another such disaster, he predicted, would result in the extinction of mankind.[17]

At the hands of these *philosophes,* the American Indians suffered a rhetorical massacre in which neither men, women, nor children were spared. Buffon described them as cowardly, shiftless weaklings: without rational powers or even activity of mind, the Indian appeared to the eminent French *savant* as "a mere animal of the first rank." De Pauw dismissed them as enervated, stupid, brutish syphilitics who mistreated their women, got drunk, made war, took scalps, tortured prisoners, practiced cannibalism, and, when not engaged in these nefarious activities, spent their days in vacuous indolence in their smoke-filled, fetid lodges. "Relieve him of hunger and thirst," said Buffon, "and you deprive him of the active principle of all his movements; he will rest stupidly upon his legs or lying down entire days." They treated their women abominably, using them as mere beasts of burden and tillers of the soil. At best, the men showed only a languid interest in their women as objects of sexual desire; their organs of generation were small and seldom used; and they had no strong family ties. Comparing the Indians with Homo sapiens Europeaneus, the *philosophes* concluded that here was an example of how Nature, "by refusing him [the Indian] the power of love, has treated him worse and lowered him deeper than an animal." And all these evidences of degeneracy were attributed to the climate of the New World, not to the pernicious influence of the white man; this poor, diseased, emasculated creature mistakenly called the Indian was Homo Americanus in his natural state.[18]

Against the aspersions of the *philosophes,* Jefferson defended the sexual prowess of the Indians: in this respect, they seemed to him to be perfectly normal, although, admittedly, they did not exhibit the inordinate sexuality he attributed to males of African descent. In consequence, Jefferson did not fear the Indians' aggressive sexual drive; unlike the blacks, they did not figure as potential rapists of white women. Being more or less the equals of whites, Indians, in Jefferson's opinion, did not lust after white women; he drew no analogy between them and orangutans.*

In praising the Indians, Jefferson was in effect vindicating his concept

---

* Thomas Malthus attributed the slow rate of population increase among the American Indians not to a constitutional "want of ardor in the men toward their women," but to the fact that like all primitive peoples, their food was poor and insufficient. The phlegmatic temperament of the Indians observed by travelers in North America "seems," said Malthus, "to be generated by the hardships and dangers of savage life, which take off the attention from the sexual passion." See Malthus 1963, p. 18.

of America as a Garden set aside by the Author of Nature for the delectation of mankind. The Garden was intended for the Chosen People of God, and the American Indians, if they did not already belong to the club, were quite capable of meeting all the entrance requirements if they settled down as farmers. Being essentially a primitive European whose only disadvantage was that he suffered from a culture lag, the American Indian, Jefferson supposed, was capable of making a great leap forward into the eighteenth century. All that was required of him was that he learn to respect property, to practice industry and frugality, and to obey the white man's laws. As hunters, warriors, and food gatherers, the Indians had no place in the Jeffersonian scheme: he demanded that they abandon their culture, their tribal organization, and their communal ownership of land and embrace without reserve the white man's culture, his farming, and his system of private ownership of land. The standard was that of the white settler of European descent: the Indian was told, in effect, to conform or suffer the consequences.

Jefferson urged the Indians to read and to profit from the clear lesson of history: upon innocent, happy, and contented primitive peoples the impact of civilization was almost always fatal. Take for example, he suggested, the conduct of Captain Cook toward the natives of Polynesia—conduct which, Jefferson said, "lessened our regrets at his fate." Unfortunately for the American Indians, Jefferson admitted, the British sea captain's attitude was all too prevalent among white men. In consequence, the Indian could survive only by adopting the defensive tactic of emulating the white man's way and becoming, to all intents and purposes, a white man himself. For the Indian, he warned, there was no security except behind the plow. And, Jefferson believed, this change from nomad hunter to farmer would accrue wholly to the Indians' benefit: after all, he was being invited to adopt the best life known to man—the life of an American farmer.

While the white man, in Jefferson's view, had by virtue of his superior civilization and by a Decree of Providence the right to dispossess the Indian, this right did not extend to the total expropriation of the aborigines. Rather, the Divine Plan called for the sharing of the Garden between whites and Indians, with the Indians getting their fair share provided that they settled down as farmers. If, on the other hand, they chose to remain hunters and gatherers, they must face the prospect of removal beyond the Mississippi. Even so, Jefferson insisted that all lands of those who chose to go West must be bought and paid for by the federal government. In his eagerness to acquire Indian lands, however, he suggested that they be induced by easy credit to go into debt at the government's Indian Trading Houses and so compelled to sell their tribal lands at bargain prices. But, at least, this was some improvement over the traditional method of getting the Indians drunk and then persuading them to sign away their tribal lands for a pittance, and an even more pronounced improvement over the time-honored custom of making war upon them and quieting their title with a bullet.[19]

As president, Jefferson delighted in doing honor to visiting Indian chiefs. When a delegation of Cherokee and Chickasaw chiefs—some with powdered hair and resplendent in military uniforms and cocked hats— came to Washington, D.C., Jefferson, the British minister complained, "paid them infinitely more attention that he ever vouchsafed to shew to a foreign Minister." On New Year's Day 1804, the British minister, Anthony Merry, and his aide Augustus John Foster, arrived at the President's House just as Jefferson was greeting some Indians; after making a formal bow to Merry and Foster and asking them "how they did," he turned his attention wholly to the Indians, saying no more to the discomfited Britons. Whereupon Merry exclaimed that no representative of His Britannic Majesty would yield the place of honor to "painted Savages"; after five minutes he stalked out in high dudgeon.[20]

Dealing with warlike, indomitable, and intelligent savages required, Jefferson said, a policy based upon "justice and fear." Even while inculcating "temperance, peace and agriculture" among the Indians, he did not allow them to suppose that he had ruled out the use of force. In 1813, after a rising of the tribes had been suppressed, Jefferson said that their "ferocious barbarities justified extermination," although he personally favored their removal beyond the Mississippi. While denying any intention of waging unprovoked war upon the Indians, he let them know that retaliation for acts against whites would be swift and terrible: "If ever we are constrained to lift the hatchet against any tribe," he warned, "we will never lay it down till that tribe is exterminated, or driven beyond the Mississippi." [21]

Although in 1796 Jefferson had opposed the establishment of federal Indian trading houses as unconstitutional—regulating trade with the Indians, he said, was beyond the powers of the federal government—his constitutional scruples vanished when he became president. He now took the position that the federal government was the protector of Indian rights, especially those guaranteed by treaty, against the states. The Indians, he declared, had a right to enjoy the occupation of their lands free of interference by the state governments. To the consternation of many of his followers, the word was handed down from Washington that no state or individual had the right to treat with the Indians without the express consent of the federal government. The Indians, Jefferson promised, could always look to the federal government for justice against the states and the frontiersmen. Killing an Indian—which many Westerners regarded as no crime at all—ought, he said, to be legally considered as no different from killing a white man.[22]

Nor did Jefferson permit his strict regard for the doctrine of the separation of powers to affect his concept of the president as the constitutionally appointed custodian of the Indians' rights; in the guise of the Great White Father he did not fear the exercise of power. "I am their father, wish their happiness and well-being and am always ready to promote their good," he said. If this was paternalism, it was an attitude Indians rarely encountered in the white man; it was far better to be considered children than "varmints." His genuine concern for the welfare of the natives is evidenced in his instructions to Lewis and Clark to use the recently introduced Jennerian method of vaccination against smallpox among the Indians and to encourage them to rely upon it rather than upon the ministrations of medicine men.[23]

Jefferson visualized the role of the federal government as teacher and guide to the Indians in the difficult art of survival in a white man's world. As he saw it, the real enemy of the Indian was "the interested and crafty individuals among them who inculcate a sanctimonious reverence for the customs of their ancestors," i.e. Indian medicine men. The function of the government was not to eradicate the Indians but to eradicate the superstitions, customs, and attitudes which impeded their transition from the state of Nature to civilized society.[24]

Accordingly, he made it the mission of the federal government rather than of religious denominations or private societies to spread civilization among the Indians. (In the eighteenth century, it was possible to speak of the white man "spreading civilization.") Like a good Deist, he feared the influence of Christian missionaries upon the Indians; indeed, he compared them to Indian medicine men as enemies of progress bent upon keeping the Indians in ignorance. Before attempting to convert the natives to Christianity, he recommended that they be taught Aesop's Fables. Rather than send missionaries to civilize the Indians, Jefferson urged that the job be assigned to anthropologists.[25]

Jefferson envisaged an orderly expansion of the white man's civilization across the North American continent, the Indians selling their land for a just price to the government and retiring to reservations or, better still, remaining as farmers within the white community. Of all the Indian tribes, he entertained the highest hopes for the Cherokees, the Chickasaws, the Creeks, and the Choctaws who showed a special aptitude as cotton growers, cattle ranchers, and farmers. When the Creeks asked to become United States citizens, Jefferson endorsed their application as the first step toward the fulfillment of his ideal of amalgamating the two peoples in a single society. The Cherokees, too, gave every sign of becoming orderly, industrious, and "virtuous" United States citizens: they created a written language, established a newspaper, and instituted a representative form of government.[26]

Few of Jefferson's contemporaries or, for that matter, his successors, shared that ideal. For the Indian had land which the white man coveted, and no treaties or guarantees of Indian "rights" were permitted to impede the march of "civilization." The Cherokees were ultimately dispossessed by the state of Georgia against the orders of the United States Supreme Court but with the approval of President Andrew Jackson, and the Indians were forced to move beyond the Mississippi. Adapting to the white man's ways and joining the "Chosen People of God" by becoming farmers did not save the Indians from expropriation, exile, and death. "The Union treats the Indians with less cupidity and violence than the several states," observed Alexis de Tocqueville, "but the two governments are alike deficient in good faith." [27]

In the case of the Indians, Jefferson, in the words of his biographer, "defended the honor of human nature and challenged the doctrine of human inequality"—something he signally failed to do as regards the blacks. He gladly admitted them to the pantheon of the white race and, as he had not done with the blacks, attributed the differences between the two races wholly to environment. Had Jefferson applied the same criteria to blacks that he did to Indians, he would have reached conclusions more favorable to the blacks than are found in the *Notes on Virginia.*[28]

9

Jefferson and
Black Intellectuals

———◆———

JEFFERSON SAID THAT NO ONE AWAITED with more anxiety and a keener sense of anticipation the appearance of convincing proof that the mental endowment of blacks was equal to that of whites and that their apparent inferiority was owing to their degraded situation, both in Africa and America, rather than to biological inequalities ordained by Nature and therefore beyond all remedy. He would be happy, he said, to see a complete refutation of the doubts expressed in the *Notes on Virginia* concerning "the grade of understanding alloted to them by Nature" and whether their laziness and improvidence were congenital or the effect of slavery.

Before these questions could be answered with scientific certitude, Jefferson said, the blacks must be studied as subjects of "natural history" by what we would now call anthropologists and sociologists—fields of inquiry into which the *philosophes* did not fear to tread—who made it their business to examine the degree of culture and intelligence exhibited by Africans in their native habitat. It was in Africa rather than the United States, it appeared, that the "natural" black was to be found and the truth regarding his genetic endowments was to be ascertained.[1]

In 1773, Dr. Benjamin Rush of Philadelphia, later a member of the Jeffersonian circle, published *An Address on the Slavery of the Negroes in America* in which he reported that travelers returning from Africa had found the natives to be ingenious, humane, and strongly attached to their family and friends—all of which proved, he contended, that "they were equal to the Europeans, when we allow for the diversity of temper and genius which is occasioned by climate. . . .We have many well-attested anecdotes of as sublime and disinterested virtue among them as ever adorned a Roman or a Christian character." The idleness, unreliability, and pilfering attributed to them by American slaveowners Rush set down as "the genuine offspring of slavery." [2]

But these travelers' accounts failed to convince Jefferson: he demanded more tangible evidence of the Africans' capacity for civilization. Late in life, he said of the questions he had raised in the *Notes on Virginia:* "We are not sufficiently acquainted with all the nations of Africa to say that there may not be some in which habits of industry are established, and the arts practiced which are necessary to render life comfortable. It would be a solecism to suppose a race of animals created, without sufficient foresight and energy, to preserve their own." The scientific caution, the insistence upon a suspension of judgment until all the evidence had been gathered, which he prided himself upon observing in the *Notes on Virginia,* applied to proof of the blacks' equality with whites.

The same inconclusive results attended, in Jefferson's opinion, the efforts of Afro-Americans to distinguish themselves in poetry, philosophy, the arts, and sciences. By the time of his death, American blacks had not yet provided him with enough evidence to make a definitive judgment.[3]

Among blacks whom Jefferson might have cited as distinguished members of their race were Lemuel Hayes, a Congregational minister; Price Hall, a pioneer black Mason; Paul Cuffee, merchant shipbuilder and philanthropist; Phillis Wheatley, a poet; and Benjamin Banneker, an astronomer and mathematician. Of these individuals, Jefferson considered only Phillis Wheatley and Benjamin Banneker worthy of attention.

A black of African birth, a woman, and a poet, Phillis Wheatley appeared to have formidable claims to the favorable attention of a man in search of evidences of black genius. But Jefferson gave her short shrift: he dismissed her poetry as unworthy of serious criticism. In the *Notes on Virginia,* Jefferson said that blacks were deficient in poetic feeling, and he stood resolutely by his critical guns. Of course, much of her poetry had a devoutly religious theme, the kind of poetry Jefferson, as a rationalist and Deist, could not endure. Jefferson did not admire John Donne or other religious poets; here, as in the architecture and the other arts, he had a limited range of appreciation. "Religion," he remarked, "produced a Phillis Wheatley, but it could not produce a poet."

Yet not all of Phillis Wheatley's poetry was an expression of her deeply felt religious convictions. She also translated part of Ovid, an achievement which might have been expected to have evoked a positive response from a classical scholar such as Jefferson. George Washington considered her patriotic poems, written during the War of Independence, worthy of high commendation. Voltaire complimented her on her "polished verse," and her book of poetry went through five editions before 1800. In 1773 she went to England where she was received in some of the noble houses and acclaimed by Lord Dartmouth, a devout follower of John Wesley. When she returned to Boston, the *Gazette* welcomed her as "the extraordinary Poetical Genius." Contrary to Jefferson's opinion, Phillis Wheatley provided an instructive example of how blacks could excel if given educational opportunity.[4]

In 1791, Benjamin Banneker, a Maryland free black who had gained a reputation as a mathematician, clockmaker, and astronomer, sent Jefferson, then secretary of state, the manuscript of an almanac he had compiled. Banneker hoped that Jefferson would accept this almanac as the long-awaited proof of the hypothesis that men were endowed by their Creator with qualities and capacities which bore no relationship to racial differences. As matters stood, Banneker said, blacks were considered "rather as brutish than human and scarcely capable of mental endowments." Having heard that Jefferson was "measurably friendly and well disposed" towards blacks, Banneker assumed that the author of the Declaration of Independence would welcome proof that, regardless of race, men were created equal.

But Banneker's letter was not in an altogether complimentary vein. He accused Jefferson of violating his own principles by holding blacks in a state of "tyrannical thralldom and inhuman captivity" and insensitivity to the "cruel oppression" under which hundreds of thousands of blacks suffered. It was a far cry, lamented Banneker, from the glorious days in 1776 when it had seemed possible to purge the land of every vestige of inhumanity.[5]

Despite the unmistakable rebuke contained in Banneker's letter, Jefferson replied courteously, apparently choosing not to take offense at the charge that he was living in violation of his own declared principles. He secured for Banneker an appointment as surveyor in the District of Columbia where the new Federal City was to be built, and he sent Banneker's almanac, together with a covering letter, to the Marquis de Condorcet, a French *philosophe* with whom Jefferson had struck up a friendship in Paris. To Condorcet he expressed his pleasure that a black had become "a very respectable mathematician" capable of "very elegant solutions of Geometrical problems." But he made clear that one black mathematician did not prove that the whole black race was equal to the white race: "I shall be delighted to see these instances of moral eminence so multiplied as to prove that the want of talents observed in them, is merely the effect of their degraded condition, and not proceeding from any difference in the structure of the parts on which intellect depends." In short, he still awaited verification of the claim that blacks were not congenitally inferior to whites, and he still insisted this proof must come from the blacks themselves despite the many disabilities they suffered in consequence of their degraded condition.

Although the transmittal of his pamphlet to the Marquis de Condorcet was accompanied by a commendatory letter from Jefferson flattering to Banneker, it was not exactly what the black mathematician expected of him. Banneker hoped that the author of the Declaration of Independence, presented with irrefutable proof of black genius, would lead a crusade for the emancipation of the blacks and their admission into American society as equals with white Americans in rights, dignity, and opportunity. Here Banneker was disappointed. Jefferson still awaited more convincing authentication of black genius. In the meantime, his position remained tentative, fluid, and not a little ambiguous.[6]

Had Banneker been privileged to read Jefferson's subsequent letters and to overhear his conversations, he would have realized how completely he had failed to persuade Jefferson that the two races were equal in intellectual powers. While admitting that Banneker appeared to have enough knowledge of trigonometry to produce an almanac, Jefferson did not conceal his suspicion that the black man was aided by a white neighbor. In 1809 he said that the letter he had received from Banneker proved that he had "a mind of very common stature indeed." And the following year he told the British minister to the United States that, except for his almanac, Banneker "appeared to little advantage, particularly in his letters, he having received several from him which were very childish and trivial."

This was the response consistently given by Jefferson to claims of black intellectual achievement: scepticism or open incredulity. In his old age he had yet to see a black "natural aristocrat." Henri Grégoire, Bishop of Blois, a noted contemporary opponent of slavery, compiled a series of case histories of distinguished blacks which proved, to the bishop's satisfaction, that Jefferson's doubts about the intellectual capabilities of blacks were without foundation. Jefferson ridiculed the project: "his [Bishop Grégoire's] credulity, "Jefferson observed, "has made him gather up every story he could find of men of color (without distinguishing whether black, or of what degree mixture) however slight the mention or light the authority on which they are quoted." But, Jefferson added, "as to Bishop Grégoire, I wrote him . . . a very soft answer." But if he gave soft answers, he demanded hard evidence—and this, he was convinced, had yet to be produced.[7]

When Jefferson heard of a colored person distinguishing himself or herself in the arts, science, or literature, his first question habitually was how much white "blood" this particular individual possessed. He was less surprised to find talent in mulattoes than in pure blacks; in his genetic scale, mulattoes were generally superior to their parents. At this point, blacks might well have protested that the decision had already been rendered against them: if they showed signs of excellence it was attributed to the white genes in their makeup; their deficiencies were ascribed to their "Africanness." [8]

Even though his appreciation of the intellectual abilities of blacks was at best guarded and qualified, Jefferson discovered that any relationship whatever with the blacks on an intellectual level could be politically damaging. His first letter to Benjamin Banneker found its way into print, and Jefferson found himself in political hot water. In the South, it was accounted almost as reprehensible to write a letter to a black man as to invite him to dinner. In 1796, when Jefferson was his party's candidate for president (although he himself said that he aspired no higher than the vice-presidency), William Smith, a South Carolina Federalist, denounced him for corresponding with Banneker. "What shall we think of a *secretary of state* thus *fraternizing* with negroes," Smith exclaimed, "writing them complimentary epistles, styling them *his black brethren*, congratulating them on the evidences of their *genius*, and assuring them of his good wishes for their speedy emancipation." Although Jefferson won the electoral votes of South Carolina, he lost the presidency to John Adams by a margin of three votes in the electoral college.

Thus it was again borne in upon Jefferson that the course of political wisdom was to ignore the blacks and the problems they created. Southerners did not relish hearing unpalatable truths about an institution which, by becoming peculiar to the South, tended to place that section of the Union in a position of moral isolation. Expediency dictated that slavery be treated as though somehow, sometime, and by means as yet undisclosed, it would go away of its own accord.

～ 10 ～

Blacks and Agriculture

◆

PERHAPS THE MOST FAMOUS PASSAGE in the *Notes on Virginia* is Jefferson's almost rhapsodic apostrophe to the joys, the spiritual gratifications, and the political benefits of farming. To Jefferson, farming was, of all the occupations known to man, the most satisfying, most spiritually rewarding, most natural, and most conducive to happiness and economic well-being. Nature intended man to be a farmer—therefore, by becoming a farmer, a man fulfilled the designs of Providence. It was especially important for Americans to become farmers because, as Jefferson interpreted the divine plan, America had been designated by Nature, above all other parts of the earth, for the pursuit of agriculture and for the happiness and contentment of mankind.[1]

The true glory of America, as it appeared to Jefferson, was that the Author of Nature had here created a bountiful New World for the special felicity of man. As John Locke said, "In the beginning all the world was America," and, Jefferson might have added, if the world were fortunate, it might again become America. The beauty of his native land seemed to him sufficient testimonial of the beneficence of the Creator. The Falls of the Potomac alone, he said, was a sublime spectacle worthy of a voyage across the Atlantic; and it is impossible to doubt that in a later age he would have been among the forefront of those opposed to the reduction of this natural wonder to a hydroelectric power site.

In this garden, Jefferson was certain that human nature would be refined and perfected. For farming ripened the "seeds of virtue" implanted in man by the Author of Nature and thereby brought the moral sense to full fruition and, at the same time, developed the qualities of self-reliance and independence. In short, farming was outdoor moral therapy designed to produce Nature's fairest work—the autonomous individual, beholden to no man, and independent of the vagaries of the marketplace. Jefferson believed that Nature intended men to work for themselves, not for others, and agriculture alone offered hope of achieving this "natural" state. The American farmer stood at the apex of creation,

79

and, if he disappeared, Jefferson offered no hope that we would ever see his like again. "Those who labour in the earth," he said, "are the chosen people of God, if ever he had a chosen people, whose breasts he has made his peculiar deposit for substantial and genuine virtue." For Jefferson, happiness could be pursued successfully only on a farm. He might well have told Napoleon Bonaparte (in the words of Madame Helvetius), "General, you cannot imagine how much happiness can be squeezed into three acres of land!" [2]

As was true of so much of Jefferson's personal philosophy, in his idealization of the agricultural way of life he reflected the prevailing attitudes of the eighteenth century Enlightenment. Especially in the latter part of that century, the pastoral eclogue of classical antiquity became the manifesto and breviary of the "back to nature" movement of the romantics.

Rousseau gave expression to the bias of his age when he asserted that farmers were the most virtuous of all human beings; Marie Antoinette and the ladies of her court played at being milkmaids and shepherdesses; and George III supervised a model farm at Windsor, thereby winning the sobriquet of "Farmer George." In France, the Physiocrats asserted that agriculture alone was productive, and even Adam Smith and Alexander Hamilton admitted that it must be given primacy over all other occupations. [3]

Jefferson viewed America not as an aggregate of natural resources waiting exploitation, but as a paradise to be cherished and cultivated in the spirit in which it was given to man by Divine Providence. He expected Americans to realize that they were the most fortunate people on earth and to comport themselves accordingly toward their environment. Without renouncing his belief in progress, Jefferson felt sure that the natural beauty of America would be preserved by the enlightened custodianship of the American people. The American, he reasoned, was not a destroyer, a pollutor, or an exploiter, but a conservator who realized that he acted under a mandate from Heaven to transform the wilderness into a garden by cultivation and art. [4]

In the interests of their own virtue and happiness, Jefferson advised young men to become farmers rather than businessmen and to buy land (which in the South also meant slaves) instead of investing in government securities or bank stock. "500 acres of land," he told a correspondent, "is of more value than the prospect of the fortune of any merchant whatever." Jefferson acted upon this maxim, and ended by becoming land and slave poor. [5]

Jefferson believed that the success of the republican experiment depended not upon the quantity of goods and services produced, but upon the production of the kind of people whose mental and moral calibre qualified them to fulfill the onerous responsibilities of citizenship. In his eyes, the supreme merit of farming was that it created men capable of conducting their own affairs as well as the affairs of government. He said that he could assay the amount of corruption in a government and the prevalence or comparative absence of self-seeking in a society by the degree to which farming was practiced by the people. The quality of man produced by an occupation or profession was all-important to Jefferson; had he believed that manufacturing created a higher type of man and more "solid happiness" for the majority than did farming, he would have been for manufacturing. He admitted that an economy heavily weighted toward agriculture might not be wholly advantageous if measured solely by material considerations, but he was convinced that any loss in national income would be "made up in happiness and permanence of government." From which he concluded that, rich as Americans might become in material goods by devoting themselves to commerce and manufacturing, happiness would forever elude them if they forsook the good American earth and the ethical values it generated.[6]

In acclaiming farming as the great, indeed, the only regenerator of mankind, Jefferson made clear that what he valued most of all was the independence—a purely psychological effect—it produced. He regarded independence as a prerequisite of virtue; any man who submitted his opinions in matters of religion, philosophy, or politics to the control of others or to the creed of a party he accounted guilty of "the last degradation of a free and moral agent." In his eyes, political parties were a form of slavery: "If I could go to heaven but with a party," he said, "I would not go at all"—especially if he thought that Heaven was also Alexander Hamilton's destination. On the other hand, freed of personal dependence upon any other person or upon a party—as Jefferson believed American farmers to be—everything was possible. In a nation of independent farmers, all of whom were able to read, and blessed with a free press, government could safely be reduced to so few functions that citizens would be scarcely aware of its existence. The minimal government favored by Jefferson presupposed a community of farmers practicing maximal virtue.[7]

Since he attributed Americans' superiority to their environment, the preservation of that environment took priority in Jefferson's plans. In large measure, his political career was an effort to preserve the America he loved—"this lovely land"—against the profane hands of speculators, bankers, profit-minded businessmen, and the centralizers of political power.

Jefferson feared government largely because he feared it would fall under the control of interests hostile to the "agricultural interest". For this reason, he urged that farmers and planters, the representatives of the general interest, ought to be elected to Congress. "Such men," he said, "are the true representatives of the great American interest, and are alone to be relied on for expressing the proper American sentiment." Paradoxically it did not occur to Jefferson that the realization in politics of this preponderance of agriculturalists would have had the effect of increasing the political power of the slaveowning interest, already the most powerful special interest in the United States.[8]

If Americans remained an agricultural people, Jefferson assumed they would eschew the pursuit of wealth and power for the modest, down-to-earth but durable pleasures of an American farmer: contentment, independence, and enough land for the needs of his family. This farmer, as Jefferson conceived him, renounced the unending striving for more; he shunned luxuries, never bought on credit, and never went into debt. He recognized that there was no happiness for him on earth unless he restrained his desire for material possessions within the compass of his actual needs, and that he must rest content with a fair share of the earth's bounty. He combined agriculture with the solid gratifications derived from literature and the contemplation of Nature: "Ours are the only farmers who read Homer," boasted Jefferson.

Jefferson's idealized farmer was, in fact, a lineal descendant of the literary shepherd of the Greek and Roman pastorals: the innocent, virtuous farmer of classical antiquity metamorphosed into the innocent, virtuous American farmer. By the same token, in his political philosophy, Jefferson fused the pastoral dream of antiquity with American democracy. He made the American farmer a figure out of Virgil's *Eclogues*. Deprived of his land and the independence it begot, the American farmer, like his Roman counterpart, became a prey to anxiety and alienated from society. The expropriated farmer lost all civic virtue: he was now willing to sell his vote to his employer or to the highest bidder. The mobs of great cities, Jefferson observed, were composed of men who had lost their independence. They were living proof of the truism that "dependence begets subservience and venality." [9]

Manifestly, although he rejected the Platonic ideal of the philosopher-king, Jefferson's conception of democracy was based upon the existence of large numbers of philosopher-farmers. From their contact with the soil, farmers were expected to develop a "philosophical turn" which enabled them to perceive that an egalitarian society in which no one would sink to the poverty level and no one would enjoy inordinate wealth was infinitely preferable to a society which practiced an unrestrained scramble for wealth.

Although he himself owned ten thousand acres of land and over a hundred and fifty slaves, Jefferson prized the small, self-sufficient, family-sized farm as the ideal agricultural unit. Simplicity, simplicity, and yet more simplicity was the burden of the message handed down from Monticello but, unhappily, not always practiced there. Jefferson wished to do away with all economic complexities and to strip down to essentials. The economy he believed to be best suited for the American people was the kind of semisubsistence farming practiced by the small yeomen farmers of western Virginia—almost devoid of money, self-sufficient except for a small surplus with which to buy salt, sugar, and coffee "and a little finery for his [the farmer's] wife and daughters." In such a society no one would want for the necessities of life and neither would any one get rich.[10]

If this were the Jeffersonian dream, it was hardly the American reality in his own day, and in the nineteenth century it bore increasingly less resemblance to the facts of American life. The future held some nasty surprises for Jefferson, but none was more shocking than the decline and fall of the virtuous American farmer who sought happiness and self-fulfillment in the cultivation of his land rather than in sharp financial practices and in the pursuit of gain. For into the Jeffersonian Arcadia of simple, hard-working, frugal subsistence farmers insidiously crept commercial agriculture—and with it the canker of money-making. And, in the South, slavery provided the indispensable base for the kind of commercial farming that spelled the end of the kind of agriculture which produced the human qualities Jefferson cherished. In the Jeffersonian script, as farmers went, so went the nation—and it became increasingly clear that farmers were straying from the path Jefferson had marked out. The American people, it seemed, were bent upon getting ahead in the world, and no amount of exhortations to practice virtue and seek happiness rather than to accumulate tangible possessions would have dissuaded them from a course of action upon which they had already eagerly embarked. The very wealth of resources which they found on every hand awaiting the vivifying touch of the entrepreneur sealed, as it were, the fate of Jeffersonian idealism based upon an agrarian way of life.

In actuality, the increasing equality of opportunity for advancement which characterized the United States and which Jefferson regarded as a prerequisite to the creation of a true democracy ultimately defeated his hopes. For it tended to produce an inward "restlessness of heart" which conspired against the kind of contentment which Jefferson knew to be essential to happiness. To Alexis de Tocqueville and many other observers of the American scene, it seemed that Americans were condemned by the logic of a situation which coupled boundless opportunities of becoming rich with egalitarian ideals; to forever seek, but never, never to attain happiness. For most Americans, equality of opportunity meant a chance to give free play to the gratification of the acquisitive instinct. And, as de Tocqueville pointed out, "The first of all distinctions in America is money," and the most compelling ambition of Americans was to become a member of the "moneyed aristocracy." In the United States, that was where true opportunity and power were to be found.[11]

Henry David Thoreau saw the American farmers in a very different light than did Jefferson. From the perspective of Walden Pond, they appeared to be quite as self-seeking, avaricious, and mean-minded as other

capitalists on the make. If they had ever been the angels of the Jeffersonian dispensation, by the middle of the nineteenth century they had
become fallen angels. Thoreau attributed this fall from grace to their
single-minded pursuit of pecuniary profit. Using language that would
have horrified Jefferson, Thoreau said of the farmer, "I respect not his
labors, his farm where everything has its price, who would carry the
landscape, who would carry his God, to market, if he could get anything
for him; who goes to market for his god as it is . . . he knows Nature but
as a robber." Jefferson was ravaged by the beauty of America: his countrymen, as Thoreau saw them, seemed bent only upon ravaging it.[12]

🍁

When Jefferson remarked that the Chosen People of God, assuming
he had a Chosen People, were those who labored in the earth, a Federalist
unkindly pointed out that if that were true, the blacks must be the
Chosen People in Virginia for they did most of that kind of labor. Certainly no group of men, women, and children in the Old Dominion lived
closer to Nature—and thereby qualified for the place of honor—than did
the black slaves. This, however, was not the message Jefferson proclaimed
from his mountaintop: in his hierarchical order, the Chosen People were
white.

Jefferson never pretended that tilling the soil sufficed in itself to inculcate virtue, promote happiness, and provide the training for citizenship necessary for a republican system of government. To achieve the
maximum benefits, it was essential, he said, for the farmer to own his own
land, to work it himself, and to live on it. Merely tilling the soil, as slaves
or even tenant farmers did, deprived agriculture of most of its regenera-
tive effect. Even European peasants who, though they owned their own
land, lived together in villages rather than on isolated homesteads, sacri-
ficed by their gregariousness much of the salutary effects of agriculture.
As for European peasants who did not own their land, Jefferson thought
that they were reduced to a state of "subservience and venality" which
effectively suffocated "the germ of virtue" that American landowners
presumably derived from contact with the soil.[13]

Accordingly, despite the fact that they labored unremittingly in the
earth, black slaves could not be counted among God's Chosen People—a
message that had already reached them by other routes. Nor apparently
were free black landowners entitled to join the goodly company; upon
them, landownership as moral therapy was wasted, at least as long as they
remained in the United States.

🍁

Because he conceived America in the image of a garden, Jefferson
recoiled from the prospect, unveiled by Alexander Hamilton, of large

industrial and commercial cities dotting the unspoiled agricultural landscape of the United States. In his dislike and fear of cities, Jefferson
epitomized the tradition which, from early classical times, had glorified
the rural life and the rural virtues while deprecating the immorality and
vice generated by cities. Jefferson's strongly held conviction that cities
were inimical to virtue and happiness reflected the eighteenth century
pattern of thought, reinforced in his case by the fact that he genuinely
loved the life of a Virginia planter and regarded the growth of Northern
cities as a political and economic threat to the South and to republicanism. His sojourn in Europe served to confirm the prejudices against
cities he had already conceived as a Virginia country gentleman and as a
student of Cicero, Horace, and Pliny.[14]

Jefferson's "antiurban bias" was actually a protest against the de-
humanization of living conditions and social relationships that followed
in the train of the Industrial Revolution. His attitude toward institutions
was generally determined by the effect he believed they had upon mankind; whether they enhanced the morally more admirable and socially
beneficial qualities of human nature or whether they brought to the fore
the evil propensities—the "darker side"—that made man the cruellest and
most remorseless destroyer of his own kind known to Nature. Another
equally crucial criterion was whether these institutions fostered the
growth of republicanism, happiness, and freedom—or the despotism and
ignorance he associated with the rule of kings, priests, and nobles. On all
these scores he found large cities inimical to the welfare of the American
people.

Since the inhabitants of cities were for the most part propertyless wage
earners, strangling in filth and misery, dependent for their livelihood
upon employers who had only their own welfare at heart, Jefferson
reasoned that these undernourished, overworked people became "vitiated
and debased by ignorance, indigence and oppression"—mere tools for "the
designs of ambition." These degraded city-dwellers Jefferson called the
canaille (a word he never applied to farmers), a breed of men capable of
every crime and prone to every vice. From the likes of these Jefferson
prayed that the United States would be forever delivered.[15]

To describe cities, Jefferson customarily used the imagery of suffoca-
tion, degeneracy, and disease; when, on the other hand, he contemplated
the rural landscape, the metaphors that came to his mind were those of
fertility, growth, and felicity. He did not admit any significant distinction
between the burgeoning American cities and the great urban centers of
the Old World. Admittedly to a lesser degree, he thought that New York
City exhibited, like London, "a Cloaca of all the depravities of human
nature." Everywhere, he lamented, cities were "pestilential to the morals,
the health and the liberties of man." In 1798 he went so far as to express
the hope that epidemics of yellow fever—presumably the work of that

overruling Providence which never ceased to work for the benefit of the United States—would effectively discourage the growth of cities.[16]

Jefferson's objective was to keep American cities small and manageable, not to eliminate them altogether. He recognized that cities served an indispensable role as commercial centers and therefore could not be dispensed with by an enlightened agricultural community; and he personally delighted in the civility and the elegance afforded by cities. He hoped to keep the proportion of urban and rural inhabitants approximately at the ratio which existed during his own lifetime—ninety percent on farms, plantation, and small rural communities. Yet Jefferson believed that with intelligent planning and a proper concern for environment, cities could be made not only habitable but compatible with social, cultural, and moral values. What must be done, he said, was to eliminate the congestion, the slums, and the foul air. He suggested that American cities be reconstructed with a view to providing clear air, living space, and public parks. Jefferson's favored plan for cities was that of a checkerboard; "let the black squares only be building squares," he recommended, "and the white ones be left open, in turf and trees. Every square of houses will be surrounded by four open squares and every house will front an open square." The atmosphere of such a city, he believed, would be like that of the country and the townspeople would be a true "yeomanry." The plans he drew up for Washington, D.C., and New Orleans incorporated this approach to city planning.[17]

Like other Americans who deplored large cities as a "canker" upon republicanism and a danger to social stability, Jefferson had a special reason, not shared by his European contemporaries, for anxiety. For American cities tended to absorb a large part of the population of free blacks who were forced to live under conditions worse than those experienced by the *canaille* of European cities. Blacks constituted a large and increasing proportion of the criminal population of the cities—or, at least, that part of the criminal population which landed in jail. In New York, for example, most of the petty crime was attributed to "the ignorance, debauchery and the idleness of the lower class of blacks." [18]

Alexis de Tocqueville, who visited the United States less than a decade after Jefferson's death, fully shared Jefferson's apprehensions about the dangers posed to American democracy by the large cities of the eastern seaboard, especially New York and Philadelphia, where, he observed, the lower class "constitute a rabble even more formidable that the populace of European towns. They consist of freed blacks, in the first place, who are condemned by the laws and by public opinion to a hereditary state of misery and degradation" and European immigrants driven to the New World by misfortune, poverty, or crime. De Tocqueville concluded that racial prejudice in the North had increased since emancipation and was more prevalent in the "free" North than in the slave South. Here blacks, though nominally free, lived in the squalor reserved for the urban poor and for those whose skin color marked them as members of a servile race. C. F. Volney, the French *philosophe,* found that the quays of New York and Philadelphia where the free blacks were housed exceeded "in public and private nastiness anything ever beheld in Turkey." [10]

Although he was not aware of it, Jefferson was witness to the creation of an Afro-American subculture, especially in the cities where blacks built their own "African" churches and organized their own schools and charitable societies. Here blacks began to emerge as a free people with a distinct Afro-American identity. In Northern and Southern cities, they enjoyed more liberty, a more varied social life, and more economic opportunity than in the more rigidly structured rural areas. As a result, the center of free black population gravitated cityward as more and more slaves received their freedom.[20]

It was not necessary for Jefferson to travel to Northern cities to observe the degradation visited upon free blacks: it was manifest on every hand in his native Virginia. Here, to a far greater degree than in the cities, blacks were reduced to the status of "slaves without masters." While a minuscule middle class was beginning to take form in the cities, no comparable movement "up from slavery" occurred in the rural areas of the South. In Virginia and Maryland the most fortunate free blacks in the rural areas became tenant farmers, replacing the white farmers who were drawn westward by the lure of cheap land. Although there was a large reservoir of free blacks upon which to draw, Jefferson made no effort to substitute free blacks for slaves. When he employed free blacks, it was as hired laborers, not as tenant farmers.[21]

Free blacks were discriminated against by laws designed to ensure that they did not rise in the economic and social scale. After 1801, free blacks who traveled from one county to another without authorization in Virginia could be arrested, fined, and even sold into slavery in default of payment of the fine they incurred. Virginia forbade the licensing of free blacks as captains and pilots. The law of 1782 which liberalized manumission also provided that free blacks could be sold into slavery if they failed to pay their taxes. The laws of Virginia punished free blacks far more severely than whites for petty crimes and permitted the jailing and enslavement of an unemployed free black and his children. Even at the height of postrevolutionary liberalism, it was declared unlawful for free blacks to organize their own schools. Free blacks and slaves alike were prohibited from meeting together in groups for educational or fraternal purposes.

"No respectability, however unquestionable,—no property, however large—no character, however unblemished," said Henry Fearon, a British traveler, "will gain a man, whose body is (in American estimation) *cursed* with even a twentieth portion of the blood of his African ancestry, admission into society. They are considered as mere Pariahs—as outcasts and vagrants upon the face of the earth!" Francis Wright, an English reformer who visited the United States in the 1820s, reported that "the free negroes of Maryland and Virginia form the most wretched and consequently the most vicious portion of the black population. I have not seen a miserable half-clad negro in either state whom I have not found, upon enquiry, to be in possession of his liberty." For the slaves, freedom in a white community was merely a change from one to another, perhaps more invidious, species of oppression.[22]

Jefferson uttered no protest against the laws of Virginia and other states which denied free blacks equality of opportunity even though, legally, they were free citizens of the United States. He did not regard them as objects of solicitude because, in his opinion, they were not permanent residents of the United States entitled to the rights and privileges of citizens; a decree of Providence had ordained that their occupation of this "lovely land" should be brief. What happened to free blacks in the United States was therefore not a vital concern: their real emancipation would occur when they were transported outside the boundaries of the Republic. For them, liberty began at the water's edge.

Nor did Jefferson take note of the fact that the repression of free blacks inevitably affected the rights of white men. In 1798, for instance, the state of Virginia enacted a law barring members of abolition societies, but not slaveowners, from sitting on juries hearing freedom suits brought by slaves—a law which made it virtually impossible for a slave to win his freedom, however just his cause, in the courts of the commonwealth. Freedom suits were tried in county courts presided over by justices who were themselves slaveowners, and few attorneys were prepared to offend public opinion by serving as counsel for blacks. Yet, at this very time— 1798—Jefferson was writing the protest (which ultimately became the Kentucky Resolutions) against the invasion of civil liberties by the federal government in the Alien and Sedition Acts. The doctrine of states' rights tended to obscure the offenses committed by the state governments while focusing attention wholly upon the wrongdoing of the federal government. And, significantly, the Virginia law against which Jefferson did *not* protest, while it discriminated against white men who expressed ideas unacceptable to the majority, was actually aimed at black men and designed to keep them in servitude, however legitimate their claims to freedom.

⮦ 11 ⮧

Slavery and the Moral Sense

———◆———

In 1785, at the age of forty-three, Jefferson told his friends not to
expect him to participate actively in the effort to abolish slavery in
Virginia. Early in his career, Jefferson had indicated that he was acutely
aware of the danger of impairing his "usefulness"—his ability to do good
for his fellow men—by engaging in a futile and unpopular effort to hasten
emancipation by governmental action. Vital as the abolition of slavery
admittedly was, the repeated rebuffs he had suffered when he had proposed plans for freeing the slaves had demonstrated to him that to press
too hard on this issue was to risk a premature end to his political career.
Jefferson still had too much work to do—there were too many reforms to
accomplish, too many wrongs to redress—to account the world well lost
in order to do justice to the blacks.

By taking himself out of the struggle against slavery, Jefferson acted
upon the maxim that one revolution in a lifetime was enough for any
man. A single generation, he believed, could effect only a certain amount
of reform that would stand the test of time. The revolutionary generation—his own—had acquitted itself nobly by successfully resisting British
tyranny, securing independence, establishing republicanism upon a solid
foundation, and procuring for future generations "the precious blessing
of liberty." It was proper, therefore, that the torch be passed on to the
younger generation and that it be allowed a fair share of the glory of
carrying the Revolution to completion.

Besides the abolition of slavery, Jefferson assigned the younger generation other unfinished business of the American Revolution: the revision of the Virginia Constitution which he believed contained the seeds
of tyranny, and the division of the commonwealth into wards. Above all,
he delegated to the young men of Virginia the task of proving that the
greatness of a nation was always in proportion to the degree of freedom
it enjoyed. Freedom, he reminded the young men, was not an opportunity
to enjoy the fruits of the labors and sacrifices of a previous generation

but an opportunity to "immortalize" themselves by completing work left unfinished by their fathers.[1]

By relinquishing leadership of the struggle against slavery, Jefferson did not believe that he was delaying in the slightest degree the eventual outcome. In 1785, when he first began to be concerned about the defection of the American people from republican virtue, he told Dr. Richard Price that the real assault upon slavery would occur in Virginia and that it would be conducted by a phalanx of young men. They, he felt sure, would make Virginia the first Southern state to abolish slavery.

These young Virginians seemed to Jefferson to be superbly qualified to bring the American Revolution to a triumphant conclusion; as he said, they had "sucked in the principles of liberty as if it were their mother's milk"—a diet he proposed to supplement with the *Notes on Virginia*. Raised upon such wholesome nutriments, the younger generation appeared to him far better equipped to abolish slavery than were their fathers who had been reared in the enervating atmosphere of monarchism which, Jefferson said, blighted everything "liberal." Owing to their early exposure to pure republicanism, these young men could be expected to be less preoccupied with money-making, less prone to avarice and self-indulgence—the fatal defects of character that seemed to keep slaveowners of the revolutionary generation as tightly shackled to their slaves as their slaves were bound to them.[2]

From the youth of Virginia Jefferson anticipated, in short, an unprecedented display of the potency of the moral sense. At the heart of Jefferson's philosophy lay his unshakable conviction that man was endowed by his Creator with a moral sense which was capable, given the right environment, of almost infinite improvement. Jefferson believed in progress—and, to him, progress meant above all the growth of man's moral sense. From the gradual ameliorative process that this all-important component of the human psyche would usher in, would come, he predicted, the reign of justice: government, advancing "hand in hand with the progress of the human mind" would become an instrument in the hands of men for achieving the kind of social and political order hitherto regarded as "visionary."

The world view of the eighteenth century Enlightenment was profoundly moralistic. The *philosophes* took it for granted that moral principles were injected by the Author of Nature into the universal scheme of things; philosophy was styled "moral science," with the implication that morality could be reduced to a science and that science itself was a branch of moral study. Religion was judged by its effect upon human conduct: if it helped to make men good, virtuous, and amenable to accepted social values and mores, it was justified on utilitarian grounds—the highest accolade the men of the Enlightenment could bestow. Edward

Gibbon judged historical characters from a moralistic point of view, and the *Decline and Fall of the Roman Empire* is embellished with moral reflections. In the *Wealth of Nations,* Adam Smith postulated a cosmic moral system as the basis of economics; the "Invisible Hand" ensured that, under certain favorable conditions, self-interest served the public good. There was, in short, a divine ordering even of the marketplace.

The eighteenth century has been aptly described as the century of man's good concept of himself, a rediscovery of the latent potentialities for good in human nature, an affirmation of man's capacity to remake society and its institutions, and a declaration of faith in man's ability to erect a Heavenly City on earth. To effect this transformation of the conditions of human life, the men of the Enlightenment relied primarily upon the unfettering of man's capacity to bring the social order into conformity with the Laws of Nature laid down by the Creator for the guidance of mankind. That capacity was believed to lie in the symbiosis of reason and the moral faculty in the human psyche.

A faithful mirror of the advanced thought of his day rather than an original creative thinker, Jefferson wholeheartedly embraced the idea of a moralistic universe and of inherent, rational, and moral constitutive parts of human nature. He assumed that the Creator, having made man a social being, had implanted in human beings faculties designed to enable them to live according to "principles which are in concert with the reason of the supreme Mind." The plan of the Heavenly City which some *philosophes* believed mankind would erect upon earth already existed in the heart and mind of man: the City needed builders, not architects, for the essential design had already been drafted in Heaven.

As contrasted with reason, the moral instinct, in Jefferson's scale of values, was clearly preeminent as a means of distinguishing between right and wrong, justice and injustice. Reason, he believed, was fallible, whereas the promptings of the moral sense could be relied upon implicitly. He feared that too much dependence upon the reasoning faculty in matters of morality could be misleading: God had taken care, he said, to impress the precepts of morality "so indelibly on our heart that they shall not be effaced by the subtleties of our brain": morality was not "left to the feeble and sophistical investigations of reason, but is impressed on the sense of every man." No wonder, therefore, that he acclaimed the moral sense as "the brightest gem with which the human character can be studded."

Yet he anticipated no conflict between reason and the moral sense: the function of reason, as he envisaged it, was to feed data to the conscience, to apprehend the laws of nature and the divine structure of the universe, and to assist in making right decisions through the exercise of common sense, "the arbiter of everything." Jefferson's advice to those in search of truth was to "fix reason firmly in her seat, and to call to her tribunal every fact, every opinion," without, however, permitting reason to usurp the empire of the moral sense.[3]

Possessed of a properly functioning moral sense, mankind, Jefferson believed, stood in little need of organized religion: "true Religion," he said, "is morality" insofar as it conformed its message to the injunction "be just and good." He regarded organized religion as a supplement to rather than as the source of virtuous living. In his opinion, even a belief in God could be dispensed with: some of his best friends in Paris were atheists and he accounted them among the most virtuous of men. "Their virtue, then," he observed, "must have had some other foundation than the love of God." It was obvious to him that this foundation was the moral sense.[4]

Since the moral sense was actually the divine spark implanted by the Creator in His creatures at the moment of genesis, its presence wonderfully simplified the choice of action. "I have ever found one and one only rule, *to do what is right*," Jefferson said, "and generally we shall disentangle ourselves without perceiving how it happened." To his daughter he prescribed this advice: "If ever you are about to say anything amiss or to do anything wrong, consider it before hand. You will feel something within you which will tell you it is wrong and ought not to be said or done; this is your conscience, and be sure to obey it." [5]

While this sense of right and wrong was common to all men, Jefferson did not assert "the moral equality of mankind." Experience taught him that it was not uniformly distributed among classes and individuals: it was weakest among the rich and politicians—most wealthy men were rogues who owed their riches to their habit of doing what they knew was wrong but profitable, while politicians, especially those who followed Alexander Hamilton, were guided by self-interest rather than by their moral sense. Generally, the moral sense was strongest among farmers who were occupationally predisposed to obey its dictates to the letter. From which it appeared that the moral sense could not be divorced from environment: it developed or atrophied, depending upon occupation, education, and the conscious exercising of this precious, God-given faculty.[6]

A deficiency of this instinct in an individual struck Jefferson as "more degrading than the most hideous of the bodily deformations." Yet these unfortunates should not be treated as moral pariahs—not, at least, until the remedial effects of education had been tried and proved unavailing. Jefferson took it for granted that in most instances the moral sense could be invigorated by education; indeed, one of education's main purposes, as he conceived it, was to keep the faculty of distinguishing right from wrong operative at all times and places. Education, therefore, by his reckoning, was vitally important in a republic where the people must constantly exercise their moral sense in making decisions affecting the public welfare. Even an atrophied moral sense might be energized by education, although Jefferson was compelled to admit that some cases, especially prominent Federalist politicans, were too far advanced to be helped even by this sovereign therapy.

The presence of this "faithful internal monitor" by which right could be clearly distinguished from wrong provided Jefferson with the vital basis of his faith in the capacity of the common man, his reliance upon the individual, and his conviction that the powers of government could be safely reduced to a minimum. For Jefferson assumed that men can decide important political questions by following the dictates of their moral sense; that they can be trusted with freedom because they are capable of making right decisions; and that they can pursue happiness in their own way with the certainty that they would find it in doing good to their fellow men. The Author of Nature had so arranged human affairs, Jefferson believed, that "as long as we may think as we will and speak as we think, the condition of man will proceed in improvement." Mankind would never be truly happy until its social and political institutions had been brought into harmony with the plans of the Creator—which meant, in effect, that the moral sense would govern the world. If man were free, he would remake his world in the image the Creator had designed for it.[7]

Jefferson did not believe that it was necessary to change human nature in order to change human behavior: human nature being already essentially good, all that was necessary was to change the environment with a view to liberating the potential for goodness inherent in man. Man was, as it were, "programmed" to engage in ethical conduct; the Creator had interwoven the moral law into the human mind as well as into the texture of the universe. For that reason, the promotion of the general interest was the highest form of self-interest; God joined them together indissolubly.[8]

In this array of beneficial instincts with which the Creator had endowed man, Jefferson gave the philanthropic urge the highest rank. This quality, present to some degree in the constitution of every human being, made men compassionate and altruistic—qualities Jefferson believed to be essential to the functioning of every democratic society. "Nature hath implanted in our breasts a love of others, a sense of duty to them, a moral instinct, in short," he said, "which prompts us irresistably to feel and succor their distresses." The Creator intended that man should seek to promote the happiness of others by acting honestly and benevolently, "respecting sacredly their rights, bodily and mental, and cherishing their freedom as we value our own." The inward gratification derived from the performance of acts of benevolence was its own reward. "Virtue and interest," he argued, "are inseparable." The Creator had ordained that men should find their true interest in exercise of sympathy, benevolence, and altruism: people really care whether they do right or wrong; and when they do right they experience the highest happiness human beings can ever know. Furthering the welfare of others was the supreme virtue and the supreme happiness.[9]

While Jefferson did not disdain the "comforts and decencies" of life which science was already beginning to confer, he emphasized the refinements of morality, ethics and virtue which would accrue from progress. He believed that the effect upon the civilized values of society would be cumulative: in the twentieth century people would distinguish more surely between right and wrong, good and evil, than in the nineteenth century, and the twenty-first century would register an even more impressive advance. Had he supposed that progress would bring only a flood of material goods, creating appetites that could be satisfied only by more and more of the same, he probably would have preferred to let things go on as they were in the eighteenth century. For the inveterate enemy of Jeffersonian idealism was the pervasive preoccupation with the output of goods and services which tends to make the gross national product the paramount index of national greatness.[10]

To Jefferson, it was "heresy"—a word he often used to stigmatize deviations from the true republican faith—to suggest that these ethical intuitions were simply man-made conventions, the evolutionary end product of many millennia of communal living. He refused to regard the moral sense as anything less than a gift from the Creator, bred, more or less uniformly, into the marrow of every individual and consisting of eternal verities that were writ in Heaven for the guidance of men on earth. In Jefferson's cosmology, a benevolent Creator had arranged everything for man's special convenience, freedom, and happiness.

For Thomas Hobbes's "egoistic morality," which made self-love the basis of morality, Jefferson had only righteous indigation—an emotion usually excited in him by the mere mention of Hobbes. He never doubted that self-love was the inveterate enemy of morality because it encouraged self-gratification "in violation of our moral duties to others" and because it gave license to avarice and greed. "Take from man his selfish propensities, and he can have nothing to seduce him from virtue," Jefferson declared. "Or subdue these propensities by education, instruction or restraint and virtue remains with a competitor." [11]

That this optimistic view of man's ability to alter fundamentally his world by the exercise of his moral and intellectual capabilities was overdrawn Jefferson emphatically denied. "I was bred to the law: that gave me a view of the dark side of humanity," he said; but he also was acquainted with some of the most moral and public-spirited men of his generation, and he lived at a time when expectations of the betterment of the human condition were rising on every hand—and that, he said, gave him a balanced point of view.[12]

From the perspective of the "due medium," slavery was a by-product of the darker side of human nature. "What a stupendous, what an incomprehensible machine is man!" Jefferson wrote in 1786, "who can endure toil, famine, stripes, imprisonment or death itself in vindication of his own liberty"—yet is also capable of inflicting upon his fellow men a bondage "one hour of which is fraught with more misery than ages of that which he rose in rebellion to oppose." Here Jefferson touched upon the supreme irony of the American Revolution, but this irony was not fully revealed to him because he believed that the anomaly of slavery in a republic of free men could not endure. "We must await with patience," he said, "the workings of an overruling providence, and hope that that is preparing the deliverance of these our suffering brethren." [13]

The "darker side" of human nature manifested itself, Jefferson believed, in three areas of human activity where the promptings of the moral sense and the affirmations of reason seemed to have little or no effect: war, racial prejudice, and the corruptive effects of political power. He observed that man was the only animal which destroyed its own kind, that racial prejudice was so deeply imbedded in both blacks and whites that the two races could not live together in harmony in the United States, and that virtually every individual entrusted with political power succumbed eventually to the worst impulses of human nature. But in all these seemingly ineradicable evils he saw evidences of Divine wisdom: man preyed upon his own species, he concluded, because war was necessary to prevent overpopulation; racial prejudice was ingrained in human nature to prevent miscegenation; and the corruptive effect of political power was designed to warn the people to keep power securely in their own hands.[14]

Among the distinguishing traits of the eighteenth century Enlightenment none was more characteristic of the age than the expectation of mankind's future felicity. Although voices of caution were not absent, in general the intellectual community of that period assumed that men had at long last broken with the past, that age-old shackles upon the mind and spirit of man had been struck off, and that mankind stood upon the threshold of a new era in which savagery, superstition, irrationality, and mindless violence would make way for reason, knowledge, and wisdom. Mankind seemed to be moving toward greater equality, social justice, morality, freedom, happiness, and greater access to the material comforts of life. The idea of progress—under the right conditions, the inevitability of progress—became an article of faith among the men of the Enlightenment hardly distinguishable from the canons of the religion with which many of them had broken.[15]

Jefferson shared to the full this faith that the future held incalculable good in store for mankind; indeed, he was more optimistic than many of the *philosophes* with whom he consorted in France. He confessed that he loved to dream of the future, under the happy persuasion that it would be far better than the present. Among the alluring vistas revealed by Jefferson's "peeps into the future" was the abolition of slavery.

When slavery came directly under the attack of the moral sense, as Jefferson believed it must, the end of that institution was predictable. For nothing in America could be more abhorrent to a fully developed moral sense than slavery. Every human being knew intuitively that it was a wrong; and Americans, being a people who, by Jefferson's reckoning, were responsive, above all other peoples, to the promptings of conscience, would surely not suffer it to exist. If the end of slavery was not imminent—in the sense that it could be confidently anticipated within his own lifetime, it was clearly immanent—in the sense that its termination had been foreordained by the Creator. There was no way slavery could successfully defy this divine interdiction. Therefore, said Jefferson, "the evil will wear off gradually and their [the slaves] places be filled up by free white laborers." [16]

This sturdy conviction that slavery was doomed despite the considerable evidence that it was alive, well, and flourishing, accounts for Jefferson's ability to make with clear conscience his resounding pronouncements about the rights of man, the Laws of Nature, and the role of the United States as moral leader of the world. It is as though when Jefferson wrote and spoke about these high matters, he experienced a convenient defect of vision which prevented him from seeing black. Certainly he enunciated American principles and ideals quite as though slavery and black Americans did not exist. He apostrophized "the people" of the United States without betraying any recognition whatever of the fact that one fifth of the inhabitants of the Republic were enslaved. "I am not among those who fear the people," he said, ". . . the people being the only safe depository of power"; "goverements are republican only in proportion as they embody the will of the people, and execute it"; "educate and inform the whole mass of the people." "The people," in Jefferson's frame of reference, were clearly composed of free white Americans.

Similarly, he left black Americans wholly out of consideration when he declared that "every man, and every body on earth possess the right of self-government; they receive it with their being from the hand of nature." And blacks were clearly nonexistent within his range of consciousness when he asserted that all governments derive their just powers from the consent of the governed and that the freedom and happiness of man were "the sole objects of all legitimate government." (The freedom and happiness of blacks were not even an incidental concern of the federal and state governments.) In America, he said in 1813, "everyone, by his property, or by his satisfactory situation, is interested in the support of law and order" without mentioning that black slaves were included among that "property." [17]

Even the affirmations of his faith in the republican experiment which seem to apply unequivocally to blacks were actually intended by Jefferson to refer to whites only. "Nothing is unchangeable," he said, "but the inherent and indivisible rights of man.... The earth is given as a common stock for men to labour and live on." If employment were not provided by landowners, he said, "the fundamental right to labour the earth returns to the unemployed." In the United States, it did not seem to him to be too soon to apply the principle that "as few as possible shall be without a little portion of land. The small land holders are the most precious part of a state." Even when he declared that he was resolved to "put it out of the power of the few to riot on the labours of the many" he meant by the "few" the merchants, speculators, and bankers of the North, and by the many he meant the white farmers and planters.[18]

Nor, obviously, did Jefferson feel that the existence of slavery on American soil impugned the position of the United States as the Heaven-designated example to all the nations, or that the United States suffered by comparison with other countries that had already abolished slavery. Republican government, he declared, was "the only form of government that is not eternally at open or secret war with the rights of mankind"— and this despite the fact that the monarchical government of Great Britain had abolished slavery in 1772 by judicial decision.[19]

Jefferson not only assumed that slavery had been placed in the course of ultimate extinguishment; he often spoke as though the event had already occurred, as if the United States had freed the slaves, removed them to another land, and made its peace with the Author of Nature. His proclivity for living in the future, reveling in the felicities that awaited mankind, sometimes obscured present realities for Jefferson. As a protective device, it had the effect of relieving him of the overpowering, paralyzing sense of guilt that a realistic contemplation of the existing state of affairs might have induced in a man less oriented toward the future; on the other hand, it tended to diminish the need for the kind of incessant, dedicated, and uncompromising action that had distinguished Jefferson's career as a revolutionary.

Jefferson's faith in the existence of a benevolent, philanthropic instinct as an integral part of the human psyche and his belief in the eventual victory of the moral sense over slavery proved to be not wholly unfounded. The "passion for benevolence" with which he credited human beings was exemplified during his lifetime in the creation of Bible and missionary societies, prison reform organizations, societies for civilizing the Indians, and groups devoted to promoting the welfare of free blacks. Moreover, during the nineteenth century, as Jefferson had predicted, western civilization was swept by a wave of moral revulsion against slavery. The Northern states wholly abolished slavery; in the 1830s Great Britain freed over eight hundred thousand slaves in its West Indian possessions; the countries of Latin America freed their slaves; and in 1861 the Czar emancipated twenty-one million serfs. But for the most part, this moral force upon which Jefferson had confidently relied bypassed Virginia and the other Southern slave states; as regards slavery, the South defected from "the party of humanity, progress and enlightenment." But the moral sense did not disappear in the South: it merely enlisted under the banner of slavery. To the end, it served loyally and well the slaveowners who claimed to be its sole custodian.[20]

～ 12 ～

Blacks as Citizens

———◆———

ALTHOUGH JEFFERSON DESCRIBED HIMSELF IN FRANCE AS "a savage from the mountains of America," no one would have suspected it from his style of living in Paris. Benjamin Franklin, during his residence in France, had lived simply and unostentatiously at his country retreat at Passy, affecting a plain Quakerlike garb and the mien of a rustic republican philosopher. Jefferson, on the other hand, seemed intent on demonstrating that a republican philosopher could also be an epicurean. In Paris, where he served as United States Minister to France, he insisted upon the best of everything, whether it was housing, wine, food, furniture, books, horses, carriages, or servants. He engaged the services of a cook, a *valet de chambre*, a *pédicure*, a *tailleur*, and a barber. He appeared in public in knee breeches, lace ruffles, silk stockings and a richly embroidered waist-coat, and powdered hair. As Lord Chesterfield said, "Fashion is more tyrannical at Paris than in any other place in the world: it governs men more absolutely than the king." To this tyranny, Jefferson submitted without a protest.[1]

While complaining of the "luxurious proclivities" of his countrymen, Jefferson offered no apologies for the resplendence with which he had surrounded himself in Paris: a little ostentation, he maintained, was necessary to support the reputation and dignity of an American minister abroad.

But he did complain of the cost. His salary as United States Minister to France, he repeatedly told the Continental Congress, was woefully in-adequate to maintain the style of living which he deemed appropriate to his official position. So hard pressed was he for funds, he lamented, that he was forced to devote "an almost womanlike attention to the details of the household, equally perplexing, disgusting and inconsistent with business." [2]

Living in a style benefitting a French nobleman, his small salary often in arrears, and burdened by debts to British merchants which he saw no

99

way of paying, Jefferson was driven to financial shifts, some of which were made at the expense of his slaves. In 1787, for example, he decided to hire out some of his slaves—a practice he had hitherto avoided because of the hardship it wreaked upon the slaves themselves. He tried to protect them by providing in the contract that the death of a slave would not mean a reduction in the payments made him: ". . . otherwise," he remarked, "it would be their interest to kill all the old and infirm by hard usage." Although selling slaves was the quickest way of raising the cash required to sustain his style of living and to placate his creditors, Jefferson tried to avoid that drastic step, and, he added, not solely because it would deprive him of the labor force upon which his income depended. "This unwillingness," he said, "is for their sake, not my own; because my debts once cleared off, I shall try some plan of making their situation happier, determined to content myself with a small portion of their labor." Unhappily for his slaves, that moment never arrived; as time went on, Jefferson needed more, not less of the usufruct of their labor.[3]

In 1788, Brissot de Warville—who had written a book about his travels in the United States and who later, during the French Revolution, became the leader of the Brissotin or Girondin faction—founded a philanthropic club in Paris called the *Société des Amis des Noirs.* The members included Jefferson's friends Lafayette, the Marquis de Condorcet, and the Duc de la Rochefoucauld-Liancourt. Brissot de Warville invited Jefferson to join the *Amis des Noirs,* but Jefferson, although he approved the primary objective of the society—the abolition of the slave trade—refused the invitation on the grounds that it was not proper for the United States minister to participate in the internal concerns of the French monarchy, and that by associating himself with French abolitionists he would impair his ability to do "good" in Virginia. Jefferson's political instinct proved sound: as a member of the *Amis des Noirs* he would have been a marked man in the Old Dominion.[4]

Nevertheless, it was in the 1780s, while he was far removed from the scene of slavery and from immediate contact with the political and economic problems that plagued his countrymen that Jefferson's moral revulsion against slavery reached its climax. In the clubs and salons frequented by Jefferson, talk about politics and the rights of man came increasingly to usurp the conversation about gardening, history, and *belles-lettres* which Jefferson had found so agreeable when he first arrived in Paris. Inspired by this highly charged political atmosphere, he startled his friend James Madison by announcing his conversion to the doctrine that "the earth belongs to the living"—that is, that every generation has the right to refashion the laws, institutions, and governments as it sees fit. This right, said Jefferson, was a Law of Nature.

The counterpoint of this radical political concept—if it were literally applied, Madison remonstrated, it would be destructive of all order, continuity, and stability in society—was Jefferson's equally startling announcement in 1788–1780 that upon his return to Virginia he would free his slaves, import as many German farmers as he had mature slaves, and settle them and the slaves as sharecroppers upon his plantations, allowing each family a tract of at least fifty acres of land. Of these black and white farmers, he said, he would ask no more than that they give him in return a moderate share of the crops they produced as "a just equivalent for the use of the lands they labored and the stocks and other necessary advances."

The idea of converting slaves into tenants had been discussed by many Virginia planters disgusted with the cost of maintaining slaves during periods of low agricultural prices and by the slaves' low rate of productivity when they were obliged to work solely for the benefit of their masters. As early as 1765, George Mason had observed that such a solution would increase the value of land while removing the curse of slavery. But Jefferson's plan was far more revolutionary than anything hitherto projected, inasmuch as he proposed to intermingle whites and blacks upon his estates. "The [black] children shall be brought up, as others are, in habits of property and foresight," he said, "and I have no doubt that they will be good citizens." [5]

For a brief time in 1788–1789, it seemed that Jefferson was about to repudiate dramatically the position he had taken in the *Notes on Virginia* and in his private correspondence: that the blacks must be removed from Virginia as soon as they were freed. He now proposed not only to let them remain but to give them the opportunity of becoming "good citizens."

While he had "no doubt" that black children, brought up in freedom, would make good farmers and good citizens, he had serious misgivings about their parents' capacity to cope with the problems created by their sudden and wholly unprepared-for emancipation. He cited the example of some Quakers who had settled their lands with black tenant farmers, with the result, Jefferson reported, that "the landlord was obliged to plant their crops for them, to direct all their operations and watch them daily to make sure they worked." To free slaves, he said, was "like abandoning children": the infantile habits and attitudes they had learned as slaves had to be unlearned when they attained freedom. [6]

The idea of using Germans as tenant farmers was open to the objection, among others, that it would have destroyed the plantation system. The Germans who settled in Pennsylvania were the best farmers in America—indeed, it was the "Pennsylvania Dutch" rather than the farmers of Virginia who practiced the agricultural methods and who exemplified the self-sufficiency praised by Jefferson in the *Notes on Virginia*. But German peasants were not content to remain tenant farmers or laborers: they had an unappeasable appetite for land ownership. While

Jefferson warmly approved of this quality in other Americans, it would have made the Germans unsatisfactory tenants over the long term. They would either have moved West where land was cheap or remained in Virginia and bought out their improvident, luxury-loving landlords. In inviting Germans into the country as tenant farmers, Southern planters might have relieved themselves of dependence upon the forced labor of blacks, but they also might have contributed to their own liquidation as a class.

Jefferson proposed this scheme of racial amalgamation at a time when radical ideas were rife among the French aristocracy in whose company he moved in Paris. These men and women of the *haut monde* were largely immune to racial fears and prejudices: many of them lived in the rarefied realm of utopian ideas. As early as 1783, Lafayette was talking about establishing a colony of free blacks in western Virginia to prove that the former slaves were as capable as whites of profiting from freedom. It would hardly do for a seasoned American revolutionary of strong anti-slavery views to permit a French nobleman to take the first step toward the large-scale emancipation of Virginia slaves.[7]

But the spectacle of Thomas Jefferson solemnly renouncing slavery and converting his plantations into enclaves of freedom in a land dominated by slave labor was never vouchsafed the American people. Much as Jefferson loved to indulge his fascination with ideas, his common sense always governed the practical implementation of those ideas. He quickly saw that by attempting the unilateral abolition of slavery he had far transcended the limits of practicality. By 1790, the idea—at least, as a plan of action—had been discarded. In that year, when his daughter Martha married Thomas Mann Randolph, Jefferson gave the happy couple, as a marriage present, one thousand acres of his best land and twenty-five "negroes little and big." He thereby implicitly acknowledged that a Virginia plantation could not function without slaves.[8]

Thus the brave new world of freedom and racial desegregation which Jefferson envisaged in 1788–1789 proved to be but a momentary aberration in his career as an antislavery leader; thereafter, he reverted to the position he had adopted in the *Notes on Virginia,* and from that position he never again departed.

Jefferson attributed this sudden change of mind to the pressure exerted by his British creditors, whose dogged persistence in collecting debts was the bane of his existence and that of many other Virginia planters. At their hands, he suffered almost as much mental anguish as he did from the moral ambiguity created by his ownership of slaves; in July 1787, for example, he said that "the torment of mind I endure till the moment shall arrive when I shall owe not a shilling on earth is such really as to render life of little value." He once defined happiness as being clear of debt, but it was his fate to owe money and to hold slaves, both circumstances being contrary to his principles. In 1789 his creditors became so importunate that, he lamented, he simply could not afford the luxury of conducting a social experiment which, he flattered himself, offered a viable substitute for slavery.

Of course, Jefferson might have paid his creditors by selling his slaves and his estates—it might have been necessary, in that case, to part even with Monticello—and retire to the Elysium, as he described it, of a small farm. But to Jefferson this solution was unthinkable: he loved the spacious life of a Virginia planter too well not to wage a lifelong but increasingly dubious battle to keep his land and slaves intact. While prescribing farming for the American people, Jefferson was not so dedicated to farming that he found happiness with one-hundred acres and a plow. As he said of himself, until he was delivered from his own bondage to his creditors, he saw no real prospect of liberating his slaves from theirs.

∽ 13 ∽

Jefferson as a Slavemaster

Although Jefferson was accused by his enemies of virtually every conceivable political and moral transgression under the sun, it was seldom said that he was a cruel master to his slaves; here his offense was said to consist in the exceptional kindness he showed his female slaves. In fact, in his bearing toward his slaves, Jefferson passed as an exemplary master. Even so, about thirty of his slaves ran off to the British army during the War of Independence, thereby depriving Jefferson of the agreeable illusion that kind treatment was a credible substitute for emancipation.

And yet, kindness and compassion did help to assuage the pangs of conscience; it eased the time on the cross for slaveowners like Jefferson who, holding slavery in abomination, nevertheless continued to own slaves and to profit from their labor. St. John Crèvecoeur, the author of the *Letters of An American Farmer,* prided himself upon his ability to make his slaves feel that they were his "friends and companions," with the happy result, he supposed, that they were as "happy and merry as if they were freemen and freeholders." The cause of abolition, in consequence, lost much of its urgency, although Crèvecoeur would doubtless have been closer to the truth had he observed that some small part of the blacks' natural gaiety, good humor, and eagerness to oblige survived even under servitude.

Moreover, treating slaves humanely tended to weaken the imperative for positive action against slavery enjoined by conscience by investing the institution with a spurious aura of benevolence. Good masters expected their "people" to be good slaves. In the hands of well-intentioned slaveowners the system created the same kind of benevolent despotism Jefferson found so reprehensible when practiced by kings, priests, and nobles.[1]

Jefferson prided himself upon being a "good" master; kindly, compassionate, and considerate of his servitors' well-being. If he were a party to the conspiracy against the natural rights of man implicit in slavery, he could at least, as he put it, place his own slaves "on the comfortable footing of the laborers of other countries." Visitors to Monticello thought he had succeeded: the Duc de la Rochefoucauld-Liancourt reported that Jefferson's slaves were "nourished, clothed and treated as well as white servants could be." He rewarded industry and obedience with incentives such as an extra ration of food and time off for the slaves to work in their own gardens. Jefferson considered his system a notable success: in 1801 he described Monticello as a place "where all is peace and harmony, where we love and are loved by every object we see." While he arraigned slavery before the bar of conscience as "a hideous evil," at Monticello its aspect was, at least outwardly, benign.

Yet Jefferson never permitted his "people" to forget who was master and who was slave. On one occasion he rebuked Jupiter, his coachman, who had been his personal attendant at the College of William and Mary, "in tones and with a look which neither he nor the terrified bystanders ever forgot." Jupiter's offense consisted in refusing to allow a slave boy who claimed to be acting on orders from Jefferson to use one of the carriage horses on an errand.[2]

In general, however, at Monticello the display of the "boisterous passions" produced by the master-slave relationship which Jefferson deplored in the *Notes on Virginia* came from visitors who habitually and notoriously mistreated their slaves. Among these visitors was George Richard Tuberville, an "imperious, haughty Virginia Lord" who made it a practice to keep his coachman chained to the chariot-box. "The Fellow is inclined to run away," said a young New Englander serving as a tutor in Virginia, "and this is a method which this Tyrant makes use of to keep him when abroad; and so soon as he goes home he is delivered into the pitiless Hands of a bloody overseer!" When Colonel Archibald Cary visited Monticello he openly flogged his slaves, a spectacle which, no doubt, made Jefferson's slaves thankful that they were the property of a humane man.[3]

Kindness to slaves was often reciprocated by loyalty and affection.* When he returned to Monticello late in 1789 after five years' absence in France, the slaves on Jefferson's estates were given a holiday to demonstrate their joy at this homecoming. They did not disappoint their master. They crowded around his carriage and drew it up the mountain by hand. "When the door of the carriage was opened, they received him in their arms and bore him to the house, crowding around and kissing his hands and feet—some blubbering and crying, others laughing. It seemed impossible to satisfy their anxiety to touch and kiss the very earth which

---

* In the American South, as in classical Greece and Rome, the highest place among the slaves was occupied by the wet nurse, or, as she was called by Southerners, "mammy." But in the South, the adage that "the hand that rocks the cradle moves the world" did not apply. Nevertheless, the "mammy" was a respected, often loved, member of the household. See Finley 1968, pp. 36–40 and *Journal of Negro History* 23, p. 349.

bore him." Had Jefferson been a god he could hardly have received more adulation, but, then, slaveowners were always playing god to their slaves, especially when dispensing rewards and punishments. Perhaps, too, they had good reason to rejoice at Jefferson's return and to pray that he would finally settle down at Monticello and give his estates his personal supervision.[4]

Because of his long absences from Virginia and his use of overseers and stewards, Jefferson was more or less insulated against the grosser aspects of slavery. His closest contacts were with household servants, who, in the hierarchy established by the slaves themselves, were far superior to field hands. As Henry Thoreau said, "It is hard to have a southern overseer; it is worse to have a northern one; but worst of all when you are the slave-driver yourself." Jefferson was spared that particular fate but neither did he attempt to escape responsibility for what went on at Monticello and his other plantations.

As an absentee owner, Jefferson could do little more than leave his field hands to the mercies of overseers with instructions not to overwork them. Although he sometimes carried a small whip which he brandished at recalcitrant slaves, Jefferson did not personally apply the lash: he left that form of correction to his overseers with the directive that slaves be whipped only in cases of extreme insubordination. And he always preferred to sell incorrigibles rather than have them flogged.[5]

Besides Monticello, Jefferson had three other plantations, totalling about ten thousand acres, each of which required an overseer. The profitability of a plantation depended largely upon the ability of the overseer to "get out the crop," and, in most instances, the overseer was paid a share. Jefferson was not always fortunate in his choice of overseers: one overworked the slaves so cruelly that he had to be dismissed. Moreover, they allowed his arable land to deteriorate for want of crop rotation and fertilizer. In 1809, when he returned to Monticello from Washington, D.C., he found his plantations run down and disorganized.

George Washington, although more reticent about the matter than Jefferson, detested slavery and was quite as eager as his fellow Virginian to see it abolished. While Washington felt the full force of the moral objection to slavery, he was more conscious than was Jefferson of the economic ill effects of depending upon slave labor. In Washington's opinion, slaves were wholly unsatisfactory as laborers: he complained of their dilatoriness, pilfering, wastefulness, and their seeming inability to perform even simple tasks without supervision. He attributed the relative backwardness of Southern agriculture to a system of labor which he could regard only as a disaster.* [6]

---

* A British traveler graphically described the tribulations experienced by slaveowners: "Nothing can be conceived more inert than a slave; his unwilling labour is discovered by every step that he takes; he moves not if he can avoid it; if the eyes of the over-

Among his neighbors Washington gained the reputation of being a strict disciplinarian, quick to order the physical punishment of disobedient slaves. He ran a tight ship at Mount Vernon, and he made obedience to his orders the first law of his plantation. Nevertheless, Washington considered slavery a dirty business and he refused either to buy or sell slaves, "as you would do cattle at a market." Were it not for this aversion to selling slaves, he said, he would dispose of every slave he owned. He had to wait for his death for that event: in his will he ordered all his slaves manumitted upon Martha Washington's death.[7]

In contrast to the master of Mount Vernon, Jefferson, even when he was president, bought and sold slaves. To conceal his part in these transactions, he used a third person. From 1784 to 1794, Jefferson sold about fifty slaves and applied most of the proceeds to the payment of his creditors. Nor did Jefferson free his slaves by his last will and testament. Slaves at Monticello may have had an easier time than at Mount Vernon, but the ending was happier for Washington's slaves.[8]

When selling slaves, Jefferson tried to dispose of families as a unit rather than to separate parents and children, husbands and wives. He was, it is true, under no obligation to keep slave families intact; the laws of the Southern states did not recognize the existence of the slave family. But, like many other slaveowners, Jefferson found it both profitable and humanitarian to give slave families *de facto* recognition: it eased the conscience of the slaveowner and made the slaves more content and therefore less disposed to run away.[9]

Because he insisted to the end– long after his dwindling resources and accumulating debts forbade it—on living in the grand style of a Virginia aristocrat, a style that put many European aristocrats to shame, Jefferson was compelled to maintain a large retinue of household slaves together with hostlers, coachmen, and grooms. Only about one third of his slaves were field hands, that is, productive workers whose labors generated the wealth upon which Jefferson's life of gentility and cultivated leisure was based. Household servants were better treated than the field hands and they had a much better chance of being manumitted by their owners. It was these household slaves by whose appearance and demeanor Jefferson was judged to be a kind and considerate master.[10]

Reflecting his passion for building—"architecture," he said, "is my delight, and putting up and pulling down one of my favorite amusements"—a large number of Jefferson's slaves were artisans: carpenters, bricklayers, cabinetmakers, and blacksmiths. During the long period required to put Monticello in its present form—it took Jefferson over forty years—these artisans were kept almost constantly at work. Although Jeffer-

---

seer be off him, he sleeps; all is listless inactivity; all motion is evidently compulsory."
See Strickland 1971, pp. 32–33.

son employed some skilled white artisans, he could scarcely have brought Monticello to completion without massive reliance upon slave labor.

🍁

Alexander Hamilton urged American manufacturers to utilize in their factories the labor of women and children; at Monticello, Jefferson made extensive use of black slave women and children in manufacturing. He did not object to manufacturing as long as it was carried on in the right place and by the right people: that is, by farmers' wives and children in the household and by slaves on a plantation. At Monticello, with slave women and children as operatives, he ran a small textile factory: by 1814 he had four spinning jennies at work. Utilizing the labor of his slaves, he built a dam, canal, and mill on his property where he ground flour, some of which he sold in Richmond.

Considering the size of his total labor force, Jefferson made extensive use of child labor. Between the ages of ten and sixteen, before they were sent into the fields, boys and girls were employed in spinning, weaving, and manufacturing nails. The naillery which Jefferson established in 1794—in 1796, he installed a cutting machine, imported from England, one of the most advanced in the United States and capable of turning out ten thousand nails a day—employed about a dozen slave boys supervised by a slave called Great George and, on occasion, by Jefferson himself, who delighted in working at the forge.[11]

Of this nail manufactory Jefferson was inordinately proud: he described himself as a nailmaker as well as a farmer, the only virtuous occupation besides farming that he was willing to admit to his pantheon. (Significantly, he never described himself as a politician). In the United States, where, he said, every employment was deemed honorable, the title of nailmaker ought to be held in as high esteem as any possessed by a European noble.[12]

For a few years the nail manufactory yielded such a handsome profit that it seemed possible that Jefferson could combine financial solvency with the felicity vouchsafed a Virginia planter—a situation which rapidly became, in his case, a contradiction in terms. He sold nails for groceries in Richmond and for cash to local retailers—virtually his only source of cash inflow. Both Monticello and James Monroe's house were built with nails produced by Jefferson's naillery. The boys who worked in the naillery shared in this newfound prosperity: they received a pound of meat a week, a dozen herrings, a quart of molasses, and a peck of meal. Those who turned out the most nails were rewarded with a suit of red or blue cloth. He did not give these rewards lightly, however; like a latter-day efficiency expert, he calculated the quantity of nails a boy ought to produce in a day's work and held him to it.[13]

But, like all of Jefferson's business enterprises (his flour mill was completely destroyed when the dam broke) the naillery was fated to fall on evil days. Retailers ceased to stock his nails, preferring British-made nails to the local product. Jefferson attributed the decline of his nail business to British merchants who, he said, were bent upon nipping in the bud all domestic manufactures in the United States. But in actuality, he himself correctly diagnosed the cause of his troubles when he admitted that, having little or no fluid capital, he could not afford to sell on credit. British merchants, on the other hand, were in a position to advance credit to their customers, and most of Virginia wholesalers and retailers needed all the credit they could get to remain in business. Despite this disadvantage, Jefferson continued to produce nails, although on a diminishing scale, until 1823—a confirmation of his faith that agriculture could be successfully combined with manufacturing, provided that the British did not deliberately cut prices in order to destroy competition. But here, again, he considered himself to be the victim of a British "conspiracy" similar to George III's deep-laid plot against American freedom.

↬ 14 ↫

Slavery and the
Treaty of 1783

———•———

LATE IN 1789, after witnessing the opening scenes of the French Revolution, Jefferson returned to Virginia, and in the spring of 1790 he went to New York to assume the post of secretary of state in the cabinet of President Washington. He brought with him to the temporary capital of the United States a retinue of household servants, footmen, and a coachman. Republican simplicity as practiced by Jefferson and other Southerners who came North to serve in Congress or the cabinet never required the renunciation of the services of slaves; and, in Jefferson's case, it did not require the sacrifice of fine furniture, French cooking, exquisite wines, horses, and carriages. On the strength of his appearance—he sported the latest fashions of the French *haut monde*— one would hardly have supposed that a great American democrat had arrived in town or, unless one had read the *Notes on Virginia,* that Jefferson felt the slightest repugnance to slavery. The truth is, that he had grown up with slavery and his "people" were essential to his comfort and well being.

Amply as his physical comforts were ministered to, Jefferson found himself involved in some very unsettling diplomatic exchanges with George Hammond, the British minister to the United States who arrived in Philadelphia in 1791 as the first official representative sent by His Brittanic Majesty to his former subjects in America. In his negotiations with Hammond, Jefferson distinguished himself as a champion of peculiarly Virginia interests and as a defender of the rights of property, especially that species of property represented by black slaves. In the first clearly defined postrevolutionary confrontation between the rights of black man and the rights of property, Jefferson aligned himself decisively on the side of property. His insistence that slaves be treated as property attributed significantly toward bringing Great Britain and the United States to an impasse from which war seemed the probable outcome.

The treaty of peace of 1783, which brought an end to the war between

the United States and Great Britain and established the independence of
the United States (a preliminary treaty had been agreed upon as early as
November 1782) was ratified by the Continental Congress in January
1784. Among other provisions, the definitive treaty prohibited the British
army, when it evacuated the United States, from carrying away "Negroes
or other property" belonging to American citizens; it required the United
States to desist from interposing any obstacles to the collection of debts
owed by Americans to British citizens; and it committed the British to
surrender the Northwest Posts (which had been ceded by the treaty of
peace) "with all convenient speed" to the United States. In the negotiations conducted by Jefferson with George Hammond in 1791–1793, these
three articles were of paramount importance.

The treaty by which the United States gained its independence proved
in retrospect to be one of the most consistently and flagrantly violated
treaties which the Republic has ever signed. Both sides infringed it freely
wherever it suited their sovereign interests. The British army transgressed
by carrying away over three thousand blacks, formerly the slaves of American patriots, most of whom were Virginians, when it evacuated New
York City and Charleston, South Carolina, in 1783. Instead of transferring
the Northwest Posts to American custody "with all convenient speed,"
the British retained possession until 1796. On their part, the Americans,
especially the Virginians, placed obstacles in the way of the collection of
prewar British debts, an action in palpable violation of the treaty.

As for the slaves carried off by the British, Jefferson considered them
in 1784–1785 to be "a mere Bagatelle." He admitted that the British had
a right to free the slaves and he would not say that they had done wrong
by giving freedom to those who had voluntarily placed themselves under
British protection. He attached far more importance to the retention by
the British of the Northwest Posts than to the "abduction" of the slaves.
But the Virginia House of Delegates was emphatic in its refusal to regard
the issue of the "abducted" slaves as a bagatelle. In 1784, it coupled the
restitution of the slaves to the payment of British debts and the surrender
of the Northwest Posts. Unitl the British fully complied with the terms of
the treaty of peace, the Virginia legislators considered themselves justified
in blocking the collection of British debts. Virginia had good reason to
take this intransigent position: the commonwealth's share of the debt
owing British merchants by American citizens was two million pounds
sterling, well over half the total.

British officials did not deny that in carrying off "Negroes, or other
property" of the American citizens they had committed an infraction of
the Treaty of Peace. But as Sir Guy Carleton, the British general under
whose command the evacuation of New York in 1783 had taken place,
pointed out, these "Negroes" were free men, having been emancipated by
the British army acting under the authority of His Britannic Majesty,

and were therefore not "the property" of Americans or of anyone else. In 1784, William Pitt, the British prime minister, told John Adams that that British army had acted in 1783 in obedience to the dictates of the higher law of humanity rather than to the letter of the treaty. But Pitt declined to equate the carrying off of the slaves with impediments placed by legislatures and courts of the American states upon the recovery of British debts. Until justice had been done these creditors, he told John Adams, the Northwest Posts would remain in British hands.[1]

In 1787, in the hope of making a commercial treaty with Great Britain and securing the cession of the Northwest Posts, John Jay, the secretary of foreign affairs, acknowledged that the United States had been guilty of the first breach of the treaty of 1783, and the Continental Congress called upon the states to repeal all legislation and to stop all practices that contravened the treaty. Three of the offending states complied, but Virginia would do no more than offer to permit the collection of British debts provided that Great Britain paid for the slaves and ceded the Northwest Posts. As a result, in 1791, when Jefferson began his talks with the British minister, Virginia was the only state still in defiance of the treaty of peace.*

The responsibility for Virginia's uncompromising stand on the debt issue lay with Governor Patrick Henry and the small farmers of the commonwealth who composed the bulk of his constituency. Henry urged the Virginia legislature to declare all debts owing British subjects extinguished by the war. The governor did not allege prior British infractions of the terms of the treaty as a justification for this arbitrary and unilateral action; he chose rather to argue that the barbarity and savagery with which Great Britain had waged war against the United States had released Americans from all obligations normally imposed by international law.[2]

Jefferson, on the other hand, while he agreed that the British were guilty of atrocities that would have stricken the conscience of a nation less hardened to wrongdoing by long and assiduous practice, did not contend that these war crimes expunged private debts owing British subjects. Nor, at this time, did he say that Great Britain's refusal to surrender the Northwest Posts justified retaliatory action against the British creditors. "Whether England gives up the Posts or not," he said in 1786, "these debts must be paid, or our character will be stained with infamy among all nations and to all times." The sequestration of British and Loyalist property by the states during the war was sufficient, Jefferson

---

* And citizens of Virginia still owed a total of 2.3 million pounds, including interest, mainly to London and Glasgow merchants. Only 150,000 pounds was owing by citizens of the Northern states.

considered, to drive home to Great Britain the long-deferred lesson that it must observe the rules of international law.

While Jefferson did not deny that these debts were legal obligations, he claimed for American debtors the right to withhold payment of interest during the War of Independence, a period of seven years. Having violated all the laws governing civilized warfare, the British, he said, could hardly expect Americans to pay interest on top of reconstructing their ruined cities, ravaged farms and plantations, and replenishing their depleted slave labor force. To pay interest during the war years, Jefferson asserted, would ruin many honest farmers and planters struggling to get on their feet.[3]

In deprecating the withholding of payment on legitimate debts contracted before the war, Jefferson was speaking for the minority of Virginians who were less concerned with immediate personal advantage than with the honor and financial probity of the commonwealth. But this was not the way to popularity in Virginia. George Mason discovered that when he advocated the repeal of all laws in contravention of the treaty of peace, he encountered the question, "If we are now to pay the debts due to British merchants, what have we been fighting for all this while?" John Marshall was confronted with this question so often that he concluded that Virginians' hostility to Great Britain, while "cloaked in the name of patriotism," was actually only an excuse to avoid paying the prewar debts.[4]

Unilateral actions by the states impeding the collection of debts owing British subjects raised the question whether treaties made by the United States Congress were in fact the supreme law of the land. If each state presumed to interpret treaties as it saw fit, the government of the United States would become "a mere government of reason and persuasion," not a government of laws. Lacking a system of courts in which the laws could be enforced and military power by which recalcitrant states could be coerced, the central government became wholly dependent upon the good will of the state governments. On this issue, critical to the continued existence of the American Union, Jefferson took his stand on the principle that the right of interpreting and executing treaties belonged exclusively to Congress and that unless the states ceased to interfere, the national honor, good faith, and the capability of making future treaties with foreign powers would be jeopardized.[5]

Nevertheless, in 1791–1793, during his negotiations with George Hammond, Jefferson swung over completely to the position taken by the Virginia legislature a decade earlier to the effect that no agreement on the debts was possible until the British had paid for the slaves illegally carried away and surrendered the Northwest Posts. Far from considering the question of the slaves a "mere Bagatelle," Jefferson now made this the central issue of the dispute. Characteristically, in his correspondence with Hammond, he referred to the objects of the controversy as "laborers," "Negroes," or "Property": he studiously avoided referring to them as "slaves." [6]

At Jefferson's insistence, these talks revolved round the pivotal question: which signatory of the treaty, Great Britain or the United States, was guilty of the first infraction? Jefferson vehemently accused the British of having committed the original breach, and the action which he cited to prove it was the "abduction" of the slaves. He peremptorily demanded that the British acknowledge their guilt, reimburse the slaveowners for their loss, and evacuate the Northwest Posts. The action taken by Virginia and other states obstructing the collection of British debts he justified on the ground of prior British violation. From the beginning to the end of his talks with Hammond, Jefferson insisted that the British acknowledge that they bore the responsibility for all American violations of the treaty. If this admission could be extracted from Great Britain, the United States would obviously stand before the world as the innocent, injured party in a dispute forced upon it by its late enemy. As secretary of state, Jefferson clearly felt that it was more important to uphold the honor, integrity, and rectitude of the United States as the most moral nation on earth than to advance the cause of Anglo-American rapprochement. Here and elsewhere, Jefferson was first and foremost an American patriot, and nowhere was this fact more vividly evidenced than in his dealings with Britons.[7]

In actuality, it was the moral position of Virginia, far more than that of the United States, that was at stake. The Continental Congress had emphatically condemned the acts of Virginia and other states by which British creditors were denied due process in the collection of debts, and Jefferson himself had previously taken the position that here his fellow Virginians were in the wrong.[8]

But as secretary of state he was under strong pressure to uphold the special interests of his native state. Had he not done so, he would have risked not only alienating his own supporters in Virginia, but, even more to the point, he would have certainly widened the already alarming breach that he had opened up between Virginia and the federal government as a result of the adoption of Alexander Hamilton's plan for the assumption of state debts, a measure for which Jefferson himself, along with James Madison, bore considerable responsibility; for it was the two Virginians who, in July 1790, struck the famous bargain with Hamilton which made possible the assumption of state debts. Even though Congress had added considerable "sweetening" to Virginia and other states with small debts, the assumption of state debts was so unpopular in Virginia that in 1791 the state legislature formally protested against what it regarded as a sellout to corrupt Northern speculators.[9]

Under these circumstances, Jefferson could hardly have taken the lofty attitude that the question of the slaves carried away by the British was of minor importance. Instead, recognizing the extreme delicacy of his position, he put the United States officially on record for the first time claiming that the onus for the first breach of the treaty of peace lay upon Great Britain, and, also for the first time, legitimizing its own infractions of the peace treaty as a morally defensible response to prior British violations. By removing the slaves contrary to the treaty, Jefferson asserted, the British had "preceded and *produced* the acts on our part complained of." Moreover, by "withdrawing the cultivators of the soil" (i.e. the slaves), "the produce of which was to pay the debts," the British themselves had put it out of the power, as well as removed the moral obligation, of Americans to honor otherwise sacred obligations.

But Jefferson discovered that to assert the culpability of the British for the first breach of the treaty was far easier than to prove it. Hammond took the position that the entire fault lay with the Americans and that nothing would be done about the slaves or the Northwest Posts until Virginia had cleared the way for the collection of British debts. In sum, Jefferson succeeded in making the question of the "abducted" slaves a major stumbling block to the settlement of Anglo-American differences.

Gratifying as this was to Virginians, who, after all, were the chief sufferers by the removal of the slaves, few Americans outside the Old Dominion were seriously agitated by this issue. Their principal concern was rather to get possession of the Northwest Posts. These strategic strongholds located along the boundary between the United States and Canada lay within the boundaries of the United States as agreed to by Great Britain in the treaty of peace; the British, therefore, were indeed in illegal occupation of American territory. The possession of the posts was vital to the Indian trade—the trade in furs alone, Jefferson calculated, amounted to one hundred thousand pounds sterling annually—and to the control of the Indians themselves. Every Indian foray against the American frontier was attributed by Americans to the influence Great Britain maintained over the Indians by virtue of its possession of the Northwest Posts.*

Had Jefferson's paramount objective been to gain possession of the Northwest Posts and to make a commercial treaty with Great Britain opening the British West Indies to American ships, he would hardly have adopted the hectoring, abrasive, and unconciliatory tone he used with Hammond. It served no constructive purpose to engage in recriminations,

---

* Although Jefferson did not know it—the fact did not come to light until long after his death—the British government had decided to retain possession of the Northwest Posts *before* it heard of American infractions of the treaty of peace. This decision was made shortly after the fall of the Shelburne ministry early in 1783. If intent is taken into account, this was the first breach of the treaty of peace.

and the question of which nation was guilty of the first infringement of the treaty inevitably degenerated into a mere exercise in mutual vituperation. Manifestly, Jefferson did not give the highest priority to effecting a settlement with Great Britain; he was far more intent upon establishing closer commercial relations with France than with Great Britain, and he was more concerned with vindicating the reputation of the United States than in promoting commercial intercourse with the former mother country—intercourse that he feared might lead to military alliance between the two countries. He still referred to Great Britain as "the enemy," and he had by no means forgotten or forgiven the slights and humiliations he had endured at the hands of high British officials in London in the spring of 1786. Great Britain's governing principles, he had long since decided, were "Conquest, Colonization, Commerce, and Monopoly of the Ocean." Nor could he be persuaded that a nation pursuing such objectives seriously intended to surrender the Northwest Posts or to make a commercial treaty with the United States.[10]

While these negotiations were in progress—if that is the right word to describe this exchange of tirades and outcries of outraged virtue on the part of both men—Alexander Hamilton, as secretary of the treasury, was doing his utmost to undermine Jefferson's position. As early as 1783, Hamilton had taken the position that the United States had no right to demand the return of the slaves. Having been emancipated by British military order, they became, he said, free men, and no compact, however solemn, made between the United States and Great Britain, could alter their status. Under these circumstances, for the United States to demand the surrender of these slaves was, in Hamilton's opinion, "as *odius* and *immoral* a thing as can be conceived." Moreover, Hamilton strongly dissented from Jefferson's view that raising legal obstacles to the collection of debts was a legitimate reprisal for prior British infractions of the treaty. "The debts of private individuals are in no case a proper object of reprisals," he declared; in international law, debts were not subject to confiscation, and public injuries could not discharge private obligations.

With convictions regarding the way American foreign policy ought to be conducted quite as strong as but completely opposite to Jefferson's governing principles, Hamilton took it upon himself to tell Hammond that the American sercretary of state was speaking for himself, not for the government of the United States. Without consulting the president, he tried to dissociate Washington and the cabinet from Jefferson's "intemperate violence" and Anglophobia. Jefferson and Madison, he told Hammond, were the victims of "a womanish attachment to France and a womanish resentment against Great Britain."[11]

Since nothing could be more inconsequential than "womanish" opinions on international affairs, Hamilton advised Hammond to pay no attention to Jefferson's demands for compensation for the slaves and he assured the British minister that His Majesty's subjects would receive justice in federal courts. Thus Hamilton and Jefferson both took their stand upon the rights of property: Hamilton upholding the rights of British creditors to their property—namely, contracts, bills of sale, notes, and other evidences of indebtedness—and Jefferson for his part insisting upon the right of Southerners to their property—namely, slaves.[12]

By intruding into the negotiations between Jefferson and Hammond, Hamilton believed that he was saving the peace between Great Britain and the United States. In disputes between nations, he observed, nothing was more common than for each to charge the other with being the aggressor or the delinquent. The acrimonious recrimination inevitably produced by such confrontations created, he pointed out, a situation in which the pride of one nation would not yield to the arguments of the other, leaving war as the only arbiter of the dispute. In Hamilton's opinion, for the United States to go to war with Great Britain over such a trivial issue as the slaves and the debts would be as great a tragedy as Jefferson believed it would be for the United States to go to war with France over French seizures of American ships. By talking directly to Hammond, behind the back of the secretary of state, Hamilton hoped to effect a compromise which waived the question of first agression or delinquency: "Compromise," he said, is "the bridge by which nations, arrayed against each other, are enabled to retire with honor and without bloodshed, from the field of combat." Mollified and put in a conciliatory frame of mind by an American display of good will, the British, Hamilton flattered himself, would surrender the Northwest Posts and make a commercial treaty with the United States.[13]

In his negotiations with George Hammond, Jefferson failed to achieve any of his objectives: the British refused to admit that they were guilty of the first breach of the treaty; they declined to compensate the slaveowners whose "property" they had carried away; and they retained possession of the Northwest Posts. To his government, Hammond described Jefferson as a perfect Frenchman, imbued with all the Frenchman's hatred of "perfidious Albion." This report of Jefferson's Anglophobism had the untoward effect of stiffening the determination of the British government to retain possession of the Northwest Posts. In February 1794, Lord Grenville, the British foreign secretary, declared that because of the refusal of the United States to honor the peace treaty over a period of nine years, Great Britain no longer considered itself obliged to abide by it. Thus, after three years of desultory negotiations, Anglo-American relations were worse than when Jefferson had assumed the office of secretary of state. The British themselves had contributed to this exacerbation of the antagonism between the two countries by seizing American ships in the West Indies in 1793 in order to cut off American trade with the French islands. In December 1793, Jefferson accompanied his resignation from the position of secretary of state with a "valedictory" calling for commercial retaliation upon Great Britain, and in January 1794, James Madison, the leader of the Jeffersonian Republicans in Congress, proposed the sequestration of British debts.

War with Great Britain—seemingly inevitable in the early spring of 1794 when news of new British seizures of American ships reached the United States—was averted by timely concessions on the part of the British government to the rights of neutral shipping and by the appointment of John Jay, the former chief justice of the United States, as envoy extraordinary to the Court of St. James's.

John Jay brought with him to London a very different frame of mind than that in which Jefferson, as secretary of state, had conducted negotiations with George Hammond: he was conciliatory, flexible, and considerate of British susceptibilities. An ardent abolitionist, Jay was hardly the man to press Virginia's case against the British government for carrying off "Negroes, and other property." He did make, however, a purely *pro forma* statement to Lord Grenville, the British foreign secretary, accusing the British of having committed the first violation of the treaty by taking away the slaves. But when Lord Grenville tesily rejected the charge, Jay freely admitted, as he had done in 1786 as secretary of foreign affairs, that the British had done right to free the slaves. He even allowed himself to be persuaded by Lord Grenville that the United States had no just claim to compensation for the loss of these "labourers." Accordingly the treaty Jay signed in November 1794 made no mention whatever of the points which Jefferson had been at such pains to establish: that the British were guilty of the first infringement of the Treaty of 1783 and that Americans (in the first instance Virginians) were justified in obstructing the collection of British debts.

Among other things, Jay's treaty assured the United States of possession of the Northwest Posts and opened the British West Indies to American ships of small tonnage—a provision later rejected by the United States Senate. But it also required the United States to make concessions on the subject of neutral rights at sea and to renounce the use of what Jefferson called the "commercial weapons"—discrimination against British ships and merchandise and sequestration of British debts. A final blow to Jeffersonian diplomatic approaches and methods was Jay's agreement to the appointment of a joint commission to assess the amount owing by American debtors to British subjects.

Jefferson considered Jay's treaty an alliance in all but name between the United States and Great Britain and, therefore, a mortal affront to France, the United States's ally since 1778. To his friends, he condemned the treaty as the work of "a vile aristocratic few who have too long governed America, and who are enemies of the equality of man." He accused John Jay of "avarice and corruption," and he pronounced him guilty of treason against his country.

Although the treaty was approved by the Senate and ratified by the president, an appropriation of money by the House of Representatives was required to carry it into effect. Urged on by Jefferson himself, the Jeffersonian Republicans in the House of Representatives asserted that the House had a concurrent right with the Senate to approve or to disapprove treaties affecting commerce. This claim of constitutional power was left to the determination of future events: by a vote of 51 to 48, the House finally voted to carry the treaty into effect. Only one representative from Virginia voted in favor of executing the treaty.

Difficult as it was for Jefferson to swallow Jay's treaty, Hamilton made the pill even more unpalatable by asserting in the newspapers under the signature "Camillus" that Jefferson and his fellow Virginians had taken "the odius and immoral" position of demanding that free men be returned to slavery. (Here Hamilton tried to score a propaganda point: Jefferson had asked for compensation for the slaves, not for their physical return.) The secretary of the treasury gave short shrift to Jefferson's contention that the British were guilty of the first infraction of the treaty of peace: the two countries had committed simultaneous violations, he declared, and therefore neither had the right to complain, much less to justify, its own noncompliance on the wholly untenable ground of the other party's guilt. In this dispute with Jefferson, Hamilton had the last word: in 1802, the United States agreed to pay 600,000 pounds sterling to the British government to extinguish all outstanding claims against American citizens, most of whom were Virginians. Jefferson's cup of humiliation was filled to the brim: not a farthing was ever paid by the British for the slaves they had carried off in 1783.[14]

∾ 15 ∾

The Decline of the
Antislavery Movement

◆

DURING THE PERIOD of the ascendancy of the Federalist party (1789–
1801), Jefferson served not only as secretary of state but, after 1797, as
vice-president of the United States. During these years, he played very
little part in the antislavery movement. He took care, in particular, not
to identify himself with the religious denominations most fervent and
uncompromising in bearing testimony against slavery. Although he had
accepted the aid of the Virginia Presbyterians, Baptists, and Methodists
in bringing about the enactment of the Statute of Religious Freedom in
1786, he shunned all association with them on the subject of slavery.
He would have found them ardent allies: "Friends of equality and
liberty" formed abolitionist societies in Delaware, Maryland, and Virginia, and many of these societies joined the American Convention of
Abolition Societies when it was organized in 1794. Toward the Quakers,
by far the most fervent and intransigent in their opposition to slavery,
Jefferson was especially aloof: he well knew how Southerners reacted to
the Quakers' methods of pointing up the iniquity of slavery by means of
petitions to Congress and the publication of antislavery tracts. Quakers
took the position, as did Jefferson, that slavery was a moral wrong as
well as a denial of natural rights, but they accepted the fact that a multiracial society had been created in the United States and that Americans
must make the best of it.[1]

Jefferson justified his refusal to speak out on the subject of slavery,
or to support those who were speaking out, by appealing to the position
he had taken as early as 1785 that the institution was in the course of
extinguishment and that premature action, especially of the kind
prompted by religious emotionalism, would serve only to "rivet closer
the chains of bondage" and to postpone the inevitable day when the
fetters would be struck off forever. This line of reasoning led Jefferson to

the conclusion that the antislavery cause could be best served by a policy of masterly inaction—a remarkable proposition coming from a revolutionary who had made masterly action the guiding principle of his struggle against British tyranny.

Washington shared Jefferson's optimistic view that slavery was best left alone to expire of its unprofitability and inherent moral and economic contradictions. In 1794, Washington said that he did not like to think and much less to talk of slavery; it was dangerous, he believed, to "strike too vigorously at a prejudice which has begun to diminish" and which "time, patience and information would not fail to vanquish." Two years later he predicted that Virginia would adopt a scheme of gradual emancipation as soon as a practicable method was proposed. In his opposition to slavery, Jefferson was concerned primarily with cleansing the land of a moral dereliction and a high offense against the rights of man; to Washington, on the other hand, the abolition of slavery was necessary to save Virginia agriculture and to preserve the federal Union.[2]

A congenitally sanguine man who had already received a Sign from Heaven that slavery would sooner or later be eradicated from the American Garden (and the slaves themselves expelled from its purlieus), Jefferson looked constantly for signs in Virginia that the process was under way. He found encouraging evidence in the growing tendency among Virginia slaveowners to treat their slaves with the humanitarianism that was an essential characteristic of the Enlightenment. Needless brutality to slaves came to be frowned upon in the best slaveholding circles, and in 1788 the Virginia legislature repealed a law which had virtually licensed a master to kill his "servant" in the course of administering punishment. The wanton killing of a slave was declared to be a heinous offense, but there was nothing in the law to prevent a jury from following its natural predilection and holding the killing of a slave to be justifiable homicide or an unfortunate accident.[3]

Nor, seemingly, had the moral revulsion many planters felt for slavery suffered any diminution. John Randolph of Roanoke, who sat in the United States Senate, William B. Giles, a Virginia delegate to the House of Representatives, and John Taylor of Caroline, the chief ideologue of Jeffersonian Republicanism, declared that they "lamented and detested slavery," although they admitted that they did not know what to do about it. As late as 1799 a British traveler reported he had not encountered a single Virginia planter who acknowledged the right to enslave blacks or defended the institution on any other ground than that it was necessary to sustain the economy of the state.[4]

During his term of office as secretary of state, and, indeed, during the entire decade of the 1790s, Jefferson was preoccupied with the struggle against Hamiltonian finance and the "monarchism" which seemed to him certain to follow in its train. By the summer of 1790, after a few months' residence in New York, he became convinced that a conspiracy against republicanism, no less formidable than the conspiracy against freedom that Americans had encountered and overcome in the British Empire, existed among highly placed officials in the new federal government and that President Washington was in danger of becoming an unsuspecting abettor of the plot.

In the course of his career, Jefferson was compelled to respond to a succession of threats to freedom and republicanism which demanded his undivided attention. At no time did he permit slavery to take precedence over what he regarded as more immediate threats to the ideals and institutions he cherished. Jefferson viewed the American scene not merely as a philosopher-statesman but, more importantly, as a political activist fighting on many fronts against a legion of enemies hostile to republicanism. Conscious of being beset by dangers on every hand, he was never able to concentrate his attention upon slavery as the paramount, all-encompassing evil of the day.

For this reason, Jefferson appeared during the 1790s to be far more eager to combat Hamiltonian finance and to liquidate the national debt than to eradicate slavery. Since he considered the assumption of state debts (to which he had been persuaded to assent) and the perpetuation of the national debt to be the prime engines of the system of corruption and centralization Hamilton was trying to foist upon the country, Jefferson naturally gave priority to his continuing struggle with the secretary of the treasury. If Hamiltonianism triumphed, the question of slavery would become academic: farmers and planters, Jefferson predicted, would then be reduced to a more cruel and certainly more exploitative form of slavery to Northern businessmen, bankers, and speculators than the relatively humane servitude experienced by Southern slaves. So fearful was he that these "conspirators against human happiness" would overthrow the republic that in the 1790s he demanded that all holders of government securities and bank stock be prohibited by federal law from sitting in Congress. Since he did not propose a similar morals test for slaveowners, many of whom were members of Congress, Jefferson put himself in the extraordinary position of holding that the ownership of human beings was less reprehensible than the ownership of stocks and bonds.

In 1799 he involved himself in a similar contradiction by insisting that foreigners, before becoming United States citizens, renounce their titles, without at the same time requiring that they divest themselves of slaves. Samuel Dexter, a Massachusetts Congressman, quickly detecting an anomaly in the Jeffersonian argument, moved that prospective citizens be required to renounce the possession of slaves as well as of titles. Whereupon John Nicholson of Virginia denounced Dexter for implying that slaveholders were not fit to be citizens or to hold public office. Dexter's motion was defeated, but the incident served to bring to light the fact that Jefferson and his partisans believed that a titled aristocrat was more of a menace to American republicanism than was a Southern slaveowner.[5]

Preoccupied with his struggle with Hamilton and the "monarchical" Federalist party, Jefferson was content to register his disapproval of slavery in various small, inconsequential ways. In 1790, for example, he began to use maple sugar which, he said, required only the labor of children, in preference to cane sugar which was produced by slave labor in the West Indies. He tried unsuccessfully to grow sugar maples at Monticello, and he requested his friend Dr. Benjamin Rush of Philadelphia (Rush declared that he contemplated sugar maples with "a species of affection and even veneration") to communicate to the American Philosophical Society an account of this useful and ornamental tree in the hope that its cultivation would weaken slavery in the West Indies. But Jefferson neither took nor advocated any action that would weaken slavery among the tobacco and cotton producers in the United States. Southern unity against Hamiltonianism was all-important: while Southerners quarreled among themselves, Northern speculator-capitalists would reap an even richer harvest than that which they had already gathered from the assumption of state debts.[6]

After 1790, when Jefferson worked against slavery at all, it was underground. He confided his thoughts to his friends and correspondents but he refrained carefully from taking a public stand. While John Jay, Benjamin Rush, Benjamin Franklin, Alexander Hamilton, and Aaron Burr joined antislavery societies, Jefferson's name was absent from the rosters. No clarion calls for action against slavery issued from Monticello; a quiet, induced in part by circumspection, had fallen upon the great champion of the rights of man. By his silence and his inaction, Jefferson tacitly acquiesced in a situation described by a Virginia emancipationist as one in which "the majority are poor; the Rich had Slaves; and the rich make the laws." [7]

It could truly be said of Virginians that while everyone talked about slavery no one did anything about it. When someone actually tried to do something the result seemed to confirm the wisdom of Jefferson's policy of saying little and doing nothing. In 1796, St. George Tucker, a professor at the College of William and Mary, proposed in a book entitled *A Dissertation on Slavery* a plan for the abolition of slavery which was presented to the Virginia legislature for immediate consideration and, hopefully, action. Arguing that slavery was wholly incompatible with Republicanism, Tucker proposed a gradual scheme of emancipation—so gradual, in fact, that it would have required almost a century to accomplish its objective—accompanied by the deportation of free blacks. Yet this proposal received short shrift from the Virginia House of Delegates: it was simply laid on the table. Not a single member spoke in support of the plan.[8]

Despite this clear sign that slavery was not on its way out—indeed, it seemed to be gravitating in exactly the opposite direction—Jefferson did not abandon hope that the institution was losing its grip upon the Southern mind and the Southern economy. In the first place, the slave trade was in the process of being abolished, and, secondly, at least from Jefferson's perspective at Monticello, it seemed to be losing its profitability—the certain prelude, he supposed, to its final extinguishment.

The abolition of the slave trade by state action—for several years between 1783 and 1808, the traffic was illegal in all the states—Jefferson took to be a sign that the "monster," deprived of sustenance in the form of fresh cargoes of Africans, would sooner or later expire in its lair. Actually, the decline demonstrated only that when the economy was depressed, as it was in the immediate postwar period, the disadvantages of slavery—especially the necessity of feeding, housing and clothing idle hands—were impressed upon slaveowners. With a surfeit of slaves and with many planters deeply in debt to British merchants for slaves and other "merchandise," it was natural that the Southern states would attempt to curtail and even to prohibit altogether a trade that had the effect of putting them deeper into debt and adding further to their surplus labor force. They had acted in the same manner and on similar grounds prior to the American Revolution.

William Loughton Smith of South Carolina, a more perceptive economist but a far less emotionally engaged moralist than Thomas Jefferson, observed that regardless of state prohibitions upon the slave trade, the institution was "so engrafted into the policy of the Southern states, that it cannot be eradicated without tearing up by the roots their happiness, tranquility, and prosperity." Moreover, despite the increasingly humane treatment of blacks, no evidence was forthcoming that whites had essentially changed their view of blacks as "an indolent people, improvident, averse to labor; when emancipated, they will either starve or plunder." [9]

Equally important was slavery's unique capacity to provide a system of social control on a restive black population. Because it kept the blacks "in their place"—which, unfortunately for them, was at the very mudsills of society—it was esteemed by a multitude of Southerners who had no direct financial stake in the institution. Moreover, slaveholding was the way to wealth in the South, and the number of slaves held by an individual helped to determine his place in the social hierarchy. Finally, the area of slavery and the number of slaveowners was constantly increasing at the expense of the pioneers and small non-slaveholding farmers who either conformed to the new planting economy and the social struc-

ture it brought in its train or moved beyond its reach—a feat which sometimes required three or four major moves in a lifetime.[10]

The unprofitability of slavery upon which Jefferson relied to activate
the sluggish moral sense of slaveowners was largely confined to the
Chesapeake tobacco planters in whose company he himself belonged.
For cotton planters the situation was radically changed in 1793 by the
invention by Eli Whitney of the cotton gin. Within a few years, the
"monster," hitherto comatose, was displaying unprecedented vitality as it
extended its sway over South Carolina and the territories of Alabama and
Mississippi. Thus, contrary to Jefferson's expectations, slavery strengthened its hold upon the Southern economy and, equally important, upon
the Southern mind. For Jefferson, the dilemma posed by slavery's manifest utility as an adjunct of agriculture was intensified. As a result of the
spread of cotton cultivation, slavery became even more inextricably
identified with agriculture than when it was confined to the production
of tabacco, rice, indigo, and naval stores. In consequence, Jefferson found
it increasingly difficult to take a stand against slavery without at the same
time delivering a mortal blow at the agricultural system upon the perpetuation of which he rested his hopes of the survival of republicanism.[11]

It was an unmistakable sign of the times that during the last decade
of the eighteenth century the evangelical sects in the South began to lose
their ardor for emancipation, until by 1810 they had ceased to equate
Christianity with abolitionism. Thus the South was divested of the
strongest force operating within the region in favor of the liberation of
the slaves. In the Southern states, antislavery sentiment reached its apex
in the 1780s, lost it dynamism in the 1790s, and visibly began to decline
in the early years of the nineteenth century. Time, in appeared, was
emphatically not on the side of the idealistic young men of Virginia upon
whom Jefferson depended to win a notable victory over greed and
avarice.

~ 16 ~

Jefferson and
Gabriel's Conspiracy

———◆———

DURING MUCH OF HIS ADULT LIFE Jefferson had the uneasy sensation of sitting on a volcano that might erupt at any moment. He never imagined that the slaves would be content with anything short of freedom, and so powerful was this instinctual desire that he believed they would sacrifice everything, including life itself, to attain it. In short, Jefferson credited blacks with possessing the same love of liberty, and in the same amplitude, that had animated white Americans during the War of Independence.[1]

Yet the nagging fear of servile uprising—a chilling prospect foreign to Jefferson's usually optimistic hope of future felicity—had less basis in historical experience than in Jefferson's own conviction that an intolerable wrong was being inflicted upon men, women, and children who, regardless of whether they were equal in intelligence to the whites, shared equally in the moral sense which told them that they had as much right to be free as the whites who held them in servitude. Moreover, as a student of Roman history, he knew that the Roman republic had been racked by servile wars that had devastated Sicily; and the French Revolution had raised the specter of American slaves donning the Liberty cap.

Although a few slaves were involved in an abortive insurrection during the colonial period, nothing occurred in Virginia until 1800 to give substance to Jefferson's apprehensions of a racial upheaval. In that year, thousands of blacks were reported to have joined a plot hatched by Gabriel, a free black, to attack Richmond and, after putting the inhabitants to the sword and burning the city, to escape to the Indian country to the west. But before the march upon Richmond had begun, a slave gave timely warning to the authorities. Hundreds of slaves were rounded up, and over thirty were given summary trial (a slave accused of such a crime seldom received more than a summary trial) and executed.[2]

When Jefferson, who was spending the summer at Monticello, learned of Gabriel's Conspiracy, his first words were, "We are truly to be pitied!" By "we" he meant of course the white inhabitants of Virginia who, he believed, merited commiseration because they were under the necessity of holding down a large population of potentially dangerous blacks. His response was, in fact, an outcry against the outrageous fate which impelled thousands of decent, moral, and compassionate men who knew in their hearts that it was wrong to hold human beings in servitude. While admitting that slavery was unjust to both races, Jefferson revealed by this remark that he was most keenly sensible of the moral harm done to the whites by slavery and by the presence of large numbers of half-mutinous black people in their midst.[3]

Gabriel's Conspiracy was followed by the Great Fear which, before it ran its course, threatened to claim the lives of hundreds of blacks charged with having taken part in the conspiracy. Joseph Jones, a Virginia planter, gave voice to the prevalent state of mind when he said that "where there is any reason to believe that any person is concerned, they ought immediately to be hanged, quartered, and hung upon trees on every road as a terror to the rest."

Jefferson had no desire to water the tree of liberty with the blood of black martyrs. He never supposed that punitive reprisals were a solution for the discontent of slaves and an effective preventative for insurrection. He had characterized capital punishment for whites as "the last melancholy resource to exterminate from society those whose continuance among us is inconsistent with the public safety. . . . It is unjustifiable to aggravate capital executions by circumstances of terror and pain." He now proposed to apply this dictum to the thirty or more blacks, in addition to those already sent to the gallows, awaiting execution in Richmond.

For the black victims of popular hysteria, Jefferson undoubtedly felt solicitude, but his paramount concern was for the good name of Virginia and the United States. As the world's preceptor in matters of morality, ethics, and virtue, the United States would appear wholly out of character if Virginians staged a bloodbath at the expense of blacks whose guilt was not proved beyond a reasonable doubt according to the rules of evidence applicable to whites. "If we indulge in a principle of revenge, or go one step beyond absolute necessity," he warned his fellow Virginians, public opinion in the other states and in the world at large would condemn the Old Dominion. Moreover, Gabriel's Conspiracy was something of a nonevent: no white person had suffered physical harm at the hands of the alleged insurrectionists.[4]

For these reasons, Jefferson recommended to Governor James Monroe that the accused slaves be deported rather than executed. He did not propose that any be released on the ground of insufficient evidence; even if he had believed that gross injustice had been done, he knew that public opinion in Virginia would never tolerate freeing the accused. However, his idea that the cause of justice and the humanitarian image of Virginia and the United States would be served by expatriating the slaves found favor with Governor Monroe and with a majority of the Virginia legislature.

Shortly after his election to the presidency, Jefferson was asked by Governor Monroe and the Virginia legislature to inquire into the possibility of sending the slaves to Sierra Leone, a colony for free blacks on the west coast of Africa established by the Sierra Leone Company, an English philanthropic society. President Jefferson was careful to assure the directors of the Sierra Leone Company that they were not being asked to receive common criminals; the United States, he made clear, had no intention of converting Sierra Leone into a black Botany Bay. These men, although guilty of a crime by the laws of Virginia, were in their own eyes the champions of the cause of freedom. Viewed in this light, Jefferson argued, they could be considered "a valuable acquisition to the settlement already existing there." [5]

Despite the character-reference given by Jefferson to the blacks, neither the Sierra Leone Company nor the British government were willing to receive them as colonists. Denied a homeland in Africa, most of Gabriel's co-conspirators were ultimately sold as slaves in the Spanish and Portuguese colonies.[6]

Jefferson hoped that Virginians would learn from Gabriel's Conspiracy that the emancipation and expulsion of the black population could no longer be delayed. In fact, however, most Virginians put a very different interpretation upon the event: to them, it proved the necessity of more stringent controls upon the blacks. Because Gabriel had been a freedman, the free blacks were singled out as objects of retaliation, and more rigorous restrictions were placed on their freedom of movement. The Old Dominion adopted a posture of defense not only against blacks (a guard was posted at the State Capitol in Richmond where it remained until the end of the Civil War), but against all ideas that tended to weaken or undermine the peculiar institution of the South. Learning that it was regarded as a subversive organization and that it was denied freedom of speech and of the press, the Virginia Abolition Society wound up its affairs and quietly passed out of existence.[7]

After Gabriel's Conspiracy, it was difficult for any but the most confirmed optimist to believe that slavery was withering away in Virginia. The abolitionist movement in the Old Dominion had, in fact, received a blow from which it never recovered. Even the manumission of slaves was discouraged by a law enacted by the Virginia legislature in 1806. The law of 1782 had authorized masters to free their slaves—provided they were not over fiifty years of age and otherwise liable to become public charges—by deed or will, as they saw fit. The law of 1806, however, reflecting the growing fear of free blacks, required all manumitted blacks to leave the state within a year after receiving their freedom on pain of being reclaimed and sold as slaves. Most of the Southern states followed the Old Dominion's example, and Georgia went so far as to prohibit masters from liberating their slaves under any conditions.

Despite the law of 1806, the number of free blacks continued to increase in Virginia, although at a perceptibly slower rate of growth. By 1810 there were 30,269 freedmen living in Virginia, compared with fewer than 3,000 in 1790. Obviously, the law of 1806 was not strictly enforced; the free black population grew, until by 1860 Virginia had the largest numbers of freedmen of any state in the union. Special permission was given by the governor and upper house to masters who wished their emancipated slaves to remain in the state, and many newly manumitted freedmen refused to obey a law which required them to leave their homes.[8]

It was one thing for Virginia to order the freed slaves to depart the state forthwith; it was a very different matter to tell them where to go. No state in the union welcomed them, and many states, including every slaveholding state, refused to receive them. Even Illinois and Indiana, free soil by virtue of the Ordinance of 1787 which had prohibited slavery in the Northwest Territory, barred their entry. Ohio, a refuge for runaway slaves and free blacks, enacted Black Laws in 1804 and 1807 designed to discourage the migration of all black people, slave or free, and to encourage free blacks to leave the state. Jefferson's plan of an overseas "homeland" for American blacks where they would be beyond the possibility of mixture seemed to accord well with the sentiments of most white Americans, Northerners as well as Southerners.[9]

ᔰ 17 ᔰ

Slavery and the
Louisiana Purchase

◆

ON MARCH 4, 1801, Thomas Jefferson became president of the largest slaveholding country in the world. Of the United States's total population of 5,308,000, about 900,000 were slaves, and eight of the sixteen states which then comprised the American Republic sanctioned slavery. Second to the United States as a slaveholding power stood the British Empire. Between them, the English-speaking peoples held 1,700,000 blacks in servitude without seriously impairing their own concept of themselves as the most truly free and enlightened people on earth.[1]

In his inaugural address Jefferson reaffirmed the ideals of the American Revolution, called for a return to first principles, and appealed for harmony after the abrasive and divisive party struggles of the Federalist era. He did not mention slavery; indeed, readers of Jefferson's inaugural would not have supposed that such a thing as slavery existed in the United States. Moreover, the president's emphasis upon the negative role of government as the guarantor of rights—the rights of property as well as the rights of man—left no reason to suppose that he would undertake the kind of positive action required to effect significant social change. Obviously, an assault upon slavery had no place in what he called "The Revolution of 1800."

Early in his first term as president, Jefferson decided to pursue a policy of strict silence on the subject of slavery: he would not see the evil, he would not speak of it, and he would not willingly hear of it. He proposed to treat slavery as though it did not exist; the "peculiar institution" of the South had become, at least publicly and officially, a non-institution; and the whole subject was, hopefully, well on its way to becoming the Great Unmentionable of American politics.[2]

So rigidly did Jefferson adhere to this program of self-imposed silence on the subject of slavery that in 1805 he even refused to subscribe to an antislavery poem entitled *Avenia, or a Tragical Poem on the Oppression of the Human Species,* the work of Thomas Brannagan of Philadelphia. "The subscription to a book on this subject," he observed, "is one of those little irritating measures which, without advancing its end at all, would by lessening the confidence and good will of a description of friends composing a large body, only lessen my powers of doing them good in the other great relations in which I stand to the public." On the other hand, he professed himself ready to act "should an occasion ever occur in which I can interpose with decisive effect"; in that event, he declared, "I should certainly . . . do my duty with promptitude and zeal." In effect, Jefferson took the position that the abolition of slavery was an idea whose time had not yet come and that it would be a mistake to try to hasten its coming by poetic effusions or other trivia. The evil was not to be destroyed by pinpricks, and he was not prepared to sacrifice his political influence even in the best of causes if it would accomplish no good purpose. Jefferson subjected all acts and even expressions of opinion to this test: would they benefit the cause they were intended to advance? He did not believe that candor required a confessional approach to politics: the politician who wore his heart upon his sleeve was often quickly remanded to private life.

Equally compelling as a reason for enjoining silence on the subject of slavery was Jefferson's unshakable conviction that the stars in their courses were moving slowly but surely toward its extirpation. Early in 1805, while he confessed that he had long since abandoned hope of the early extinguishment of slavery, he continued to detect signs that public opinion, the most reliable barometer of coming events, had begun to turn against it. Especially among the young men, he said, interest seemed to be working hand in hand with morality; the forces of greed and avarice were being weakened by the declining profitability of slavery in Virginia. "The value of the slave is every day lessening," he noted with satisfaction, although he himself stood to suffer financial loss from this event, "his burden on his master dayly increasing. Interest is therefore preparing the disposition to be just." He failed to sufficiently heed the fact that cotton cultivation was having quite the opposite effect upon the young men of South Carolina and the Southwest; there "greed and avarice," the eternal enemies of the moral sense, were striking a new and seemingly invincible alliance with slavery.[3]

At the same time he sensed a mounting impatience among the slaves to see justice done and a growing determination to take matters into their own hands if white men failed to act upon their responsibility. The "insurrectionary spirit," he predicted, would either result in the voluntary abolition of slavery or in "dreadful scenes and sufferings" which would force masters to release their slaves on their own terms. And, in that event, instead of leaving the state, they would form an indigestible and corruptive element within the body politic.

Jefferson's critics charged that he was mute on the subject of slavery because, while he loved the rights of man, he loved popularity more. Yet it is true that most of those who accused him of political cowardice would have been overjoyed to see him destroy himself politically by beating his head against the wall of slavery. As a political leader, Jefferson never fell victim to the illusion that he would gain the North if he lost the South on the slavery issue: a sectional schism on that issue would simply open the door to the return of the Federalist party. A political realist rather than the impractical visionary pictured by Federalist propaganda busying himself with divising whirligig chairs and carts that went before the horse, Jefferson's attitude toward the slavery question was governed not so much by love of popularity as by fear of an ineffaceable unpopularity that would preclude him from accomplishing any constructive purpose whatever.

Even so, Jefferson's decision to make expediency his guide and to adopt officially a neutral attitude toward slavery probably prevented the enactment in 1806 of a bill to exclude slavery from the District of Columbia. Had the president exerted himself on this issue—his influence over Congress was greater than that enjoyed by any other president prior to 1933—he might have spared the country the spectacle of a slavemarket in the shadow of the Capitol and gangs of manacled slaves being driven through the streets of the nation's capital.[4]

Yet, despite the President's best efforts to take refuge from it in silence and inaction, the slavery issue pursued him remorselessly. While he said little, events forced him to act—and his actions had portentous consequences for both slavery and sectional conflict which, for the most part, he did not foresee.

❧

By making the removal of blacks from the United States a precondition of their emancipation, Jefferson made it imperative to find a new homeland for them. Africa could not be counted upon to provide a refuge: Sierra Leone, the only place where American slaves had found sanctuary in Africa, had closed its doors to further settlement from the United States. Thus the perennial quandary of emancipationists like Jefferson was rendered even more perplexing: where to dispose of the unwanted blacks after they had been freed?

By 1802, Jefferson had received strong intimations that Providence (which had already decreed that the United States should be reserved for whites and Indians) had provided a convenient refuge for the blacks who were destined to be uprooted from American soil. The place designated for this purpose was the island of Santo Domingo. Columbus, who discovered the island, named it Hispaniola. A Spanish colony for several centuries, by the end of the eighteenth century, when it entered the orbit of American politics, it consisted of two colonies: Saint Domingue (French) and Santo Domingo (Spanish). Americans called the entire island St. Domingo.

In 1791 the black slaves and free mulattoes in the French colony of Saint Domingue rose in rebellion in order to secure for themselves the rights promised by the Declaration of the Rights of Man, "the first great shock between the ideals of white supremacy and race equality." Several thousand refugees fled from the island to the United States. Since many of them were hostile to the French Revolution—they were, after all, victims of the revolutionaries' racial policies—Jefferson was not disposed to welcome them to the United States lest they create an antirepublican element in a country already suffering from a surfeit of "monarchical" Federalists. He suggested, therefore, that several hundreds of these "aristocrats" be distributed among the Indians, "who would teach them lessons of liberty and equality." As for federal aid to refugees, Jefferson opposed it on constitutional grounds: he found no warrant in the Constitution for such humanitarian outlays of federal funds.[5]

By 1793, Jefferson had decided in his own mind that France could not reconquer St. Domingo from "the people of color." Even the abolition of slavery by the French government in 1793 did not change his opinion; he predicted that all the islands of the West Indies would expel the whites and set up independent governments of their own. It was not a prospect that the United States could view with indifference: Nature, he observed, had connected the United States and those islands "by the strong link of mutual necessity."[6]

Many Southern slaveowners saw in the establishment of black power on St. Domingo an imminent threat to the security of the United States. Presumably the emancipated blacks on St. Domingo, aided and abetted by the *Amis des Noirs,* would not rest content until slavery had been totally exitrpated from the western hemisphere—in which event, the United States, the largest slaveholding power in the world, would be a prime target and, ultimately, the principal loser. "Liberty, equality, and fraternity" was a dangerous slogan when applied to racial relations; in 1797, Jefferson predicted that "the revolutionary storm, now sweeping the globe, will be upon us" in the form of racial massacres and counter-massacres. By 1799 he was convinced that black crews and supercargoes from St. Domingo would soon be at work spreading subversive notions among American slaves. John Wayles Eppes, Jefferson's son-in-law, declared in Congress that if St. Domingo became independent it would create a system "that will bring immediate and horrible destruction to the fairest portion of America"—by which he meant, of course, the Southern slaveholding states.[7]

The lesson Jefferson drew from this turn of events in St. Domingo was that Americans ought to emancipate and deport their black slaves without delay: "If something is not done, and soon done," he said in 1797, "we shall be the murderers of our own children." The intentions of Providence seemed clearly writ, but Jefferson's fellow Southerners preferred to follow another directive: to forestall racial war by repressing libertarian ideas among both whites and blacks in the Southern states.[8]

During the administration of John Adams, St. Domingo became an issue in American politics. The Federalists, spokesmen of the commercial interests of the Northern states, tried to increase American trade in molasses, sugar, coffee, indigo, and cotton—in exchange for large quantities of arms and ammunition—with the black insurgents on St. Domingo led by Toussaint Louverture, himself a former slave. Secretary of State Timothy Pickering opened negotiations with the "amiable and respectable Toussaint," as he was known in Federalist circles, and dined in Philadelphia with Toussaint's emissary. For the Northern Federalists, far less agitated than Southern Jeffersonian Republicans by the prospect of black rule in St. Domingo, the hope of commercial gain outweighed all other considerations. However, President Adams and Secretary of State Pickering preferred a "Negro republic" to a continuance of French control. If the island remained under the sovereignty of France, Pickering warned, the French could recruit from the blacks a "military corps of such strength in a future war, as no European or other white people could resist." With the aid of this army, the French might hope to conquer all the West Indies and eventually attack the United States in the hope of establishing by force of arms the principles of liberty, equality, and fraternity on American soil under the French *tricolore*.[9] In 1800, to forestall this danger, Alexander Hamilton drew up a constitution for what he hoped would become the black republic of St. Domingo with Toussaint Louverture as its first president.[10]

During 1798–1800, with the United States engaged in an undeclared war with France, the Adams administration was prepared to make an agreement with Great Britain by which the two countries would monopolize the trade of St. Domingo—the certain prelude, Jefferson believed, to an Anglo-American alliance. Jefferson and his partisans therefore opposed United States trade with St. Domingo as part and parcel of a Federalist plot to produce an open, declared war with France and an alliance with Great Britain against the French Republic.[11]

🍁

As president, Jefferson gave high importance to the restoration of good relations with France. Although hostilities between the two countries had been terminated by the Convention of 1800 (which, among other things, abrogated the Franco-American alliance of 1778), the trade fostered by the Adams administration between Toussaint Louverture and the United States continued to serve as an impediment to the kind of comity with France Jefferson desired.

The president therefore moved quickly to demonstrate to Napoleon Bonaparte, recently elevated to the rank of first consul of the French Republic, that Toussaint Louverture and the black rebels he led could no longer count on aid from the United States. When, as directed by Bonaparte, the French *chargé d'affaires,* Louis Pichon, asked President Jefferson what the United States's attitude toward a French effort to reconquer St. Domingo would be, Jefferson replied that if Great Britain and France made peace (as they soon did in 1801 at Amiens), "then nothing will be easier than to furnish your army and fleet with everything and to reduce Toussaint to starvation." By Toussaint, of course, Jefferson meant all the former slaves who had joined the black leader's standard, not simply Toussaint himself. Overjoyed by the green light Jefferson had seemingly given to a French reconquest of St. Domingo, Pichon wrote to the first consul that, at long last, France had a whole-hearted friend in the president of the United States.[12]

Although the people of the United States did not know of their president's commitment to the first consul by which a French triumph over the black revolutionaries on St. Domingo seemed assured, they derived a strong impression from the debates in Congress that the Jefferson administration was strongly opposed to the establishment of a black republic on that island. Albert Gallatin, the floor leader of the Jeffersonian Republicans in the House of Representatives and later secretary of the treasury, declared that "no man would be more unwilling than I to constitute a whole nation of freed slaves ... and thus to throw so many wild Tigers on society." [13]

In his interview with the French minister, Jefferson left no doubt in Pichon's mind that he believed that the security of the United States, not merely Franco-American friendship, required the forcible termination of black domination in St. Domingo. He rehearsed the familiar argument that an independent, black-controlled St. Domingo would menace the slaveholding states and, he added disingenuously, the American people did not love Toussaint and would welcome his elimination. At this point Jefferson seemed prepared to embark upon a policy which was quite as much antiblack as it was pro-French.[14]

This news, relayed to Paris, was especially gratifying to Bonaparte because he badly needed the cooperation of the United States to implement his plans for a new transAtlantic French empire. As the first consul envisaged it, France, after making peace with Great Britain, would turn its energies to the restoration of French power in the western hemisphere. Bonaparte intended that Louisiana would serve as one pillar of the restored French empire; St. Domingo would constitute its other main support.

In May 1801, Jefferson and James Madison, the secretary of state, picked up the first signals that the first consul was harboring designs upon the western hemisphere. They learned of the retrocession of Louisiana to France by the "secret" treaty of San Ildefonso of October 1800, an event which presaged a French occupation of this vast territory, including the port of New Orleans, the vital lifeline of the American West to the outside world. Instead of a weak vacillating neighbor, Spain, which since 1796 had permitted American trade through New Orleans, the United States seemed destined to acquire a strong, militarily aggressive neighbor, France, with the disquieting prospect that the port of New Orleans might be closed to American goods and ships at any time.

Since Jefferson knew of the secret treaty of San Ildefonso in July 1801, when he offered American cooperation in "starving" Toussaint—a prospect he seemed positively to relish—it appeared that he was prepared to further Bonaparte's grandiose scheme to make France the dominant power in North America. But Jefferson had no love for Bonaparte, and by July 1801 he had begun seriously to question the capacity of the French to maintain a republican form of government. In any case, he had no intention of welcoming the French to Louisiana. His objective in encouraging Bonaparte to expend his fleet and army upon the conquest of St. Domingo, it seems clear, was to offer a bargain whereby the United States helped France by supplying its fleets and armies in the West Indies in exchange for a hands-off policy toward Louisiana. His offer of American aid in the reconquest of St. Domingo was coupled with a warning that the United States did not approve of French occupation of Louisiana.

In 1801, after the signing of the Peace of Amiens with Great Britain, the British government told Bonaparte that it had no objections to a French reconquest of St. Domingo, although stopping short of Jefferson's commitment to participate actively in the enterprise. Thus the first consul, uninformed of Jefferson's reservations, was led to believe that he had been given a free hand in St. Domingo by both the British and United States governments. Late in 1801 he sent his brother-in-law, General Victor Leclerc, to St. Domingo with ten thousand men to dispose of Toussaint Louverture, "the black Bonaparte of the Antilles." General Leclerc was given to understand by Bonaparte that he could safely depend on the Americans to supply the French army and navy. Acting in the spirit of these instructions he seized twenty American ships and confiscated their cargoes of arms, ammunition, and merchandise. He justified this action on the ground that these cargoes were about to be delivered to the black insurgents and that he would be applauded by the Jefferson administration for stopping a trade of which it presumably disapproved.

Much to the French general's surprise, the United States government, instead of thanking him for executing its policies, protested vigorously against what it termed a flagrant violation of its sovereign rights. A similar shock was in store for the French *chargé d'affaires* who, when he approached Jefferson with a request for aid in money and supplies, was rebuffed. Abruptly and seemingly without warning, Jefferson had reversed himself in the matter of limited cooperation with the French in the reconquest of St. Domingo.

This singular *volte-face* in the president's attitude, so dismaying to Pichon, was occasioned by his realization that Bonaparte was deadly serious about adding Louisiana to the French empire. In the winter of 1801–1802, news reached Washington of a fleet and army equipping in Holland with Louisiana as their destination. (Later this report was confirmed: General Victor, at the head of a large expeditionary force, was stationed in Holland with instructions to embark for Louisiana.) Obviously, there was to be no trade-off of St. Domingo in exchange for Louisiana as Jefferson had implicitly proposed to the first consul. It dawned on the president that St. Domingo and Louisiana were part of a master plan so inimical to the interests of the United States that it must be thwarted at all cost. Once the prevention of French occupation of Louisiana became the cardinal objective of the United States, St. Domingo, now viewed as a stepping-stone to Louisiana, acquired a significance wholly unperceived by Jefferson when he first took office and rashly promised his administration's cooperation in the French military effort on the island.

The president's change of heart was quickly evidenced in American foreign policy. Instead of trying to starve Toussaint, the United States began to supply impartially both the black insurgents and the French armed forces. The Jefferson administration did not even tilt its neutrality in favor of the French. When General Leclerc proclaimed that all rebel-held ports were in a state of blockade, the United States insisted upon the right of its shipowners and merchants to trade freely with the rebels.[15]

To the French, Jefferson explained his administration's sudden conversion to even-handed neutrality on the ground that the United States could not afford to risk a breach with Toussaint. If, therefore, France failed to reconquer St. Domingo—and Jefferson still considered this to be the most likely outcome—the United States, were it aligned with France, would lose its markets in St. Domingo and risk alienating the free blacks on the island to such an extent that they might make common cause with their enslaved brethren in the United States. In short, Jefferson paid the Federalists the backhanded compliment of adopting the substance of their policy toward Toussaint Louverture.

But Jefferson's plans for St. Domingo went far beyond anything dreamed of by the Federalists. In the autumn of 1802 he began to contemplate converting the island into a sanctuary for displaced American blacks. The same "overruling Providence" which had decreed that the blacks should be expelled from the United States must, he concluded, have provided a convenient refuge for them.

In 1802, instead of complying with the wishes of the Virginia legislature and sending to the American West the slaves accused of involvement in Gabriel's Conspiracy after they had been turned away by Sierra Leone, Jefferson urged that they be sent to St. Domingo. Nature, he told Governor James Monroe, had created the West Indies "to become the receptacle of the blacks transplanted into this hemisphere." He now dismissed as frivolous the fear that free, independent blacks in the West Indies would subvert slavery in the United States; the "contemplation of our relative strength, and of the disproportion daily growing" ensured the impotence of black armies or black "missionaries of sedition." Compared with the advantages of making St. Domingo a black homeland, Africa, for him, was a second choice. He turned to Sierra Leone in 1802 only because the Virginia legislature made its preference for Africa unmistakable.[16]

✤

It was becoming agonizingly clear to Jefferson that whatever the designs of Providence for St. Domingo, he must first cope with Napoleon Bonaparte's grand design for the western hemisphere. While American ships continued to supply the black insurgents with arms and ammunition for killing Frenchmen, the president initiated efforts in Paris to buy New Orleans and West Florida from France. For this comparatively small enclave of territory he was willing to pay almost as much as the United States later paid for the whole of Louisiana. If Bonaparte insisted on occupying Louisiana, Jefferson was prepared as a last resort to "marry" the United States to the British fleet and nation. He did not add, probably because he could not bring himself to face the fact that the prerogative for giving away the bride would, in that case, fall to George III.

It was the black insurgents on St. Domingo who dispelled the spectre of this marriage of convenience so dreaded by Jefferson. The former slaves, the French commander told Napoleon, fought and died "with unbelievable fanaticism; they laugh at death. It is the same with the women." Leclerc saw no hope of victory short of killing all the men and women, "retaining only children under twelve years old, destroy half of those in the plains; and not leave in the colony a single colored man who has worn an epaulet." [17]

But it was the French army, not the blacks, that suffered annihilation: by October 1802, when General Leclerc himself died of fever, the French had lost twenty-four thousand men to guerrilla warfare, dysentery, and yellow fever. By early 1803 the French position on St. Domingo was no longer tenable: General Rochambeau was forced to surrender the remnant of his army to the British rather than face massacre at the hands of the triumphant blacks.[18]

These events lent credibility to Jefferson's prediction that France could never regain control of St. Domingo. The capture of Toussaint did not shake his conviction that the French cause was hopeless: "Some other black leader will arise," he said, "and a war of extermination will ensue: for no second capitulation will ever be trusted by the blacks." He was right about the war of extermination: in 1804 almost the entire remaining white population was massacred by the blacks. Both races practiced genocide, and there opened up on St. Domingo a scene of horrors not matched since the conquest and destruction of Aztec civilization by the *conquistadores.*[19]

The catastrophe that befell French arms in St. Domingo, coupled with Bonaparte's decision to resume the war with Great Britain in 1803, radically changed his plans with regard to Louisiana. France's North American empire followed into limbo Bonaparte's dream of a Middle Eastern empire with Egypt as its pivot. Rather than see Great Britain and the United States jointly or severally, possess themselves of Louisiana by force, the first consul sold the entire province, including the vital port city of New Orleans, to the United States for fifteen million dollars.

Thus, by their long and bitter struggle for independence, St. Domingo's blacks were instrumental in allowing the United States to more than double the size of its territory at a bargain price. But while American diplomats vied for the honor of having made the Louisiana Purchase and Thomas Jefferson was inclined to see in the transaction the handiwork of that beneficent Providence that shaped events in favor of the United States, the decisive contribution made by the black freedom fighters of St. Domingo went almost unnoticed by the Jeffersonian administration. Napoleon, however, was more generous. He later listed among the most costly errors of his career—second only to the invasion of Spain in 1808 and of Russia in 1812 his failure to make Toussaint Louverture an ally and to rule St. Domingo through the "black Bonaparte."

Despite the fact that the blacks were now in full control of St. Domingo (in 1804 Jean Jacques Dessalines proclaimed himself emperor of Haiti, the name given the island by the Indians), the United States refused to recognize the independence of the island or the legitimacy of the black regime—in marked contrast to the position taken by Jefferson when, as secretary of state, he urged the recognition of the new French Republic on the ground that it represented the will of the people. But Jefferson was not actuated by aversion to blacks: he feared that an independent Haiti would fall under the sway of Great Britain. To prevent that dire event—certain, he believed, to result in a British monopoly of the island's commerce—he preferred to maintain the fiction of French sovereignty. Against the counsels of experience and the weight of evidence, Jefferson hoped that Napoleon would open the island to United States trade after it had been pacified.

And so, instead of receiving tokens of gratitude from the United States, Haiti was consigned to the role of pawn in the game Jefferson began to play after the Louisiana Purchase for the further territorial aggrandizement of the United States. Despite the crushing reverse suffered by the French army in St. Domingo, Bonaparte, crowned in 1804 as the emperor of France, could not bring himself to abandon the island to the "gilded Africans" who succeeded Toussaint Louverture. Officially, therefore, Haiti remained a part of the French empire, and the French emperor bided his time, hoping for an opportunity to recoup his losses in the West Indies. If Haiti were to be reconquered, as Napoleon did not cease to hope it would be, France must clearly rely to an even greater degree upon American aid than in 1801 when it first embarked upon its ill-fated adventure in the western hemisphere. Above all, Napoleon needed an embargo imposed by the United States upon its trade with the blacks on the revolted island.[20]

As in 1801, Jefferson seemed eager to cooperate with the French ruler. In February 1806, Congress passed the Logan Bill, an administration-sponsored embargo which, at least on paper, did everything Napoleon had asked of the American president. The United States ostensibly committed itself to the course of starving the Haitians into submission at the bidding of the French emperor.

Seemingly, Jefferson was prepared to sacrifice Haiti as a refuge for American slaves and even willing to aid Napoleon in reducing the Haitians themselves to slavery. There could be no doubt what lay in store for them if they fell under French rule: Napoleon's racism was direct and simplistic: "I am for the whites because I am white. I have no other reason. That one suffices." The French emperor's ardor for restoring slavery was matched by that of John Wayles Eppes, Jefferson's son-in-law, who declared in Congress that he would pledge the entire Treasury of the United States so that "the Negro government should be destroyed." [21]

In actuality, President Jefferson was playing a deep and devious game with Napoleon—the kind of game in which the French emperor, a master of the art of double-dealing and intrigue, usually succeeded in stripping his adversary of all his worldly goods. Jefferson played with concealed cards; neither American nor French policy was what it appeared to be. He had no intention of enforcing the Logan Act so rigorously that it cut off American trade with Haiti, thereby compelling the blacks to return to French rule—slavery and all. The president never supposed that Northern Jeffersonian Republicans, many of whom were merchants, bankers, and shipowners, would willingly forego the profits of a lucrative trade with Haiti; he refrained, therefore, from denouncing the "mercantile avarice" of his Northern supporters lest he drive them back into the Federalist fold. Keeping the sea lanes open to Haiti was as important to him from the point of view of domestic politics as appearing to close those lanes was to the success of his foreign policy.

Although Timothy Pickering declared that the Logan Act carried on it the stamp "Made in France," Jefferson expected a major *quid pro quo* from Napoleon. The American president went through the motions of yielding to Napoleon because he believed that by conciliating the emperor he could be induced to underwrite American claims to West Florida and Texas, both of which Jefferson supposed had been included in the Louisiana Purchase. For these provinces, although he thought of himself as a buyer compelled to buy the same horse twice, Jefferson was prepared to bribe Napoleon in order to secure his commitment to bring pressure upon Spain to surrender East and West Florida to the United States. Here, as always, Jefferson gave priority to the interests of his own country; he was never, as the Federalists said, a conscious instrument of French imperialism.

But Napoleon, despite the United States's offer of a *douceur* of two million dollars cash, refused to *sell* the same horse twice. He gladly received the administration's money and the embargo upon American trade with Haiti, but while he continued to dangle these territorial sweets before the fascinated American administration, the Floridas and Texas remained in Spanish possession. In the meantime, as Jefferson disconsolately admitted, the British were the chief beneficiaries of the American partial embargo of trade with Haiti; they preempted much of the sugar, molasses, and coffee which had hitherto gone to the United States.[22]

Disappointed in his efforts to acquire West Florida and Texas by pretending to deliver Haiti to the tender mercies of Napoleon, Jefferson returned to the idea that the island would someday serve as a sanctuary for uprooted American slaves and as an experimental laboratory that would demonstrate the black man's capacity for self-government and, perhaps, even prove his equality with white men. Even so, Jefferson never proposed any concrete measure which might have contributed toward the amelioration of the condition of the blacks on Haiti, thereby improving their chances of demonstrating their potentialities. On the contrary, the embargo on trade with St. Domingo remained in force until 1810, and the United States did not recognize the independence of Haiti, the second republic in the New World, until 1862. Jefferson never said of the Haitians as he said of the white Latin Americans, "They have a right to be free, and we a right to aid them, as a strong man has a right to assist a weak one assaulted by a robber or murderer." In American foreign policy, Haiti remained the orphan of the revolutionary storm of liberty which, beginning with the American Revolution, swept over western Europe and the New World.[23]

ᴄ 18 ᴄ

The Abolition
of the Slave Trade

———◆———

THE TWO MAJOR ACHIEVEMENTS OF JEFFERSON'S PRESIDENCY were the Louisiana Purchase and the abolition of the slave trade. In their effect upon American slavery, these two events complemented each other: while the Louisiana Purchase opened up an immense area to the introduction of slavery, the cloture of the slave trade ensured that this ever-expanding market for slaves would be preempted by slave-exporting states like Virginia and Maryland. Paradoxically, some of the accomplishments in which Jefferson took the greatest pride tended to consolidate and perpetuate the institution he abhorred.

In the perspective of history, the most important question raised by the Louisiana Purchase was not whether the federal government possessed a constitutional right to acquire and govern territory outside the boundaries of the United States, but whether the territory bought from France in 1803 should be slave or free soil. In that part of the Louisiana Purchase settled by France and Spain, slavery had flourished. Particularly in the area around New Orleans where most of the sugar of the colony was produced, slaves were so numerous that they composed a majority of the population. Nevertheless, in 1804, James Hillhouse of Connecticut, a Federalist member of Congress, offered an amendment to the bill organizing the territory of Louisiana which would have prohibited slavery in the entire area ceded by France. Joel Barlow, a poet, diplomat, and confidant of the president, urged Jefferson to cross party and sectional lines by supporting the Hillhouse amendment. And, in 1805, Tom Paine added his voice to those who wished Jefferson to take a firm antislavery stand in Louisiana: Paine pointed out that settling Louisiana with Germans rather than with black slaves would serve the national interest by increasing the revenues of the government and the cultivation of sugar.[1]

Since 1784, when he had proposed to exclude slavery from all the territories of the United States, Jefferson had, however, lost some of his antislavery zeal. As president, he made no protest when William Henry Harrison, governor of Indiana Territory permitted the establishment of a form of servitude akin to slavery contrary to Article VI of the Northwest Ordinance of 1787. Despite Tom Paine's enthusiasm for German immigrants, Jefferson was aware that the abolition of slavery in Louisiana would, at least temporarily, cripple the production of sugar— and he depended upon Louisiana sugar to relieve the United States of its dependence upon precarious foreign supplies from the West Indies. Finally, he believed that the terms of the treaty with France by which the United States acquired Louisiana in 1803 precluded the abolition of slavery, at least in the settled parts of that region. Napoleon had insisted upon writing into the treaty a provision stipulating that the inhabitants of Louisiana would enjoy all the rights and immunities of citizens of the United States. Since citizens of the United States, unless prohibited by state law, had the right to hold slaves, the inhabitants of Louisiana citizens of the United States by virtue of the treaty of cession, could not legally be deprived of their slaves or of their right to acquire slaves in future by the Federal government.[2]

Nevertheless, had the spirit that possessed Jefferson in 1784 moved him in 1803–1805, he might have proposed to Congress a bargain whereby in exchange for confirming the existence of slavery in the territory of Orleans, the rest of the Louisiana Purchase would be forever free soil. By this expedient Jefferson might have averted the struggle between the North and South, free and slave labor, for primacy in the national domain—the immediate, and probably the only truly irrepressible, cause of the Civil War.

Instead, Jefferson raised no objections to the continued existence of slavery in the Louisiana Purchase. But he did refuse to allow citizens of Louisiana the right, guaranteed all citizens of the United States unless prohibited by state law, to buy slaves imported from abroad.* This prohibition, while it created indignation and resentment among the Louisianans, was popular in Congress where Southern and Northern factions joined forces for radically different reasons to deprive these new citizens of a right they had enjoyed under French and Spanish rule and upon which they insisted as their due under the government of the United States. But this was hardly a triumph of morality and justice: the South-

---

* A precedent for prohibiting the foreign slave trade from a territory of the United States had been established in 1798 when that trade had been barred from the Mississippi Territory. But a motion to exclude slavery altogether from that territory on the precedent of the Northwest Ordinance of 1787 received only twelve affirmative votes in the House.

erners' major objective was to secure for themselves the prerogative to supply at high prices from their own stocks of surplus slaves the labor needs of the Louisianans.[3]

And so, while President Jefferson won the plaudits of most Southern members of Congress (except those from South Carolina) by his stand against the foreign slave trade, had he had the temerity to propose that Louisiana be excluded from the domestic slave trade he would have encountered a solid bloc of hostile votes from south of the Mason-Dixon line. Jefferson was fond of saying that he never tilted against windmills, especially those that seemed certain to unhorse him. Accordingly, the system of slave labor, already in force in parts of the Louisiana Purchase, was perpetuated under American rule. While a "republican form of government" guaranteed by the Constitution was held in the case of Louisiana to require the establishment of trial by jury and the use of English as an official language, it did not necessitate the abolition of slavery or the abrogation of the domestic slave trade.

Although Jefferson never publicly admitted the fact, the lot of the slaves in Louisiana deteriorated as a result of the American occupation. Prior to 1803, slaves had been guaranteed certain rights by the *Code Noir:* to be instructed in religion, to cultivate a plot of ground for their own sustenance, to testify in court when white witnesses were not available (not, however, against masters), to observe Sundays as holidays, and to be buried in consecrated ground. Under the *Code Noir,* husbands and wives could not be sold separately, nor could a child under fourteen years of age be sold away from his or her mother; and slaves could, if mistreated, appeal to the colonial authorities. The Americans changed all that: the first territorial legislature under the new administration designated slaves as real estate, and the Black Code adopted by the Territory of Orleans in 1806 abolished the requirement that slaves be instructed in religion; deprived slave marriages of legal status; prohibited blacks from testifying against whites; and rescinded the obligation formerly imposed upon masters to provide their slaves with plots of ground. The Black Code likewise permitted the selling of husbands and wives separately and authorized the sale of any child over ten years of age without its mother.[4]

These drastic changes in the status of slaves drew no protest from the white inhabitants of Louisiana; their indignation was reserved for the prohibition of the foreign slave trade—an act of tyranny which, they alleged, was contrary to the principles of the Declaration of Independence.[5]

In 1783, Jefferson had acclaimed the United States as an "Empire of Liberty," and, after the Louisiana Purchase, it seemed to him that the Republic had consolidated its claim to that designation. "By enlarging the empire of liberty," he said, "we multiply its auxiliaries, and provide new sources of renovation, should its principles at any time degenerate, in those portions of our country which gave them birth." The way was now clear, he declared, for the orderly possession of the continent, "advancing compactly as we multiply."

But the question remained whether Americans would, as they advanced, bring their slaves with them? Would the "Empire of Liberty" prove to be an "Empire of Slavery"? Did the expansion of agriculture in itself ensure the perpetuation of republicanism, as Jefferson seemed to believe—or was there a type of agriculture inexorably hostile to the political and social order Jefferson hoped to create in the United States? Was the real enemy of the Jeffersonian dispensation large-scale, profit-minded agriculture rather than "Hamiltonianism?"

Certainly the answer to these fateful questions would be necessarily in the affirmative if the plantation system and the slave labor upon which it depended were permitted to expand over the entire area comprised within the Louisiana Purchase. By not making the exclusion of slavery from that region an administration measure, President Jefferson seemed to have opened up a new world for the plantation system and slavery, the "malign twins," to conquer. And had Jefferson's plan of adding West Florida, Texas, and Cuba to the Union, and thereby more than doubling the living space of slavery, been adopted, he would in effect have contributed to the destruction of his own Elysium of small, independent yeomen farmers living austerely, autonomously, and virtuously, happily removed from the "hideous evil" of slavery.

Jefferson might have answered that in 1803 he did not envisage the northern half of the Louisiana Purchase—the area north of the thirty-first parallel—as a living-space for slavery but as a huge reservation for displaced Indians. While Jefferson gave blacks no choice but to leave the United States, he allowed Indians to choose between conforming to the white man's ways by becoming farmers or moving westward beyond the Mississippi. Although the Indians could hardly have been aware of it, they were, at least in President Jefferson's counsels, not to be treated by whites as aliens in their own land but as potential participants in the march of progress.

If Jefferson did not include the cloture of the foreign slave trade among the three major achievements by which he wished to be remembered by posterity, this was because it was not really his handiwork: he simply recommended, in March 1807, that Congress act upon the authority granted it under the Constitution, and there was very little opposition to his request. In 1807 only South Carolina still permitted the entry of slaves from outside the borders of the United States. Yet, thanks to President Jefferson's initiative, Congress abolished the foreign slave trade at the earliest possible date, on the first of January, 1808, thereby officially terminating a traffic which, as Jefferson said, "the morality, the reputation, and the best interests of our country have long been eager to proscribe." [6]

Jefferson regarded the act of Congress halting the slave trade as a long stride toward the inevitable abolition of slavery. But he had always tended to indulge the comforting illusion that hostility to the slave trade could be equated with hostility to slavery itself. Yet, contrary to Jefferson's expectations, the stoppage of the slave trade by Virginia in 1778 had not noticeably weakened the institution. So with the abolition of the slave trade in 1808: by putting the United States on the side of the angels, it helped to dull the prickings of conscience. The sedated moral sense took a long holiday to celebrate its great and glorious victory over the forces of evil, while slavery fastened its hold more firmly upon the economic and social structure of the South.

Equally illusory was the idea that the abolition of the foreign slave trade ensured a long, perhaps permanent, period of sectional peace. It was widely supposed that the South, having contributed to appeasing the national conscience by supporting the enactment of the law of January 1, 1808, would no longer be accused of maintaining a regressive attitude toward an institution which, as a result of the abolition of domestic slavery by the Northern states, had become peculiar to the South. Although this was not perceived at the time, the prospect of sectional concord based upon a consensus toward slavery had been effectively blasted by the Louisiana Purchase: as a result of that massive acquisition of territory, slavery had acquired new powers of setting Americans against each other and of ultimately rending the Union in fratricidal war.

Nor, finally, did the law of January 1, 1808, have the effect of tightly sealing the United States against the introduction of African slaves. In part, this failure was owing to the fact that the act of Congress abolishing the slave trade could not avoid paying obeisance to the doctrine of states' rights. The custody of Africans removed from slave ships by the United States Navy and the punishment of offenders under the law were given to the states, some of which had no interest in enforcing the law. Even more injurious was the failure of successive American administrations to station a squadron off the coast of Africa to intercept and seize American ships illegally carrying slaves. In the absence of vigorous American action, the only power capable of ridding the seas of slavers was the British navy. Wilberforce urged President Jefferson to agree to permit seizures by either navy of the slave ships of the other country, but Jefferson stood firmly by the doctrine of the freedom of the seas; in no circumstances, he declared, could a British man-of-war send a boarding party to inspect the crew or cargo of an American ship. As a result, the American flag, along with that of Portugal, became a cover for slave runners of all nationalities, and thousands of slaves were transported to the western hemisphere after 1808 under the protective cloak of the Stars and Stripes. Even after 1820, when Congress made direct participation in the slave trade an act of piracy punishable by death and stationed a squadron off the African

Edmund Pendleton by Thomas Sully. (Reproduced through courtesy of the
Virginia Historical Society.)

George Wythe by J. B. Longacre. (Virginia State Library.)

Facing page, Title page of Jefferson's pamphlet, *A Summary View* (1774). (Courtesy of the Library of Congress.)

Presented to Joseph C. Cabell

A

SUMMARY VIEW

OF THE

RIGHTS

OF

BRITISH AMERICA.

SET FORTH IN SOME

RESOLUTIONS

INTENDED FOR THE

INSPECTION

OF THE PRESENT

DELEGATES

OF THE

PEOPLE OF VIRGINIA.

NOW IN

CONVENTION.

BY A NATIVE, AND MEMBER OF THE
HOUSE OF BURGESSES.
Mr. Jefferson.

WILLIAMSBURG:
PRINTED BY CLEMENTINA RIND
1774.

John Marshall by Chester Harding. (Collection of Washington and Lee University, Virginia.)

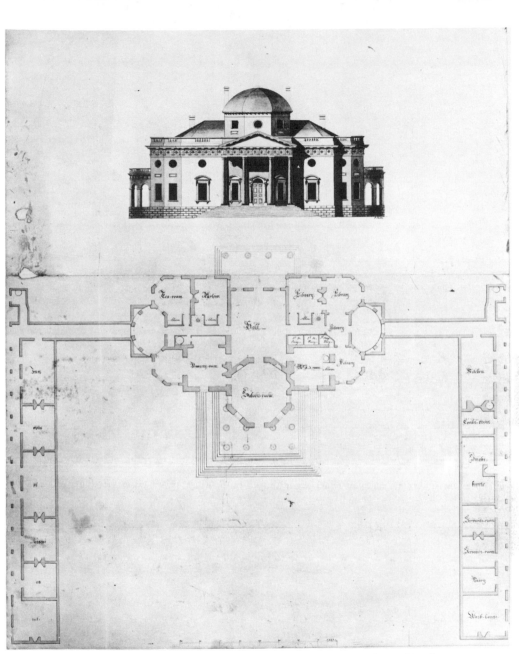

Design for remodeling Monticello, drawn by Robert Mills in 1803. (Courtesy Massachusetts Historical Society.)

TOUSSAINT LOUVERTURE
Warrior, Statesman, Liberator, Founder of State, Martyr

Toussaint Louverture. (Musée de la Nation Haitienne.)

Paragraph concerning slavery in Jefferson's "original rough draft" of the Declaration of Independence. (Courtesy of the Library of Congress.)

he has incited treasonable insurrections of our fellow-citizens, with the allurements of forfeiture & confiscation of our property. he has waged cruel war against human nature itself, violating it's most sacred rights of life & liberty in the persons of a distant people who never offended him, captivating & carrying them into slavery in another hemisphere, or to incur miserable death in their transportation thither. this piratical warfare, the opprobrium of infidel powers, is the warfare of the Christian king of Great Britain. determined to keep open a market where MEN should be bought & sold he has prostituted his negative for suppressing every legislative attempt to prohibit or to restrain this execrable commerce: and that this assemblage of horrors might want no fact of distinguished die, he is now exciting those very people to rise in arms among us, and to purchase that liberty of which he has deprived them, by murdering the people upon whom he also obtruded them: thus paying off former crimes committed against the liberties of one people, with crimes which he urges them to commit against the lives of another.

coast, abuses of the American flag continued. It was not until 1862 that the United States entered into a convention with Great Britain providing for mutual visit, search and detention.* [7]

Cloture of the slave trade, however imperfectly realized and enforced, saved millions of Africans from servitude on American plantations. Occurring on the eve of the massive expansion of cotton and slavery into the Southwest (the Southwest then being the present states of Mississippi and Alabama) and the insatiable demand for slaves that followed that event, the official stoppage of the trade took place just in time to prevent a massive influx of blacks from Africa and the West Indies. For nothing— not even the prospect of "darkening half a continent" and the aggravation of the danger of servile insurrection—would have prevailed against the greed and self-aggrandizement unleashed by the cotton boom. [8]

---

* In 1842 the Treaty of Washington provided for joint operations by British and American cruisers off the African coast, but the American participation was neither consistent nor effective. In 1858 a concerted effort was made in some Southern states to reopen the African slave trade.

❧ 19 ❧

Jefferson and James Callender:
The Politics of
Character Assassination

———◆———

DURING THE PRESIDENTIAL CAMPAIGN OF 1800, Jefferson was arraigned in the Federalist newspapers as an atheist, a traitorous Francophile (at this time the United States was involved in an undeclared war with France), a "philosopher," and an enemy of the powers of the federal government and of commerce. Even so, his private life had remained relatively unscathed. But midway through his first administration, a concerted effort was made to drive him from the presidency on the grounds that enormities were being committed at Monticello from which even a Roman emperor of the decadence would have recoiled. Leading the pack of journalists in full cry against the president was one of Jefferson's erstwhile votaries whose redoubtable talents for character assassination had helped bring down the Federalist party in 1800.

James Callender first came to Jefferson's attention as the author of *The Political Progress of Britain,* a political tract that might more aptly have been entitled *The Political Decline and Fall of Britain.* An exercise in vilification and propaganda rather than a serious work of history, Callender's book castigated "the ruffian race of British kings," most of whom, it appeared, richly deserved hanging; Prime Minister William Pitt was called "a hardened swindler"; the Prince of Wales was described as a murderer; the British Parliament was pictured as "a phalanx of mercenaries" who represented hell rather than any British constituency; the English Constitution was characterized as "a conspiracy of the rich against the poor"; and the British Empire was portrayed as a scene of "horrid enormities in the four quarters of the globe." Among their more notorious accomplishments, British imperialists had wantonly "strewn the plains of Indostan with 15–20 million carcasses." Such carnage, corruption, and bestiality could only end, Callender assured his readers, in the speedy downfall of Great Britain.[1]

Jefferson was captivated by Callender's diatribe against Great Britain and "the ruffian race of British kings" because it confirmed everything he had been saying since 1776. Moreover, his view of Great Britain as the inveterate enemy of the rights of man had been given reinforcement by the outbreak of war between Great Britain and the French republic early in 1793. His state of mind was, perhaps, most strikingly revealed in 1795 when he said that although he had never planned to go abroad again, he would gladly go to London to take tea with a conquering French general. He expected that the French, having beaten the British to their knees and dethroned George III, would retire voluntarily from England, leaving the English people to enjoy the liberty, equality, and fraternity of French-style republicanism.

Not surprisingly, therefore, Jefferson concluded that Callender was a "man of genius," "a man of science fled from persecution," and an "unjustly persecuted" martyr. *The Political Progress of Britain* was reprinted in Philadephia at Jefferson's recommendation. Half-apologetically, Jefferson later said that Callender "told some useful truths in his coarse way"— as compared with the Federalist Journalists who lied with urbanity and finesse.[2]

Under indictment for sedition, and facing almost certain conviction and a long prison term, Callender fled to the United States where he joined the sizable colony of expatriated British journalists whose attacks upon the government of William Pitt had brought them into conflict with the law. In the United States, Callender, like other fugitive British newspapermen and pamphleteers, involved himself in the struggle between the Federalists and Jeffersonian Republicans—on the side of the Jeffersonians. But he never admitted to being a political partisan: he was, he said, an "historian" conducting impartial "researches into American history." He proposed to focus his historical scholarship upon American history, as he had already done upon British.[3]

In 1797, Jefferson met Callender for the first time at Francis's Hotel in Philadelphia. Despite Callender's unprepossessing appearance—even his admirers admitted that he was an uncommonly "mean-looking" man— Jefferson, now vice-president of the United States, promised to assist Callender in his next publication.

The first fruit of Callender's researches into American history was *The History of the United States for 1796*. Here he presented "proof" that Alexander Hamilton, as secretary of the treasury, had been personally involved in corrupt practices, including illegal speculation in government securities, and exposed Hamilton's illicit affair with Mrs. James Reynolds. The historical material from which Callender worked had been supplied by John Beckley, the late clerk of the House of Representatives and a close friend of Thomas Jefferson. Hamilton publicly confessed that he had been involved in "an irregular and indelicate amour" with Mrs. Reynolds, but Jefferson dismissed Hamilton's confession as an attempt to escape prosecution on a criminal charge—stealing from the United States Treasury—by pleading guilty to a less heinous offense.[4]

Jefferson was so pleased with *The History of the United States for 1796* that he bought fifteen copies which he distributed among his friends, and he sent Callender fifty dollars, the first of ten payments totalling two hundred dollars made the journalist by Jefferson. He flattered himself that Callender's book would "inform the thinking part of the nation" and enable these molders of public opinion "to set the people to rights." In 1798, Callender told Jefferson that his next book would produce "such a Tornado as no Government ever got before," whereupon the vice-president sent him another fifty dollars as down payment on the sowing of a whirlwind that promised to sweep President John Adams into limbo.[5]

Despite his deserved reputation as a "manager of men," Jefferson, on occasion, was deceived by the men he sought to manage. Gouverneur Morris, who had an opportunity to observe him at close range in Paris, remarked that "he does not form very just estimates of character, but rather assigns too many to the humble rank of fools. . . ." In the case of James Callender, however, Jefferson's fault lay in elevating a mountebank to the rank of honest men. But his motive in offering to subsidize Callender's future publications is clear: he overlooked the journalist's unsavory appearance, his drunkenness, and his dirty habits, because he saw in Callender an instrument for bringing down an administration Jefferson believed to be committed to war with France, alliance with Great Britain, the ascendancy of commerce, speculation, and banking over the "agricultural interest," and the erection of a monarchy upon the ruins of the American Republic.[6]

James Callender found American history a congenial field for the exercise of his peculiar talents, "for," he said, "there is in American history a species of ignorance, absurdity, and imbecility unknown to the annals of any other," and to this was added a system of robbery, corruption, and rapine as vicious and pervasive as anything he had encountered in Great Britain.[7]

The deeper he delved into this chamber of horrors otherwise known as the United States government, the more crimes and follies he discovered—all of which he duly noted in his next volume, eagerly awaited at Monticello.

This volume was entitled *The Prospect Before Us*. It opened up vistas of American history and contemporary politics which left no doubt that unless there was an immediate change in the government the American Republic would go down in corruption, crime, and dishonor. Cal-

lender brushed aside Hamilton's confession that he was guilty only of
marital infidelity: the former secretary of the treasury, Callender insisted,
was a corrupt, pro-British monarchist who despised Washington as "an
old damned fool." As for Washington, he was, according to Callender,
the dupe of Hamilton, "a scandalous hypocrite" and a self-serving
scoundrel who, during the darkest days of the Revolutionary War, had
"authorized the robbery and ruin of the remnants of his own army" for
his own financial advantage. President Adams was a "British Spy" who
consciously served the British interest in the United States; the Judas of
his country; "one of the most egregious fools upon the continent"; "a
hoary-headed incendiary" who had "completed the scenes of ignominy
which Washington began"; "a wretch, whose soul came blasted from the
hand of nature"; "the apostle of royalty and aristocracy" who deserved to
swing from a gibbet; and the "blasted tyrant of America" who richly
merited "the curses of mankind." Among other traitors in high places
who deserved punishment according to Callender's lights was John Jay,
the former chief justice of the United States Supreme Court, who only
offense was that he had negotiated a treaty with Great Britain in 1794.
Jay, said Callender, ought to be impeached and brought to trial on the
charge of high treason.[8]

Jefferson was more than Callender's financial angel: he read large
sections of the second part of *The Prospect Before Us* in proof, and he
supplied Callender with useful information regarding the inner workings
of the government. The journalist's inimitable hyperbolic style were of
course his own but there was an uncomfortable amount of truth in Callender's later claim that "Jefferson's political ideas are, to the minutest
ramification, precisely mine."

Although Callender denied that he was a "hireling," he sang Jefferson's praises in *The Prospect Before Us*. Jefferson's mind, said Callender,
"Is the essence of innocence and candour," and he compared him with
Xenophon and Polybius, the classical Greek historians. *The Prospect Before Us*, in short, cast a resounding vote for Jefferson in the presidential
election of 1800.

Despite these panegyrics, Jefferson was warned by his friends not to
become intimate with Callender, and Jefferson heeded these admonitions
to the extent of attempting to conceal his cash gifts to the journalist. On
one occasion he drew a check in favor of a third person, "my name," as
he put it, "not being proper to appear." Even so, he insisted that the
money he sent Callender was "charity." "My charities to him," he later
asserted, "were no more meant as encouragement to his scurrilities than
those I gave to the beggar at my door are meant as rewards for the vices
of his life and to make them chargeable to myself." Yet he insisted to the
end that Callender acted from "an honest conviction in his own mind
that he was right." It does not appear, however, that Jefferson ever tried

to tone down Callender's flagrantly mendacious attack upon John Adam's honesty and patriotism; indeed, had he done so, little of Callender's work would have remained intact.[9] No more than when he dealt with the character of George III in the Declaration of Independence was Jefferson restrained by the danger of propagandistic overkill.

The Prospect Before Us opened for Callender personally the prospect of a long term in prison. Despite his efforts to escape indictment under the Sedition Act—he walked all the way from Philadelphia to Virginia where he found sanctuary with Senator Stephen Thomas Mason—he was indicted in the Richmond Federal District Court. Although Governor James Monroe, at Jefferson's suggestion, enlisted some of the best legal talent in the Old Dominion for the defense, Callender was found guilty and sentenced by Justice Samuel Chase to serve a prison term of nine months and to pay a fine of two hundred dollars.[10]

In the elation of victory in the presidential election of 1800, Jefferson did not forget the numerous journalists who had been convicted, fined, and imprisoned for violating the Sedition Act. Among others, James Callender was pardoned and the president ordered the fine imposed upon Callender refunded. In the president's opinion this action was no more than the due of a man who had suffered martyrdom at the hands of a Federalist judge and jury for defending the freedom of the press.[11]

But an unexpected difficulty developed when the United States marshal at Richmond, a Federalist holdover, refused to accept the opinion of the United States attorney general that Callender's fine could be legally remitted. Callender, who was possessed of a powerful if disordered imagination, concluded that President Jefferson was trying to hold out on him. To persuade Callender that he was acting in good faith, Jefferson, at Governor James Monroe's suggestion, established a fund from contributions by Callender's friends, including Jefferson himself who gave fifty dollars to the cause, to pay the journalist's fine. But Callender, his suspicions now thoroughly aroused, refused to be bought off so cheaply: though he did not refuse the money, he said that he accepted it not as charity but as "hush-money." He demanded to be appointed postmaster at Richmond, Virginia, where, secure in a federal job, he said that he would marry, settle down on a farm, and "bid adieu to the rascally society of men" of which he himself, it might be said, was a conspicuous member.[12]

Unless he received the Richmond postmastership, he warned Jefferson, he would regale the president's "numerous and implacable enemies" with some tidbits of history of the same kind that had ruined the reputations of John Adams and Alexander Hamilton. "I am not the man, who is either oppressed or plundered with impunity," he told Jefferson. He strongly advised the president not to alienate him: the time might come, he said, when his services might again be required to raise another "political Tornado" against Jefferson's enemies.

The Richmond postmastership was not an unreasonable reward for the very considerable services Callender had rendered the president in the campaign of 1800. Jefferson was never averse to rewarding his friends for their political aid, but he would not yield to blackmail by a man he considered to be wholly unfit for any political office whatever. But even had he been inclined to buy off Callender, Jefferson knew that if it ever became public knowledge that he had used a federal office to purchase Callender's silence, the consequences were likely to be worse than anything Callender could do to him. As he said, Callender had completely mistaken his character. For his part, however, Callender believed that he knew Jefferson very well—a timid, devious man who customarily worked through others to achieve his political ends and who would pay any price to avoid being dragged kicking and screaming into the limelight.

Jefferson was the more inclined to reject Callender's demand for a political job because he believed that he had carefully prepared his defenses against all the accusations of wrongdoing Callender was likely to bring. The president clearly expected that Callender would accuse him of complicity in the publication of *The Prospect Before Us* and other writings judged libelous by the federal courts. While it would certainly be embarrassing to Jefferson to find himself charged, while serving as vice-president of the United States, with subsidizing a renegade journalist to subvert the administration of President John Adams, Jefferson was ready to state in his own defense that the payments he had made to Callender were charitable contributions. Only in his correspondence with Callender did he believe himself vulnerable; to make sure that Callender did not misuse the letters Jefferson had written him, the president tried unsuccessfully to recover them from Callender's possession.

Certain of his ability to prove his innocence—he had already prepared his defense—Jefferson deprecated Callender's threat to "tell all." "He knows nothing of me," Jefferson told his friends, "which I am not willing to declare to the world myself." But, as the event proved, Jefferson reckoned too much on his own sense of rectitude, forgetting that his career had come under the scrutiny of the most unscrupulous scandalmonger of the day. As Jefferson ought to have known, and as Hamilton certainly knew, James Callender was a journalist who stopped at nothing and stooped to anything.

In 1802, Callender was given a job by the *Richmond Recorder: or Lady's and Gentleman's Miscellany,* a Federalist newspaper which made no pretense of publishing only news that was fit to print. Callender converted the *Richmond Recorder* into an anti-Jefferson scandal sheet. From this congenial forum, he asserted that Jefferson had aided in the publication of the pamphlets—and he printed the president's letters to prove it—that had led to Callender's prosecution under the Sedition Act and had then denied him the honors and emoluments he deserved as "a martyr to liberty." It was shabby treatment, Callender complained, from a man who had complimented him upon editing "the best newspaper in America" and had subsidized his efforts to demolish Alexander Hamilton, the colossus of Federalism.[13]

In his probings into the career of Alexander Hamilton, Callender acted upon the maxim "cherchez la femme," and by diligently following this line of approach, he had been led to the person of Mrs. James Reynolds. Applied to Thomas Jefferson, this method opened up an even richer vein of scandal. For, Callender announced triumphantly in September 1802, in the pages of the *Richmond Recorder,* Jefferson was involved with two, and probably more, women; not only that, but one of these women, a slave girl named Sally Hemings, had borne him several mulatto children who were kept at Monticello as slaves.

Callender made his charges against Jefferson without fear and without research. He had never visited Monticello; he had never spoken to Sally Hemings; and he never made the slightest effort to verify the "facts" he so stridently proclaimed. It was "journalism" at its most reckless, wildly irresponsible, and scurrilous. Callender was not an investigative journalist; he never bothered to investigate anything. For him, the story, especially if it reeked of scandal, was everything; truth, if it stood in his way, was summarily mowed down.

Callender turned against Jefferson the principles of freedom of the press and of the right of the people to be informed about the conduct of public servants. "Until the people are well informed," Callender intoned in the true Jeffersonian spirit, "there cannot be a correct and free government." He invoked the sacred principle that The People Must Know—in this case that their president was not fit to enter the company of self-respecting citizens, and that the virtue of no woman, white or black, was safe from his lubricity.[14]

Warming to his theme, Callender pictured Jefferson, before the agonized gaze of his daughters, sending out to the kitchen "or perhaps to his pigstye, for this Mahogany coloured charmer" (Sally Hemings) and frolicking with "the black wench and her mulatto litter." No longer need the American people wonder why President Jefferson insisted upon taking such long vacations at Monticello: it was to enjoy the favors of the "black Venus." If eighty thousand white men in Virginia followed Jefferson's example, Callender warned, the commonwealth would soon have an additional four hundred thousand mulattoes to worry about. In that event, Callender predicted, "the country would no longer be habitable, till after a civil war, and a series of massacres. We all know with absolute certainty that the contest would end in the utter extinction of both blacks and mulattoes." Thus, according to Callender, Jefferson was helping to bring on the racial war he professed to dread.[15]

Magnified in the telling and retelling, Callender's story grew into the tale of a voluptuary in the Executive Mansion who maintained a "Congo Harem" and who kept his numerous offspring by black women as slaves at Monticello until they were ready for the auction block. In her book *The Democratic Manners of the Americans* (1832), Mrs. Frances Trollope reported it as common knowledge that Jefferson was the progenitor of "unnumbered generations of slaves." It was his special delight, Mrs. Trollope declared, to be waited upon at table by his slave-children, "and the hospitable orgies for which Monticello was so celebrated were incomplete, unless the goblets he quaffed were tendered by the trembling hand of his own slave offspring," and she reveled in the story that Jefferson had forced Harriet Hemings, Sally's sister, into a life of prostitution in Baltimore. By reviling Jefferson, Mrs. Trollope gratified her hatred of American democracy and the principles of the Declaration of Independence. In her opinion, those principles—especially the assertion that men were created equal—could be most effectively assailed by showing how the author himself had made a mockery of them.[16]

The titillating theme of a beautiful slave girl—and even an entire bevy of voluptuous Congo nymphs—prostituted to the lust of an American president even inspired poetry. Jefferson complained that American slaves did not write poetry; with more propriety, he might have lamented that Englishmen and Americans insisted on writing it—at the expense of his good name. At the tender age of twelve years, when proper Bostonians were not expected to know anything of such matters, William Cullen Bryant made his reputation as a poet in Federalist Boston by his verses adjuring Jefferson to

> Go wretch, resign the presidential chair,
> . . . .Go, scan, Philosophist, thy Sally's charms,
> And sink supinely in her sable arms;
> But quit to abler hands the helm of state.[17]

John Quincy Adams published anonymous verses depicting a brazen hypocrite who mouthed platitudes about freedom while enjoying the favors of his slave concubines. (Adams repented of this foray into "poison pen" poetasting when he became a Jeffersonian Republican.) The English poet Tom Moore apostrophized

> The patriot, fresh from Freedom's councils come,
> Now pleas'd, retires to lash his slaves at home;
> Or woo some black Aspasia's charms
> And dreams of freedom in his bondsmaid's arms.

Moore made it appear that Jefferson was a sadist as well as a libertine, and thereby doubly damned in the eyes of all decent people.[18]

It is revelatory of the state of journalism in the early nineteenth century that no newspaper sent a reporter to Monticello to interview Sally Hemings or, indeed, took any action whatever to ascertain the truth of Callender's allegations. There was no wall of brass around Monticello; Sally Hemings was not held incommunicado by her master. She was, in fact, freely accessible to journalists of both parties, Federalist and Republican alike, yet they seemed strangely uninterested in getting her side of the story. Clearly, Sally was ignored by Republicans because they did not believe Callender's allegations and because Jefferson himself adopted the posture of neither hearing nor seeing evil. The Federalists, on the other hand, valued the story as propaganda that might, if judiciously exploited, encompass Jefferson's defeat in the presidential election of 1804; with this joyful prospect before them, they had no desire to press for an investigation which, by revealing the truth, might destroy a perfectly good, politically serviceable lie.

Yet it would have been easy to have established the truth of the "Black Sally" and "Congo Harem" stories. Callender himself provided the clue that would have enabled an enterprising journalist, assuming Callender's story were true, to produce the evidence of Jefferson's guilt. Among Jefferson's offspring by Sally Hemings, Callender identified Tom, Jr., whom he called "Yellow Tom" or "President Tom," presumably because Jefferson planned to make his son his successor in the presidency, thereby inflicting upon the United States the ultimate horror of a "Negro President." Callender credited Tom, whom he had never seen, with bearing a striking resemblance to the president. But no trace of the existence of "Yellow Tom" has ever been discovered; even Sally Hemings's alleged confession makes no mention of this shadowy individual. In actuality "Yellow Tom" never existed, but in Callender's hands he became one of the most famous nonpersons in American history.[19]

Had "Yellow Tom" existed, proof of his identity would have gone far toward confirming that "Black Sally" was the president's concubine. In her recent biography of Thomas Jefferson, Fawn Brodie maintains that "Yellow Tom" was whisked out of sight by the president as soon as Callender's story appeared in the *Richmond Recorder* lest irrefutable evidence of his carnal relationship with Sally Hemings should come to light. And so Thomas Jefferson banished his only begotten son who had survived infancy and never saw him again simply in order to conceal the proof of his own guilt and to continue his illicit love affair with Sally Hemings without interruption.

Ms. Brodie adduces no evidence for this extraordinary incident; we are back with Callender and his dark surmises. The only real difference between Ms. Brodie and Callender is that she dignifies Jefferson's relations with Sally Hemings as a true love affair, one of the grand passions of the American presidency. With Sally, Jefferson experienced a "secret happiness"—"love without debauchery"—that transcended all other sources of happiness known to him. For Ms. Brodie, as for Callender, "Yellow Tom" is an essential character in the story of Jefferson's relations with Sally Hemings. But Ms. Brodie goes beyond Callender: could anything be more monstrous, as she alleged, than for Jefferson to ostracize his son from Monticello and to cut off contact with him in order to conceal evidence of the liaison with Sally Hemings? From Jefferson's point of view insofar as it is known to us, this would be the act of an utterly immoral monster.[20]

There actually was a slave living at Monticello named Thomas Jefferson, but he was an old man and no one accused the white Thomas Jefferson of being *his* father. The death of the black Thomas Jefferson in 1800 gave rise to the report—glad tidings to the Federalists—that Thomas Jefferson, "the great arch priest of Jacobinism and infidelity and a base plotter against the peace, safety and felicity of the United States" had passed to his reward.[21]

A renegade, down-at-heels, villainous-looking journalist who had accused Washington of profiting financially from the privations of his soldiers at Valley Forge, President John Adams of being in the pay of the British Crown, and Alexander Hamilton of having committed grand theft while secretary of the treasury—such a man might have been thought to be lacking in credibility. Indeed, Callender might have provided an instructive case history in the abnormal psychology symptomatic of the state of contemporary politics and journalism. In the early Republic political passions ran as high and generated the same kind of ferocity and intolerance—although, happily, without the bloodshed—as religious bigotry had in the seventeenth century. So surcharged with passion was the political atmosphere that credulity frequently was carried to the point of fatuity. Nothing, however improbable or fantastical, was rejected as grist for the propaganda mills of the Federalists and the Jeffersonian Republicans. As Abigail Adams said, party spirit on both sides was "blind, malevolent, uncandid, ungenerous, unjust and unforgiving." [22]

Yet not all Federalists took advantage of this opportunity to defame the president. Alexander Hamilton, the leader of the party, advised the editor of a Federalist newspaper not to publish Callender's libels. His own feelings in the matter, he said, were that politics ought to be divorced from private life except where it was directly connected with public considerations. Hamilton spoke from bitter experience of how private life—in his case, his affair with Mrs. Reynolds—had wrecked his political career. He recommended that President Jefferson emulate the example of Federalist officeholders when they were vilified by Republican editors—hale the culprit into federal court and charge him with seditious libel. But Hamilton's influence over the Federalist party had been shattered by his own misadventures and abortive political intrigues, and few

Federalists could refrain from wallowing with Callender in the delightful ordure.

Nor did Jefferson take Hamilton's advice: he neither instituted legal proceedings against Callender nor responded in any way to the attacks upon him appearing in the *Richmond Recorder*. As he had done on several occasions before, he remained in the Olympian calm of Monticello wrapped in impenetrable silence while the political storms raged below.

The fact that President Jefferson took no public notice of Callender's libels does not mean that he suffered from a guilty conscience. Early in his career, feeling "an insuperable aversion to be drawn into controversy in the public papers," he resolved never to write for the newspapers—a resolution to which, with minor exceptions, he adhered. At the same time, he decided not to permit calumny, no matter how great the provocation, to disturb his peace of mind. Denial, no matter how vehement or often repeated, seemed to offer no defense against character assassins. "Were I to undertake to answer the calumnies of the newspapers," he remarked, "it would be more than all my own time, and that of 20 aids could effect. . . . For while I should be answering one, twenty new ones would be invented." [23]

Jefferson, would not, in fact, bring himself to believe that any decent man, regardless of his party affiliation, would believe Callender; and for the good opinion of indecent men he cared not a farthing. The Callender story consequently became in Jefferson's mind a test not only of political orthodoxy but of moral integrity. For this reason, no delegation of anguished Jeffersonian Republicans journeyed to Monticello to beseech the love-struck President to put away his "black" concubine lest he bring ruin upon himself and his party. Jeffersonian Republicans did not believe the story and had any appeared on Jefferson's threshold on such a mission they would probably have found the door slammed in their faces.

No doubt, Jefferson was correct in believing that a public denial on his part would have made no difference; "President Tom," the "Congo Harem," and his illicit passion for Sally Hemings were designed to portray him to the American people as a moral and political monster. While Jefferson's assessment of Federalist motives was often tinctured with his own irrepressible partisanship, he did them no wrong when he said that "Federalist bitterness increases with their desperation. They are trying slanders now which nothing could prompt but a guilt which blinds their judgment as well as their consciences." As the Federalists retreated to their final enclave in New England before the sweep of Jeffersonian Republicanism, they clutched at any means, fair or foul, to destroy Jefferson. In such a poisonously partisan atmosphere, political discourse quickly degenerated into vilification, scurrility, and calumny; truth figured only as the first casualty in a war waged to destroy the enemy at any cost. [24]

Jefferson took comfort in the reflection that his enemies did not really know him and therefore had not succeeded in injuring him: they had merely manufactured an odious, utterly repellent scarecrow at which they had spat their venom under the illusion that they were soiling Thomas Jefferson. The real Thomas Jefferson, however, remained unscathed: he was to be found at Monticello with his books, his scientific apparatus, his garden, and his friends, daughters, and grandchildren. Anyone who saw him at Monticello surrounded by the things in which he most delighted would never, he felt sure, pay the slightest heed to malicious stories spread by his political enemies.[25]

To preserve his reputation from the slings and arrows of outrageous journalists, Jefferson characteristically chose to trust to the justice, common sense, and fairness of his fellow countrymen. He asked them to judge him by what they saw of his conduct on the public stage rather than by the vilification of his political enemies. In short, rather than go down into the gutter with Callender and his Federalist colleagues, Jefferson stood upon his record, his public character, and on his reputation for probity—and he let the people judge. He said that he would gladly submit his reputation to "the umpirage of public opinion," confident of the justice of "the republican mass of our citizens." "Their approbation," he continued, "has taught a lesson, useful to the world, that the man who fears no truths has nothing to fear from lies. I should have fancied myself half guilty, had I condescended to put pen to paper in refutation of their falsehoods, or drawn to them respect by any notice from myself." [26]

Alexander Hamilton tried to observe the same rule. "It has been a general maxim with me," he said, "to leave the evidence of my conduct and character to answer the calumnies which party spirit is so incessantly busied in heaping upon me." But Hamilton was unable to take refuge in silence: his political enemies succeeded in putting him in a position in which he had no recourse but to confess his relations with Mrs. Reynolds: "I have paid pretty severely for the folly," Hamilton told the American people, "and can never recollect it without disgust and self-condemnation." [27]

Jefferson's closest friends—James Madison and James Monroe, in particular—did not rush into print with attestations of the president's innocence, for that would have defeated Jefferson's strategy of killing the scandal by salutary neglect. But David Humphreys, who had been in France when Jefferson was United States minister, branded Callender's story a barefaced lie, and Tom Paine, after visiting the president in Washington, declared that to link Jefferson with Sally Hemings was "the blackest effusions of the blackest calumny that ever escaped the envenomed pen of a villain." To which the Federalists countered that the word of two atheists was no better than the word of one atheist; and, for good measure, they concocted a lurid story in which Paine figured as the seducer of the "African Venus," thereby, like a true infidel, cuckolding his best friend.[28]

No doubt, Jefferson's reputed atheism predisposed many pious people to believe him guilty as charged; after all, every atheist was supposed to be a reprobate capable of violating the laws of God and man with equal impunity. A New England Federalist congressman spoke for many of his fellow Down Easters when he delivered himself of a damning indictment of Jefferson: the president, he declared, was immoral; he questioned the existence of God; and he had dismantled the United States Navy.[29]

The notion that Jefferson was guilty of the grosser forms of moral turpitude—cohabiting with his own slave-woman—was clearly a source of intense gratification to his political enemies. What they found most objectionable in Jefferson—it really set their teeth on edge—was his insufferable, unctuous self-righteousness; more than even the seventeenth century New England Puritans he seemed to walk in a "holier-than-thou" aura. Federalists complained that Jefferson appeared to think that he had never done a wrong or even committed a mistake: he was virtue incarnate, inviolate, and immaculate. Moreover, he had always portrayed his own party as the Heaven-appointed custodian of virtue, rectitude, idealism, and true republicanism" while stigmatizing the Federalists, at least in the higher echelons, as the party of vice, corruption, and monarchism. Sensing an opportunity to pull down this pillar of rectitude, the Federalists gave ready credence to the story of "Black Sally," "the Congo Harem," and the "mulatto litter."

Just as the Salem witchcraft craze of the previous century had ultimately brought under suspicion divers clergymen and magistrates, so the frenzy unleashed by Callender spared no one. Among others, Chief Justice John Marshall was accused of keeping a black mistress. Not even the pillars of the Federalist Establishment could escape the contagious virus of vilification.

🍁

Clearly, Jefferson paid a heavy price by any standards for his charitable "benefactions" to James Callender, the erstwhile persecuted "man of genius" and "martyr" of liberty. Angered by what he regarded as Callender's base ingratitude, Jefferson now called him "a lying renegade from republicanism"; "a poor creature, hypochondriac, drunken, penniless and unprincipled." Jefferson was inclined to believe that the greatest rogues were profit-minded businessmen, but, obviously, he had to make an exception in the case of James Callender.

To Jefferson's discomfiture, some of his critics detected the retributive hand of the same Providence he was so fond of discovering in the misfortunes of his enemies. Abigail Adams, for example, said that Jefferson had been bitten by a serpent he had "cherished and warmed" in his bosom as long as it confined its venom to Federalists. Outraged by the libels Callender had uttered against her husband, Mrs. Adams read Jefferson a lecture on political morality, a subject on which the sage of Monticello considered himself to be a peerless authority. "When such vipers are let loose upon society," she admonished him, "all distinctions between virtue and vice are levelled, all respect for character is lost in the overwhelming deluge of calumny, that respect which is a necessary bond in the social union and which gives efficacy to laws, and teaches the subject to obey the magistrates, and the child to submit to the parent." Stung by this rebuke, Jefferson assured Mrs. Adams that he was utterly incapable of taking part in such "dirty work." His only offense, he maintained, consisted in extending charity to an ingrate and a blackguard: he kept no vipers at Monticello.[30]

∼ 20 ∼

The Sally Hemings Story

———◆———

SALLY HEMINGS entered Jefferson's life in 1787 when she was chosen to accompany Jefferson's younger daughter to join her father in France. Although she was sometimes called a "black," she was actually a quadroon, who bore little trace of her African ancestry. She was the daughter of Betty Hemings, herself the daughter of an English sea captain and an African slave woman. Betty Hemings bore fourteen children of varying shades of color, most of whom served Jefferson as slaves. She and her children became Jefferson's property in 1773 upon the death of his father-in-law, John Wayles, a wealthy Virginia planter.[1]

At Monticello, Betty Hemings and her quadroon children received favored treatment. Instead of being put to work in the fields, they were trained as household servants and artisans. Moreover, most of them, with the notable exception of Sally, were freed during Jefferson's lifetime or by his will.

The explanation given in the slave quarters at Monticello for the singular partiality shown by Jefferson to Betty Hemings and her children was that some of them were the progeny of the late Colonel Wayles who, exercising the traditional *droit du seigneur* to the full, had in the process added notably to his contingent of slaves. If the Monticello slaves were correct, Sally Hemings was Jefferson's wife's half-sister and her brothers were Mrs. Jefferson's half-brothers. As Alice might have said, in the Wonderland of a Virginia plantation life became curiouser and curiouser.

There is nothing inherently implausible in the gossip of the Monticello slaves. It was not uncommon for slaveowners to make slave women their concubines, and, of course, the children born of such unions were legally slaves and could be sold. One of the most formidable obstacles in the way of a male slave gaining status in his own family was his inability to protect his wife and daughters from the sexual aggression of whites, including, sometimes, the slaveowner himself. David Ramsay of South

Carolina, a contemporary of Jefferson's and a historian of the American Revolution, predicted that in a few centuries the blackness of the Afro-American would be washed white by miscegenation. Alliances between young white men and slave girls were described by a Virginia judge as "imprudent (though not uncommon) temporary connections." Yet, widespread as was the practice, it bore a heavy social stigma: no planter would admit to cohabiting with his slaves unless, of course, he was discovered *in flagrante delicto*. Mulatto children were usually attributed to overseers, white indentured servants, and poor whites.[2]

Thus, by marrying into the Wayles family and accepting his wife's inheritance of land and slaves, Jefferson involved himself in a web of highly anomalous racial and familial relationships. He tried to meet the situation by making slavery as easy as possible for the Hemings. In 1784 he took James Hemings with him to France in order to learn French cookery. James's brothers and sisters were trained as household servants and artisans, and Betty Hemings attended Mrs. Jefferson in her last illness. The only child of Betty Hemings sold by Jefferson was Thenia, who became the property of James Monroe.[3]

The special treatment meted out to Betty Hemings and her offspring by Jefferson may have assuaged but it hardly could have removed the harrowing sense of guilt Jefferson experienced by holding his late wife's half-brothers and half-sisters in servitude, particularly since he could see in these mulattoes the lineaments of his own wife. It is no wonder, therefore, that he conceived the overwhelming antipathy toward miscegenation which led him to favor putting all Afro-Americans beyond the possibility of admixture with whites. If, as the evidence indicates, his attitude toward mulattoes underwent a radical change in 1772–1773, it was probably owing to the astonishing discovery he made at that time of the sexual practices of his late father-in-law and the tangible evidence of his aberration Jefferson had acquired as a result of his marriage.[4]

If Sally Hemings were actually the natural daughter of John Wayles, she was the last of his children, conceived in the last year of his life. She came to Monticello in 1774 as an infant. She apparently assisted her mother Betty in the sickroom during Mrs. Jefferson's illness in 1782. Thereafter she remained at Monticello doing light housework until 1786 when she was unexpectedly called upon to accompany Mary Jefferson to France. Jefferson had asked that his daughter be entrusted, under the supervision of a gentleman, to the care of "a careful negro woman, Isabel, for instance, if she has had the small-pox." Had he known that his sister had consigned his daughter to the care of a fourteen-year-old girl, he probably would have spent many sleepless nights. Abigail Adams, who took charge of Mary Jefferson when she arrived in England on her way to Paris, wrote Jefferson that Sally Hemings was much too young and inexperienced for her charge: she "wants more care than the child, and is wholly incapable of looking after her without some superior to direct her." [5]

Jefferson impatiently awaited Mary's arrival in Paris. "Then, indeed," he said, "shall I be the happiest of mortals, united to what I have the dearest in the world, nothing more will be requisite to render my happiness complete." But according to the account publicized by James Callender and, later, allegedly corroborated by Sally Hemings herself, Jefferson quickly acquired a new love, dearer to him than anything else in the world. And his happiness was at long last rendered complete—but not, however, as he had expected, by the reunion with his younger daughter: he made Sally Hemings, whom Mrs. John Adams had considered to be too young and inexperienced to take care of Mary Jefferson, his mistress. [6]

According to the story reputedly told by Sally Hemings herself, this conquest was not effected without some difficulty. Sally wanted to learn to speak French and to remain in France where she would become a free woman and, perhaps, marry a Frenchman. But the amorous statesman, goaded by an overmastering passion, refused to take no for an answer: he persuaded her to submit to his desire under the promise of freeing, when they reached adulthood, any children born to them.

If this account can be believed, Jefferson emerges as the seducer of a young, innocent, attractive colored girl, hardly out of puberty, who yearned only to be free and to remain in a country where she would not be despised as a "Negress" and humiliated as a slave.

At Monticello, after Jefferson's return from France, Sally Hemings became Jefferson's chambermaid—a circumstance later cited as "evidence" of the illicit relationship between the slave girl and her master. The presence of this near-white girl and her mulatto brothers and sisters startled some visitors at Monticello who had innocently supposed that all Virginia slaves were black. The Duc de la Rochefoucauld-Liancourt, for example, who visited Monticello in 1796, reported that he had seen "slaves, who, neither in point of color nor features, showed the least trace of their original descent"; and the Comte de Volney, the French *philosophe,* remarked a few years later upon the phenomenon of slaves who appeared to be more white than black. Yet neither of Jefferson's French visitors detected any evidence of a permanent connection between a white man and a slave woman at Monticello. It never entered their minds that Jefferson himself had breached the color line.

Certainly there were mulatto children being born at Monticello who, although slaves, were given a special category. The same consideration shown by Jefferson to Betty Hemings and her children was extended to the second generation. It was these children, especially the imaginary "President Tom," that Callender imagined to have been sired by Jefferson. The work load of these light-skinned slaves was deliberately lightened, and they were neither sold nor hired out as laborers—a significant advantage inasmuch as hired slaves were often cruelly overworked. Harriet Hemings was taught to spin and weave in the little factory at Monticello; Beverly, Madison, and Eston Hemings became carpenters. Two of Sally's children were permitted to leave Monticello: Harriet was given fifty dollars and put aboard a stagecoach to ·Philadelphia, and her brother Beverly was allowed to "run away" to Philadelphia. Both Harriet and Beverly married whites and passed into the Caucasian community.[7]

If this version of Jefferson's relationship with Sally Hemings is true, he risked the loss of the presidency in 1804 by continuing to father her children even after his "exposure" by James Callender. It would appear that he reckoned the world well lost for the gratification of his all-consuming love for Sally Hemings.*

If Jefferson can, in fact, be assumed to have been the lover of Sally Hemings and the father of her children, it must be admitted that he behaved toward these children in a very uncharacteristic manner. Jefferson was an intensely domestic man who always regarded public service as a duty thrust upon him by a not altogether kind destiny; to him, New York, Philadelphia, and Washington were places of exile from Monticello, his true spiritual home, a refuge for replenishment after the gladiatorial combats of the political arena. Above all he delighted in the company of his daughters and grandchildren and he seemed unable to conceive of true happiness away from his family. Upon his two surviving daughters and his twelve grandchildren he lavished his watchful attention, overseeing their education, dress, deportment, their health, and, indeed, every detail of their lives. It could, in fact, be argued that he carried this solicitude too far, that he was too possessive, too sententious, too preceptorial, and too sensitive to even trivial things that concerned their welfare.

Yet toward Sally Hemings's children Jefferson showed no affection whatever. Madison Hemings, the only child of Sally Hemings who left a record of his life at Monticello—its authenticity, like everything else relating to Sally Hemings, is problematical said that he would never have known from Jefferson's bearing toward him that Jefferson was his father. Madison Hemings was twenty years old when Jefferson died yet he could not recall a single act of paternal affection in all that time.†

---

* In her book *Thomas Jefferson: An Intimate History*, Fawn Brodie conceded that this was truly "a dangerous decision of the heart." At Monticello, in her script the scene of Jefferson's grand passion, love triumphed over all and the infatuated president found solace from the cares of state in the arms of his slave mistress whom he loved more deeply than reputation, honor, and political power. Still, caution was not wholly thrown to the winds for the president did not at any time take Sally Hemings to Washington to share the presidential mansion with him. It was a small, but vital, concession to public opinion. See Brodie 1974, p. 359.

† Madison Hemings claimed to have been named by Dolley Madison who, he said, promised Sally "a fine present for the honor . . . but like many promises of whites to the slaves, she never gave my mother anything." James Madison was in a position to

A methodical man who made a practice, almost a fetish, of putting down the most minute and trivial matters in his voluminous notebooks, Jefferson failed to record the birth of several of Sally's children, especially those who died in infancy. For example, Beverly Hemings, a son, born in 1798, received little notice either in Jefferson's correspondence or in the records he kept of events at Monticello even though Beverly was the first son born to Sally. While it is true that Jefferson was in residence at Monticello nine months before each of Sally's children was born, he was not present at the time each of her children were delivered. Their births and even their deaths received only cursory notice in his journals. Two of Sally's children who died in infancy were buried in the slave burying-ground at Monticello; there is no record of Jefferson's presence at the interment. If these were actually his children, the conclusion is inescapable that he must be portrayed as a cold, heartless and callous man— the very antithesis of the Thomas Jefferson that emerges from the historical record.

In marked contrast to the dry, factual manner in which he recorded the birth or death of Sally Hemings's children, Jefferson was overjoyed at the birth of his own children and prostrated with grief if they died. "There is no degree of affliction, produced by the loss of those dear to us, which experience has not taught me to estimate," he said. Nevertheless he appears in a recent biography turning, in the anguish of bereavement occasioned by the death of his youngest surviving daughter, to Sally Hemings, "the source of continuing life"— a happy event that led to the conception of Madison Hemings, born in January 1805.[8]

No less anomalous was Jefferson's manifest disinterest in educating the mulatto children born to Sally Hemings. The man who, above all his contemporaries, put his faith in raising the level of the mass of the people by education and who conceived of the educative process as the best way of bringing genius to the fore and of developing the moral sense, was, we are asked to believe, wholly unconcerned with giving his own children, if they were actually such, an opportunity to demonstrate the talents they might have inherited from him. As it was, what little education Sally Hemings's children received was picked up from Jefferson's white grandchildren.

Had Jefferson loved Sally Hemings in the deeper sense of that word, he would surely have loved the children she bore him. It was not in Jefferson's nature, nor is it in the nature of most men, to show indiffer-

---

know the true nature of Jefferson's relations with Sally Hemings. Had he believed that Jefferson's son and his (Madison's) namesake was living at Monticello is it credible that he would have treated him with the indifference of which Madison Hemings later complained? Unless, of course, we are prepared to accept the only conclusion possible if the Callender-Brodie thesis is correct: namely, that James Madison himself was a party to the cover-up masterminded by Jefferson. See Brodie 1974, p. 473.

ence to the children born of a love match. If his treatment of the children is any indicator, Jefferson's feeling for Sally Hemings—assuming that he had any feeling for her other than the regard a master feels for a loyal, devoted servant and half-sister of his deceased wife—must have been purely carnal. The children did not concern him at all; he was solely preoccupied in indulging his passion for the "African Venus."

It was impossible for Jefferson to carry on a romance or even a friendship without constant letter-writing. Jefferson not only wrote voluminously but he kept a record of every letter he sent or received. He was in the habit of using the polygraph and stylograph to make copies of his own letters, and he carefully preserved the letters addressed to him. In all this correspondence there is only the most casual and infrequent mention of Sally Hemings. She produced no letter written by Jefferson which would have set at rest all doubts of the paternity of her children and the depth of Jefferson's feeling for her. She apparently was not literate; at least, she did not teach her children to read and write. ('When he called her a "Black Aspasia," Tom Moore was stretching poetic license to the utmost latitude.*⁹') Of course, if Sally could not read, the absence of letters from Jefferson is explicable; but this explanation requires a suspension of disbelief in the idea that Jefferson loved an illiterate slave woman for over thirty years.

Jefferson's real love-letters were written to his daughters and to his wife, Martha, not to Sally Hemings or to any other woman. "I deem the composition of my family the most precious of all the kindnesses of fortune," he said, and he referred frequently in his correspondence to "the ineffable pleasures of my family society." In 1797 he wrote to his daughter Martha Randolph that "the bloom of Monticello is chilled by my solitude. . . . I value the enjoyments of this life only in proportion as you participate in them with me." He bewailed his "solitude" yet he had Sally Hemings at his side!

When Jefferson spoke of happiness, he meant, above all, the pleasure he derived from the presence of his daughters and his grandchildren. He never included specifically or by fair inference Sally Hemings in this familial felicity. When he lost his daughter Mary in 1804, he lamented that "others may lose of their abundance, but I, of my want, have lost even the half of all I had. My evening prospects now hang on the slender thread of a single life." It is beyond all credibility that Jefferson was here referring to Sally Hemings rather than to his surviving daughter, Martha Randolph.¹⁰

Had Jefferson wanted to devote himself to the unalloyed happiness he allegedly found in the company and arms of Sally Hemings, it is

* Aspasia was the beautiful, talented courtesan who became the mistress and later the wife of Pericles, the Athenian statesman and war leader.

extraordinary that he should have made such a point of urging his married daughters and their husbands to live with him at Monticello. Lovers usually wish to be alone, but in Jefferson's case he seemed deliberately to have courted exposure of his affair by surrounding himself with as many members of his family as possible. In this respect, at least, Jefferson appears to have been unique among the Great Lovers of history.

Since Jefferson's daughters were not aware of their father's alleged relations with Sally Hemings—even though Mary Jefferson lived at Monticello much of the time her father is supposed to have been intimate with Sally and while several of her children were born—a new dimension ought to be added to Jefferson's fame: he was a master, unequalled in American history, of the art of dissimulation. His bearing toward Sally Hemings's children was simply part of an elaborately contrived cover-up sustained for a period of over thirty years. Keeping them as slaves, even though they were well treated, was part of the cover-up; the traumatic experience of growing up on a Virginia plantation as slaves had to be inflicted upon them in order that Jefferson could enjoy the favors of Sally Hemings with impunity.

Perhaps the most inexplicable event in the Sally Hemings story as the Callender-Brodie script unfolds is Jefferson's failure to give freedom upon his death to the woman who as a young girl, allegedly had renounced her opportunity of freedom and returned to Monticello in order to satisfy his desires. In his will, Jefferson freed five slaves, all Hemingses, and he petitioned the state legislature, as the law required, for permission for these freed slaves to remain in Virginia. But Sally Hemings was not among those manumitted: her name appeared on the slave inventory of his estate and her value was set at fifty dollars, although she might have been regarded as a collector's item by anyone who believed Callender's story. A few years later she was freed by Martha Jefferson, and she spent her last years living with her sons. She died in 1835 and was buried in a Negro burying ground, not at Monticello with Jefferson.[11]

If Jefferson were actually trying to conceal his liaison with Sally Hemings and the existence of his slave children, this must be regarded as the final step in the cover-up. The very enormity of the offense with which he was certain to be charged after his will had been made public provided Jefferson with a plausible argument in favor of his innocence, for who would believe that he failed to free a slave woman with whom, according to Fawn Brodie, he had enjoyed decades of idyllic bliss and for whose love he had risked the presidency and the good opinion of posterity; and how could it be explained that he had not stipulated that she be buried in the family plot at Monticello rather than in an obscure Negro cemetery? Obviously, the answer is that no decent-minded person would believe this of Jefferson—indeed, it would be difficult to believe it of any man—and so Callender's charges would almost certainly be dismissed by posterity as the work of a unprincipled traducer of a great and good man whose conduct offered convincing proof of his innocence. And so Jefferson would be gathered to history, immaculate, virtuous, and above suspicion.

🍁

What incriminated Jefferson according to Callender—indeed, this was the only "evidence" he cited to support his allegations—was the resemblance Sally Hemings's children, especially "Yellow Tom," bore to the president. Callender's case was seriously weakened by the fact that "Yellow Tom" never existed except in his imagination, but Madison Hemings, born in 1805 after Callender's death, was said to resemble Jefferson and, like Jefferson, he played the fiddle: *ergo,* he must have been Jefferson's son. If Jefferson had been the object of a paternity suit, the prosecution would doubtless have made Madison Hemings its chief exhibit.[12]

Yet something more than this kind of circumstantial evidence is required in a court of law. A superficial physical resemblance is too widespread a phenomenon to serve as irrefutable evidence of paternity. Edward Coles, Jefferson's neighbor and Madison's one-time secretary, closely resembled Jefferson in stature, form, and features; and Dr. Edward Stevens bore such a striking resemblance to Alexander Hamilton that they were thought to be brothers.

There were, however, two persons, frequent visitors at Monticello, who bore a close resemblance to Thomas Jefferson. These were Peter and Samuel Carr, Jefferson's nephews, both strongly built men whose physiques were similar to that of their paternal grandfather, Peter Jefferson.

During Jefferson's youth and young manhood, his closest friend was Dabney Carr, the son of a wealthy Virginia planter, and a classmate at the College of William and Mary. Rambling together in the forests near Shadwell, Jefferson's birthplace, they discovered a huge oak on the slopes of the hill Jefferson later named Monticello. Here they romantically vowed that they would be buried together.

In 1765 this Damon and Pythias relationship was reinforced by the marriage of Dabney Carr to Jefferson's sister, Martha. But in 1773, shortly after Jefferson's own marriage, Dabney Carr died at the age of thirty, leaving six children, and it became Jefferson's melancholy duty to bury his friend. Dabney Carr was the first to be interred in the small private cemetery at Monticello. Over a half century later, Jefferson himself fulfilled the compact he had made with Dabney Carr.

Dabney Carr's sons, Peter and Samuel, became Jefferson's favorite nephews, and upon them he lavished a wealth of sententious advice with respect to their reading, their morals, and their behavior. He was resolved to make them paragons of the Virginia gentry, combining the manners of gentlemen with the erudition of scholars. The moral code he laid down for their guidance was so exacting that, had they followed it implicitly, they would indeed have been cynosures. To fully develop the virtuous propensities of these young Virginia nonesuches, Jefferson recommended the reading of the ancient moralists: Epictetus, Plato's Socratic Dialogues, and Cicero. "When tempted to any thing in secret," he told Peter Carr, "ask yourself if you would do it in public; if you would not, be sure it is wrong." [13]

Of the two brothers, Peter was singled out by Jefferson for special attention. When he went to France, he consigned the boy to the care of James Madison with instructions that he be taught Latin, Greek, French, Italian, and Anglo-Saxon. To Madison, Jefferson described Peter Carr as "a boy of fine disposition and sound masculine talents." [14]

From Paris, Jefferson preached to the Carr brothers what he called "sermons" upon the perils of the Grand Tour and its almost certain adverse effects upon morals, health, and happiness. In 1787, when Peter asked Jefferson to permit him to make the Grand Tour, Jefferson refused. "There is no place where your pursuit of knowledge will be as little obstructed by foreign objects as in your own country," he told young Carr, "nor any wherein the virtues of the heart will be less exposed to be weakened. Be good, be learned, and be industrious, and you will not want the aid of traveling to render you precious to your country, dear to your friends, happy within yourself." [15]

But, as Jefferson learned, a Virginia plantation could be quite as destructive of morals as the Grand Tour. For slave women offered a constant temptation to white men, and the Carr brothers did not permit their studies, their uncle's exhortations, or, apparently, their moral sense, to stand in way of the gratification of their sexual desires. They sowed their wild oats at Monticello and brought forth an abundant crop of slave mulatto children.

It has been established by diligent research that Jefferson's presence at Monticello coincided approximately with the time of the conception of Sally's children, but no attention has been given to the whereabouts of Peter and Samuel Carr during these critical periods. It is probable that these were the occasions when the two brothers would have been at Monticello visiting their uncle and their cousins and, at the same time, enjoying surreptitiously the favors of the Hemings girls.

The only question in the minds of those who lived at Monticello was whether Peter or Samuel Carr was the father of Sally Hemings's children. Ellen Randolph Coolidge, Jefferson's granddaughter who grew up at Monticello, pointed to Samuel Carr as "the most notorious good-natured Turk that ever was master of a black seraglio kept at other men's expense." Samuel Carr certainly had the opportunity to disport himself in the slave quarters at Monticello: he lived either at Monticello or nearby during most of his life; after his marriage, he had a house near Charlottesville, only a short ride from Monticello. Peter Carr, on the other hand, before he moved to Baltimore, may have been linked with Sally Hemings's sister. In any event, when Jefferson praised Peter Carr's "sound masculine talents" he had no idea that the Carr brothers' masculinity would be instrumental in drawing down upon his head one of the great scandals of the American presidency.[16]

The Carr brothers later expressed repentance to Thomas Jefferson Randolph for having caused distress to their uncle but neither of them came forward in 1802–1803 when scandal was at its height and when a confession would have been of most help to Jefferson. But it is doubtful if Jefferson would have consented under any circumstances to throw his nephews to Callender and the other journalist-wolves in order to refute their calumnies: he took the attitude that what went on at Monticello was no outsider's business. Accordingly, although he no doubt knew of what was going on, he maintained a tight-lipped silence toward the whole affair. The sexual escapades of the Carr brothers in the slave quarters was something one simply did not talk about at Monticello— no more than one talked about two other nephews who killed a black man or about the insanity of Thomas Mann Randolph or about the drunken tavern brawls of the wastrel who married one of Jefferson's granddaughters. Jefferson preserved his equanimity and his optimism by closing his mind to disagreeable events; the problem, as he saw it, was to derive instructive moral lessons even from misfortune when it came.

Nevertheless, if Jefferson can convincingly be absolved of the charge of being the father of five mulatto children, the fact remains that at Monticello he presided over a scene of miscegenation. If he made any effort to stop the Carr brothers, he was certainly not successful in the attempt. Possibly he could not prevent it: Sally may have been truly in love with Samuel or Peter Carr. Although Jefferson's daughters wished that he would send all the Hemingses away, he refused to part with them probably because, as his late wife's relatives, he felt responsible for them and because they did not wish to go. Moreover, ordering them to leave Monticello might have been construed as a capitulation to Callender and his calumnies. And to bid them begone would, at least by implication, confirm Callender's charge that Jefferson had something shameful to conceal.

If Callender's version of Jefferson's relations with "Dusky Sally" is given the accreditation of historical scholarship, the Jefferson family cannot escape complicity: its members either resolutely closed their eyes to what was going on at Monticello, were completely deceived by the wily president, or deliberately lied to aid in the cover-up. This is a serious charge to bring upon the testimony of James Callender and of the tale allegedly told by Sally Hemings to her son. There is no instance in American history where the reputation of an American president and the honor, integrity, and credibility of his family have been impugned by such flimsy evidence.*

🍁

Conceived in malice and disappointed ambition, the "Dusky Sally" story lent itself admirably to the cause of political partisanship, and it served that cause loyally and well for almost a century. In the presidential campaign of 1860, for example, Abraham Lincoln was falsely reported in Republican newspapers to have expressed his detestation of Thomas Jefferson for having a black mistress and keeping as slaves the children she conceived by him. The clear intent of this fabrication was to make it appear that the patron saint of Southern Democrats had feet of Virginia clay and that he and his party deserved the contempt and abhorrence of all decent Americans. It made no difference to Republican journalists that in actuality Lincoln admired Jefferson and gave no credence whatever to the lurid tales of the moral aberrations and sexual escapades of the author of the Declaration of Independence.

During the Reconstruction period, the Sally Hemings scandal and the "Congo Harem" myth again surfaced in the newspapers. The hoary canard had not outlived its political usefulness, for the name of Thomas Jefferson was still a force to be reckoned with by politicians of both parties. The exigencies of the Republican "Southern Strategy" of the postwar years required that the former slaveholding aristocrats of the South who, beaten and discredited as they were, still constituted a threat to Republican hegemony in the states of the late Confederacy be portrayed as monsters of lubricity who prostituted slave women to their

---

* Dumas Malone, the leading contemporary authority on Jefferson, rejects James Callender's erotic connection of Jefferson and Sally Hemings as the work of "the vengeful pen of an unscrupulous man. . . . promulgated in a spirit of bitter partisanship." But Fawn Brodie is conspicuously free of the rancor and partisanship that actuated Callender. Her efforts are directed toward "humanizing" the master of Monticello by portraying him as the ardent and devoted lover of an attractive slave woman. To explain the eager popular acceptance of this new perception of Jefferson requires recognition of the fact that in the post-Watergate, post-Vietnam era there exists a strong compulsion to belittle the great men of the past, not excluding the Founding Fathers of the American Republic, to the stature of contemporary politicians. It is somehow consoling to believe that Jefferson had a slave mistress, that he brought up his own children as slaves and succeeded in concealing the fact from the American people by lies, evasions, and subterfuges. Finally, Jefferson's romantic involvement with a "black" slave woman serves dramatically to refute his often-expressed conviction that whites and blacks could not live together in the United States in amity and concord. By virtue of practicing integration at Monticello, regardless of what he preached, Jefferson becomes in Ms. Brodie's book one of the culture-heroes of the present-day integration movement—and this despite the "fact" that he raised five of his natural children as slaves.

lust and consigned their mulatto children to the auction-block or the brothel. If Thomas Jefferson, the exemplar of all virtues to which the Southern leadership had laid claim, could be shown to have deceived the American people about his intimacy with a slave girl, Southern Democrats were in deep trouble indeed. To the slogan used by Republicans during Reconstruction—"vote as you shot"—could be added the equally cogent exhortation—vote against the party of white debauchers of black women.[16]

The Gilded Age was distinguished, among other things, by the journalistic hoax and stunt, and the newspapers of that period were no less sensational, bitterly partisan, and irresponsible than those of Jefferson's day. It was in this prostituted press that the Sally Hemings story was revived, embellished, and given, at least to credulous political partisans, the final seal of authenticity.

In 1873, after the congressional and presidential elections of 1872 had demonstrated that the Democratic Party, despite the best efforts of the Republicans to brand it as "the party of rebellion," was not yet prepared to lie down and die, the Republican party sorely needed a new accession of propaganda against the Southern aristocracy. An enterprising journalist who was more than incidentally a rabid Republican unearthed a veritable trove of propaganda in an unlikely spot: Pee Wee, Pike County, Ohio.

Pee Wee was the home of Madison Hemings. He and his brother Eston, after being freed by Jefferson's will, remained in Albemarle County, Virginia, with their mother until she died in 1836. Eston married a white woman and "passed" into the white community, but Madison married a black before moving to Pike County, Ohio, where he appeared on the census records as a "Negro." Actually, he was seven-eighths Caucasian.

In 1873 the editor of the Pike County *Republican* published a journalistic scoop: an interview with Madison Hemings in which he asserted that before she died his mother had told him that he and his brothers and sisters were the children of Thomas Jefferson; that she had conceived her first child by Jefferson in France in 1789 (the child, born in 1790, had died in infancy); and that Jefferson, while minister to France, had entered into a bargain with Sally Hemings to the effect that in exchange for her favors all the children born of this union would eventually be set free.* [17]

Whatever its claim to authenticity, this is strictly an "as told to" account. Madison Hemings had only a rudimentary education, and he

---

* In Callender's version, this child must have been "Yellow Tom" or "President Tom." But Madison Hemings made no mention of an older brother of that name; on the contrary, he specifically claimed to have been told by his mother that her first child by Jefferson had died. Her first surviving child, Harriet, was born in 1795.

could not possibly have used the stilted overblown "literary" language in which the "interview" is couched: among other things, he is made to say that Sally Hemings was "enciente" (sic) by Thomas Jefferson when they returned to Monticello in 1789 and that his brother and sister who went North were never "suspected of being tainted with African blood." Did Madison Hemings, who was of African descent on his mother's side and who had married a black, really consider "African blood" a taint or did the editor of the Pike County *Republican* simply reveal his bias? [18] His objective is clear enough: to induce the newly enfranchised Southern blacks to vote Republican and to destroy all possibility that the Southern aristocracy could resume its position as the titular leader of its section against the North. But, as sometimes occurs when politicians and journalists deplore racial discrimination, equality is something to be exported, not practiced at home.

If Madison Hemings actually told this story to the editor of the Pike County *Republican,* doubtless he hoped to achieve instant fame as the unacknowledged natural son of Thomas Jefferson. Madison was now an old man and, like most blacks and mulattoes in nineteenth century America, he probably felt cheated by life. In the community in which he lived, he was classed as "colored" and no doubt was treated as such by his white neighbors—which meant that they had nothing to do with him. But if he could prove that he were a natural son of a president of the United States, his position would change dramatically overnight: he would appear not only as good as a white man but as the white man's superior and, as such, entitled to the respect and consideration that had hitherto been denied him.

It was clearly this desire to gain social standing and respectability that prompted slaves to assume the family name of their master: for example, Isaac Jefferson, one of Jefferson's slaves whose life story appeared in the Pike County *Republican* along with Madison Hemings's, took the surname of Jefferson because, as he said, "it would give me more dignity to be called after so eminent a man." (For the same reason, slaves in classical antiquity, upon receiving their freedom, often took the name of their master.)

What is at issue in the Madison Hemings interview is not his claim to be related to Thomas Jefferson (since he was almost certainly the natural son of one or the other of the Carr brothers, who were themselves blood relations of Jefferson) but his claim to be the natural son of Jefferson himself. It is this assertion which tends to place him in the company of those who, for whatever motives, have throughout history laid claim of descent from famous men without producing evidence which would establish its validity in a court of law. His unsupported, undocumented testimony, conveyed in a politically suspect vehicle, the Pike

County *Republican,* would certainly not carry conviction in such a court.* [19]

Even if Sally Hemings did, in fact, relate the story printed in the Pike County *Republican* to her son, the possibility remains that her purpose was to raise him in his own sadly battered esteem and to conceal her own dereliction in having children out of wedlock by one of the Carr brothers. The offense of going "outside her race" (legally, of course, she was both a "black" and a slave) might be mitigated by the exalted station occupied by her paramour. Her story conveys the clear impression that she submitted, not altogether willingly and not without exacting conditions, to the then United States minister to France and later president of the United States, not to just an ordinary white man. On the other hand, as the mistress of Samuel Carr and the mother of his children, she lost the stature bestowed upon her by James Callender. Manifestly, if she is acknowledged to have been the concubine of a president of United States, she acquires an éclat denied every other slave woman in American history.[20] For that reason alone, the temptation on her part to confirm Callender's allegations must have been very strong. It is true that one American vice-president, Richard Johnson, admitted to having a slave mistress and to having children by her, but no president confessed to it or, except for President Jefferson, was ever so accused. We know virtually nothing of Sally Hemings or her motives: she is hardly more than a name, "Dusky Sally." Except by making a leap of the imagination far beyond the confines of historical fact, we cannot make her the heroine of a great American love story or as a paragon of purity, self-sacrifice, and tender devotion. And yet it is not beyond the realm of possibility that she was all these things to Samuel Carr.

As regards Jefferson, on the other hand, we know a great deal about his character, motives, ideals, preoccupations, and attitudes. It is on the basis of this knowledge that the man should—indeed, must—be gauged by successive generations of Americans. Jefferson should be—indeed, he asked to be—judged by the moral standards he preached to his daughters, his grandchildren, and the American people in general and by which he judged others, especially Alexander Hamilton. If, then, he is to be ac-

* In *American Heritage,* October 1976, Fawn Brodie presents new "evidence" bearing upon the claims of certain individuals to be the descendants of Thomas Jefferson. On the basis of interviews with and materials provided by people living in California, Pennsylvania, New York, and New Jersey, Ms. Brodie identifies two groups or "families" who claim descent from Eston and Madison Hemings respectively. Instead, however, of exploring the possibility that these individuals might be related to Thomas Jefferson through his nephews Peter and Samuel Carr, she represents them as direct lineal descendants of Jefferson himself. In her "humanized" perception of Jefferson, his paternity of the Hemings children is raised to the dignity of an irrefutable fact, a conclusion which is not established in *American Heritage* or in her *Intimate History.*

cused of seducing a sixteen-year-old slave girl and having children by her whom he held as slaves, it is in utter defiance of the testimony he bore over the course of a long lifetime of the primacy of the moral sense and his loathing of racial mixture. How could Jefferson hope to escape the avenging Deity who, he believed, struck down whole nations as well as individuals who closed their ears to the injunctions of the moral sense? How can his frequent assertions that his conscience was clear and that his enemies did him a cruel and wholly unmerited injustice be reconciled with the Jefferson of the Sally Hemings story?—unless, of course, Jefferson is set down as a practitioner of pharisaical holiness who loved to preach to others what he himself did not practice?

If the answer to these questions is that Jefferson was simply trying to cover up his illicit relations with Sally Hemings—not to mention the "Congo Harem" he allegedly maintained at Monticello—he deserves to be regarded as one of the most profligate liars and consummate hypocrites ever to occupy the presidency. To give credence to the Sally Hemings story is, in effect, to question the authenticity of Jefferson's faith in freedom, the rights of man, and the innate controlling faculty of reason and the sense of right and wrong. It is to infer that there were no principles to which he was inviolably committed, that what he acclaimed as morality was no more than a rhetorical facade for self-indulgence, and that he was always prepared to make exceptions in his own case when it suited his purpose. In short, beneath his sanctimonious and sententious exterior lay a thoroughly adaptive and amoral public figure—like so many of those of the present day. Even conceding that Jefferson was deeply in love with Sally Hemings does not essentially alter the case: love does not sanctify such an egregious violation of his own principles and preachments and the shifts and dodges, the paltry artifices, to which he was compelled to resort in order to fool the American people. "There is no vice that doth so cover a man with shame," said Francis Bacon, whom Jefferson accounted one of the three greatest men who ever lived, "as to be found false and perfidious." *

---

* Professor Page Smith, elaborating in his *Revealing Biography* upon the theses advanced by Fawn Brodie in her *Intimate History*, concludes that Sally Hemings was "in one sense the perfect mate. She belonged to Jefferson in two ways: she was his lover and his property." (The contemporary reader will observe with interest what constitutes the "perfect mate.") Without citing his sources (Professor Smith cheerfully dispenses with footnotes, citations of sources, bibliographies, and the other irksome appurtenances of historical scholarship) he describes Sally as "intelligent, handsome, perhaps beautiful," and, above all, good in bed where Jefferson, too, apparently excelled. According to Professor Smith, Jefferson derived peculiar pleasure from this relationship because "for a man bitterly opposed to slavery, the taking of a slave woman as a mistress was both a kind of expiation for his guilt and a self-crucifying act." By this logic, Jefferson's tormented passion for Sally Hemings caused him to experience delight in penitentially abasing himself before his own slave. The ecstacy and the agony must have become almost unbearably exquisite when he made his own children slaves. See Smith 1976, pp. 206–211.

~ 21 ~

Jefferson and Maria Cosway

———◆———

FOR JEFFERSON TO HAVE CONDUCTED A CLANDESTINE LOVE AFFAIR with a slave woman and to have raised his children as slaves is completely at variance with his character, insofar as it can be determined by his acts and words, the strict moral code by which he professed to live and which he constantly enjoined upon others, especially young men and women, and his conception of women and their place in society. He was not a womanizer; in his relations with the opposite sex he was temperate to the point of continence. On the one occasion when he was tempted to transgress the bounds of discretion and propriety, he curbed his sexual desire—with the result that the love affair did not go beyond a romantic friendship. After the death of his wife, his "affairs of the heart" did not usually involve more than his affections. This circumstance served as his answer to his calumniators: those who knew him, he said, could not believe him guilty of the crimes, follies, and flagrant immorality of which he stood accused by his political enemies.

At bottom, Jefferson was far more a representative figure of the Romantic Enlightenment than of the Age of Reason. As a young man he had abandoned himself to literary raptures over his love for "Belinda" (Rebecca Burwell), and he always spoke of himself as being peculiarly susceptible to passion: "When I was young, mathematics were the passion of my life"; he was "passionately" fond of the poetry of Ossian, a legendary Celtic bard of the third century B.C. (Jefferson never realized that the wild and romantic poetry he so much admired was wholly the work of James Macpherson, a minor Scottish poet and a contemporary of Jefferson himself); he was "passionately" in love with poetry, music, painting and sculpture. An inveterate and incorrigible romantic, he romanticized farming, the noble savage, the common people, and the natural scenery of the United States. He discerned grandeur and beauty in mountains when to most men of the eighteenth century they were simply repulsive and inconvenient excrescences upon the landscape. He declared that the

177

passage of the Potomac River through the Blue Ridge was "one of the most stupendous scenes in nature" and that the spectacle of the Natural Bridge near Lexington, Virginia produced in him an indescribable rapture. Who but a romantic would have built his house upon a mountaintop and would have described Monticello in such terms as did Jefferson: "With what majesty do we there ride above the storms! How sublime to look down into the workshop of Nature, to see her clouds, hail, snow, rain, thunder, all fabricated at our feet!" In nature, Jefferson discovered an awesome beauty, not merely immutable laws.[1]

As a man of feeling, Jefferson enjoyed, especially in early manhood, a rich emotional life: he "melted into tenderness" easily, he rejoiced in the opportunity of mingling his tears with those of a friend who had met with misfortune, and he delighted in "a feast of sentiment." His favorite novelist was Lawrence Sterne who coined the word "sentimental." From early life onward, he recognized that the romantic side of his nature threatened to undermine and even to usurp the high place the early eighteenth century assigned to pure reason.

As a young man, Jefferson rejected the Stoic ideal of disdain for human passion, desire, and enjoyment of the things usually accounted good in this world; in his opinion, the Stoics mistook the nature of the real world and the nature of man. Instead, Jefferson found himself drawn to the Epicurean ethic which, while admitting the reality and the necessity of the passions, sought to control them by the exercise of reason. The Epicureans taught that while the passions constituted the true life of man, they must be kept under tight rein in order to attain the serenity, tranquillity, happiness, and right conduct sought by every man.[2]

The Epicurean ideal of dynamic passions harnessed and directed by reason became the ideal of the eighteenth century Enlightenment. Diderot, for example, recognized that "it is only the passions, and the great passions, that can raise the soul to great things" in poetry, painting, rhetoric, and music; but, Lord Bolingbroke cautioned, virtue consisted in "the wise use and application of these appetites, desires and passions, according to the laws of reason; and therefore often in opposition to their own blind impulse." Although he was not insensitive to the glorification of sensibility and untrammeled freedom of the passions that marked the transition from the Age of Reason to the Romantic Rebellion, Jefferson stood midway between the earlier implicit trust in reason and the later exaltation of uninhibited emotionalism; he remained an Epicurean cast in the eighteenth century mold who never abandoned his faith in the utility of the directive power of Reason.[3]

Since the sexual drive is among the most powerful and least tractable of the passions, Jefferson was especially concerned lest reason lose control—as, indeed, it did in one instance in his early life. From a relatively early age, he seems to have known exactly what he wanted in a woman—

and he waited until he was thirty years old for the right one to come along. His future wife, he decided, must be intelligent, talented, a good companion, and, withal, a good homemaker. (He did not add that she must be rich, but it cannot be entirely fortuitous that he married an heiress.) He found these qualities in his wife Martha, widow of Bathurst Skelton and daughter of John Wayles, with whom he enjoyed, in his own words, ten years of "unchequered happiness" until her death in 1782. Little is known of Martha Jefferson because Jefferson destroyed all the correspondence that had passed between them; apparently the memory of her was too poignant to be recalled by a single line she had written. Like her husband, Martha Jefferson loved music, and they spent many hours playing duets, she at the pianoforte, he on the violin. It was a source of mutual gratification and happiness which he recommended to all married couples: music, he said, "furnishes a delightful recreation for the hours of respite from the cares of the day." [4]

Martha Jefferson bore Thomas Jefferson six children in ten years (a child by her previous marriage died before her marriage to Jefferson). Only two of these children survived infancy. Martha died at the age of thirty-three, worn out with childbearing. Jefferson never acknowledged any responsibility for his wife's premature death: in the eighteenth century, a woman was expected to bear as many children as Nature allowed. Although she had been ill and confined to her bed for months, he was so distraught by her death that he fainted and for several months remained in the seclusion of his chamber at Monticello. The Man of Feeling was plunged from the heights of personal happiness to the abyss of loneliness and despair.[5]

It was widely believed by Jefferson's close friends and by the slaves at Monticello that on her deathbed Martha Jefferson exacted of her husband a promise that would never put their children under the care of a stepmother. This was usually given as the reason for Jefferson's failure to remarry. It is an explanation entirely in accord with his romantic idiosyncrasy: by remaining true to the promise given his dying wife, he could be true to the essence of the romantic spirit. This decision was made easier for him because the ten years of unalloyed happiness with Martha had made it impossible for him really to love another woman. He had expended so much of his emotional life upon his wife that it might be truly said that no other woman could take her place. And, finally, the too few years of bliss abruptly terminated by Martha's death, taught him that happiness, when once attained, is exceedingly fragile and evanescent.[6]

❧

In France Jefferson discovered a new world—a world of attractive, intelligent, emancipated, and sophisticated women who presided over the salons. Many of them—Madame Helvetius, Madame Brillon, the Duchesse de Deux Ponts, the Comtesse de Polignac, Madame d'Houdelot—were admirers of Franklin whom Jefferson "inherited" when the former returned to the United States. While Jefferson paid his devoirs to these ladies and even added a few more to his own coterie, he never pretended to be at ease in salon society; for he was profoundly disturbed by the fact that these women, stepping out of their "natural" role as housewives and mothers, had extended their influence over politics to such a degree that Jefferson feared that France was in danger of becoming a matriarchy. From the influence of women upon politics he apprehended every evil; "female intrigue" in matters of state seemed to portend the downfall of the French monarchy. "The tender breasts of ladies were not formed for political convulsions," he declared, "and the French ladies miscalculate much their own happiness when they wander from the true field of their influence into that of politicks." [7]

To this idea of woman as a domestic being removed by an ordinance of Nature from the intrigue, acrimony, and brawls of politics Jefferson adhered throughout his life; to him it was a self-evident truth certified by both reason and the moral sense. In every society, primitive or civilized, in which men and women lived as Nature intended, it appeared that the two sexes had separate functions to which they were genetically adapted: to women were consigned the domestic duties, whereas men were constituted for the task of providing food, shelter, and protection. "Men," said Antoine Louis Claude Destutt de Tracy, a French economist and sociologist whose work Jefferson translated and pronounced to be superior even to Montesquieu, "are the natural representatives and defenders of those they love; these should not assume their place, nor contend with them. There is between beings of constitutions so different and so necessary to each other, a dissimilitude, but not an inequality." [8]

Although Jefferson praised the Indians for their "masculine sound Understanding" (and thereby tacitly indicated that the reasoning faculties were essentially a male faculty and attribute), he never expressed the "suspicion" as he allowed himself in the case of blacks and whites, that men and women were unequal in intellectual capacity. Nor, on the other hand, did he every say that they were equal. To him the question was unimportant: it was only necessary to realize that Nature had ordained that the aptitudes of the two sexes should complement each other in order to create a harmonious whole—the family. In Jefferson's opinion, the family was one of the supreme achievements of the Author of Nature, and it was up to man—and also to woman—to keep it free of jars, rivalry, and contention.

In his attitude toward women and their place in society, it could be argued that Jefferson was simply reflecting the conventional wisdom of the eighteenth century. As Rousseau said, "the education of women should be always relative to the men. To please, to be useful to us, to make us love and esteem, to educate us when young, and to take care of us when we grow up, to advise, to console us, to render our lives easy and agreeable." Edward Gibbon declared that the "female virtues" were primarily those of chastity, obedience, and domesticity; domestic enjoyments, he said, were the source of every other pleasure. (But Gibbon never married; hence he did not experience personally the felicity of which he spoke so magisterially.) [9]

In America, Jefferson rejoiced, women knew their place—which was in the home and, more specifically, in the nursery. For him it was one of the special charms of the United States that there the female "does not endeavor to extend herself beyond the domestic line." And, instead of gadding frivolously about town as did Parisian women in a frenetic, empty-headed pursuit of pleasure which they confused with happiness, "some on foot, some on horses, and some in carriage hunting pleasure in the streets, in routs and assemblies, and forgetting that they have left it behind in their nurseries," American women were content with "the tender and tranquil amusements of domestic life," and never troubled their pretty heads about politics. In this blessed land where men and women had learned to stay out of each others' affairs, women were content to "soothe and calm the minds of their husbands returning ruffled from political debate" rather than starting an argument over politics or, indeed, over anything else.* [10]

In the United States, during Jefferson's presidency, a female politician was said to be only slightly less disgusting than a female infidel. Dolley Madison, although she knew more public men than any other woman of her day, never talked politics and never tried to influence her husband's political decisions. Her discretion and forbearance won for her the reputation of a model wife. Captain Basil Hall, an English traveler, remarked upon the rigid line of demarcation between the sexes in the United States: in New England, he observed, men and women were separated in church "as if they had belonged to different races," and everywhere in the Republic women were denied "the virtual control which women in England exercise over the conduct of men." In the United States, women seemed to be wholly occupied with replenishing the earth: the country swarmed with children. But Captain Hall found that the American Republic was the loser by wholly excluding the tenderness, the compassion, and the civilizing, emolliative influence of women from public affairs.[11]

Since women were not called upon even to discuss politics, Jefferson

* Here Jefferson echoed Joseph Addison who in the *Spectator* advised the "dear creatures" to eschew politics since, he said, "there is nothing as bad for the Face as Party-zeal. It gives an ill-natured Cast to the Eye, and a disagreeable Sourness to the Look, besides that it makes the Lines too strong, and flushes them more than Brandy." See Willey 1964, p. 247.

saw no reason to give them the vote. Moreover—and this prospect gave Jefferson qualms—enfranchised women might take it into their heads to run for political office. "The appointment of a woman to office," Jefferson declared, "is an innovation for which the public is not prepared, nor am I." Women being thus excluded from public affairs, no effort need be made, Jefferson said, to educate them in any subjects which did not seem likely to be useful in their "natural" place as wives and mothers. They could profit from French, English grammar and spelling, arithmetic, letter writing, music, and dancing, but not from much more. The objective was to give them enough education so that they could instruct their children in the rudiments. Above all, Jefferson said, women must be taught to be industrious, for, as he observed, "no laborious person was ever yet hysterical." * [12]

Blacks might have taken a small measure of comfort from Jefferson's attitude toward women: if blacks were debarred from all participation in political affairs, they were not alone. Sex, like color, was a highly visible and no less decisive determinant. Still, Jefferson wished to encourage the development of the artistic talents of women and generally those aspects of their intelligence that made them worthy companions for their husbands and satisfactory tutors of their children.

If this were male chauvinism, Jefferson, in effect, defied his critics to make the most of it. In 1816 he declared that for men and women to mix promiscuously in public meetings with men would inevitably produce "deprivation of morals and ambiguity of issue." In plain English, bastards. During the American Revolution, John Adams said that bastards and legislators were begotten in Boston taverns, but Jefferson seemed to fear the same result if town meetings were opened to women. He apprehended a similar disconcerting outcome from the popular religious revivals held at night in Richmond, Virginia, where women "attended by their priests and sometimes henpecked husband, pour forth the effusions of their love of Jesus, in terms so amatory and carnal, as their modesty would permit them to use to a mere earthly lover." [13]

As Harriet Martineau pointed out, if the principle of equality between men and women were admitted, there was no way of conducting public affairs except by "promiscuous meetings," and these assemblages were no more likely to produce "ambiguity of issue" than meetings for worship, music, or dramatic entertainment. And if women were denied

---

* One of Jefferson's objections to the Indian way of life was that it reduced women to the status of beasts of burden, a degradation which he believed to be universally characteristic of the state of nature. Only in civilized society, he reasoned, could women attain their natural equality with men. In Jefferson's view, women, far more than men, had a vital need to escape from the state of nature.

  This idea was probably derived from John Millar's *Observations Concerning the Distinction of Ranks in Society* (1771). But Millar's surmise had been disproved by subsequent research. See Boyd 11, p. 420, 446n, 458 and M. Harris 1968, p. 31.

the right to participate in the government of the nation, how, she asked, could the position of women be reconciled with the principle that all governments derive their just powers from the consent of the governed? After all, women were taxed, punished for crimes and misdemeanors, and required to obey the laws without having given, either actually or virtually, their assent to any law. On this issue, she sorrowfully concluded, Jefferson was the advocate of the tyranny of man over woman.* [14]

🍁

In France, Jefferson was scandalized by the "depravity" of morals exhibited by men and women in the high social circles in which he moved. As he saw it, fidelity to the marriage bed was such a rarity as to be accounted an extraordinary event: the only fidelity recognized by these fine ladies and gentlemen was faithfulness to a mistress or to a lover observed over the course of a year or more.

The fervor and sense of outraged righteousness with which Jefferson castigated the French aristocracy for their laxness of morals, tended to create the impression that he was a New World Puritan in an Old World Babylon. Actually, Jefferson was displaying the animus characteristic of most revolutionaries and social reformers, Nazis and Communists included, against moral laxness, especially sexual license. While it is hardly true to say that revolutionaries are themselves moralists, they are usually outraged by immorality in other people and are quick to straighten them out. John Adams, too, was scandalized by the "profligate females" he saw in Paris, but Adams, of course, was from Boston. Jefferson would probably not have objected to the comparison between himself and an Old Roman—Cato, for example, inveighing against vice and moral corruption of the Roman aristocracy—but he certainly would have rejected any comparison with the Reverend Cotton Mather.

Even Gouverneur Morris, who succeeded Jefferson as minister to France and who was never accused of being a Puritan, reported that an American mind boggled at "the Degree of Depravity" which prevailed in aristocratic French society. But Morris was shocked not so much by sexual license as by the lack of truthfulness and fidelity to promises he found in Paris and Versailles. In other respects, however, he entered fully into the spirit of the *haut monde:* he promptly took a mistress, and before he was recalled by the United States government he had cut a wide swath through the upper crust of French society. Morris had no reason

---

* In the matter of women's rights, Jefferson was far from being abreast of the most advanced thought of his day. In 1792, Mary Wollstonecraft published *Vindication of the Rights of Women* in which she demanded equality of opportunity with men in work and in the professions; educational reforms, including coeducation in state-supported schools equality in the custody of the children of a marriage; and the responsibility by the father in the case of illegitimate children.

to lament the lack of conjugal fidelity of the fashionable ladies whose boudoirs he frequented.[15]

Of course, Jefferson's and Gouverneur Morris's strictures really applied only to that part of upper-class society with which they were acquainted; Jefferson knew little of the bourgeoisie because he did not move in their circle. When Jefferson spoke of "the world," he meant that small part of it he knew from experience; and in France it was almost wholly confined to the intellectual, the aristocratic, and the artistic community. Had Jefferson extended the circle of his acquaintances beyond the confines of the Parisian *haut monde,* he might have found among middle-class French men and women the same straitlaced, puritanical attitude he prized among Americans.

In America, Jefferson's friend Brissot de Warville said, men did not "make it a business to pay court to the women"; in France, on the other hand, Jefferson complained, they did little else. Every man was expected to play the gallant, to compliment women fulsomely, and to pretend to be a little in love with every woman under the age of eighty. Jefferson never succeeded in matching Franklin's skill in making women feel that they were special objects of his devotion (he conspicuously lacked the touch of "roguishness" that made Franklin irresistible to women), but he did conform to the dictates of fashion by paying court to women he specially admired.[16]

Without exception, the women singled out by Jefferson for special attention, besides being intelligent, artistic, or gifted in some other way, were either young or old—young enough to be his daughter or old enough to be his aunt, and usually with husbands lurking somewhere in the background. With married women he felt secure against embarrassing complications; he trusted their husbands to understand that his intentions were platonic. Every woman, American, English, or French, with whom he was on familiar terms in Paris, was married. As a young man he "offered love" to a married lady, and he married a widow. Except for a brief and abortive adolescent affair with "Belinda," Jefferson fought shy of virgins. In Paris the roster of his "female friends" included Madame de Tesse, Lafayette's cousin but so advanced in years that she was usually mistaken for his aunt; Mrs. Anne Bingham of Philadelphia, a vivacious beauty half Jefferson's age; Madame de Corny, a beautiful young woman with a husband much older than herself (with her Jefferson frequently took walks in the Bois de Boulogne) ; and the Comtesse d'Houdelot, the former mistress of Saint-Lambert, but now well into middle age.

With these women Jefferson shared common interests in history, gardening, art, and architecture; politics alone was a forbidden subject. Jefferson was not attracted to women who could not converse well and whose intellect did not in some way complement his own. His friendship with Madame de Tesse, for example, was based upon her expertise in gardening and architecture and her affection for "whatever is Roman and noble." On his tour of France, he wrote her that he thought of her frequently in southern France "where Roman taste, genius, and magnificence excites [sic] ideas analogous to yours at every step." But the woman who came closest to fulfilling his ideal of womanhood, with the exception of his own wife, was Abigail Adams, the wife of John Adams. With her, Jefferson maintained a close friendship. The admiration was mutual: Abigail Adams said that Jefferson was "one of the choice ones of the earth"—until politics did them part.[17]

The woman with whom Jefferson conducted his most intimate romantic liaison in Paris met, in most respects, the exacting standards he always maintained in affairs of the heart. Maria Cosway was the wife of Richard Cosway, a fashionable painter and miniaturist. Born in Italy, the daughter of an English hotel-keeper named Hadfield, she was an artist in her own right: an accomplished musician and painter, she had exhibited at the Royal Academy, and she was a member of the Florentine Academy of Fine Arts. Among her works was a set of aquatints depicting "The Progress of Female Virtue and of Female Dissipation." In London, she presided over a salon where some of the most brilliant and socially eminent of the *bon ton* congregated. A young, beautiful, and talented woman, she moved with poise and assurance in the artistic and half-artistic, half-Bohemian worlds of London and Paris.[18]

In August 1786, Maria Cosway and her husband came to Paris where they were introduced to Jefferson by Colonel John Trumbull of Connecticut who had known the Cosways in London and who was then engaged in painting the signing of the Declaration of Independence. The result was electrifying: Jefferson, who hitherto had confined himself largely to business and enjoyment of the art and architecture of Paris, suddenly shed his stiffness and reserve and became a man-about-town, a gallant who dressed in the latest French fashions, dashed about Paris in his phaeton, and frequented the Palais-Royal and the Bois de Boulogne.

With the Cosways, Jefferson for the first time since his wife's death felt gay, carefree, and lighthearted. For a few weeks the pall that had lain for four years upon his spirit lifted: during "those charming moments" when they sallied forth in his phaeton to visit St. Cloud, Marly, and St. Germain, "hills, valleys, chateaux, gardens, rivers, every object," he said, "wore its liveliest hue." At least part of the happiness he had lost on that dreadful day in 1782 seemed to have been recovered in the company of the Cosways.[19]

One of Mrs. Cosway's qualities that Jefferson found especially endearing was her complete indifference to politics: she never stirred up controversies by advancing an opinion upon subjects over which, Jefferson thought, ladies ought not to "wrinkle their foreheads." As a result, he found her house "an asylum for tranquillity," very unlike the salons where politically minded ladies held forth on affairs of state as though France were under a petticoat regime.[20]

With Mrs. Cosway, Jefferson established what in the eighteenth century was called a romantic friendship. It was a relationship with erotic overtones, replete with professions of love, but based mainly upon mutual self-esteem, common intellectual and artistic interests—a conjoining of spirits in which physical passion, while an essential ingredient, was subordinate and kept under strict control. In England, if not in France, it was not expected to lead to adultery, divorce, or other unseemly complications. One of the cardinal rules of romantic friendship was that the lady's virtue remained intact.

Jefferson's friendship embraced both Mr. and Mrs. Cosway: during their rambles into the country and when in the evenings they dined together, Richard Cosway was usually present. When Jefferson declared that he loved "the Cosways," that he would continue to love them all his life and that "if fortune should dispose them or me on one side of the globe, and me on the other, my affections shall pervade its whole mass to reach them," he was of course indulging, although with perfect sincerity, in the wildest romantic hyperbole: in these verbal effusions, Jefferson gave vent to the sentimental romanticism that welled up from the depth of his being. He loved the Cosways' talk about art, their sallies of wit, and the kindness and consideration they always showed him. His hope was to become a part of their charmed circle. Although Richard Cosway was much older than his wife (as, indeed, was Jefferson himself) and his wife was obviously not in love with him, Jefferson's game plan, at least in the beginning, was not to usurp Mr. Cosway's place in Mrs. Cosway's affections; the rules of romantic friendship required that he profess his devotion to both husband and wife.

After almost a month in the company of the Cosways, the idyll was rudely interrupted by an accident. In the middle of September, Jefferson tried to leap a fence in the *Petit Cours*; he fell and dislocated his right wrist which, not being properly set, never completely healed. For the rest of his life Jefferson suffered pain in his wrist, and he was even compelled to learn to write with his left hand. Jumping fences, he decided, was "one of those follies from which good cannot come, but ill may." [21]

During the late summer days with the Cosways, Jefferson received an unmistakable warning signal: a "generous spasm of the heart" told him that he was in danger of losing control of that organ. This premonition was confirmed when the Cosways left Paris: the night of their departure, Jefferson later wrote Mrs. Cosway, he tossed and turned from one side of the bed to the other all night, but he rather spoiled the effect by saying that his discomfort was partly owing to the pain from his "poor crippled wrist." But he left no doubt that their departure had desolated him: he pictured himself "rent into fragments by the force of my grief" and as the most wretched of all earthly beings—the kind of license allowed romantic as well as poetic spirits. In a calmer vein, he said that he had spent hours talking with his friends "of the goodness, the amiability and talents of Mr. and Mrs. Cosway." It was still "Mr. and Mrs. Cosway," not Maria Cosway alone, who had captured his heart.[22]

But this fiction was becoming increasingly difficult to maintain. Jefferson could hardly conceal from himself the perturbing truth that it was not "Mr. and Mrs. Cosway" but Maria Cosway who monopolized his affections. His feelings for her had clearly passed beyond the metes and bounds established by the conventions of romantic friendship: as a result, he was compelled to choose between beating a strategic retreat or permitting himself to be drawn into a love affair with all the complications it inevitably entailed. After all, he had no reason to believe that Mr. Cosway would obligingly play the role of the complaisant husband if Jefferson, throwing caution to the winds, made Mrs. Cosway his mistress.

With the Cosways gone, the gaiety, irresponsibility, and exuberance he had experienced in their company quickly vanished. He again felt the oppressive sense of lost happiness, of a bliss that had ended forever at Monticello; as he wrote Mrs. Cosway, he feared that he was destined to lose everything he loved. And, he added, he had already lost so much that he could not bear to lose more. True happiness with other human beings, he had learned, required the knowledge that there would be no parting. As the remembrance of things past gained ascendancy, Jefferson was reminded that "the present joys are damped by a consciousness that they are passing from us; and past ones are only the subjects of sorrow and regret."[23]

In short, Jefferson's quandary was not merely that he felt a strong desire to make Mrs. Cosway his mistress but that he feared that the romantic friendship upon which he had embarked might involve him too deeply in an emotional attachment which carried a high risk of being incontinently terminated. The question was whether the evanescent joys of this relationship were worth the pain, sorrow, and sense of deprivation to which it might lead.

On October 12, 1786, Jefferson set forth his dilemma to Maria Cosway in *A Dialogue Between the Head and the Heart*. The Head spoke in the name of reason; the Heart replied in the very different language of emotion. This dialogue was not, however, written under the spell which Mrs. Cosway had momentarily cast upon Jefferson but under the far more profound and enduring sense of his love for Martha Jefferson. If the *Dialogue Between the Head and the Heart* is, as Charles C. Tansill has written, "one of the notable love letters in the English language," its tone and much of its substance are derived from the ten years of "unchequered happiness" Jefferson spent at Monticello with his wife, not from the few weeks of enchantment he experienced in Paris during the summer of

1786. It is a nostalgic pavane, pervaded by the melancholy tenderness which since 1782 had invaded and tempered his naturally sanguine temperament.[24]

In the *Dialogue between the Head and the Heart,* the Head was the voice of Jefferson's experience telling him that "pleasure is always before us; but misfortune is at our side"; "there is no pleasure without pain, for such is the law of our existence; "do not bite at the bait of pleasure till you know there is no hook beneath it"; it was folly "to place your affections without reserve, on objects which you must so soon lose and whose loss when it comes must cost you such severe pangs"; and "nothing is ours which another may deprive us of." The counsel given by the Head was not to engage his affections deeply for he knew all too well that by following that course he had laid himself open to one of the severest blows fate can deal a man. When the Head told him that "the most effectual means of being secure against harm is to retire within ourself, and to suffice for your happiness," the reference is unmistakably in the first instance to Martha Jefferson and not to Maria Cosway. Jefferson had learned from bitter experience that to love without reserve is to risk being maimed emotionally for the remainder of one's life.

Surmising the truth, Mrs. Cosway realized that her real rival was not a living woman but the memory of Martha Jefferson. To her, it was incredible that Jefferson could spend his life mourning a dead woman. In February 1787, she bluntly asked him, "Are you to be painted in future ages sitting solitary and sad, on the beautiful Monticello tormented by the shadow of a woman?" Jefferson made no reply, mercifully unaware that he was to be painted in future ages as sitting happy and sexually satisfied on "the beautiful Monticello" with a slave mistress and a brood of illegitimate slave children.[25]

With the Head firmly in command, the now chastened and circumspect Heart was ready to resume the romantic friendship. There is no evidence that this relationship ever became more than an affair of the mind. Amid the effusive professions of love and devotion in Jefferson's correspondence with Mrs. Cosway there is no mention of kisses, caresses, and other overt acts of endearment. On his part, the tone is almost ethereal—which, indeed, is the modulation prescribed by romantic friendship. When Jefferson asked Maria Cosway to "love me much, and love me always" and complained that he loved her more than she loved him, he used the word "love" in its eighteenth century, not in its twentieth century, sense: it was interchangeable with "esteem," "friendship," and "affection." As he made clear in the *Notes on Virginia,* to him love was far more a spiritual relationship than the gratification of carnal appetite.

Soon after the Cosways left Paris, sober second thought seems to have given Jefferson a new perspective on the pair. Richard Cosway had the unfortunate trait of chattering like a monkey, and he was openly jealous of his wife's talent, even to the extent of begrudging her success at public exhibitions. Maria Cosway, after the initial euphoria had worn away, while admittedly talented, beautiful, amiable, good, and redolent of "that softness of disposition which is the ornament of her sex and the charms of ours," began to seem more and more a social butterfly, a species to which Jefferson was not strongly attracted. She dressed in the height of fashion, she was elaborately coiffured, pampered, and constantly surrounded by a "domestic cortege" of admirers. Finally, she was a devout Roman Catholic; she had been educated in a convent school and she had expressed the wish to become a nun. Most disconcerting of all, she submitted herself wholly to priests. In Jefferson's words, she "joined enthusiasm and religion." As a deist, Jefferson held religious enthusiasm in very low esteem. Understandably, Jefferson seems to have decided that the kind of social whirl in which he had been caught up with the Cosways was wholly out of character; he was not the Playboy of the Western World and he had business to do which he had sadly neglected.[26]

Even though London was only four days' journey from Paris, Jefferson made no effort to see Maria Cosway in the English capital. Instead, at this stage of his relations with Maria Cosway, he resembled one of Rousseau's characters who delighted in his absence from his inamorata because it provided him with an opportunity of writing letters to her. It has been said of Jefferson by one of his biographers that he was the sort of man who loves to play chess by correspondence; although he never played chess by that method, he certainly played at love by correspondence. In this particular, he was in rapport with the spirit of the eighteenth century, when the epistolary art was brought to perfection. Lord Chesterfield's *Letters to his Son* became a classic; and Samuel Richardson wrote entire novels in the form of letters. For Jefferson, in 1786–1789, letter writing provided a release from the inhibitions imposed upon personal relationships by his natural reserve and reticence; he found it far easier to make his declarations of love and affection to Mrs. Cosway and his other "female friends" in letters than in person.[27]

Despite the apparent triumph of Jefferson's Head over his Heart, Mrs. Cosway continued to hope that the Heart would prevail. She had no intention of allowing the affair to stop at mere romantic friendship and to expend itself in an exchange of letters. Instead, she invited Jefferson to embark upon the pursuit of happiness, and perhaps the game she offered was worth the candle. "Why," she asked plaintively, "do you say so many kind things" and yet do nothing to follow them up? She told Jefferson that when his Head said, "That is enough," his Heart ought to have told him that she wished for more substantial testimonials of his affection than letters. Seemingly, her obvious eagerness to bring the affair to a physical climax was whetted by Jefferson's elusiveness.[28]

Early in 1787, Jefferson began to tire even of the correspondence: he was too busy, too fatigued, his wrist pained him too much, the post office was too unreliable, for him to write. He seems to have supposed that he had said the last word in the *Dialogue* and that Mrs. Cosway ought to understand that the Head had prevailed. While he did not propose to put an end to the romantic friendship that had sprung up between them, he obviously intended to dispel any idea that the relationship would go beyond that stage.

In August 1787, Mrs. Cosway returned to Paris—this time without her husband. Apparently she was ready to place herself at Jefferson's disposal, and he might have made her his mistress without raising a single eyebrow in Paris. But if the lady was willing, Jefferson was not. Although they went for a few drives together and Jefferson gave a dinner party in her honor, he saw much less of her than during the summer of 1786. Jefferson excused his neglect of her on the ground that she was always surrounded by such a crowd of admirers that he could not break through. When he called on her, she was out; when she called on him, he was away on business. "You make every body love you," he told her. "You are sought and surrounded by all." Jefferson, who much preferred the social mode of "petit comité" to the "bustle and tumult" of large crowds, avoided the press of admirers at Mrs. Cosway's salon. "A fatality has attended my wishes," he said, but there was an element of deliberate design on his part in this chapter of misadventures; if he remained on the periphery of her entourage, it was because, as Mrs. Cosway said, he did not tell her that he wished to see her alone. Actually, the absence of Richard Cosway may have constrained rather than released Jefferson from his inhibitions; the presence of the husband was an implied guarantee that the affair would not get out of hand.[29]

The tender idyll of 1786 ended anticlimactically in the winter of 1787. In December, Mrs. Cosway invited Jefferson to a farewell breakfast, but when he arrived she had already left for London: she could not, confessed later, bear the pain of another parting; but Jefferson complained that by sparing him that pain she had deprived him of "the comfort of recollecting that pain." Parting was such sweet sorrow, but sweeter than parting was the memory of it. Only a confirmed Romantic could have said that.[30]

🍁

In December 1787, Maria Cosway acquired a rival for the Head and Heart of Thomas Jefferson. Mrs. Angelica Schuyler Church, Alexander Hamilton's sister-in-law, arrived in Paris with her daughter in the company of Colonel John Trumbull. Jefferson quickly struck up a romantic friendship with Angelica who, when she left Paris a few months later, put her daughter in his care. To Angelica Church he wrote letters in the same strain of devoted admiration, esteem, and affection that he assumed toward Mrs. Cosway. "I esteem you infinitely," he wrote; "I am with you always in spirit; be you with me sometimes." "The morning you left us," he wrote Mrs. Church in February 1788, "all was wrong. Even the sun shine was provoking, with which I never quarreled before. I took it into my head he shone only to throw light on our loss. . . . I mounted my horse earlier than common, and took by instinct the road you had taken." That evening he spent at Madame de Corny's talking about their loss, just as a little over a year before he had bewailed the loss of the Cosways.

Maria Cosway and Angelica Church knew each other well—they called each other sister—and they frequently talked about this strange, enigmatic, yet lovable and highly intelligent man. Had they exchanged the letters they received from him that would not have noticed much difference in content or in style for Jefferson addressed them both in the same playful tone and with the same delicate touch of Eros. Mrs. Cosway said that she was resigned to losing Jefferson: "If I did not love her [Angelica] so much I should fear her rivalship, but no I give you free permission to love her with all your heart, and I shall feel happy if I think you keep me in a little corner of it, when you admit her even to reigning Queen." But Mrs. Cosway's subsequent letters, replete with upbraidings for not writing more frequently and pleadings for him to come to London, belie her willingness to take second place in his affections.[31]

She found confirmation of her fears that she had been supplanted not only by the infrequency but by the changed tone of Jefferson's letters. Although he continued to assure Mrs. Cosway of his "sincere esteem," he now addressed her more frequently as "My dear Madam" and "my dear friend." Vexed with Jefferson for neglecting her, she said that she was a "Lady in a Passion" (of anger). "Your long silence is unpardonable," she declared, but she made clear that he would be pardoned if he came to London. She gave Colonel John Trumbull no peace until he had completed a portrait of Jefferson for her—no doubt, said Trumbull, "that she may scold *it*."[32]

Whatever she may have done to his portrait, she certainly scolded him in her letters. But she mixed her upbraidings with desperate appeals. "Pray write, pray write, pray write, and dont go to America without coming to England," she wrote in November 1788. She offered to dismiss her entourage of admirers and to see Jefferson alone, and, knowing Jefferson's opinion of England, especially after his humiliations at the hands of English officials when he visited that country in the spring of 1786, she deferred to his opinion in the obvious hope of endearing herself to him. She was disgusted, she told Jefferson, by the corruption, immorality, and intrigue that prevailed in English politics and by the capriciousness of the English people. But nothing seemed to work for her: Jefferson made a tour of Europe but he always contrived to be too busy to come to London.

As is permitted by the rules of the game of romantic friendship, Jefferson pursued two affairs simultaneously and with complete impartiality. When both Mrs. Cosway and Mrs. Church asked for a miniature portrait, Jefferson commissioned Col. Trumbull to paint portraits for each of them. When he rode alone in the Bois de Boulogne, Jefferson said that his thoughts turned irresistibly to both Angelica and Maria and that when he traveled up the Rhine he held Angelica by one hand and Maria by the other. In July 1788 he wrote almost identical letters to the ladies on the same day, urging them both to come to America and join him at Monticello.[33]

In the classic romantic friendship, it is *de rigueur* to dream impossible dreams and, half-playfully, to propose things that can never be. Jefferson, for instance, told Maria Cosway that when she came to the United States they would "make together the tour of the curiosities of that country." He offered her nothing more, however, than some excellent sites for sketching. "There you find original scenes for your pencil," especially the Natural Bridge and Niagara Falls. If she could not make the trip, "let us," he said, "be together in spirit"—a relationship which Jefferson seemed to prefer to her actual presence.[34]

It hardly could have raised Mrs. Cosway's spirits when Jefferson suggested in 1789 that she join him and Mrs. Church at Le Havre and embark with them for the United States. Mrs. Church, he was happy to say, had definitely decided to accompany him on the voyage, and with Mrs. Cosway along his pleasure would be doubled. But Mrs. Cosway had hoped to be alone with Jefferson, not to make the third member of a *ménage à trois*.

Had all the women Jefferson invited to make the tour of America with him accepted his offer, he would have suffered from an embarrassing plethora of female company. How this guided tour would have been received by the folks back home, Jefferson never seems to have considered, but, then, of course, he did not intend to be taken literally: it was all proposed in the spirit of romantic friendship. Had Jefferson been serious, he might have been given pause by the experience of the Comte de Moustier, the French minister to the United States, who in 1788 scandalized Americans by traveling about the country with his sister-in-law. Gossip immediately made her his mistress, and he had to be recalled to placate public opinion. Fortunately for Jefferson, none of the ladies insisted on holding him to his promise: had any one of them done so, his political career would have unceremoniously ended.[35]

After his return to the United States in 1789, Jefferson wisely abstained from indulging in future romantic friendships. The American public, he realized, might not understand that it was all innocent diversion: in the United States, as he well knew, "gallant adventures are little known and still less practiced" and "conjugal disloyalties, on either side, are punished by ineffaceable infamy." In Philadelphia his evenings were spent not in soirées with vivacious, talented, and beautiful women but with politicians and members of the American Philosophical Society. In this chaste company of kindred spirits, no female pundit ever appeared.[36]

✿

While Jefferson, after second thoughts, decided against proceeding with Mrs. Cosway beyond the strict confines of romantic friendship, he clearly wished to preserve that kind of friendship. Psychologically, it was imperative for him to enjoy a semierotic relationship with beautiful, talented, and preferably married women. The key to Jefferson's relations with Maria Cosway and Angelica Church lies, perhaps, in one line he wrote to Mrs. Church: "I am your brother." He could love them as sisters with violating the compact he had made with Martha. Many years before, he had lost the sister to whom he felt a closer attachment than to any other member of his family except his father. Jefferson needed the kind of affection he received from Maria Cosway and Angelica Church, and he needed to have an outlet for the superabundant affection that he felt for the people he loved.[37]

The romantic friendships carried on by Jefferson with Maria Cosway and Angelica Church reveal him as a man of delicate, aesthetic, fastidious, highly refined, almost feminine sensibility. If, at the same time that he was writing letters expressing a highly rarified affection for these two women, he descended to the grosser forms of sensuality, without any pretence whatever of romantic attachment, with a sixteen-year-old slave girl who wanted to be free rather than to become his mistress, then there must have been two very distinct Thomas Jeffersons inhabiting the same body.

Jefferson's passion for Sally Hemings is attributed by his most recent biographer, Fawn Brodie, to his "normal need for sexual fulfillment, coupled with the attraction of the forbidden." But the truth is, Jefferson was not an ordinary man and there is nothing in his career, other than his putative passion for Sally Hemings, to indicate that the forbidden had an unholy attraction for him.[38]

Almost certainly, after his wife's death, he sublimated the sexual drive in such activities as music—"the favorite passion of my soul"; architecture—building Monticello took over thirty years; gardening and farming; exercise (he spent one to three hours a day on horseback); reading, science, and philosophy; his love for his daughters and grandchildren and delight in the company of his friends. He was never bored; he habitually rose at dawn and a change of his work was his recreation. "A man em-

ployed is always happy," he said. ". . . the idle are the only wretched."
Jefferson's description of the pleasures derived from intellectual activity
reveal how it served, at least in his own case, as a compensation for other
pleasures. "Ever in our power," he said of the human mind, "always leading us to something new, never cloying, we ride, serene and sublime,
above the concerns of the mortal world, contemplating truth and nature,
matter and motion, the laws which bind up their existence, and that
eternal being who made and bound them up by these laws."

The art and architecture of France, together with his romantic friendships, afforded Jefferson some release from the emotional tensions generated by enforced sexual continence. He seemed to be as much affected
by the beauty of statues and buildings as by that of women. He said that
in France he had two love affairs—one with the statue of Diana at the
Château de Laye, and the other with the Maison Quarrée at Nimes where
he spent hours gazing "like a lover at his mistress." But he had many
other objects of love with which he kept trysts: the Pont de Neuilly, which
he regarded as the most handsome bridge in the world; the Hôtel de
Salm, where he was "violently smitten" with love at first sight, and which
he looked at almost daily sitting on the parapet of the Palais de Tuileries—
"twisting my neck to see the object of my admiration." Here there was
no dialogue between the Head and the Heart—the Heart triumphed
without a struggle. In an English garden he found a statute of Venus
Pudique "turned half round as if inviting you with her into the recess."
This is the strongest physical attraction Jefferson ever admitted to feeling
about a woman—and it was a statue! [39]

Perhaps, above all, Jefferson found his avocation in leading a political
party in a struggle upon the outcome of which depended, he supposed,
the fate of republican government and with it the hopes of mankind.
Such a transcendant cause served in some measure as a surrogate for the
conjugal happiness he had lost in 1782.

Still, this is obviously the portrait of a man cruelly, perhaps irrep-
arably, seared and scarred by the premature loss of a beloved wife. It is
not the Jefferson of early manhood, the Jefferson who brought his bride
to Monticello and who spent ten years of "unchequered happiness" there.
This part of his life—emotionally the richest part—remains tightly shut-
tered from view; but had his letters to Martha been preserved it would
not be necessary or even possible for his biographer to "humanize" him
by linking him romantically wth Sally Hemings.

∾ 22 ∾

Jefferson, Mrs. Walker, and the Freedom of the Press

◆

JAMES CALLENDER SERVED Jefferson's enemies with not one, but two, hot, spicy, and wholly delectable scandals. Besides making Sally Hemings his concubine and maintaining a "Congo Harem," Jefferson, according to Callender, had attempted to seduce the wife of one of his close friends and former classmates at the College of William and Mary, John Walker. In 1769, while Walker was away from home attending a conference with the Six Nations at Albany, Jefferson, then a young bachelor, "offered love," in his own words, "to a handsome lady." His methods reveal at this early age a strong literary bent: he wrote notes to Mrs. Walker in which he seemed to argue that there was no harm in a little promiscuity among friends, and then furtively attempted to insert these missives in various parts of Mrs. Walker's dress. On one occasion Jefferson was said to have stolen into Mrs. Walker's bedroom prepared to take her by force, only to be repulsed by a pair of scissors. Walker later asserted that his wife had been besieged by Jefferson for over ten years—longer than the siege of Troy—but in the end Mrs. Walker's virtue remained intact. In 1779, seven years after his own marriage, Jefferson was seen, according to Walker, prowling the halls near her bedroom, presumably with amorous intent. But Mrs. Walker's trepidation on this occasion was almost certainly groundless; Jefferson was now happily married and he had long since lost interest in assailing such an impregnable fortress.[1]

In any event, Mrs. Walker did not tell her husband of her narrow escape from Jefferson's unwelcome advances until 1785 when John Walker proposed to make his friend, now minister to France, executor of his will. Mrs. Walker informed her astonished husband that he presumed too much in supposing Jefferson to be his friend, whereupon the whole story came out. Fortunately for Jefferson, Walker was satisfied of his wife's innocence, and, perhaps also fortunately, Jefferson was three thousand miles away.

This nonevent might have ended there, for neither Jefferson nor Walker had any interest in bringing it into the open. It was, in fact, a singularly inept performance on Jefferson's part: eighteenth century gallants who prided themselves on their finesse would have dismissed him as a rank amateur. But partisan politics subsequently accomplished what Jefferson's youthful indiscretion could not. In 1790–1791, Jefferson helped defeat John Walker's bid for reelection to the United States Senate from Virginia. This act of political "treachery," as Walker regarded it, broke up the friendship between the old school chums.

All this had occurred many years before Callender picked up the scent. (Possibly he read it in the *Gazette of the United States*, but it is more probable that he had learned of it from Jefferson's political enemies; it had long been heard in the whispering galleries, and apparently Alexander Hamilton knew about it as early as 1792.) But there is no statute of limitations upon moral transgressions, and scandal does not necessarily lose its savor with the passage of time. In 1802, when Callender broke the story of Jefferson's assault upon Mrs. Walker's virtue, it was eagerly seized upon by the Federalists as proof of what they had been saying all along about Jefferson: that he was a libertine in morals as well as in philosophy, and they applauded Callender for having stripped the mask of hypocrisy from this Virginia "Jacobin" and enemy of female virtue.

Whipped up by the Federalist press, the Walker affair became a *cause célèbre* and Mrs. Walker was converted into the personification of Virtue Assailed by Lechery. In 1805 the Massachusetts legislature gravely debated the question whether Thomas Jefferson was fit to be president of the United States because of the offense against the moral code of a God-fearing people which he had committed thirty-five years previously. In actuality the concern of the legislators was owing less to the resurrection of Puritan morality than to the persistence of political rancor among the Yankees. Of course, none of those who shuddered at the iniquity of Thomas Jefferson admitted that *they* had ever lusted after the wives of their friends; his offense was made to appear unprecedented in the recorded history of mankind. Like all infidels, Jefferson was believed to act upon the principle that adultery, when known, was a small crime; when unknown, it was not crime at all.[2]

Finally the pressure generated by the press reached such a pitch of intensity that Walker demanded—and he threatened Jefferson with a duel unless the president met his terms—a public statement absolving Mrs. Walker and admitting his own culpability. In 1806, Jefferson admitted his transgression in a private letter sent to several of his friends (and attested to by two witnesses to forestall possible claims of forgery), fully acquitting Mrs. Walker. "I plead guilty to one of their [the Federalists'] charges" (the other charge related to Sally Hemings and the "Congo

Harem"), Jefferson confessed, "that when young and single I offered love to a handsome lady. I acknowledge its incorrectness. It is the only one founded in truth among all their allegations against me." Walker accepted this private plea of guilt and dropped his demand for a public confession.[3]

When Jefferson became president in 1801, he had resolved to conduct an experiment unique in the history of modern western civilization. Having experienced the "Reign of Terror" directed against Jeffersonian Republican politicians, press, and newspaper editors by the federal government under the powers granted by the Sedition Act of 1798, he decided that this violation of the First Amendment (as he regarded it) must never occur again in the United States. He therefore proposed to act upon the doctrine he and James Madison had promulgated in the Kentucky and Virginia Resolutions of 1798–1800—namely, that the federal government had no authority whatever under the Constitution to punish individuals for seditious libel: that function was the exclusive prerogative of the state governments acting through the state courts.

While admitting that the states had jurisdiction over slander and libel, Jefferson hoped that they would stay their hand against offenders of either political party. He would cherish it as one of the great achievements of his presidency, he said, if it could be demonstrated that "freedom of the press is compatible with orderly government" and that men could be governed by reason and truth arrived at by free inquiry. Admittedly, it would require an almost inexhaustible fund of patience and self-denial on the part of the federal and state governments, but, he believed, the success or failure of this experiment would determine the outcome of the even greater experiment upon which the American people had embarked—whether a country as large and diversified as the United States could actually be governed upon republican principles.

For this reason, among others, Jefferson remained silent under the calumnies propagated by his political enemies. "I shall take no other revenge," he said, "than, by a steady pursuit of economy and peace and by the establishment of republican principles to sink federalism into an abyss from which there shall be no resurrection for it." The most effective answer to their abuse, he decided, was the honesty, integrity, purity, and uprightness of the government over which he had assumed command. He proposed to leave malicious journalists to the reproof of their own consciences. "If these do not condemn them," he predicted, "there will yet come a day when the false witness will meet a Judge who has not slept over this slander." In the meantime, while they were waiting to meet their justly incensed Maker, he would protect them even in "the right of lying and calumniating," treating their censures as a form of praise.[4]

By making this "fair and full experiment" Jefferson hoped to demon-

strate the validity of one of several of his most cherished convictions—
that "truth is great and will prevail if left to itself," that error was not
dangerous as long as reason was free to contradict it, that free discussion—"the unbounded exercise of freedom and opinion"—was the only
way to attain and defend truth, and that a government that did right
could not be battered down by the falsehoods of a "licentious press." The
theory upon which Jefferson acted was founded upon his conviction that
if an educated people were permitted to hear everything, true and false,
they would infallibly arrive, sooner or later, at a correct judgment; for
Nature had given to men the ability to sift out truth from error, whether
in religion, law, or politics.[5]

If Jefferson were right, freedom of the press and of speech could be
expected to produce an agreement among Americans upon the basic
principles of government—a republican consensus—for truth, he was certain, lay on the side of republicanism. It was because of this firm conviction that he could declare, "I have sworn upon the altar of God eternal
hostility against every form of tyranny over the mind of man."

Still, Jefferson acknowledged that even with this agreement upon
fundamentals, there would always be differences of opinion within the
republican consensus requiring free expression of opinion. He likewise
recognized that a free press was essential to keep a republican government clear of corruption and responsive to the will of the people. Every
government, he admitted, needed vigilant censors and sentinels, and, he
added, it would not lack for them as long as the press remained free. As
president, he expected to be brought by a free press before the tribunal
of public opinion and to be reminded frequently of the temptation every
government is under to exceed and to abuse its powers. This, in his
opinion, was the legitimate function of a free press.[6]

Although in making his pronouncements Jefferson sometimes gave the
impression that he believed in the absolute, unqualified, and uncon-
trollable freedom of the press, in actuality he, like all eighteenth century
lawyers, distinguished between the "freedom" and the "licentiousness" of
the press. He never asserted that the press was above the law; on the contrary, he always insisted that the press must be held responsible for
slander, seditious libel, and other publications dangerous to the public
peace. The only absolute freedom he was prepared to concede to the
press was freedom from prior constraint or control: any form of censor-
ship was repugnant to his concept of the press as a critic and sentinel of
government wrongdoing.* [7]

* The United States Supreme Court has gone far beyond Jefferson's position. In March
1964 the Court declared that "debate on public issues should be uninhibited, robust,
and wide-open"—which the Court held to mean that even falsehoods relating to
official conduct should not be punished if published without "actual malice"—i.e.,
knowledge that a statement was false or a "reckless disregard of whether it was false

The freedom of the press, as Jefferson saw it, entailed an obligation by the press to conduct itself responsibly; it could not expect to publish with impunity defamation and sedition. If it disregarded this stipulation—the condition upon which it held its tenure of freedom—it must be disciplined by government. While Jefferson had no desire to invoke the powers of government—he preferred to assign the overseeing of the press to public opinion—he acknowledged that to keep it within the "legal and wholesome bounds of truth" the coercive power of authority must be retained—although, preferably, kept in abeyance.[8]

In short, Jefferson recognized that liberty must be reconciled with the legitimate right of government to maintain the public peace and order. Viewed in this light, authority was necessary to the preservation of freedom. Liberty did not exclude restraint; it merely excluded unreasonable or arbitrary restraint. Reasonable restraint did not impair freedom, for no individual had the right to publish arrant libels and sedition. The "licentiousness" of the press tended to destroy freedom of the press as surely as did restraint prior to publication—for both destroyed the credibility of the press. If it came to the point that no one could believe what he or she read in the newspapers, they would have ceased to fulfill the purposes for which Jefferson believed they had been established. This line of reasoning led inevitably to the conclusion already reached by Sir William Blackstone that "to censure the licentiousness of the press is to maintain the liberty of the press." [9]

Early in his administration, Jefferson announced that it would be his policy never to recommend the institution of actions in the courts when his personal reputation—as distinguished from the peace and safety of the community—was concerned. But he quickly found that he had embarked upon "an ocean of slander, of falsehood and of malice," and that the waves made by James Callender with the Sally Hemings and Mrs. John Walker scandals could not be calmed merely by doing good works and forgiving his traducers. In spite of his profound admiration for the moral teachings of Jesus of Nazareth, Jefferson was not a man to shrug off calumny and defamation and to turn the other check meekly to his vilifiers. Sensitive and thin-skinned, with an easily bruised ego, he admitted that "unmerited abuse wounds, while unmerited praise has not the power to heal." When he was threatened with impeachment in 1781 for his failure as governor of Virginia to oppose effectively the incursions of the British army into the commonwealth, he agonized over what he regarded as a maneuver engineered by Patrick Henry to destroy him politically. "I stood arraigned for treasons of the heart and not mere

---

or not." The First Amendment, the Court said, was "fashioned to assure the unfettered interchange of ideas for the bringing about of political and social changes desired by the people."

weaknesses of the head," he said. Even the vote of the Virginia legislature to conduct an inquiry, Jefferson added hyperbolically, "inflicted a wound on my spirit which will only be cured by the all-healing grave." To clear his name he returned to the legislature as a delegate, insisting that the charges be read in order that he could answer them sequentially.[10]

The question, as it presented itself to Jefferson in 1803–1808, was whether his "usefulness" (a consideration which largely determined his decision against taking an active part in the antislavery movement) would be fatally impaired by submitting to vilification at the hands of unconscionable Federalist journalists. Truth would no doubt prevail in the long run, but the long run might be too late. For a president of the United States bent upon achieving high and noble goals in his own lifetime, it was not enough to be vindicated by posterity. Jefferson knew that men were not elevated to the pantheon merely because their intentions were good or their hearts were pure.

At first, Jefferson had regarded the Federalist newspapers as chimneys which served "to carry off noxious vapors and smoke," but by 1803 it was clear that they themselves were polluting the political atmosphere with the Sally Hemings, "Congo Harem," and Walker scandals. The chimneys themselves, it appeared, must be abated as nuisances which threatened the basic quality of civic and political life.

Accordingly, in 1803, President Jefferson recommended to key Republican officials to begin prosecutions in the state courts against the most egregious disseminators of "false facts." This was not to be "a general prosecution" of Federalist newspapers, for that, he warned, "would look like persecution." He prescribed instead a selective approach; by making a few examples, he hoped to dissuade the others from a course of action that must inevitably destroy the credibility of the press under the mistaken idea that it was upholding the freedom of the press.* [11]

James Callender himself was beyond the reach of federal or state courts. He did not long enjoy the exhilarating sensation of having raised a political tempest that threatened to topple the president of the United States. Falling upon evil days, he took to drink and sodomy, disgusting even his Federalist colleagues on the Richmond *Register*. In 1803 the Republican "martyr" met his end: he fell from his horse, apparently in a drunken seizure, and drowned in three feet of water in the James River. He died, as he lived, in the congenial muck.

By recommending even a selective action against Federalist newspapers, Jefferson in effect admitted the defeat of his hope that his

---

* The state governments were not averse to instituting prosecutions. In 1802, Seth Webster was fined $100 by the Connecticut Supreme Court for sedition; the charge against him was that he had advocated "equal representation which we fought for in the Revolution and universal suffrage." Connecticut was a rockbound Federalist state. See Williamson 1960, p. 170.

administration would be wholly free of prosecutions for seditious libel. But he did remain true to his conviction that such actions, if and when they did occur, must take place in the state rather than in the federal courts. In his view, the federal courts were wholly lacking in constitutional authority to impose "the salutary coercions of the law"; citizens and even federal officials could seek redress in the state courts but in no others. And Jefferson cleaved to this doctrine, which he believed essential to the preservation of republicanism in the United States, despite the fact that in the federal courts truth was a valid defense in cases involving seditious libel, whereas in the state courts, where the common law generally prevailed, the truth of actionable allegations could not be admitted as a defense. Jefferson's solution was to urge the state courts to emulate, in this respect, the federal courts.

In conformity with the president's wishes, all the actions brought against Federalist printers on the charge of seditious libel were initiated in the state courts. In 1806–1807, when suit was begun in the Federal District Court in Connecticut (the case involved Jefferson's attempt to seduce Mrs. Walker), Jefferson stopped the proceedings. He acted belatedly, it is true, but that was clearly because he did not wish to offend his overzealous partisans who had brought the action in the first place.

At the end of his second administration, Jefferson prided himself upon having treated his vilifiers with "the utmost latitude." Only a handful of actions for seditious libel had been brought, and he had steadfastly resisted demands from his own partisans that the federal government be given authority to suppress all offending newspapers and that the federal courts be opened, under Republican auspices, to cases involving libels judged to be "destructive of the public peace, and dangerous to the public safety." By 1806, even Thomas Paine, generally regarded as a thoroughgoing libertarian, felt that Jefferson had carried freedom of the press too far and had failed to draw a sufficiently sharp distinction between freedom and licentiousness.[12]

Nevertheless, in his later years Jefferson was compelled to admit that the great experiment which he had begun in 1801 had not vindicated his hopes. The man who had said that if he were forced to choose between a government without newspapers and no government at all with newspapers would choose the latter, ended by saying that he scarcely looked at newspapers, that nothing in them except possibly the advertisements could be believed, that they had become "prostituted vehicles of passion," and that even truth itself became suspicious by appearing in the company of "daring and atrocious lies." "The man who never looks into a newspaper," he said, "is better informed than he who reads; inasmuch as he who knows nothing is nearer to truth than he whose mind is filled with falsehood and errors." Newspapers, he lamented, seemed to "raven on the agonies of the victims, as wolves do on the blood of the lamb." He compared the lot of an American politician to that of the early Christians: thrown to rapacious journalistic lions, wolves, and tigers.

Harriet Martineau, who visited the United States at approximately this time, pronounced American newspapers to be the most profligate, and therefore the least credible, in the world. Many educated, principled, and honorable men who valued their reputations avoided politics, she reported, as they avoided an open sewer. She believed that it was a testimony to the strength and durability of democracy in the United States that the Republic had not succumbed to its newspapers. Miss Martineau put the responsibility for this state of affairs where Jefferson himself could never bring himself to place it: upon the people of the United States. "Whenever the many demand truth and justice in their journals and neglect falsehood and calumny," she observed, "they will be served according to their desire." [13]

Wherever the fault lay, Jefferson retained to the end his basic faith in the people and in the beneficence of a free press. For him, freedom of the press remained the sheet anchor of American republicanism. If it were futile to expect to find reasoned discussion, common sense, and ordinary civility in those soiled sheets, the agitation they produced, he told Lafayette in 1823, must be submitted to as an inseparable part of the democratic process. Stirring the water constantly, he said, had the highly salutary effect of keeping it "pure." [14]

~ 23 ~

Jefferson, John Marshall,
and Slavery

———◆———

IN MARCH 1809, Jefferson left the "splendid misery" of the presidency and returned to Monticello to pursue, as he said, "the tranquil pursuits of science" in an "Elysium of domestic affections." He bade farewell to politics under the persuasion that he had served his country well and that he had left the Republic's affairs in the capable hands of James Madison, "the greatest man in the world." Confident that integrity and wisdom reigned in both the executive and legislative branches, Jefferson believed that he could sleep soundly at Monticello "perfectly secure that our rulers and fellow-citizens are taking all possible care of us." The precautions he had recommended that the American people adopt against Hamilton and the Federalist party—eternal vigilance against the corruptive effects of power and unremitting opposition to the encroachments of the federal government (although in his efforts to enforce the embargo of 1808–1809 he had stretched the powers of that government far beyond anything advocated by Hamilton) —could now safely be dispensed with. In Jefferson's view, it made a great deal of difference whether James Madison or John Adams was president and whether Albert Gallatin or Alexander Hamilton occupied the office of secretary of the treasury.[1]

Jefferson departed Washington, D.C.—never to return—with no feeling of remorse that he had not done more for the abolition of slavery; that task, he continued to believe, was the responsibility of younger men. His chief regret was that Congress had not persisted in the embargo until Great Britain and France had been forced to yield to the American doctrine of the freedom of the seas and that he had been unable to acquire West Florida and Texas through the good offices of his favorite real estate broker, Napoleon Bonaparte. It seemed to be a matter of no concern to President Jefferson that had the United States obtained West

Florida and Texas, they, like the rest of the Louisiana Purchase, would have been opened to slavery and to the creation of new slave states.[2]

At Monticello, Jefferson rejoiced in the long-deferred opportunity to indulge in the occupations—music, farming, reading, and philosophizing—which he found most congenial to his "physical and moral constitution." To his friends he pictured himself living like an "antediluvian patriarch" (as early as 1796 he had described himself as "old and infirm") among his children and grandchildren.*

Jefferson had no intention of permitting politics to obtrude upon his Elysium. Yet he could hardly avoid the role of an elder statesman, and his advice, when it was given, was carefully weighed in Washington. He strongly backed every move made by the administration in defense of American neutral rights against the European belligerents, especially Great Britain. Foreign affairs effectively dominated the administration of President James Madison, and during this period Jefferson gave hardly a thought to the abolition of slavery. He rejoiced to see his countrymen reacting to the seizure of American ships and the impressment of American seamen by Great Britain as they had responded, forty years before, at Lexington and Concord. Once again Great Britain assumed in his mind the guise of the inveterate enemy of the Rights of Man, and Jefferson welcomed the war which began in 1812 as a second war of American independence. He predicted that the conquest of Canada would be hardly more than a summer's campaign—a mere "walk" by the seemingly invincible American army.

The ending of the War of 1812—and the American peace negotiators at Ghent, far from repining over their failure to secure the cession of Canada, accounted themselves fortunate to retain the prewar territorial boundaries of the United States—did not revive Jefferson's antislavery zeal. And this despite mounting evidence that slavery was stubbornly resisting the advance of the moral sense. In 1814 he was compelled to acknowledge that slavery was taking an unconscionably long time in dying and, indeed, that it appeared to have taken up its deathbed and walked. Since it now seemed clear that this "moral and political depravity" would outlive him, Jefferson said that he did not want to think about it any longer: he told his friends that he would dismiss it from his mind and enjoy the "summum bonum" of a pastoral life at Monticello. It appeared, he reluctantly admitted, that "morals do not necessarily advance hand in hand with the sciences"—the proposition upon which he

---

* By describing himself as living like one of the patriarchs of old, Jefferson did not mean, as Fawn Brodie suggests, to consecrate his secret idyll with Sally Hemings and the children that had blessed their union. William Byrd II, who did not consort with black slave women, used the identical expression in 1726. "Like one of the Patriarchs," he said, "I have my Flocks and my Herds, my Bond-men and Bond-women. . . . I live in a kind of Independence on everyone but Providence." See Mullin 1972, p. vii.

had founded his hopes of the ultimate triumph of the moral sense over greed and avarice.[3]

Particularly disconcerting to Jefferson was the failure of the young men of Virginia to let their consciences be their guides in the matter of slavery. Since 1785, when he had relinquished any active role in the antislavery movement, he had watched with mingled hope and anxiety the progress of the moral sense among these arbiters of the commonwealth's future. In 1814 he confessed for the first time that he was disappointed by their performance as the agents of an "overruling Providence" entrusted with the solemn duty of cleansing the land of slavery. Instead, he lamented, the postrevolutionary generation seemed less moral and less idealistic than the generation which had fought the Revolution. Among other things, they ignored his exhortations to "immortalize" themselves by dividing the states into wards "as the basis of our political edifice" and thereby ensuring that local government would not succumb to the overweening power of the state government. And they had treated with equal indifference his pleas to democratize the Virginia Constitution of 1776.[4]

If the young men of Virginia seemed more interested in profiting from slavery than in eradicating it, and more bent upon the pursuit of pleasure than upon practicing the frugality and devotion to the public weal Jefferson expected of true republicans (some observers of the Virginia scene reported that these young men were preoccupied with horse raising, cockfighting, gaming, and drinking, "the fruit of indolence and luxury, which arise from the system of African slavery") perhaps they were not to be blamed for ignoring the still, small voice of conscience which told them that slavery was a wrong to be extirpated forthwith. The comfort, stability, and opportunities for pleasure enjoyed by upper-class Virginians—particularly after the sale of surplus slaves restored a measure of the prosperity that had been lost as a result of the economic decline of the Old Dominion—conspired to make slavery appear to be essential to their way of life. It might have been said in their defense that those who did not live in the Old Dominion during the antebellum days did not know the true sweetness of life. At Monticello, Jefferson himself believed himself to be closer to Heaven than anywhere in the world, and the young men of Virginia might be pardoned for supposing that the pursuit of happiness consisted in possessing a large plantation and scores, even hundreds, of slaves. Jefferson's life-style carried more weight with them than did his pronouncements, especially when his only public words on the subject had been written thirty years before in the *Notes on Virginia*.[5]

Ironically, at the very time that Jefferson was becoming disillusioned about the young men of Virginia, one of these young men urged Jefferson to act upon his professed ideals. Edward Coles, onetime private secretary to James Madison and a neighbor of Jefferson's at Monticello, called upon Jefferson, "the revered father of all our political and social bless-

ings," to sound the tocsin for the gradual emancipation of the slaves in
Virginia and thereby remove what Coles called—and here he took the
words from Jefferson himself—"this degrading feature of British colonial
policy." Coles argued that if Jefferson put the full weight of his immense
prestige unequivocally on the side of the antislavery movement, he would
crown all his achievements and consecrate his memory for all eternity. In
the hope of bestirring the "patriarch" at Monticello, Coles used a familiar
Jeffersonian argument: the people must be led by an elite of natural
aristocrats whose function, said Coles, was "to arouse and enlighten the
public sentiment which in matters of this kind ought not to be expected
to lead, but to be led." [6]

Even if Jefferson remained quiescent at Monticello, Coles declared
his intention of actually doing something about slavery: he would sell his
estate near Charlottesville and establish his slaves as free men on farms on
the free soil of Illinois. What did Thomas Jefferson think of this idea
which, if it did nothing more, would set an example to Virginia slaveowners, afflicted, as was Jefferson himself, by the pangs of conscience?

Knowing Jefferson's strong aversion to slavery, Coles could hardly
have expected the reply he received. Instead of approving Coles's plan
and giving him his blessing, Jefferson dashed cold water on the whole
idea. The slaves, he said, would fail as free farmers because their previous
condition of servitude had made them as "incapable as children of taking
care of themselves." Since the experiment was certain to collapse, he advised Coles to remain in Virginia and "come forward in the public councils, become the missionary of this doctrine [emancipation] truly christian; insinuate and inculcate it softly but steadily." In short, he counseled
Coles to become an apostle but to keep his profile low—the course of
action Jefferson had pursued for thirty years without visible effect.

Perhaps even more astonishing to Coles was Jefferson's refusal to permit his name to figure at all in this enterprise. He found the appropriate
analogy in the Iliad: "This, my dear sir," he told Coles, "is like bidding
Old Priam to buckle [on] the armour of Hector. . . . The enterprise is for
the young. . . . It shall have all my prayers, and they are the only weapons
of an old man." Never before had he expressed such confidence in the
efficacy of prayers.

To Coles, Jefferson repeated the maxim he had consistently acted
upon in dealing with slavery: nothing was to be gained, and much might
be lost, by moving too precipitately. A successful social reformer did not
rush in where revolutionaries might fear to tread: he carefully prepared
and cautiously tested the ground before he ventured upon it, and, above
all, he made sure that public opinion was prepared to follow him. He
recited the familiar litany: the only thing that could prevent the eventual
overthrow of slavery was a premature effort on the part of overeager
zealots to hasten the inevitable day of deliverance. In the meantime, it

made no sense to preach to scoffing nonbelievers, especially as the effect of such exhortations would almost certainly delay the emancipation of the slaves and thereby aggravate the risk of a slave insurrection.[7]

A second and probably more decisive reason for Jefferson's rejection of Coles's plan was that it treated free blacks as permanent residents of the United States and even raised the disquieting possibility that they might become active citizens. As he grew older, the impossibility of the two races coexisting in the same country became to him increasingly self-evident. No plan of emancipation that did not provide for the removal of the blacks from the United States had the slightest interest for him. His abhorrence of miscegenation intensified, if that were possible, with the passage of time. "The amalgamation of whites with blacks," he told Coles, "produces a degradation to which no lover of his country, no lover of excellence in the human character, can innocently consent." The admixture of "Negro blood" would prove fatal to the republic.[*]

Had Coles followed Jefferson's advice and remained in Virginia in the forlorn hope of persuading slaveowners to see the error of their ways he would have condemned himself to the same course of frustration and powerlessness that Jefferson himself experienced. Apart from this discouraging prospect, there was a compelling reason for Coles to go to Illinois. If the region north of the Ohio were to be preserved for free labor, the presence of men like Coles with strong antislavery views was indispensable. Although the Northwest Ordinance of 1787 provided for the gradual abolition of slavery, Southern settlers introduced a system of servitude which differed only slightly from that "peculiar institution." Blacks were held as laborers under contract for as long as twenty years; they were brought and sold as servants; and when their terms of service expired they were sometimes kidnapped and sold down the river as slaves. Thanks to this subterfuge, the plantation system flourished in southern Illinois. When Illinois entered the Union in 1818 it was required by Congress to adopt a constitution barring slavery, but a concerted effort was made in 1824 by the proslavery elements in the state to legalize slavery by means of a constitutional amendment. As governor of Illinois, Edward Coles led the forces which, by a narrow margin, kept Illinois from retrograding into slavery. As a result of this defeat, immigration

---

[*] In her interpretation of this passage, Fawn Brodie strains credulity by piling implausibility upon implausibility. Ms. Brodie argues that the insertion of the word "innocently" was deliberately contrived by Jefferson because he regarded himself innocent of any wrongdoing with Sally Hemings: his love for her was undefiled by lust. It is by the use of this kind of "evidence" that she establishes her case for a romantic love affair between Jefferson and Sally Hemings. Jefferson's meaning was perfectly clear to Coles as it is to any other reader: although Coles had no intention of abetting miscegenation—he was acting "innocently" in that respect—that circumstance did not relieve him of the guilt of inadvertently encouraging racial amalgamation—a crime, as Jefferson saw it, against both his country and his race. See Brodie 1974, pp. 423–433.

from the South was checked and northern Illinois became a bastion of free-soil sentiment. Even so, it was not until 1844 that the indenture system for blacks was abolished in this so-called free state.[8]

In Illinois, Coles enjoyed the peace of mind and clear conscience forever denied Jefferson. He settled seventeen former slaves as tenant farmers on a tract of land near Edwardsville, Illinois, and gave them an opportunity to acquire ownership of 160-acre tracts on easy terms. When Frances Wright visited Edwardsville in the 1820s, she reported that "the liberated blacks spoke of their former master with tears of gratitude and affection." Several paid daily visits to Coles to inquire if there were anything they could do for their former master.[9]

Edward Coles really struck a blow for freedom; Jefferson's hand remained poised for a blow he never found an opportunity to strike. The vital difference between the two men as exponents of the rights of man was that whereas Coles did not insist upon removing the free blacks from the United States, Jefferson made it a *sine qua non* of emancipation.

In discouraging Edward Coles from going to Illinois and declining to bestir himself in the antislavery cause, Jefferson did not admit that he was letting down the friends of freedom. He believed that by publishing his opinions in the *Notes on Virginia* he had done all that he could do and, indeed, all that he could reasonably be expected to do, against slavery; the passage of thirty years had merely confirmed the views he had then expressed. Anyone who wished to discover how he felt about slavery had only to consult the *Notes on Virginia*: there, set down in print, was everything he thought about slavery, the blacks themselves, and the manner in which the institution could be most efficaciously abolished. In short, Jefferson was on record, and no good purpose could be served by repeating the sentiments and arguments already advanced in the *Notes on Virginia*. It was, he made clear, his final sermon from his Virginia mount.

In Jefferson's opinion, the sum and substance of the matter was that the facts were known; the iniquity of slavery had been laid bare; and the danger of divine retribution had been revealed. The rest was up to the moral sense. Despite his feeling of having been let down by the younger generation, Jefferson still felt sure that slavery would succumb to "temperate and steady pursuit, to the enlargement of the human mind, and its advancement in science." "When I contemplate the immense advances in science* and discoveries in the arts which have been made within the period of my life," he said in 1817, "I look forward with confidence to equal advances by the present generation, and have no doubt they will consequently be as much wiser than we have been as we than our fathers were, and they than the burners of witches." If slavery were not abolished

---

* Jefferson here uses "science" as a synonym for "knowledge."

by the present generation, it would be accomplished by the next or by some subsequent generation. Knowledge was cumulative and, barring some unforseen setback, the advance of mankind would be uninterrupted.[10]

Jefferson was fond of saying that when in doubt he rested his head upon the soft pillow of hope considerately provided for mankind by the Author of Nature. That "pillow" enabled him to dream of and believe in a future in which Americans would become progressively more responsive to the promptings of the moral sense, more disposed to seek the welfare of their fellow men, and more intent upon making justice their guide in all things. But, as Jefferson himself would have said, the realization of this dream of future felicity depended upon the existence of an elite which would set the example to the American people of devotion to the public good, the practice of self-denial, and disdain of "mere money-making."

The course of political events after the War of 1812 profoundly affected Jefferson's attitude toward the expansion of slavery into the territories of the United States. With President Jefferson's acquiescence, the territory acquired from France in 1803 had been opened to the introduction of slavery even where it was not already in existence. But after 1819, as a result of the political changes that had occurred since 1815 and decisions handed down by the Supreme Court bearing upon the constitutional relations between the states and the federal government, Jefferson became an ardent exponent of the establishment of slavery in the entire Louisiana Purchase.

For a few years after the restoration of peace between Great Britain and the United States, the prospects of the Jeffersonian Republican party had never seemed more auspicious. The Federalists, as a result of their opposition to the patriotic "Second War of American Independence" and their participation in the Hartford Convention called in 1814 to protest against the war and to demand, under the implied threat of secession, constitutional amendments to strengthen the position of New England in the Union, had succeeded in branding themselves with the stigma of factionalism and disloyalty. In consequence, after the end of the war, the Federalist party began to disintegrate rapidly and the Jeffersonian Republicans picked up the pieces in the form of political converts to the Jeffersonian creed—a process which the Federalist leaders watched with impotent anguish.

At first, Jefferson welcomed the rank-and-file Federalists into the party fold: it vindicated the assertion he had made in his first inaugural that the American people were basically all Republicans and all Federalists. With a single party enjoying undisputed ascendancy, Jefferson could hope that American politics might become a decorous exercise in mutual civility and that presidential elections would occasion no more than a ripple on the placid surface. His ideal was achieved in 1820 when James Monroe, without stirring from the White House, received every electoral vote except one—and that single dissenting vote was cast merely to prevent him from achieving the unanimous vote of the electoral college received by George Washington.

Initially, Jefferson was disposed to believe that the absorption of the Federalists by the Jeffersonian Republican party strengthened "the genuine principles of republicanism," but he was soon asking himself anxiously just who had been absorbed by whom. He began to wonder if the Federalists, "like the fox pursued by the dog," had not taken shelter in the midst of the Republican sheep—with fatal results to the sheep.[11]

Certainly by 1817 the Jeffersonian Republicans had "out-Federalized Federalism" by adopting the entire Federalist program—the Bank of the United States, a protective tariff, the buildup of the army and navy, and the encouragement of manufactures. The dismaying fact was that the Jeffersonian Republicans conquered Federalism by stooping to embrace its policies. When Jefferson said, "We are all Republicans; we are all Federalists," he had not expected that Republicans would become Federalists in everything but name. The ideological apostasy of many Jeffersonian Republicans to the worship of strange Federalist gods admonished Jefferson that there were more insidious dangers to the "revolution of 1800" than organized opposition to his policies. He himself stood unyieldingly upon the principles he had proclaimed in the Kentucky Resolutions of 1798–1799; in his eyes. Henry Clay's "American system"—a protective tariff, a second Bank of the United States, and internal improvements at the expense of the federal government—was an abominable "heresy." The only concession he made to the changed circumstances in which the republic found itself after the War of 1812 was to give grudging approval to manufacturing in factories. But even here he hedged his concession: the United States ought, he said, to manufacture for its domestic needs only: if it ever undertook to export manufactured goods, the delicate balance between commerce, manufactures, and agriculture would be upset—and agriculture, and with it republicanism, would be the certain loser. While conceding that some industrialization was essential to national defense, Jefferson felt that the wisest course for the great majority of Americans was to stay on their farms and pursue household manufactures.

Politically, the postwar resurgence of Federalist ideology was manifest especially in the House of Representatives, where the South—the bastion of "true" Jeffersonian Republicanism—was rapidly becoming a minority section. On many occasions Jefferson had described the House of Representatives as the only truly representative branch of the federal government, but on these occasions the House had been comfortably under the control of the Jeffersonian Republicans. After 1815, however, when the pure Jeffersonian creed was cast aside by eager young national-minded Republicans, he began to reconsider the wisdom of concentrating power in the House of Representatives. Unfortunately for him, the process which he had once described as essential to the preservation of republicanism had already succeeded even beyond his hopes: the House of Representatives had absorbed most of the powers of government; the speaker of the house was more powerful than the president of the United States; and the Senate, as Justice Joseph Story said, concurred supinely in the representatives' "lofty pretensions to be the guardians of the people and its rights." [12]

Much as Jefferson feared the specter of Federalism *redivivus* in Congress, he feared it more in the United States Supreme Court. From the perspective of Monticello, the conspirators against "true Republicanism" had merely shifted their headquarters from the office of the secretary of the treasury to the chambers of the Supreme Court, and Chief Justice John Marshall had grasped the torch of "consolidationism" and "monarchism" from the hand of the fallen Hamilton. The tactics had changed too: in place of Hamilton's open "corruption" of members of Congress, the Supreme Court had gone underground: the justices had embodied themselves, in Jefferson's words, into a corps of sappers and miners, steadily working "to undermine the independent rights of the States and to consolidate all power in the hands of that government." [13]

But the ultimate goal, Jefferson felt certain, was unchanged: consolidationism was no more than the first step toward the establishment of a monarchy upon the ruins of American republicanism. As its fortunes declined, Federalism had become more subtle and insidious, not less wicked: it marched to the beat of a different drummer and under a different banner toward the same objective of an American king, lords, and commons.

The Supreme Court had to be watched narrowly because, Jefferson believed, judges were possessed to an extraordinary degree of the all-too-human avidity for power, and this propensity was aggravated by an *esprit de corps* that prompted them to act as a phalanx. In the progress of the federal judiciary from its original position (it was first housed in the basement of an office building in Washington, D.C.) "without power, without patronage, without the legitimate means of ingratiating itself with the people," to a position of supremacy over the other branches of the federal government, Jefferson discerned a classic example of how the lust for power on the part of a few determined men could achieve results which, he declared, "open force would not have dared to attempt." [14]

Jefferson had no hope that the Supreme Court justices could be dissuaded from their fatal course by reasoned argument. "You may as well reason and argue with the marble columns encircling them," he said. Since the acquittal in 1805 of Justice Samuel Chase on charges of high crimes and misdemeanors, Jefferson had come to consider impeachment as a mere "scare-crow" utterly incapable of frightening any of the birds of ill omen perched on the bench of the Supreme Court. For this reason, he advocated in his later years the adoption of a constitutional amendment making judges removable by the president on the vote of a majority of both houses of Congress. But even that drastic expedient seemed to have lost much of its efficacy: Congress, Jefferson said, was "part of the conspiracy" to sweep all power into the vortex of the federal government.[15]

In the decisions handed down by the Supreme Court, John Marshall revealed to Jefferson that the Chief Justice was actuated by "venality," "personal malice," and detestation of republicanism. Marshall, he said, bore a "rancorous hatred" toward the established government of the United States, and he gave vent to his "gloomy malignity" by treating the Consitution as "a mere thing of wax." The only hope of saving republicanism from the profane hands of monarchists was to "pulverize" Marshall's arguments in the newspapers or, better still, to remove him from the high bench from which he conducted his attack upon the American Constitution.[16]

In politics, as Alexander Hamilton, Aaron Burr, and John Marshall could attest, Jefferson was not an indulgent, gentle, charitable, above-the-storm "philosopher"; on the contrary, he was, as a political partisan, a "true believer," fervent, impassioned, and intolerant of dissent toward what he regarded as the fundamentals of the Republican creed. Among those fundamentals was the doctrine expressed in the Virginia and Kentucky Resolutions that the United States was essentially a league of sovereign states—a doctrine which, in Jefferson's words "contains the catholic faith, which whosoever doth not keep whole and undefiled, without doubt, he shall perish everlastingly." There was a little of the medieval pope in the great American democrat who professed to hold the keys of political salvation. Yet it is also true that it was his fervency, his conviction that he was absolutely right and that his political opponents were as absolutely wrong which made him an effective political leader. Had Jefferson been merely a retiring, tolerant, unimpassioned philosopher, the patriarch and sage of Monticello, he would never have made his mark upon American politics.

❧

As a political strategist and proponent of a coherent philosophy of the use of a political power, John Marshall was the most redoubtable antagonist Jefferson ever encountered. He did not conveniently ruin himself politically as Hamilton had done; he avoided, as Hamilton had not, pushing his program too fast and too far; he did not reveal personal idiosyncracies and military ambitions, which had cost Hamilton heavily; and he did not engage in a sordid extramarital affair to which he felt obliged to confess in the newspapers. As Jefferson ruefully admitted, "It will be difficult to find a man who will be able to hold his own on the bench with John Marshall." Even his own handpicked appointee to the high bench, Justice William Johnson, the first great dissenter on the Supreme Court, did not dissent nearly often enough to suit Jefferson. By uniting the Supreme Court into an almost solid phalanx of like-minded justices and by his skillful domination of this body, Marshall made the Supreme Court an institution and a power—perhaps, as Jefferson said, the supreme power—in the land.[17]

While it is true that Marshall had carefully pondered Hamilton's state papers and his essays in *The Federalist* and, in his judicial opinions, had read Hamilton's opinions into the Constitution, he was a nationalist in his own right; his views of the proper relationship between the states and the general government were derived from experience rather than from his reading. As an officer in the Continental army during the War of Independence, Marshall had been exposed to the same nationalizing influences that molded Hamilton's ideas. But while Jefferson could account for Hamilton—a West Indian "adventurer" goaded by ambition, unscrupulous in attaining his ends, and wholly devoid of state loyalties—he could not understand how John Marshall, a Virginian who, under happier circumstances, Jefferson might have called "cousin John," could cast off all feeling for his "country" (i.e., Virginia) and go over to the "enemy"—the monstrous regiment of bankers, speculators, businessmen, and other vultures bent upon sucking the very lifeblood from the Old Dominion.

Although Marshall steadfastly denied that he was seeking to establish a consolidated government and ridiculed the idea that he was a monarchist, he did insist that the United States Constitution created a government supreme within its sphere and not a mere league of sovereign states based upon a covenant. This Constitution represented the will of the people of the United States, not contractual arrangements into which the several states had entered, and the government thus established worked directly upon the people, not through the medium of the state government. And, Marshall added, since this Constitution was intended to endure for centuries, it was "adapted to the various crises of human affairs." [18]

The crisis that produced most of Marshall's epochal constitutional opinions during his career on the Supreme Court stemmed from the necessity, as he saw it, of finding a final resolution to the question first raised during the period of the Articles of Confederation but not decided during Jefferson's lifetime: whether the states had the constitutional right to interfere with vested property rights and the power to defy the will and encroach upon the jurisdiction of the general government with impunity. Marshall took property under the protection of the Supreme Court by invalidating decisions of state courts and acts of state legislatures which in his opinion denied individuals and business corporations due process under the supreme law of the land. His constituency was the post-War of 1812 generation of Americans who had wholeheartedly embraced the nationalism generated by the second "War of National Independence," the generation that rejected the Jeffersonian philosophy of limited government, agrarianism and dedication of all surplus revenue to the extinguishment of the public debt, in favor of the American System advocated by Henry Clay.[19]

Chief Justice Marshall adjudicated in the interests of *laissez-faire* as it is traditionally understood in the United States: freedom for entrepreneurs from state control coupled with a helping hand from the state and Federal governments. In *Fletcher v. Peck* (1810), for example, he extended the contracts clause to cover the rights of "innocent purchasers" of real estate (in this instance the Yazoo lands later incorporated in the states of Mississippi and Alabama) originally granted to speculative land companies by a corrupt Georgia state legislature whose action had been subsequently repudiated by an honest legislature. In *Gibbons v. Ogden* (1824), he interpreted the commerce clause to vest exclusive power in Congress to regulate interstate commerce which, as defined by Marshall, included navigation. His objective in these and other decisions was to put business under the benign custodianship of the Federal government with the Federal judiciary acting as watchdogs against any untoward interference by the states. In this sense he was the prophet of the later generation of Americans that acted upon the maxim that "the business of America is business."[20]

Like Jefferson, Marshall generally found what he sought in the Laws of Nature—which made him, from Jefferson's point of view, a particularly tricky adversary who weaved and bobbed so adroitly that no one could pin him down in debate. For example, Marshall traced the obligation to observe contracts to "the original and pre-existing principle anterior to and independent of society." While Jefferson endorsed this Lockean principle, he objected that Marshall singled out the wrong kind of property for the patronage of government: bank and corporation stocks and bonds, contracts, and speculative investments rather than the property owned by the "producing interest" (i.e. agriculture).[21]

During the thirty-five years John Marshall presided over the Supreme Court, no less than thirteen laws, duly enacted by the state governments, were invalidated by the federal tribunal on the ground that they were in violation of the United States Constitution; and during the period 1818–1821 alone, the Supreme Court handed down five decisions which had the effect of expanding the legislative powers of the federal government. The manifest tendency of Marshall's policy was not only to make the Supreme Court the sole arbiter and interpreter of the Constitution but to make the federal government supreme over the states. To that end he declared that even though laws duly enacted by Congress were opposed to the wishes and directives of every state legislature in the Union, they were nevertheless the supreme law of the land. The full force of Marshall's principle of national supremacy fell upon Virginia. In *Cohen v. Virginia* (1821), the "sovereign" state of Virginia was made a defendant in a federal court where it was sued without its own consent. In this case the Marshall Court upheld the right of appeal from the decisions of state courts to the United States Supreme Court.[22]

Jefferson not only rejected the idea that the Constitution was what John Marshall said it was—"the battle of Bunker Hill," Jefferson declared, "was not fought to set up a Pope"—but he denied Marshall's premise, the basis of the doctrine of judicial review, that the people's will is embodied in the Constitution and is discoverable only by judges. He contended that each of the three great departments of government was "rightful expositor" of the constitutionality of its acts. Thus Congress itself had the sole right, pending the final arbitration of the people, to pass upon the constitutionality of acts of Congress. In interpreting the Constitution, Jefferson advised the justices of the Supreme Court to stay within the narrow limits of their own bailiwick; they were competent to decide only upon the constitutionality of matters relating to the federal judiciary. "Each department," he declared, "has an equal right to decide for itself what is the meaning of the Constitution in the case submitted to its action." [23]

Jefferson took the position that appeals from decisions of the state courts to federal courts were unconstitutional: no appeal could carry over from the courts of one independent government to the courts of another government. He thereby effectively expunged the appellate jurisdiction of the Supreme Court granted by the Judiciary Act of 1789. Yet he contended that state courts retained the prerogative of declaring acts of Congress unconstitutional, and from their decisions there could be no appeal except to the people.* [24]

The decisions emanating from the Marshall Court had the effect of

---

* The Constitution does not give the Supreme Court absolute appellate jurisdiction. Article III of the Constitution declares that "the Supreme Court shall have appellate jurisdiction, both as to law and fact, with such exceptions and under such regulations as the Congress shall make." It can be argued that Article III does not answer the question whether the Court is empowered to declare that a duly enacted state law violates the Constitution any more than it declares that the Court is empowered to declare a violation by an act of the Federal government. But Article III cannot be read in isolation from Article VI which defines the "supreme law" to include laws "in pursuance" of the Constitution. Article VI thus implies that laws not in pursuance of the Constitution shall not be given effect. See Berger 1969, pp. 3, 213–216.

reinvigorating Jefferson's devotion to state's rights, temporarily eclipsed by the exigencies of enforcing the embargo in 1808–1809. He now reverted to his earlier view that the states constituted the only effective barrier to the onrushing Leviathan State which, he lamented, many of his own former followers seemed eager to mount and ride to power.

Against "consolidationism" Jefferson reasserted the theory of the nature of the federal "compact" he had deployed against Alexander Hamilton and, later, against the Alien and Sedition Acts. The American Union, as he conceived it, was a confederation based upon a compact between "independent nations"; the general government, being the creation of the states, possessed only enumerated powers which ought to be construed strictly and carried into effect only by means which were expressly granted or were absolutely necessary to their execution. If the federal government chose to exercise a questionable power, the burden of proof was upon it to prove that it was acting constitutionally. If any doubt existed as to the constitutionality of any act contemplated by the federal government, the safest rule, he argued, was not to exercise it; only by observing this injunction could the federal government avoid the danger of overstepping the constitutional bounds set upon its authority.[25]

Had Jefferson's theory of the "beautiful equilibrium" established by the Constitution between the federal government and the states prevailed, the positive role of the federal government would have been restricted almost wholly to the conduct of foreign affairs. His method of interpreting the Constitution would have reduced the functions of the federal government to largely negative, regulative functions. But this concept of the Constitution as a self-denying ordinance imposed upon the federal government by "sovereign" states was theory only; as president, Jefferson had effectively used the powers of the national government to achieve ends which he believed to be essential to the national security and welfare.[26]

But with an Imperial Judiciary riding, as he saw it, roughshod over the rights of the states, Jefferson beheld in his imagination "a single and splendid government of an aristocracy, founded on banking corporations . . . riding and ruling over the plundered ploughman and beggared yeomanry." Monarchism, he feared, could not be very far down the garden path along which John Marshall was leading the American people.[27]

With good reason, John Marshall considered Jefferson to be the most inveterate enemy of the powers of the Supreme Court as he had himself interpreted and exercised them. (In 1800 he had called Jefferson a visionary theorist and subsequent events had not wholly disproved that opinion.) He complained that the "Grand Lama" of Monticello was setting himself up as an oracle of the Constitution and summoning the faithful to hear the Word that issued from the mountaintop. As Marshall saw it, Jefferson was trying to turn the clock back to the Articles of Confederation—a regression that would totally paralyze the federal government. "The government of the whole will be prostrated at the feet of the members," Marshall predicted, "and the grand effort of wisdom, virtue, and patriotism, which produced it, will be totally defeated." [28]

🍁

The question of slavery never bulked larger on Jefferson's horizon than when John Marshall, from the eminence of the Supreme Court, struck down acts of the state legislatures and aggrandized the powers of the federal government. For slavery could not be divorced from the conflict between the states and the general government: as the Supreme Court went, so might slavery itself go. States' rights were the first line of defense of slavery against antislavery sentiment in Congress, and Jefferson had no intention of standing by idly while this vital perimeter was breached by a troop of black-robed jurists.

Although John Marshall was quite as confirmed an enemy of slavery as was Jefferson—it was, he said, a violation of every man's "natural right to the fruits of his own labor"—he did not comfort himself with the pleasing fancy that it was in the course of extinction from the inexorable advance of science, reason, and the moral sense. "Nothing," he said, "portends more calamity and mischief to the Southern States than their slave population. Yet they seem to cherish the evil and to view with immovable prejudice and dislike everything which may tend to diminish it." At the same time, he agreed with Jefferson that the constitution and the statute law of Virginia had legalized property in human beings (he himself was a slaveowner) and that "this right could not be drawn into question" by the courts. [29]

While the Marshall Court championed the cause of businessmen, bankers, and speculators, rather than that of agriculture and farmers, it did not at any time threaten the form of property in which the South was peculiarly interested—the ownership of slaves. Despite his "spacious view" of the powers of the federal government, at no time did Marshall claim that it had the constitutional power to act upon slavery in the States where it was established by state law.

Yet Jefferson found no comfort in Marshall's inhibitions regarding this exercise of the powers of the federal government. John Taylor of Caroline, to whose opinions he increasingly deferred, declared that the principles enunciated by Marshall in *McCulloch v. Maryland* (1819) gave the federal government the right to free every slave in the Union. Even more alarming to Southerners was the opinion expressed elsewhere by Marshall to the effect that in many instances "the wisdom and discretion" of Congress and the check imposed by public opinion were the "sole restraint" upon the House and Senate. To Jefferson, this dictum constituted a sinister threat to an autonomous Southern way of life within the American Union. The very existence of power invited its abuse, and, as Hamilton had amply demonstrated, the federal government abhorred any vacuums created by the self-denial of the states. "Were we directed from Washington when to sow, and when to reap, we shall soon want bread," he said; and, he might have added, Southerners would in that event soon want slaves as well.* [30]

For the federal government to undertake the emancipation of the slaves would be far worse for the South, in Jefferson's opinion, than the continuation of slavery. If Congress freed the slaves, he predicted, "all the whites south of the Potomac and Ohio must evacuate their States, and most fortunate those who can do it first." The freedmen, he believed, would be presented with a dagger with their freedom—and Jefferson had no doubt that they would use it mercilessly against the former master race. The South, in short, would become the scene of a racial Armageddon.†

Jefferson's besetting fear was not that the Supreme Court itself would attempt to destroy slavery by judicial fiat but that the constitutional interpretations proceeding from that Court would provide Congress with a sanction for doing "what they shall think or pretend will be for the general welfare." Besides the general welfare clause, there was the supremacy clause, the necessary proper clause and the commerce clause—any one of which might serve to justify congressional interference with the domestic slave trade and ultimately with slavery itself.‡ [31]

Confronted by a Supreme Court and a Congress which he judged to be animated by hostility to every Southern interest and disdainful of constitutional restraints upon the exercise of their powers, Jefferson

---

* Slavery was abolished in England by the decision of Lord Mansfield in the Somerset Case (1772), a decision that freed fifteen thousand slaves. In 1782 the highest court in Massachusetts ruled that slavery was incompatible with the Massachusetts Constitution of 1780 which declared all men to be created free and equal. Jefferson did not regard these judicial actions as viable precedents for United States federal courts.

† John Randolph, whose views Jefferson was finding increasingly congenial, had already warned Southerners that emancipation by Congress was certain to produce a servile war: even allowing the blacks to believe that they were the equals of whites, he said, in effect "advising them to cut their masters' throats." He was also one of the first to sound the alarm against increasing the powers of Congress: if Congress gained power to appropriate money to survey roads and canals, he declared, "they may emancipate every slave in the United States."

‡ The most vehement opponent of slavery on the Supreme Court was Associate Justice Joseph Story of Massachusetts, whose appointment had been strenuously resisted by Jefferson in 1810–1811. In 1819–1821, in charges to various juries, Story asserted that the existence of slavery "under any shape is so repugnant to the natural rights of man and the dictates of justice, that it seems difficult to find for it any adequate justification." When Story declared the slave trade contrary to international law, John Marshall—and with him, the majority of the Court—disagreed. See McClellan 1971, p. 247.

began to calculate the value of union. The question he asked himself was: under the kind of centralized government John Marshall seemed bent upon establishing was the Union worth preserving? In 1776, faced with a choice between freedom and "slavery" to a "foreign government," Jefferson had unhesitatingly chosen freedom. Ominously, he now occasionally referred to the federal government as a "foreign government."

Jefferson did not, in fact, regard the Union as indivisible and indestructible; as he saw it, the several states were held together primarily by reason rather than by the "mystic chords of memory." He found no Law of Nature which decreed that the United States must remain a united nation under all circumstances. When a government ceased to fulfill the purposes for which it was instituted, the right of the people to effect fundamental changes became operative. In the case of the federal government, he could easily imagine circumstances—perhaps they had already been produced by John Marshall—which justified secession: among them was the emergence of a central government so powerful that it could trample willfully upon the rights of the states and destroy any institution, including slavery, which it judged to be immoral, improper, or inimical to the national welfare as defined in Washington, D.C. He preferred to live, however uncomfortably, with slavery than under the tyranny of such an all-powerful federal government—even though he admitted that the dissolution of the union would make the work of emancipation infinitely more difficult and militate decisively against the eventual fulfillment of the hopes of mankind. Confronted by such a concentration of power, Jefferson believed that the South would have no real option but to go its own way. In that event, he hoped that the West would throw in its lot with the agricultural South rather than with the commercial, industrial North. "I would rather the States should withdraw [from those] which are for unlimited commerce and war [the Northern states]," he said in 1816, "and confederate with those which are for peace and agriculture." [32]

All that he asked of Southerners, if and when they were faced with this stark choice, was that they should exercise patience and forbearance "and separate from our companions when the sole alternative left us is the dissolution of the union with them or submission to a government without limitation of powers." One of the consolations Jefferson found in growing old was that in all probability he would not be required to make that choice; the deluge might come, but he would not be here to see it. "I scarcely know myself," he said, "which is most to be deprecated, a consolidation, or dissolution of the states. The horrors of both are beyond the reach of human thought." [33]

What Jefferson failed to recognize, however, was that the burgeoning capitalism of the North, of which John Marshall was the apologist and spokesman, had no intention of directing the newfound powers of the federal government against slavery: those powers were to be used for the benefit of manufacturing, transportation, and banking, not for prosecuting a moral crusade against slavery. Large segments of Northern business—cotton manufacturers, bankers, shippers, and brokers—had acquired a vested interest in slavery; they had no desire to unsettle or disrupt an institution which they found becoming increasingly profitable to themselves. If Northern buisnessmen, especially those who traded with the South, felt the stirrings of moral indignation when they thought of the slaves, conscience was more often than not drowned out by the clamor of what Jefferson called greed and avarice. He did not fully appreciate the strength and durability of the material interests which cemented the sections and which provided continuing security to slavery.

The clash, when it came, was not over slavery per se, but over the extension of slavery into the territories. Here the Union revealed its vulnerability to a contest for preeminence between two expanding sections in which slavery stood arrayed against freedom and in which "the safety and happiness" of Southerners seemed diametrically opposed to the "safety and happiness" of Northerners. As the spokesman of a section whose influence was dwindling steadily in the national counsels and which was threatened with the "tyranny" of a consolidated government dominated by a section hostile to the institutions and interests of the South, Jefferson not only took the side of slavery, he demanded that the right of slavery to expand at will everywhere in the national domain be acknowledged by the Northern majority.[34]

ᗒ 24 ᗕ

The Missouri Controversy

<hr>

IN 1819, while Jefferson was bracing himself against new assaults on the Constitution by the Supreme Court, he was startled by what he called "a firebell in the night," which, as he listened in an anguish of spirit to the tolling, began to sound more and more like the death knell of the Union. It was for the American Republic and for the hopes of millions, born and unborn, that the bell tolled.

Ironically, the firebell that so profoundly alarmed Jefferson was occasioned by an effort in Congress to halt the spread of slavery into the territories and to prevent the admission of Missouri into the Union as a slave state; and the bill that caused this onset of fear and foreboding was introduced into the House of Representatives by a Jeffersonian Republican.

The closing of the slave trade in 1808 put the South at a disadvantage *vis-à-vis* the North: whereas the South was legally closed to the influx of black slaves, it principal external source of labor and population increase, no restrictions were placed upon the entry of white immigrants in the North. Because slavery tended to repel white labor (except in the cities where whites competed with black artisans) the South received a disproportionately small share of European immigrants. Not even the fecundity of the slave women, encouraged as it was by the planters, could maintain a parity of population between the two sections. Long before, Patrick Henry had pointed out the source of the South's vulnerability: though the majority of the white population and the bulk of the wealth, especially the fluid capital, was in the North, the slaves were concentrated in the South and safeguarded against emancipation by the will of the majority only by the paper barrier of the United States Constitution.

In the House of Representatives and in the electoral college, the South enjoyed a special advantage which made the acquisition of new slave states vital to its political viability. By virtue of the three-fifths rule written into the Constitution in 1787, three-fifths of the slaves were counted as the equivalent of citizens in apportioning seats in the House of Representatives and votes in the electoral college. By this means, James Madison wrote in the *Federalist,* the Constitution was leavened with the representation of property, not merely of persons. "Government," he said, "is instituted no less for the protection of the property, than of the persons, of individuals." Next to land, slaves were the preeminent form of property in the South. The Constitution thereby not only sanctioned, at least by implication, the existence of slavery but encouraged its perpetuation by giving the Southern states a positive political incentive to increase the number of slaves within their jurisdictions.[1]

By 1820, as a result of the increase of this form of property, the Southern states sent to Congress twenty representatives in addition to those to which they were entitled on the basis of their white population. Two million slaves became the equivalent of 1,200,000 white freemen, and every slaveholder who owned one hundred slaves enjoyed sixty votes. In the electoral college, the three-fifths rule made possible the election of Thomas Jefferson as president of the United States in 1800—a circumstance which led the Federalists to denigrate him as a "Negro President." Thanks to the fifteen electoral votes contributed by the black slaves of the Southern states, Jefferson and Burr, it was said, "rode into the Temple of Liberty upon the shoulders of slaves." [2]

In the North, the three-fifths rule had long been resented as a highly discriminatory method of giving the South a political bonus for its slaves. Northern senators and representatives jealously observed the swollen numbers of their Southern counterparts and calculated how many were the representatives of slaves who enjoyed none of the rights of citizenship. Some asserted that Northern horses, cows, and oxen had as much right to be represented in Congress as did Southern slaves; all were property in the eyes of the law. In 1804, exasperated by the political success of the Jeffersonian Republicans, the Massachusetts legislature submitted a proposed constitutional amendment to the other state legislatures calling for the repeal of the three-fifths rule. Not surprisingly, it failed of adoption: the South would have seceded from the Union rather than surrender the political power it derived from the ownership of slaves.[3]

🍁

To Jefferson, rule by the majority was the sacred principle of democracy and "a fundamental law of nature." The will of the majority—"if only by the majority of a single vote"—must be regarded, he argued, as no less binding than if it were unanimous; the only alternative was rule by force. Nevertheless, in his political practice, Jefferson had not always observed this inviolable rule. During the period of Alexander Hamilton's ascendancy as secretary of the treasury, Jefferson had faced a hostile majority in the House of Representatives. He had then rejected rule by that majority on the ground that it was not "a disinterested majority." "These were no longer the votes of the representatives of the people," he said, "but of deserters from the rights and interest of the people." The congressional adherents of the secretary of the treasury he stigmatized as venal and corrupt; they voted in favor of the measures proposed by Hamilton because they hoped to profit personally from their enactment; therefore their acts could not be regarded as expressive of the will of the majority of the people of the United States. While the principle of majority rule was sacrosanct, the majority, he insisted, must be "virtuous" and "reasonable" and willing to accord the minority *its* constitutional rights.[4]

Although the three-fifths rule, by giving representation to a certain "species of property," violated the principle of majority rule, Jefferson defended it as essentially no different from the practice then observed in Connecticut towns of denying freemanship to some citizens on the ground that they did not possess sufficient property to qualify them as voters—yet at the same time including them, like the slaves of the Southern states, in the census for congressional and electoral college apportionment. He did not consider it important to point out that in New England the voters did not buy and sell the nonvoters as slaves.

In actuality, in vindicating the three-fifths rule, Jefferson was engaged in special pleading—and his client was the South. Like many Southerners of his generation and background, Jefferson saw that the principle of majority rule, if literally applied, would leave the South at the mercy of the more populous North. If the three-fifths rule gave a political dividend to the ownership of slaves, that, he persuaded himself, was no more than justice to the outnumbered and politically vulnerable South. From a Northern majority, especially if it embodied the "consolidationist" views of Chief Justice John Marshall, Jefferson believed that the South could expect no mercy. Not even perfunctory regard would be shown the rights of the minority section. By the time of Jefferson's death, the slaveholding South was in the process of abandoning the principle of majority rule in favor of the doctrine of concurrent majorities—a system whereby one section of the Union would be able to negate action by the other section by means of veto, interposition, check, or nullification.[5]

In addition to the three-fifths rule, the Constitution contained a provision which made it doubly imperative for the South to acquire new slave states. The Founding Fathers, in order to enable the small states to protect themselves against the large states, had provided for state equality in the United States Senate; each state, regardless of its size and population, was entitled to two senators. While equality in the United States Senate did little for the small states—they were never in danger of absorption by aggressive, land-hungry large states—it was of vital importance to the South, especially after it had been welded into a distinct section of the Union with its own special needs and aspirations and, above all, its own "peculiar institution."

Despite the three-fifths rule, the South did not enjoy equality with the North in the House of Representatives and in the electoral college: there it was distinctly a minority section. Only in the Senate did it preserve a semblance of parity with the North. By 1819 eleven free states and eleven slave states stood arrayed against each other in the United States Senate. To maintain that equality the South had to add new slave states to the Union: the territories carved out of the region north of the Ohio and east of the Mississippi, closed to slavery by the Northwest Ordinance, were rapidly approaching or had already attained statehood. Thus, national growth tended to undermine national unity by threatening to upset the delicate balance between the two sections in the United States Senate.[6]

Even so, the South was still capable of counterbalancing with a new slave state each new free state added to the Union. In 1819, Alabama was admitted as a slave state, and, in that same year, Florida, a potential slave state, was acquired by treaty from Spain. Another potential slave state on the agenda of American expansionists was Cuba, the acquisition of which had long been advocated by Jefferson. Cuba was the only offshore territory which fulfilled his specification of not requiring a navy to protect it. And, waiting on the threshold of the Union was Missouri.

In 1819 the territory of Missouri, carved out of the Louisiana Purchase, applied for admission as a state with a constitution sanctioning slavery. As a territory, Missouri had been open to slavery, with the result that of its total population of sixty-six thousand, over ten thousand were black slaves. If Missouri were admitted as a slave state, the South would gain preponderance in the Senate, but there was an easy solution to that problem: Maine, at this time a district of Massachusetts, was knocking on the door for admission as a separate state. The practice of bringing in slave and free states simultaneously, adopted in the early period of the history of the Republic, provided a valid precedent for the concurrent admission of Missouri and Maine.

The real obstacle to the admission of Missouri was that it lay north of the Mason-Dixon line, assuming that that line extended westward from its original termination, the Appalachian mountain barrier, and followed thereafter the Ohio River boundary established by the Northwest Ordinance. If Missouri were admitted as a slave state, the line of demarcation between freedom and slavery would be breached west of the Mississippi River. Moreover, in that event, the entire area of the Louisiana Purchase would presumably be eligible for conversion into an indeterminate number of new slave states.

James Tallmadge, a Jeffersonian Republican but a member of the faction headed by Governor De Witt Clinton of New York—which meant that he looked to Albany rather than to Monticello for political guidance—offered an amendment to the bill admitting Missouri as a slave state. This so-called Tallmadge Amendment required that Missouri, as a condition of its admission as a state, adopt a constitution barring the further admission of slaves and providing for the gradual emancipation of the slaves already there. Although Tallmadge disclaimed any intention of empowering the federal government to interfere with slavery in the states where it was already established, his amendment would have meant that Missouri and, in all probability, other states created from the Louisiana Purchase north of the Mason-Dixon line, would eventually enter the Union as free states. In words disturbingly reminiscent of Jefferson's own earlier warnings, Tallmadge declared that "the extension of this evil must be now prevented, or the opportunity will be lost forever." [7]

Despite the advantage derived by the South from the three-fifths rule, the Tallmadge Amendment passed the House of Representatives by a vote of 87 to 76. It was a purely sectional test of power: every representative from states south of the Mason-Dixon line voted in the negative. Clearly, a majority of the American people, speaking through their elected representatives, wished to prohibit slavery in Missouri and, presumably, to close the territories to any further expansion of the South's "peculiar institution." But the Senate, whose members were elected by the state legislatures, proved to be less responsive to the majority will and, perhaps, more sensitive to the threat posed by the Tallmadge Amendment to the Union: here the Tallmadge Amendment was defeated by a vote of 22 to 16. [8]

But the Missouri dispute did not end with this deadlock between the House of Representatives and the Senate: the opponents of admitting Missouri as a slave state adamantly stood their ground while the proponents of slavery expansion continued to insist upon the unqualified admission of Missouri as a slave state.

In view of Jefferson's early record as an opponent of slavery in the territories, he might have been expected to support the Tallmadge Amendment. In 1784 he had tried to exclude slavery from all the territories of the United States and he had unqualifiedly endorsed the antislavery provision of the Northwest Ordinance of 1787. He had repeatedly said that he relied upon the West to preserve republicanism in its pristine purity after it had been corrupted by luxury, commerce, and urbanization in the East. The original political basis of Jeffersonian democracy was the alliance of the two agricultural sections of the Union, the South and the West, against the commercial and industrial Northeast. Since the preservation of this alliance had always been one of Jefferson's paramount objectives, it seemed logical that he would do everything in his power to keep the West a stronghold of the yeomen farmers upon whose shoulders he thought the fate of democracy rested.[9]

Considering Jefferson's hopes and aspirations for the American Republic, it could hardly be supposed that he would willingly abet the expansion of the plantation system. He knew from experience that slave labor tended to drive out free labor and that the prime instrument in effecting this expulsion was the plantation system of agriculture. Inevitably, therefore, the spread of slavery over the American Garden meant enlarging the sphere of the plantation system based on slave labor, of all methods of agricultural production the most inimical to the kind of small-scale family farming Jefferson cherished.

The "Empire of Liberty," as Jefferson always envisioned it, was to take the form of an irresistible expansion of white Americans over the entire western hemisphere. Even during the period of the Articles of Confederation when the survival of the fledgling Union was in doubt, he declared that "our confederacy must be viewed as the nest from which all America, North or South, is to be peopled," and in the first year of his presidency he said that he awaited with impatience the day when the two continents would be settled by a people "speaking the same language, governed in similar forms, and by similar laws." At this time, certainly, Jefferson did not intend that slavery should be one of the institutions carried by English-speaking settlers to the farthest reaches of the hemisphere; indeed, it was an essential part of his plan that as whites spread themselves over the continents, the blacks would stay where they were, awaiting transportation to Africa or Haiti.[10]

As Jefferson himself had once admitted, the only effective way of destroying slavery was to confine it to its existing geographical limits, east of the Appalachians. Almost from the beginning, slavery had been faced with the choice to expand or perish. If it failed to enlarge its orbit, the surplus population of slaves would become a dead weight of fixed charges under which no agricultural system could long survive. Moreover, without the constant addition of new territory, the domestic slave trade, the lifeblood of the "peculiar institution," would wither and die.[11]

Nevertheless, Jefferson lost no time in branding the Tallmadge Amendment as a "mere party trick," a patent power play concocted by the Federalist remnant in Congress in the hope of creating a wholly Northern party made up of Federalists and dissident Jeffersonian Republicans. These Federalist politicians, despairing of erecting a monarchy, had been compelled to lower their sights temporarily to the creation of a consolidated government in which the states would be reduced to mere subdivisions of the government in Washington, D.C. Chief among these plotters against the peace and order of the United States, Jefferson singled out Senator Rufus King of New York, an unreconstructed Federalist who was prepared, Jefferson declared, "to risk the union for any chance of restoring his party to power and wriggling himself to the head of it." [12]

Had the Federalists stood alone, Jefferson could have calmly observed events from the vantage point of Monticello, for they spoke in the name of the mere shadow of a party that became more attenuated at every election. Except for its domination of the Supreme Court through Chief Justice John Marshall who, Jefferson ruefully conceded, was a host in himself, the Federalist party could be written off as a national political force. Had the Missouri crisis been solely the work of Federalists, it might have been dismissed as the last shriek of an expiring party as it went under for the fifth straight presidential election.

But on the Missouri question the Federalists were joined by a large number of dissident Jeffersonian Republicans led by Governor DeWitt Clinton of New York, who, in 1812, had been backed in his bid for the presidency by a coalition of Federalists and anti-Madison Republicans. Clinton and his followers were in open revolt against "Virginia domination" of the Jeffersonian Republican party on the issues of federally financed internal improvements and the tariff. Their opposition to the admission of Missouri as a slave state—which, were it to occur, would be certain to strengthen Southern control of the party—no doubt was in part inspired by political considerations. Yet antagonism toward the political power conferred by slavery and toward the institution itself had always existed among Northern Federalists. The adoption of a plan of gradual emancipation by the state of New York in 1801, for example, was the work of Federalists; the New York Jeffersonian Republicans fought the measure to the bitter end. In 1819–1821 the Clintonians and Federalists spoke for an important segment of public opinion in the North hostile for various reasons to the expansion of slavery into the national domain.

Jefferson's "conspiracy theory" notwithstanding, the Tallmadge Amendment was not a Federalist plot to subvert republicanism in the United States but essentially a revolt within the Jeffersonian Republican party itself designed to create a viable counterforce to the ideologically outmoded, sterile, "Virginia-dynasty" brand of Republicanism. Without encouragement from Rufus King or, indeed, any other Federalist, the Pennsylvania and New York Republicans had spontaneously broken away from Virginia leadership. The opposition to the admission of Missouri as a slave state was the result of political and economic discontents which had long been gestating in the Jeffersonian Republican party.

This does not mean that as the crisis intensified Rufus King and other Federalist leaders did not try to exploit the situation by forming a new Northern party composed of Federalists and disaffected Northern

Jeffersonian Republicans. But this was a legitimate effort, however much it excited the disapproval of former President Jefferson; it was not outside the ground rules of American politics to attempt to bring the federal government under Northern hegemony (during Jefferson's and Madison's administrations it had been under Southern hegemony) or to prevent the admission of a slave state north of the line usually regarded as the boundary of slavery.[13]

Certain in his own mind that the Missouri dispute was the work of men who were willing to play politics with the Union, Jefferson could not bring himeslf to believe that any large number of people in the North were as sincerely concerned as he had once been, and for the same reasons, to keep slavery out of the territories. As he saw it, those politicians who opposed the admission of Missouri as a slave state did not care anything about slavery or the misery of the slaves except insofar as it could be made to serve their baneful political purposes: their whole objective, he said, was to poison the minds of the Northern people against Southerners as cruel, oppressive, unconscionable slave drivers who richly deserved to be taken in hand by the federal government. By driving a wedge between Northern and Southern Jeffersonian Republicans and by creating a wholly Northern party, they proposed to put the Northern majority in a position to impose its will, in the fullest latitude, upon the defenseless South.

By adopting this point of view, Jefferson succeeded in concealing from himself the true irony of the situation: after the Jeffersonian Republicans had adopted so many of the Federalists' policies that the two parties had become almost indistinguishable ideologically, the Federalists and Northern Jeffersonians had preempted one of the policies Jefferson himself had discarded—the preservation of the West for free labor.[14]

❧

With the alarm bell sounding in his ears, Jefferson buckled on the armor of Hector which in 1815 he had deemed far too heavy for his ancient frame, and took up the shield of states' rights which he had laid aside during the embargo and the War of 1812. Jefferson, in short, assumed the accoutrements of an ardent and an uncompromising champion of Southern rights.[15]

Possessed by this martial spirit, Jefferson now asserted—with the same force of conviction that he had once denied Congress power over freedom of speech, of the press, and of religion—that Congress had no power over slavery in the territories. In effect, he applied the doctrine of the Virginia and Kentucky Resolutions of 1798–1799—that the Union was essentially a confederation based upon a compact, that it was the creation of the people of the several states rather than of a united American people, that the authority of the general government was limited to the enumerated powers, narrowly interpreted, and that the residue of powers including everything pertaining to domestic affairs were retained by the states—to the Missouri controversy. Thus Jefferson demonstrated that his constitutional theories were convertible and that, depending upon the exigencies of the occasion, they were as serviceable to the advocates of slavery as to the advocates of freedom.

As the author of the Declaration of Independence, Jefferson was unavoidably involved in the Missouri debate. Supporters of the Tallmadge Amendment cited the Declaration to prove their point that a "republican form of government" was not compatible with slavery. The Jeffersonian Republicans, on the other hand, argued that the Declaration consisted of metaphysical abstractions without legal standing or relevance to the definition of republicanism. Upon this question, Jefferson offered no authoritative exegesis. Nor did he respond when Northern congressmen quoted his contention in the *Notes on Virginia* that "the whole commerce between master and slave is a perpetual exercise of the most boisterous passions," and he preserved his inscrutable silence when Southern congressmen replied that the *Notes on Virginia* were no more than "the effusions of the speculative philosophy of his young and ardent mind, and which his riper years have corrected." [16]

Jefferson did not deny that Congress had the right to require that a republican form of government be established in the several states—the Constitution is unequivocal on that point. But he did not say that slavery was incompatible with republican government; in effect, he took the position that the two had long coexisted in the slave states without doing violence to the Constitution and they could similarly coexist in the territories. Indeed, he found in the Constitution a positive mandate for the admission of Missouri to the Union under its proslavery constitution: when a state was admitted to the Union, Congress could not prescribe conditions or restrictions not imposed upon the original thirteen states. The original states had sanctioned slavery—therefore the same right must be accorded the people of Missouri when they applied for statehood. Slaves, moreover, were property, and the federal government could not interfere with property either in the territories or in the states.[17]

But the federal government was clearly empowered and even obligated to protect property, including slaves, everywhere American citizens chose to take it. Jefferson had endorsed the Fugitive Slave Act of 1793 by which the federal government underwrote the system of involuntary servitude by commiting itself to aiding in the return of fugitive slaves to their masters. To those who abhorred slavery, this law was flagrantly immoral because it offended *their* sense of right and wrong even though Jefferson's conscience was unaffected and because, as Harriet Martineau observed, it compelled every man "to deliver up to the owner a slave whose act of absconding he approves." The Act of Congress of 1793 included fugitives from justice as well as from the service of their masters but its effects were more severe toward the black who fled from slavery than toward the criminal who fled from justice. A black fugitive was not entitled to a trial by jury and conviction could be based on the oral testimony of the claimant (the master) or on an affidavit certified by a magistrate of the state from which the slave was alleged to have fled.[18]

Clearly, Jefferson had jettisoned his earlier notion that property must be legitimately acquired in order to merit the protection of the laws. In effect, he now said that since slavery was a legal institution established by the laws of Virginia and other states and its existence was guaranteed by the United States Constitution, the rights of slaveowners must be respected as long as those laws and that Constitution existed, regardless of the fact that property in human beings originated in force and deprived its victims of an inalienable right. He did not apply to these statutes of the commonwealth of Virginia the same criterion that he had earlier used against the Alien and Sedition Acts: that acts of government which were patently unconstitutional were illegal and of no force *ab initio*. Increasingly, as regards slavery, he relied upon man-made, legal forms rather than upon natural rights, and he referred more frequently to the authors of the Constitution than to the Author of Nature. He set all doubts concerning his own position at rest by declaring that slaves were unquestionably property—"for actual property has been lawfully vested in that form, and who can lawfully take it from the possessor?" Even in times of peace, the written laws of *meum* and *teum* began to take precedence in his mind over the unwritten Laws of Nature, however compelling and self-evident.[19]

Probably Jefferson would have been less emotionally agitated by the Missouri controversy—the firebell in the night might have seemed no more than a minor alarm—had it not been for two circumstances which augmented the trepidation with which he usually regarded the expansion of powers of the federal government. In the first place, it was apparent that an ominous fissure had begun to open up between the South and the West, the "natural" allies against the commercial, manufacturing North; and secondly, the constitutional decisions being handed down by John Marshall from the seemingly inviolable sanctum of the United States Supreme Court presaged a new era of aggressive federal and Northern expansionism which seemed to threaten not only the future of Jeffersonian Republicanism, but the survival of the South itself. The Missouri controversy was merely the culmination of a succession of untoward events that had sent shock waves through Thomas Jefferson.

In 1816, when the lines between Jeffersonianism and Hamiltonianism were beginning to be redrawn in consequence of the nationalizing experience of the War of 1812 and the rapid growth of the American economy, Jefferson had taken comfort in the special relationship between the South and the West. But by 1820, to Jefferson's dismay, the West had begun to defect from the canons of true republicanism laid down by Jefferson himself—opposition to tariffs, urbanization, banking, and internal improvements undertaken by the federal government. In this fateful "apostasy" Jefferson beheld the "manufacturing and consolidation parties" making large strides toward the complete domination of the social, political, and economic life of the Union. Under these circumstances, any strengthening of the powers of the federal government seemed certain to weaken further the South and hasten the final disruption of the "beautiful" equilibrium which made possible the coexistence of the Northern and Southern states in a single nation.[20]

The signs that the alliance between the South and West was weakening gave added credibility to Jefferson's fear that an isolated, defenseless South would be delivered into the hands of an implacable Northern majority. Today slavery was under attack in the territories; tomorrow it would be assailed in the states themselves. John Marshall had prepared the way: it remained only for Congress to act upon the plenitude of power with which he had invested it by establishing a consolidated government capable of doing anything it pleased. In such a perverted and prostituted Union, the South could expect no regard to be paid its rights as a minority section: it would stand arraigned as an immoral, reprobate section upon which a self-righteous, morally superior majority could work its will under the sanction of doing "right." Among the acts of such a government, Jefferson felt sure, would be a law proclaiming that "the condition of all men within the United States shall be that of freedom." Then, truly, the death knell of the Union would be heard throughout the land.[21]

Manifestly, by 1819–1821, Jefferson had moved a long way from the position he had taken in 1784 when he sought to exclude slavery from the territories of the United States and also from the position he had taken in 1798–1799 when through the Kentucky Resolutions he had tried to make the states a bulwark against the encroachments of the federal government upon the civil liberties of the American people. Now he was willing to accord Congress power only to protect slavery in the territories and he converted the doctrine of states' rights into a protective shield for slavery against interference by a hostile federal government. He was no longer concerned primarily with civil liberties or with the equalization of the ownership of property but in insuring that slave-owners were protected in the full plenitude of their property rights. The

Missouri dispute seemed to mark the strange death of Jeffersonian liberalism.[22]

Yet Jefferson himself would certainly have responded that Jeffersonian liberalism was alive and well at Monticello, although, unfortunately, he could not give an equally good report for the rest of the country, especially Congress. The conditions that had prevailed in 1784 and in 1798–1799 were very dissimilar to the intellectual, political, and economic environment of 1819–1821. The South was now in mortal danger, and the focus of Jeffersonian liberalism had consequently shifted from the individual, whose civil rights were no longer in imminent jeopardy, to the states, and from the rights of man to the rights of property owners. Despite this change of emphasis, the Jeffersonian objective remained substantially unaltered: to preserve the agricultural way of life and the virtues it engendered and to uphold the United States Constitution in the pure form in which it had come from the hands of the Framers. The admission of Missouri under its proslavery constitution and the unfettered expansion of slavery into the territories had become essential to avert the triumph of "consolidationism." The only way of averting that catastrophe, as Jefferson saw it, was for the South, the bastion of true republicanism, to maintain parity with the North. Thus it became necessary to admit Missouri as a slave state and to spread slavery over the territories in order, paradoxically, to uphold the rights and freedoms guaranteed by the Constitution.

Finally, Jefferson could say in his own defense that despite appearances to the contrary he had not abated in the slightest degree his detestation of slavery and the fervency of his desire to see "the hideous evil" obliterated. He continued to insist, as he had always done, that if any action were taken against slavery, it must be by Virginia gentlemen, not by outsiders, and, above all, not by a Northern majority acting through Congress. To the end, he maintained that while no man had the right to appropriate to himself the fruits of the labor of another without his consent, third persons "had no right to interfere between the parties." Slavery, in short, was a wholly domestic affair of the states, and the federal government was reduced to the role of bystander.[23]

Nor did Jefferson admit any diminution of his own zeal to put slavery in the course of extinguishment. "I am ready and desirous," Jefferson wrote in 1817, "to make any sacrifice which will ensure their [the blacks'] gradual but complete retirement from the state, effectually, at the same time, establish[ing] them elsewhere in freedom and safety." The word he emphasized here was "elsewhere."

Perhaps the truth is that as a result of the presence of a large population of black slaves and its devotion to an agricultural way of life, the South was in the process of creating a distinct, specialized socio-economic culture that was to become increasingly unique as the South became more and more ingrown and isolated. In the nineteenth century it resisted the advent of the modern age not merely by refusing to dispense with slave labor but by rejecting industrialism and the values and ethos associated with a system of free labor. In 1819–1821, responding to the alarm sounded by the Missouri dispute, Jefferson rushed to the aid of his beleaguered section under the conviction that the future of American republicanism and the fate of the American Union hung in the balance.* [24]

* I do not mean to imply that the South, as compared with the North, had created a truly distinctive, full-fledged culture. As David Potter observed, while the differences between the two sections were of fundamental importance psychologically, they shared a common language, a political commitment to democratic institutions, and a system of values which exalted progress, material success, individual self-reliance, and distrust of authority. See Henretta 1973, p. 112, and Potter 1968, pp. 69–70.

∽ 25 ∾

The Diffusion of Slavery

◆

In 1819–1821, Jefferson was not content merely to assert that slave-owners had the right to take their "property" everywhere in the territories of the United States: by exercising this constitutional right, he argued, they conferred a positive benefit upon the entire country, ameliorated the condition of the slaves, and hastened the advent of the day of jubilee when slavery would be wholly extirpated from the United States.[1]

The theory that the people of the United States, white and black alike, would profit from the diffusion of slavery over the national domain did not originate with Thomas Jefferson. It had first been voiced in 1798 during the debate over slavery in the Mississippi Territory. At that time, Representatives William Giles and George Nicholas of Virginia had argued that enlarging the area of slavery would ameliorate the condition of slaves both in the Mississippi Territory and in the settled parts of the South. Jefferson appropriated this argument in the debate over slavery in the Louisiana Territory in 1804: by opening Louisiana to the domestic slave trade, he said, a safety valve would be created to relieve the dangerous pressures building up in the areas of large concentrations of blacks. Although he did not foresee it at the time, it was with this argument for the extension of slavery into the Louisiana Purchase that Jefferson struck out on the tortuous road that led him to Missouri and the theory of "diffusionism."[2]

As president, Jefferson was a national, not a sectional leader, and his chief objective in foreign affairs was to increase the territory not of a particular section, but of the United States as a whole. Nevertheless, the overall effect of his actions as president was manifestly to foster the spread of slavery and thereby enhance the political power of the South. The Louisiana Purchase, no doubt inadvertently and incidentally, as Jefferson might have said, opened up a new world for slavery to conquer. But in 1819–1821, in retirement at Monticello, Jefferson made it plain that he regarded the spread of slavery into the region he had acquired from France in 1803 as both desirable and salutary.

Among the arguments they adduced in 1787–1788 for the adoption of the federal Constitution, Madison and Jefferson had broached the doctrine that the immense territorial expanse of the United States in itself provided "a republican remedy for the disease most incident to republican government." Now, in 1819–1821, they prescribed the diffusion of slavery over the national domain as a "republican remedy" for the diseases most incident to the Southern slave economy.[3]

In espousing the diffusionist theory, Jefferson did not admit that he was in any way compromising his position as a champion of freedom. He never pretended that diffusion was a substitute for the emancipation and deportation of the slaves. He assumed that slavery would be mitigated, weakened, and ultimately destroyed if it were permitted to spread over the territories of the United States without congressional hindrance. He succeeded in persuading himself that by dispersing the slaves the number of slaveowners would be increased, large concentrations of slaves would be broken up, and the lot of the slaves would be actually improved. Nor did he ignore the fact that the danger of servile insurrection in the older sections of the Union where large numbers of blacks were held in servitude—Virginia was a conspicuous example—would be lessened. Moreover, he portrayed diffusion as the most practical way of facilitating the deportation of blacks, although he could hardly deny that dispersing them over the American West was a circuitous way to their final destination in Africa or Haiti. Finally, Jefferson argued, the diffusion and the dilution of ownership of slaves would promote their "happiness" by intermingling them temporarily with the white population and disseminating them among humane owners whose moral sense was relatively free of greed and avarice.[4]

Jefferson saw nothing paradoxical in the idea that slavery could be weakened and ultimately destroyed by giving it free rein to expand over the national domain. From the vantage point of Monticello, it appeared that the greatest obstacle to emancipation was the concentration of slaves in the hands of a comparatively few wealthy owners who, it seemed, would never willingly sacrifice their property for the good of the community. One of the most salutary effects of the abolition of primogeniture and entail in Virginia, James Madison said, was the breakup and dispersal of large slaveholdings. Jefferson and Madison expected that this process would be accelerated by opening the territories to slaveowners. In that event, they supposed, the ownership of slaves would be diffused among a multitude of small farmers, none of whom would possess more than a few "servants." Being the owners of a small number of slaves, they would suffer less financial loss than would large owners when faced with the prospect of emancipation and deportation. Slavery would consequently be weakened at its core, within the slaveholding community itself.[5]

Thus the Jeffersonian concept of the American Democrat shifted from a freedom-loving yeoman farmer to an incipient capitalist who invested his money in slaves as well as land but who, on the other hand, remained so keenly sensitive to the stirrings of conscience that he was prepared to give his slaves their freedom when the moral onus of holding them in servitude became insupportable.

At bottom, Jefferson's faith in the efficacy of diffusionism was a reflection of his faith in the inherent goodness and essential rationality of the common man. If the common man were given both education and political power, and stayed close to his farm, he would usher in the reign of justice, freedom, and democracy; if the common man were entrusted with slaves, he would treat them humanely and, ultimately, in accord with the decree of Providence, he would gladly give them their freedom.

Yet Jefferson had once said that slavery atrophied the moral sense, that greed and avarice were joined with the possession of slaves, and that it placed a stigma among whites upon manual labor as "nigger's work." Nor had he ceased to believe that this was so, but he now added the proviso that the owner of three or four slaves would be more responsive to the promptings of the moral sense than the owner of large numbers of slaves, and that the small owners would therefore be disposed to alleviate the "miseries of Slavery" and to emancipate their slaves—in whom, after all, they had comparatively little capital invested.[6]

While it was true, as George Washington pointed out, that slaves who worked on large plantations under the direction of an overseer whose sole objective was to "get out the crop" were generally more harshly treated than those who worked under the personal supervision of the owner himself, there were many exceptions to this general proposition. John Randolph of Roanoke, who owned scores of slaves, made it a point as a Virginia gentleman to treat his "people" with kindness and consideration; whereas English travelers observed that blacks who fell into the hands of lower-class whites were often maltreated.* For the slave, it was no guarantee of good treatment to be installed on a small farm rather than on a large plantation; and, in fact, the patriarchal style of slavery practiced in Tidewater Virginia was more concerned with the

---

* In *Time On The Cross,* Robert Fogel and Stanley Engerman argue that the large plantation worked by slave labor was one of the most efficient units of production created by capitalism. The "agricultural capitalists" of the South, in their view, could hold their own with Northern manufacturers; they were "shrewd capitalistic businessmen" who worked their plantations like a modern assembly line and who prospered exceedingly in the process. See Fogel and Engerman 1974, vol. 1, pp. 195–214, 230–240.

welfare of the slave than was the exploitative type of slavery conducted by get-rich-quick entrepreneurs regardless of whether they owned few slaves or many.

To Jefferson, it was not a matter of "sharing the wealth" in the form of slaves but of dividing the "burden" of slaveownership. He supposed that those who carried this burden would rejoice in an opportunity to divest themselves of it. The fallacy here was that what Jefferson conceived of as a burden most Southerners regarded as lucrative, respectable, and an entirely happy solution to both the labor and the race problem. The possession of this species of property gave a sense of power, of pride of ownership, and of importance in the community. Men who could refer to their "people"—by which they meant several hundred slaves—were exalted above ordinary citizens, who owned few or no slaves, in worth and precedence; to them were allotted the posts of honor and emolument. The deference paid in the North to successful businessmen, bankers, lawyers, and wealthy men in general was transferred in the South to men who computed their wealth in terms of land and slaves. Moreover, slavery helped consolidate aristocratic leadership in Virginia by "ennobling" all white men on the basis of their skin color alone, thus effectively establishing racial consciousness in place of class consciousness—all of which constituted a powerful recommendation to its beneficiaries for the perpetuation of the institution. Just as there could be little real opposition to capitalism in a capitalistic society in which every man hoped to become a capitalist, so there was little antagonism to slavery in a society where every man hoped to become a slaveowner. A British traveler reported that he had seen in the South poor people who had hardly a roof over their heads living under conditions that would be considered unthinkable in Pennsylvania, yet who were nevertheless the proud owners of slaves. Both capitalism and slavery owed their durability at least in part to this omnipresent expectancy factor.

Thus entrenched psychologically, economically, and socially in the South, slavery, if it were permitted to diffuse itself over the territories, seemed likely to repeat in the West the pattern of events already experienced in Virginia, where the Piedmont and, to a lesser degree, the Shenandoah Valley, had been brought within the gravitational orbit of the institution. Wherever it could gain a foothold, slavery and its concomitant, the plantation system, tended to crowd out free labor.[7]

Despite the incontrovertible evidence that slavery and the plantation system were implacably hostile to the realization of Jefferson's hopes for the American Republic—hardly less hostile in fact than the industrial order projected by Alexander Hamilton—Jefferson fancied that in the benign environment of the tramontane West, the slaves would be "happier" than those who remained in the eastern part of the Union. In effect, Jefferson's advice to the new generation of slaves coming up on the plantations of the South was, "Go West, young slave, go West. There you will find kind treatment, more humane masters, a more abundant life, more happiness, and a better chance of eventual emancipation."

Never before had Jefferson suggested that happiness was compatible with slavery: he had always condemned the institution as an unmitigated curse to master and slave alike. Now it appeared, however, that under certain conditions blacks could find a modicum of happiness and contentment in slavery. Although he never asserted that slavery was a positive good—as yet, few Southerners went that far—he took a long stride toward harmonizing the institution with the principles of the Declaration of Independence. If blacks could find even a small measure of happiness as slaves, the inescapable inference was that they were natural slaves. The Quakers and other religious denominations that emphasized the miseries inflicted by slavery upon the blacks rather than upon the whites, found their case appreciably weakened by Jefferson's discovery that slavery need not be wholly oppressive and might, under the right conditions, be positively conducive to happiness.

At no time did Jefferson put the case for diffusion upon the ground that it would profit the South economically and politically. In his exposition, the fact that new slave states would strengthen the South in the councils of the federal government and increase the wealth as well as the power of the "slavocracy" received little mention. While he was certainly aware of the political advantages that would be conferred upon the South by the expansion of slavery, he seemed to prize diffusion almost wholly for its moral effect—its tendency to "dilute the evil everywhere" and to activate the moral sense in the hearts and minds of slaveowners themselves.

With his didactic, moralistic cast of mind and his conviction that the universe was governed by immutable moral laws, Jefferson could not dispense with the assurance that what he did accorded with the intentions of the Author of Nature. It was, therefore, not enough to portray the expansion of slavery into the territories as a program designed merely to bolster the economic and political position of the slave states; to be worthy of serious consideration it had to partake of the nature of a moral crusade. Accordingly, he was constrained to enlist the moral sense in support of the diffusion of slavery and to surround diffusionism with the aura of righteousness, humanitarianism, and divine approbation. It was no small achievement to put a moral imprimatur, peculiarly soothing to the uneasy consciences of moral-minded Southerners, upon the untrammeled expansion of slavery. And he executed this feat without appearing as an apologist for the "peculiar institution." Indeed, Jefferson viewed himself and his "countrymen" as upholders of virtue, humanitarianism, and constitutionalism. Slavery, it seems, was capable of appropriating and bending to its own ends idealistic impulses, and it is a tribute to its power that in 1819–1821 Jefferson marshaled the full force of his moral idealism to insure its expansion.

Despite their opposition to the spread of slavery, Northerners, as viewed from Monticello, possessed none of the positive moral and political virtues Jefferson attributed so liberally to his fellow Virginians. They were simply playing politics with human misery—not only the misery of the slaves but the equally galling misery inflicted by slavery upon conscientious slaveowners—whereas Southern gentlemen, true to the humanitarian creed of the Enlightenment, were trying to ameliorate the condition of the slaves and to augment their happiness by opening the West to their settlement. Jefferson thus turned the tables upon the anti-Missourians: he arrayed the South in the mantle of altruism and benevolence while stigmatizing Northerners as mere party hacks whose preachments against the expansion of slavery were nothing more than low, sectional electioneering politics.

The diffusion of slavery, Jefferson argued, gave the North no ground whatever for moral umbrage because, instead of increasing the number of slaves it merely redistributed the existing population over a wider area and thereby benefited the slaves, the white population, the South, and the country as a whole. On the other hand, to fence slavery behind a geographical line would not free a single human being and not bring general emancipation a moment closer.[8]

Lafayette, whose opposition to slavery was unalloyed by the states' rights dogma and who had no personal interest in bolstering the South against its rival section, regarded the diffusion theory as the last infirmity of a noble mind. In his correspondence and in the conversation he held with Jefferson in 1825, Lafayette argued against the idea that the spread of slavery over the American West would ameliorate the condition of the slaves and hasten the extinction of "this blot upon American philanthropy." To Lafayette it seemed self-evident that the more slavery expanded, the more unappeasable would become the demand for slaves, and the more ruthlessly their labor would be exploited. In his opinion, Jefferson had fallen victim to a grand illusion.[9]

No doubt Jefferson sincerely believed that the diffusion of slavery would accomplish everything he anticipated from it. And in this he had some illustrious company: James Madison, Henry Clay, and President James Monroe, among others, shared Jefferson's conviction that if the slaves were excluded from the territories they would suffer misery, destitution, and, finally, starvation. But Jefferson's fervent advocacy of diffusion put him at the forefront of the Southern militant proslavery faction in the South which paid mere lip service to his hopes of promoting the happiness of slaves and of ultimately putting an end to slavery itself.

When these proslavery activists spoke of bettering the condition of the slaves they were actually thinking of bettering the condition of slave-owners, especially those with surplus stocks of slaves. For them, the voice of conscience was less a guide than an accomplice in the struggle with the North: the moral sanctions with which Jefferson invested the diffusionist theory were for them merely a subterfuge to conceal the fact that since the South had to expand territorially in order to maintain even a semblance of political parity with the North, the "peculiar institution" must prevail over free labor in as many of the new states as possible.[10]

Although his contribution to the Missouri debate failed to give expression to the American mind—that was becoming hopelessly divided over the questions raised by the expansion of slavery into the territories—he succeeded in giving a remarkably precise expression to the Virginia mind, and this in marked contrast to 1784, when his efforts to close the territories to slavery had made him a maverick among Virginia politicians. In 1819–1821, diffusion was widely deemed essential to the material interests of the Old Dominion. For Virginia had come to live in large measure by the export of its burgeoning slave population. Rapidly acquiring a reputation as the "Guinea of the Union," Virginia annually exported large numbers of its surplus slaves, some of them bred deliberately for that purpose, to the newer regions of the South, especially the cotton fields of Mississippi and Alabama. This traffic in human beings permitted the Old Dominion to retrieve part of the prosperity it had lost as a result of the decline of tobacco exports. Virginia planters kept as close an account of the current selling price of slaves as they did of tobacco. In March 1820, Jefferson lamented that, as a result of the financial panic that swept the country in 1819, "beyond the mountains we have good slaves selling for one hundred dollars, good horses for five dollars, and the sheriffs generally the purchaser." The admission of Missouri as a slave state and the opening of all the territories to forced labor promised to enhance the profitability of the increasingly important business of breeding slaves.[11]

Undoubtedly, the most effective way of destroying slavery in Virginia was to deny the state a market for its unwanted slaves; in that event, the economy of the commonwealth might have been brought to such a pass that slaveowners would have run away from their slaves in order to be free of such troublesome and ruinously expensive property. But shutting off Virginia from its lucrative out-of-state markets would have required action by the federal government against the domestic slave trade—an exercise of power that was certain to be denounced in Virginia and other slave states as worse than any crime against liberty committed by George III and the British Parliament. Moreover, it seemed certain to produce the very thing Jefferson feared most of all—a bloody slave insurrection. Deprived of an outlet for its slave population, Virginia would experience a catastrophic economic decline at the very time that a population explosion was occurring among its black inhabitants. In the *Notes on Virginia*, Jefferson had warned his "countrymen" that they would assuredly suffer the wrath of Heaven in the form of a servile uprising unless they liberated their slaves. But by 1819–1821, the export of surplus slaves seemed to be the only practicable means, in default of emancipation, of averting racial war. "We have the wolf by the ears," Jefferson said in 1820, "and we can neither hold him, nor safely let him go. Justice is in one scale, and self-preservation in the other." Freeing the wolf to roam the western prairies seemed likely to make him less dangerous to Virginians at home.[12]

John Randolph of Roanoke, who despised slavery yet insisted upon its right to expand into the national domain, suffered from no illusion that the diffusion of the "peculiar institution" would spread sweetness and light and hasten the day of emancipation. On the other hand, he agreed that it would benefit Virginia, where "men are raised for the market, like oxen for the shambles." This was an aspect of slavery from which Jefferson preferred to avert his eyes: it was utterly antithetical to his moral outlook. Yet from 1830 to 1860, Virginia sold over three hundred thousand slaves to buyers outside the state—a diaspora comparable in scope to some of the great mass migrations of history.

The steady and increasing emigration of slaves from Virginia occasioned by their sale outside the state saved the Old Dominion from joining South Carolina in shifting from a predominantly white to a predominantly black population. In 1800 the census showed that Virginia contained 4,109 fewer whites than blacks, but by 1810 the situation had been dramatically reversed: whites outnumbered blacks by 128,446 out of a total population of almost a million.

While the mass export of slaves may have been Virginia's economic salvation, the process was costly in the long run. For Virginia, the mother of commonwealths, did not export merely its surplus slaves: it endowed the South and the West with a large part of its wealth, its talent, and its white population. The loss of some of its most enterprising citizens to competing agricultural areas no doubt accelerated the decline of the oldest and hitherto most prosperous section—the Tidewater. There, worn-out fields, unable to compete with the newer tobacco-producing regions in Kentucky and North Carolina, produced an exodus of planters who left behind them abandoned plantations, dilapidated houses and churches, and fields overgrown with sedge, briars, and pine. Plantations were sold for taxes at public auction. Nor did the Piedmont escape this economic blight: Jefferson felt its full effect when, at the end of his financial tether, he put some of his nest land on the market: he found few buyers for land that could not match the productivity of the new land in the West and Southwest being opened up to cultivation.[13]

Thus, as the event proved, the diffusion of slavery was not the benign, "humanizing" dispersal that Jefferson pictured. The thrust of slavery expansion was toward the cotton fields of Mississippi and Alabama and the sugar plantations of Louisiana. And it is difficult to believe that many of the slaves who were transported from the comparatively patriarchal society of Maryland and Virginia to the Southwest could have been persuaded that they had embarked upon the pursuit of happiness. Robert Sutcliffe, a British traveler, met on a Maryland road a party of slaves on their way South, "chained together under the watchful eye of a white man with a pistol in his hand. Behind was a cart, in which were some negro children, who had been torn from their parents." It was a familiar sight, visible to Jefferson when, as president of the United States, he had made the journey between Monticello and Washington, D.C.[14]

The opening of the national domain to slavery, while it did not accomplish any of Jefferson's moral and humanitarian objectives, helped to prolong the South's political power in the national government despite its failure to keep pace with the North in wealth, population, commerce, and manufacturing. The West did not attract large numbers of slaves (in 1860 there were only two slaves in all of New Mexico), but it did attract Southern settlers who, despite their change of residence, continued to think and vote as Southerners. To that degree, part of the West was tied ideologically to the South even after it became bound economically to the North. Although settlers from the South brought with them comparatively few slaves, they carried a partiality for slavery which was translated into local ordinances favorable to that institution. But, happily, the "peculiar institution" of the South did not become, as Jefferson's plan would have made it, the "peculiar institution" of the West also.

✒ 26 ✒

The Missouri Compromise

———◆———

DESPITE THE ANXIETY created by the Missouri controversy, Jefferson refused to be stampeded by the cry "the Union is in danger" into sacrificing the constitutional rights of the South to a parcel of Northern "tricksters." A compromise on the issue of slavery in Missouri and the territories was not the Jeffersonian solution: his strategy was to present the anti-Missourians with a set of nonnegotiable demands. If this intransigent posture led to the dissolution of the Union, Jefferson thought that the entire responsibility would rest upon the Federalists and renegade Republicans who insisted upon making Missouri a free state; while history would absolve Southerners of any blame, it would hold their Northern opponents guilty of "an act of suicide . . . an act of Treason against the hopes of the world." He rejected any sectional bargain which, in exchange for the admission of Missouri as a slave state, permitted Congress to draw a geographical line between slavery and freedom. In effect, Jefferson ranged himself alongside John Randolph of Roanoke when he defiantly declared that "God has given us the Missouri and the devil shall not take it from us." [1]

George Washington had taken the position that only the rooting out of slavery could save the Union "by uniting in one common bond of principle" all the people of the United States; Benjamin Rush declared that "freedom and slavery cannot long exist together"; and Joseph Parrish asserted in 1806 (fifty years before Abraham Lincoln) that "a house divided against itself cannot stand." Yet in 1819–1821, Jefferson took the position that only the spread of slavery over the national domain could preserve the Union. If, conversely, the territories were closed to slave labor and only free labor permitted, the contest for power between the two sections—in Jefferson's mind, the crux of the Missouri controversy—would infallibly be decided in favor of the North. [2]

As long as opposition to the admission of Missouri was confined to Senator Rufus King and Governor DeWitt Clinton and their adherents,

Jefferson did not seriously fear for the Union: it would take much more than a self-seeking faction to rend the seamless garment of the American empire. What he dreaded above all was the possibility that anti-Missourianism would be taken up by committed Northern idealists and that the essentially political idea of closing the territories to slavery would be converted to a quasireligious moral crusade. He had, it is true, already preempted the moral ground for the South, but the danger could not be lightly dismissed that Northern zealots would not try to oust the South from its eminence—that, in short, the struggle for economic and political power might erupt into a war of principle. "A geographical line, coinciding with a marked principle, moral and political," he declared, "once held up to the angry passions of men, will never be obliterated; and every new irritation will mark it deeper and deeper." At every crisis, the "angry passions of men" on both sides of this geographical line would be aroused—with the result, he predicted, that such mortal hatred between the sections would be created that separation would become preferable to "eternal discord." For he knew that the South would never accept the status of the morally unregenerate section of the Union and concede that all virtue and righteousness lay north of the Mason-Dixon line.[3]

Jefferson had good reason to fear that the moral issue would not be kept out of the dispute between the North and the South over slavery in the territories. Not only had he been the first to put it there but he, more than any other president with the possible exception of Woodrow Wilson, had arrogated to himself the mantle of moral leadership of the nation. He was a compulsive preacher and, as he himself admitted, homilies flowed freely from his pen. From the beginning he had sought to invest American politics with the overtones of a great moral drama in which good stood arrayed against evil. Against the Federalists he brought to bear the full force of his conviction that pure righteousness was wholly in the leadership of one political party, black abominations wholly in the leadership of the opposing party. Alexander Hamilton would have been startled to hear his old adversary proclaiming in 1819–1821 the doctrine that questions of morality had no place in a mere power struggle between the sections.

Quite correctly, Jefferson pointed out that in 1819–1821 there was little humanitarian concern for the welfare of the blacks, whether free or slave, among the Northern antislavery advocates in Congress. But that circumstance did not divest the anti-Missouri movement of all moral content. These Northern Jeffersonian Republicans and Federalists were in deadly earnest about the welfare of the white man in the territories. The real issue was free labor versus slave labor, and the territories were the battleground. Jefferson failed to see that moral repugnance to slavery, while in itself incapable of creating a viable sectional party, became a formidable political force when united with a determination to preserve the national domain exclusively for white men.

Looking into the future was usually Jefferson's keenest delight, but he recoiled from what he saw in 1819–1821. Prior to the Missouri controversy, his private vision of the American Armageddon had been a racial war of extermination in the South between whites and blacks, but after 1819, the doomsday vision began to assume the shape of a civil war between the North and the South over slavery. Prone to draw analogies between his own day and classical antiquity, he viewed it as a reenactment of the Peloponnesian War, with the South presumably cast in the role of the Athens of the American Republic. He did not doubt that this struggle would mark both the end of slavery and of the Republic: the South, fighting against the simultaneous thrust of Northern armies and its own slaves, would succumb to the Leviathan State. The real victors would be Alexander Hamilton and John Marshall, the architect and chief builder of a monolithic, consolidated government.[4]

It was one of the few occasions during his long life when his habitual optimism seems to have deserted him; no defeat suffered by American armies during the War of Independence, he said, caused him as much apprehension as did the Missouri dispute. In 1820 he expressed the fear that the labors and sacrifices of the revolutionary generation had been "thrown away by the unwise and unworthy passions of their sons"; and his only consolation was that he would not live to see the dreadful consummation—the suicide of the Republic. "I have been among the most sanguine," he said during the height of the Missouri controversy, "in believing that our Union would be of long duration. I now doubt it much, and see the event at no great distance." His faith in human nature was temporarily shaken. "What a Bedlamite is man!" he exclaimed. But he continued to believe that the Bedlamites were north of the Mason-Dixon line. The view he had expressed in 1801 that most of the Federalist leaders ought to be confined to asylums seemed to him to have been fully vindicated by later events.[5]

Still, while lamenting that so many Bedlamites were running around loose among the American people, Jefferson could not bring himself to believe that the people themselves would lose their sanity. His fears of a sectional war over slavery were so radically opposed to his belief in a beneficent Creator and Governor who watched over the United States with special care that his apprehensions could not long prevail against his congenital sanguinity. Even during the most critical period of the controversy, he pointed out that the United States, committed as it was to ride "the boisterous sea of liberty," must expect to encounter some rough passages; queasy patriots might give up the ship but he himself was made of sterner stuff. Yet, momentarily, Jefferson had glimpsed the real

American future: a civil war between North and South over the question whether the territories should be free or slave soil.

But that was far in the future; in 1819–1821, war between the two sections seemed almost unthinkable. However one looked at it, the South appeared to be in an almost invulnerable poistion: the crisis was largely in the minds of Southern leaders alert to even the most remote threat to the "peculiar institution." In the United States Senate, where party lines held firmer than in the House of Representatives, the proslavery forces had an unshakable majority; and President Monroe let it be known that he would veto any bills hostile to Southern interests—and no one supposed that his veto could be overridden. Still, President Monroe did not think of himself as a proponent of slavery: in 1820 he told Frances Wright, the English reformer, that "the day is not far distant when a slave will not be found in America." [6]

🍁

Virginia had long regarded itself as the shield and buckler of Southern rights, and the Old Dominion was not willing in 1819–1821 to relinquish this place of honor. By his insistence upon a policy of no compromise with Northern "political tricksters," Jefferson helped to make the Missouri dispute a test of Virginia's leadership; at his urging, the state adopted a posture of intransigence comparable in some respects to that assumed by South Carolina in 1860–1861. But in 1819–1821, there was no Solid South ready to follow Virginia wherever it might lead. On the contrary, the Jeffersonian "Virginia doctrine" of 1819–1821, like the Virginia and Kentucky Resolutions of 1798–1800, proved too radical to serve as the basis for a Southern strategy. Whereas Jefferson flatly denied that Congress had any authority whatever to interfere with slavery in the territories, the majority of Southern congressmen, however reluctantly, conceded that power to Congress as the only way of breaking the deadlock that was preventing Missouri from achieving statehood.[7]

Fortunately for the American Union, voices other than Jefferson's were heard above the sectional dissonance in Congress. Henry Clay, the Great Compromiser, guided a series of bills through Congress which in their totality became known as the Missouri Compromise. These bills were the work of a coalition consisting of a small majority of Southern and a minority of Northern senators and representatives. The Southerners made very real concessions: to secure the admission of Missouri as a slave state they agreed to the exclusion of slavery in the territories north of the line 36/30, west of Missouri, thereby, in effect, extending the Mason-Dixon line westward to the Rocky Mountains. In terms of sheer expanse of territory, free labor was given an area several times as large as that allotted to slave labor. Nor did the South gain the ascendancy in the United States Senate that the admission of Missouri alone would have given it; Maine was admitted as a free state and the equilibrium in the Senate was maintained.

Although public opinion throughout the country as a whole clearly approved the Missouri Compromise—indeed, the excitement over Missouri had been largely confined to Congress itself—Jefferson refused to endorse the settlement on that account. In the matter of the rights of slaveowners he was not willing to submit to the dictates of national public opinion: here, he argued, was one instance in which the rule of the majority—especially the majority of Congress—did not apply. For no majority, however constituted, had the right to impose restraints upon the mobility of United States citizens and their lawful property. Jefferson had begun his career by asserting the right of Virginia and the other colonies to autonomy and self-determination against the British king and Parliament. In 1819–1821 he asserted the right of Virginia and all other slaveholding states to autonomy and self-determination against the United States Congress.[8]

In taking this stand, Jefferson expressed the prevailing opinion in Virginia. In the House of Representatives, members from the Old Dominion cast fourteen votes against the Compromise, and only four members voted in favor. Only in Virginia did the leading newspapers condemn the Compromise as a sellout of the South, and there alone was President Monroe attacked for giving his approval to the Compromise. It was not the Old Dominion but the more moderate slaveholding states, joined by Northern Federalists and some Republicans, that made possible the adoption of the Compromise. Since the Deep South competed with the West for the surplus slaves of the Upper South, it had far less cause to demand the unlimited expansion of slavery and was, accordingly, more disposed to compromise than was Virginia.[9]

Essentially, the Missouri Compromise created—or was intended to create—spheres of influence between the rival sections. Jefferson's real objective—the opening of the entire national domain to slavery—was not attained until 1854 with the enactment of the Kansas-Nebraska Act. And it was not until 1858, in the Dred Scott decision, that the United States Supreme Court, Chief Justice Roger Taney presiding, declared the Northwest Ordinance unconstitutional *ab initio*. Congress, said Chief Justice Taney, had no power to delimit the spread of slavery in the territories of the United States. Ironically, it was the Supreme Court, the tribunal Jefferson had always viewed with distrust and suspicion, which vindicated the position he had taken during the Missouri dispute.[10]

But the country had not heard the last of Missouri: a second crisis developed in that trouble spot when the territorial legislature adopted a constitution which barred free blacks and mulattoes from entering the state. Not that Missouri hereby did anything out of the ordinary; several states had enacted such laws, especially after Virginia ordered all blacks emacipated after 1806 to leave the state. In all these laws there was, however, a serious hitch: the United States Constitution made free blacks citizens of the United States entitled to all the privileges and immunities of white men. As a result, the anti-Missouri coalition in Congress regrouped and demanded the deletion of this discriminatory article as the precondition of Missouri's admission to the Union. Once again the proponents of slavery were compelled, at least ostensibly, to yield: Congress authorized the president to admit Missouri to statehood by proclamation as soon as the Missouri legislature gave assurances that the state would never discriminate against the citizens of other states. In June 1821 the Missouri legislature, in defiant and minatory language, adopted the requisite legislation. Subterfuge proved more effective than outright defiance: the state was able to practice *de facto* exclusion of free blacks and mulattoes, and in 1847 the Missouri legislature passed with impunity an act declaring that "no free negro or mulatto shall, under any pretext, emigrate to this State from any other State or territory." [11]

Jefferson registered no protest against the efforts of the Missourians to prevent the entry of free blacks.* He shivered no lances for free blacks anywhere in the Union, much less in Missouri where, presumably, they would create discontent and perhaps even an insurrectionary spirit among the slaves. He could not believe that permitting free blacks to go West would accelerate emancipation; indeed, as he had frequently said, his objective was to remove them from the United States, not to encourage them to settle down as citizens. And so, by his silence on this issue, Jefferson put himself in the anomalous and morally untenable position of advocating the opening of the West to black slaves and closing it to free blacks. Truly, for Jefferson, the Missouri controversy proved to be a Pandora's box filled with ambiguities, contradictions, paradoxes, and not a few sheer fantasies.

Yet, at no time during the Missouri controversy, however, did Jefferson depart in the slightest from his conviction that slavery was a terminal evil in the process of working its own destruction. "Nothing is more certainly written in the Book of Fate," he said in 1821, "than that these people are to be free." It was also written, he added, that they were to depart the United States as soon as they received their freedom. To Jefferson this assurance carried all the force of a divine decree: it was the spiritual equivalent of the Moslems' "It is written." Yet there remained

---

* Any Southerner who valued his popularity or, indeed, his standing in society, was well advised to remain silent on this issue. When Justice William Johnson, Jefferson's appointee to the Supreme Court, ruled that a South Carolina law prohibiting the entry of free blacks into the state was unconstitutional, he became the target of a campaign of vilification throughout the South. South Carolina simply disregarded his ruling, as did Virginia and every other state in the Union with similar laws. See Bates 1963, pp. 127–128.

a disquieting ambiguity in the Book of Fate. It did not specify whether the slaves were to receive their freedom as a voluntary gift from their masters or win it for themselves in a servile war. Nor did the Book of Fate say how the freedmen, millions strong, were to be removed from American soil. Jefferson had to be content with the assurance from on high that they would go free and that they would go.[12]

During the Missouri controversy, even though it was clearly not his intention, Jefferson became the spokesman of the planter-aristocrats, the very class which during the revolutionary period he had sworn to liquidate by breaking up their large estates and slaveholdings. No less inadvertently, by coupling the expansion of slavery with Southern security in a union of unequal, adversary sections, Jefferson helped to prepare for the day when slavery would be acclaimed, in the words of John C. Calhoun, as "natural, salutary, productive of harmony, union, stability, conservation." Calhoun and other Southern champions eulogized slavery as a positive good for both races: a civilizing institution which enobled the white man by giving scope to his finest instincts and which raised the African from the degradation of barbarism. While the civilized world became increasingly hostile to slavery, the South exalted its "peculiar institution" to the position of a cornerstone of free government, sanctioned by the Laws of Nature and energized by the dynamic force of Manifest Destiny. And, not the least of these many paradoxes, the agricultural virtues prized by Jefferson were believed to attain their finest flowering in a society based upon slavery.[10]

Although the reality was concealed from Jefferson, slavery, while it was dividing the Union was also uniting the South. Under its powerful integrating influence, aided by the presence of a hostile phalanx of states to the North, the several "Souths" of the early Republic were being welded into a single section. Jefferson did not, it is true, admit to being a Southern nationalist but in the crisis he committed himself to the expansion of the one institution capable of making the South a nation. Nor did he realize that Virginians' insistence upon enlarging the sphere of slavery revealed that they had no intention of abolishing slavery of their own accord. Thus the "greed and avarice" engendered by slavery were linked indissolubly to the prosperity and perhaps even the survival of the South in a union of increasingly unequal partners.[14]

To his fellow Southerners, Jefferson bequeathed, among his other legacies, the idea that the antislavery movement in the North was politically motivated and designed not to benefit the slave or the white man but to prostrate the South politically and economically before a Northern majority bent upon despoiling the "agrarian interest" of planters and farmers. In retrospect, it was a fatal misreading of the real nature and intentions of those Northerners who opposed the expansion of slavery into the territories, and it ill prepared the South to cope realistically with the crisis of the Union when it finally arrived in 1860 with the election of Abraham Lincoln to the presidency.[15]

Increasingly, after the Missouri dispute, Jefferson withdrew into a kind of isolationism in which parochial Southern interests assumed paramount importance. He confessed that he read only one newspaper, Thomas Ritchie's Richmond *Enquirer,* "the best that is published or ever has been published in America." Stridently pro-Missouri, the Richmond *Enquirer* faithfully reflected Jefferson's uncompromising insistence upon the removal of all restrictions upon the spread of slavery.[16]

By his stand during the Missouri crisis, Jefferson succeeded in dispelling all doubts that he was not "orthodox" on the subject of slavery. A Southern congressman, rising to the defense of the sage of Monticello, asserted that Jefferson's position on Missouri had wiped clean the slate which the *Notes on Virginia* had obscured: Southerners could now set their doubts at rest, for Jefferson had proved that "the effusions of his speculative philosophy of his young and ardent mind" had been happily corrected. A large part of Jefferson's fortune was in slaves: therefore it seemed impossible that "when his mind became enlarged by reflection and informed by observation, that he could entertain such sentiments, and hold slaves at the same time." Thus Jefferson redeemed himself as a Southern leader but at the expense of his reputation as an opponent of slavery.[17]

※

The position taken by Jefferson during the Missouri crisis inevitably invites the question: was he becoming "soft on slavery"? Was the "hideous evil" assuming a more pleasing visage which would become even more pleasing if it were permitted to spread across the territories of the Republic? Were greed and avarice beginning to extend their dominion over Jefferson himself, thereby routing the moral sense even from its citadel at Monticello?

Certainly it is true that Jefferson had begun to recalculate the financial advantages of slave over free labor. Early in his career he had concluded that slave labor was more expensive and less efficient than free labor, but in 1815 he remarked that white laborers were "less subordinate [than slaves or free blacks], their wages higher, and their nourishment much more expensive." Indeed, what could be cheaper than the labor of a free black man who, as Jefferson said, could be hired for sixty dollars a year and a free black woman who cost her employer only half that amount? But there were problems with free blacks—especially their alleged unreliability and their disposition to shirk hard work—which made slave labor more attractive. Jefferson proposed, therefore, to increase the productivity of his slaves by closer supervision of their work and by determining scientifically the amount of time required for a particular task by a given number of slaves—and by holding them to the schedule.[18]

After his retirement to Monticello, Jefferson became increasingly fond of drawing comparisons between the lot of American slaves and European peasants, factory workers, and British soldiers and seamen. In 1814, for example, he argued that slaves were better fed, better clad and housed, and better rewarded for their labor than were the day laborers of Great Britain. "They" [the slaves], he observed, "have the comfort of numerous families in the midst of whom they live without want or fear of it [destitution] a solace which few laborers of England possess." In the same vein he pointed out that while slaves were subject to physical coercion, so were British soldiers and seamen; the only difference was that the soldiers and seamen were denied the certainty, enjoyed by slaves, that at the end of their long career of service they would never suffer want. "And," he asked with the triumphant air of one who has just clinched the argument, "has not the British seaman, as much as the African, been reduced to this bondage by force, in flagrant violation of human consent, and of his natural right in his own person?" [19]

Although Jefferson cautioned against assuming that this comparison was an argument for slavery—"there is nothing I would not sacrifice to a practicable plan of abolishing every vestige of this moral and political depravity," he averred ultimately this line of argument proved fatal to the nascent antislavery impulse in the South. Later defenders of slavery, contrasting the felicity enjoyed by American slaves with the merciless exploitation to which the "wage slaves" of Northern and British factories were subjected, concluded that American slavery exemplified in its most humane form the Law of Nature that ordained that some men should be masters and other slaves. The conclusion was inescapable: only in the Southern slave states was the social and economic order truly in harmony with natural law.

Even more startling was a remark made privately by Jefferson in June 1820, rejoicing in the fecundity of his female slaves who added to his capital assets. "I consider a woman who brings a child every two years," he said, "as more profitable than the best man of the farm, what she produces is an addition to the capital, while his labors disappear in mere consumption." [20]

It was not the belated triumph of greed and avarice that accounted for Jefferson's reappraisal of the benefits conferred upon himself and other slaveowners by the labor of slaves and free blacks, the amenities enjoyed by those workers, and the rejoicing occasioned by the fecundity of slave women at Monticello. For him it had become a matter of sheer financial survival and of living out his last years at Monticello rather than being forced to live, as he said, in a hut "like a Negro."

Jefferson's last years were a race between insolvency and death, with insolvency gaining at every stride. He feared his creditors more than death itself, for although he had resigned himself to death, he could not endure the prospect of selling Monticello. Although Lafayette was munificently rewarded by Congress for his services in the War of Independence when he visited the United States in 1824–1825 (he was given $200,000 and an entire township), Jefferson secured no financial aid whatever from that source. (Pensions were not paid by the United States government to former presidents until 1958.) He had, he said, retired from the presidency poorer than when he entered office, and he ended his life far poorer than when he left the presidency. It was a financial shipwreck, ending not in "genteel poverty" but in "nasty poverty," a distinction made by David Hume, the Scottish philosopher, who knew both forms intimately.

Living opulently on their estates, surrounded by their black servitors, and entertaining a constant stream of visitors, the members of the Virginia dynasty went down like gentlemen to financial ruin. James Madison was unable to procure a bank loan because the only security he had to offer was land and slaves—yet Jefferson said that Madison was "the best farmer in the world" as well as the greatest statesman. James Monroe, also land and slave poor, became dependent in his later years upon the charity of friends and relatives; in the end, he was forced to sell his estate, Oak Hill.[21]

In Jefferson's case, his financial distress was compounded by unlucky investments, unsecured loans, and the vast expenditures required in the building of Monticello. Although slaves supplied the bulk of the labor force, he had no system of cost-control; at one point, he was even obliged to mortgage many of his slaves to pay the debts he had incurred in constructing Monticello. Being his own architect and builder, Jefferson was privileged to change his plans as fancy dictated, to tear down, to rip out, and to add otherwise to his already staggering costs and mounting deficits.

As a result, in his old age Jefferson was faced with the alternative of giving up Monticello or running his estates more efficiently with slave labor and cherishing each slave child born on his estates for its cash-surrender value. Although he admitted of no diminution in his zeal to eradicate slavery and his willingness to sacrifice his own financial stake in the institution—and thereby certainly to complete his financial ruin— he seemed inclined to make the best of the "peculiar institution" while it lasted. Penury, it appeared, as well as greed and avarice, was capable of dulling even the most finely honed moral sense.

~ 27 ~

Slavery and
"The Illimitable Freedom of the
Human Mind"

———◆———

FOR THE MANIFOLD ILLS of society, Jefferson prescribed a standard "sovereign remedy": "Educate and inform the whole mass of the people." Any nation that expected to be both ignorant and free, he said, simply did not know history: ignorance and despotism always went hand in hand. Ignorance, or even dependence upon another for one's livelihood, he warned, made people pliable to the designs of power and willing votaries of the cult of personality which led inevitably to the usurpation of power by a single individual. The only way government could be kept free, he declared, was by means of an informed citizenry's "vigilant and distrustful superintendence." "Enlighten the people generally, and tyranny and oppression of body and mind will vanish like evil spirits at the dawn of day." [1]

Upon education as well as upon truth itself, Jefferson put utilitarian value: it was good because it did good. Among other things, education served to alert people to the first approaches of tyranny and oppression; it strengthened the moral sense; and it taught people that happiness depended not upon their station in life but upon the possession of a good conscience, good health, a satisfying occupation, and "freedom in all just pursuits." Education, he said, "engrafts a new man on the native stock, and improves what in his nature was vicious and perverse into qualities of virtue and social worth." As well, it opened the road to "prosperity, the power, and happiness of a nation." An educated people, he felt sure, would recognize that it was to their interest to preserve peace, order, and liberty. For this reason, he came to the conclusion late in life that education was more important than the ownership of property as the major qualification for voting.

By means of a comprehensive tax-supported educational system extending from grammar schools to postgraduate schools, Jefferson intended to prepare the people for citizenship by at least three years of formal education and to facilitate the emergence and utilization of talents hitherto submerged by a social structure unduly based upon wealth and family. By Jefferson's own definition, the paramount objective of mass education was not to make men equal but to enable them to judge of public affairs and to bring to the fore the "natural geniuses" qualified by their ability and virtue, as distinct from their inherited social and financial status, to serve as the educators, administrators, and preceptors of the community. "The object," he said, "is to bring into action that mass of talents which lies buried in poverty in every country, for want of the means of development." [2]

While Jefferson was an enemy of the existing elite based upon wealth and social position, he was not an enemy of elitism per se. His efforts were directed toward improving the quality of the higher echelons of the social and political order under the conviction that the "natural" elite (clearly intended by nature to occupy the seats of power) would devote itself to the work of social betterment rather than to furthering its own interests, especially its financial position, at the expense of the people— as did the existing "unnatural" elite.

Jefferson did not expect that the impulse to abolish slavery or, indeed, to effect any reform whatever, was likely to come from the mass of the people. In his opinion the majority were slow to learn and even slower to unlearn. "It is very difficult," he discovered, "to persuade the great body of mankind to give up what they have once learned," even though that knowledge was patently false or obsolete. He complained that "the task of persuading those of the benefits of science [i.e. knowledge] who possess none is a slow operation." No statesman, he said, ought to presume to "advance the notions of a whole people suddenly to ideal right. . . . There is a snail-paced gait for the advance of new ideas on the general mind under which we must acquiesce." [3]

To prepare the public mind for the unsettling changes required by progress, Jefferson depended upon this perceptive elite—"the intelligent part of mankind"—who, he observed, were usually a century or more ahead of government, controlled, as it usually was, by an obtuse, self-seeking ruling class. The function of these superiors was to instruct their intellectual inferiors—the majority—in the "progressive advances of the human mind, or changes in human affairs." Only an educated citizenry would be capable of electing to office and following the guidance of these "natural aristocrats"; and the sole guarantor of this enlightened electorate was a free and universal system of education. Jefferson's social and political thinking was largely directed toward facilitating the upward mobility of skilled administrators and movers and shakers of public opinion—a true meritocracy—upon whom, in his way of thinking, the success of republicanism depended, and toward giving the masses at least enough education to spot a natural artistocrat when they saw one, and, even more important, to elect him to office.[4]

🍁

In 1797, when Jefferson assumed the presidency of the American Philosophical Society, he said that he had "an ardent desire to see knowledge so disseminated through the mass of mankind thiat it may at last reach the extremes of society, beggars and kings." Significantly, he made no mention of another extreme more relevant to the American scene—the black slaves and free blacks in the United States. Jefferson's educational plans were designed for whites only: in his voluminous correspondence there are only two or three references to the education of blacks. In the *Notes on Virginia* he suggested that black children be educated at the public expense preparatory to being expatriated to Africa or Haiti. In 1815 he stipulated that "the slave is to be prepared by instruction and habit for self-government, and for the honest pursuits of industry and social duty. The former must precede the latter." But the kind of instruction he envisaged was in the skills required of artisans.[5]

Because he could not conceive of an orderly, egalitarian, biracial society in the United States, and because all his programs for the nation's future were predicated upon the relocation of the Afro-Americans, Jefferson made no effort to narrow the gap between the two races by means of education. Instead, the educational program he presented to the people of Virginia ensured that whites would become better educated, whereas blacks, if they were educated at all, would be prepared only for eventual deportation. And yet, if slavery were to be abolished peacefully in the United States, and if the freedmen were to remain, it was essential to bridge the chasm that separated the two races. A master race, firmly persuaded of its inherent superiority and enjoying a monopoly of educational facilities would never permit an ignorant, degraded, laboring people to enjoy any semblance of equality.[6]

Since he conceived of blacks as merely temporary residents of the United States whose tenancy would soon be foreclosed, Jefferson did not contribute to the support of Quaker schools for black children. Emancipationists in Virginia appealed in vain for funds to maintain a black orphan school in Richmond; when the requisite financial support was not forthcoming it was forced to close. From Jefferson's correspondence, it would not be guessed that such efforts to aid the blacks were being made in Virginia. And, although he regarded the United States as a laboratory for the implementation and testing of Enlightenment ideas, he made no effort to convert Monticello into a laboratory for measuring the slaves' intellectual capacity. He established no plantation schools where his slaves could be taught to read and write; an irrepressible pedagogue where his own children and grandchildren were concerned, he devoted no time to furthering the education of his slaves except in menial or mechanical skills. He had one black overseer at Monticello, but he did not make it a practice to put blacks in positions of responsibility. He was content to leave to others the conducting of the experiment which would determine if, "equally cultivated for a few generations," colored people would become equals of the whites.[7]

In 1817, in his capacity as executor of the estate of his late friend General Thaddeus Kosciusko, the Polish hero of the War of American Independence, Jefferson discovered that he had been directed by the general's will to sell about seventeen thousand dollars in government securities and to devote the proceeds to the purchase, manumission, and education of young blacks. He refused to execute this project and as a result the bequest was diverted to other purposes which had nothing to do with furthering the education of blacks.

Jefferson's attitude in this instance represents a regression from the assessment made by the New England Puritans of the potentialities of blacks. The Puritans did not fear the education of their slaves, and freedmen and freedwomen were occasionally admitted to membership in the Congregational churches—an evidence of "election" (i.e. spiritual regeneracy) denied the majority of the white population. The Reverend Cotton Mather, often portrayed as the incarnation of bigotry, was a pioneer in the education of slaves; as he said, their education could not be omitted because "there might be some elected ones among the Negroes." But it should be remembered that the Reverend Cotton Mather, unlike Thomas Jefferson, did not grow up in a community where black slaves, by sheer force of numbers, constituted a constant threat to the established order.* [8]

By avoiding even the pretense of educating his own slaves and by refusing to execute the provisions of General Kosciusko's will, Jefferson was obeying the laws of the commonwealth of Virginia at a time when it was particularly important to him not to appear to be a lawbreaker. Had he had the temerity to make the education of blacks an integral part of his educational plan for Virginia he would have ensured its defeat and, equally certainly, forfeited his good name in the opinion of his fellow Virginians. To most Virginians a black who could read and write was a dangerous subversive who threatened the established order by the very

---

* In prerevolutionary Virginia, the Church of England had provided some education for blacks. The all-black school at Williamsburg had about thirty pupils. The Reverend Jonathan Boucher, although himself a slaveowner, urged Marylanders and Virginians "to make some amends for the drudgery of their [the slaves'] bodies by cultivating their minds." See Brown and Brown 1964, pp. 276–277 and *Virginia Magazine* 46 (1938), p. 4.

fact that he was educated. They knew all too well that education developed in people of color the qualities of ambition, discontent, and independence. In this spirit the Virginia legislature enacted a law in 1819 denying readmission to the state to any free black who left the commonwealth in order to secure an education. This was the same legislative body which chartered the University of Virginia.

Even though Jefferson scrupulously avoided extending his efforts to establish a state-supported educational system in Virginia beyond the white community, he fell lamentably short of achieving his goal. As he said, he encountered on every hand "ignorance, malice, egoism, fanaticism, political and local perversities." He compared himself to a physician "pouring medicine down the throat of a patient insensible of needing it." The only medicine the people were ready to swallow, he complained, was roads, canals, and other tangible public improvements. In 1820, after the Virginia legislature had refused for the third time to adopt his plan of a general system of tax-supported primary school education, Jefferson lamented that "Virginia is fast becoming the Barbary of the union and in danger of falling into the ranks of our own negroes." Thus, a rough equality was being established between whites and blacks in the field of public education: for both races it was nonexistent.[9]

This state of affairs was, of course, contrary to the order of priorities devised by Jefferson: while the emancipation of slaves could, in good conscience, be handed on to the next generation, the opening of tax-supported public schools could not be deferred without endangering the freedom for which the Revolution had been fought. Republicanism could not long survive without an educated people and a "natural aristocracy" to lead them. Nor could the peaceful freeing and deportation of the slaves be accomplished without an educated people and a guiding "natural aristocracy."

Even though his fears of a sectional war over slavery had subsided, Jefferson believed that the Missouri controversy had cut such a deep ideological chasm between the North and South that the trust and affection that had formerly prevailed—exemplified notably in the national organization of the Jeffersonian Republican party—might never be restored. While the North had embraced the "heresies" promulgated by Alexander Hamilton and John Marshall, the South assumed sole custody of the true republican tablets handed down by the Founding Fathers. Despite the North's apostasy from states' rights and strict constructionism—the essence of the Virginia creed—Jefferson feared that in the coming struggle for political power between the sections the North would prevail. The issue would be decided, he believed, not by the biggest battalions but by knowledge—for knowledge was the principal weapon of power. With its superior educational system, the North possessed an inestimable advantage over the South.

In Virginia, despite Jefferson's efforts over a period of almost fifty years, the system of public education remained essentially unchanged since the American Revolution. In 1819, despairing of the adoption of his overall plan for overhauling the entire educational structure, Jefferson was forced to settle for the establishment of the capstone of his grand design—the University of Virginia.

Although Jefferson had for many years included in his educational plans the idea of a great state university which would serve as "the future bulwark of the mind in this hemisphere," the Missouri controversy made the creation of such a center of learning imperative. The tragedy of the South, in Jefferson's estimation, was that it was compelled to entrust the molding of the minds of its most promising young men to those who were opposed to its basic economic and political interests. So wantonly had the South neglected its educational needs that young Southerners were obligated to go to Northern colleges and universities for their education. In these institutions, Jefferson lamented, they imbibed "opinions and principles in discord with those of their own country," i.e. the South. Particularly if they attended Harvard University, they returned home imbued with "anti-Missourism," dazzled by the vision of "a single and splendid government of an aristocracy, founded on banking institutions and moneyed corporations" and utterly indifferent to or even contemptuous of the old-fashioned Southern patriots who still manned the defenses of freedom, equality, and democracy. "This canker is eating on the vitals of our existence," Jefferson warned his fellow Virginians, "and if not arrested at once will be beyond remedy." [10]

Jefferson had no intention of making the University of Virginia a school for rich mens' sons, although, obviously, he devised no way of keeping them out. The University of Virginia was intended to be a monument to Jefferson's conviction that intelligence and ability were "sown as liberally among the poor as the rich" and that this fund of talent would perish unrecognized and unused if not revealed by competitive examinations in the lower grades and matured and brought to fruition in institutions of higher learning. But he pointedly refrained from adding that intelligence and ability were sown as liberally among blacks as among whites, and that the black community might properly be regarded as a reservoir of latent ability, intelligence, and talent which lay buried under racial prejudice and poverty—in short, a source of genuine "natural aristocrats."

The University of Virginia also exemplified the strong and increasingly partisan ideological bent of Jefferson's mind and personality. Political ideas were hardly less important to him than were religious tenets to seventeenth century theologians who believed that salvation depended upon them. After the Missouri crisis with the threat of "consolidation" growing apace, Jefferson tended more and more to invest political—specifically, republican—ideas with a quasireligious gloss deriving from Nature and Nature's God. As he became increasingly intolerant of deviations from what he asserted to be the true republican creed—his letters abound with fulminations against "heresy" and "apostasy," and with acclamations of "orthodoxy," a nomenclature usually reserved for religious controversy—he tended to transfer to the South the role he had formerly assigned to the United States as a whole: the guardian of the republican faith, the hope of mankind, and the chosen people who enjoyed a special relationship with the Author of Nature. Jefferson began his career as a Virginian; he became an American; and in his old age he was in the process of becoming a Southern nationalist.

As the guiding principle of the University of Virginia, Jefferson took the highest ground that any statesman-educator has ever assumed; this institution, he proclaimed, would be based "on the illimitable freedom of the human mind. For here we are not afraid to follow truth wherever it may lead, not to tolerate error so long as reason is free to combat it." And, in most respects, the University of Virginia lived up to the ideals proclaimed in its prospectus: it offered a wider choice of courses; the students enjoyed more freedom (there were no examinations, and attendance at lectures was voluntary); the professors were generally of high caliber, Jefferson having ruled out "aspiring mediocrity" from the faculty; and, with one notable exception, they were permitted a degree of academic freedom unexampled in American education at that time.

Even though Jefferson did not doubt that Truth would ultimately prevail, as a political leader he felt a strong sense of duty to do everything in his power to facilitate its triumph. The University of Virginia was designed to bring the day of victory appreciably nearer by actively proselyting for the truth. Jefferson felt that in the United States in the first decades of the nineteenth century the truth stood in urgent need of some outside assistance. All the Northern universities, acting upon the principle that knowledge is power, seemed to be actively propagating anti-Missourism; therefore there ought to be at least one university where Missourism, the true republican faith, was taught. Truth was perfectly capable of competing in the marketplace, but there had to be someone to sell it—particularly since there were so many salesmen around hawking spurious products which all bore the label, "truth."

In order to discriminate between the true and the false in the realm of ideas, Jefferson felt that extreme vigilance must be observed in the appointment of the professors of law and political science and in the selection of texbooks. With the forces of antirepublicanism gaining ascendancy in the North, the principle of "the illimitable freedom of the human mind" could not be applied as liberally and as literally as Jefferson originally intended. He was not afraid to follow truth "wherever it may lead," but it seemed obvious to him that young Southerners needed some expert guidance to counteract the influence of Northern professors who pontificated upon states' rights and other high matters from academic podiums.

At the University of Virginia, Jefferson resolved that Missourism and only Missourism, the true constitutional doctrine, would be taught. As James Madison said, Jefferson intended that the institution should be a "nursery of Republican patriots as well as genuine scholars." [11]

Of the three American-born professors (only two of whom were educated in the United States) appointed to teaching posts at the University of Virginia, all were politically sound according to the criteria laid down by Jefferson. The vigilance of the overseers of the University was rewarded: not a trace of political "heresy" could be detected in the tight-knit little "academic village" created at Charlottesville. If any professor had had the temerity to raise the standard of anti-Missourism on that campus he would have found that "the illimitable freedom of the human mind" did not extend *that* far.[12]

If Jefferson's fondest hopes were realized, from the University of Virginia would go forth legions of young men, imbued with missionary zeal, to disseminate the true republican doctrine set forth in the Virginia and Kentucky Resolutions of 1798–1800. Jefferson even ventured to hope that by preserving the "vestal flame" at Charlottesville its light might be transmitted to the benighted Northern universities.

Nor did Jefferson overlook the financial, as well as political, benefits that would accrue to the South from establishing a first-rate center of higher learning south of the Mason-Dixon line. When the University of Virginia opened its doors, Jefferson assured his Southern compatriots that they could bring home all the young men attending Princeton, Harvard, Columbia, and the University of Pennsylvania, thereby rescuing them from the antirepublican indoctrination they were presently undergoing, and, incidentally, saving the $300,000 it cost every year to maintain Southern students in Northern schools.[13]

🍁

An incurably bookish man, Jefferson once said that he could not live without books. In the course of his lifetime he accumulated three libraries, one of which he sold for a pittance to the Library of Congress to replace the books destroyed by the British during the War of 1812. Not surprisingly, Jefferson attached critical importance to the ideas disseminated by books: books, he said on one occasion, "have done more towards the suppression of the liberties of man, than all the millions of men in arms of Bonaparte." On the other hand, he acknowledged that they had contributed mightily to the establishment and preservation of the liberties of mankind. Books, it appeared, were an incalculable power for both good and evil, and educators would do well to distinguish clearly between the two.[14]

Jefferson was far more greatly concerned with what books were read by the intellectual elite than with the reading matter which found its way into the hands of the common people. He believed that public opinion was made at the top—by the educated, the talented, the born leaders whom Nature had clearly designated as superiors. It was with the best interests of this "natural aristocracy" in mind that he compiled a list of good and bad books designed to serve as a guide to students at the University of Virginia.

Among the "good" books on Jefferson's agenda was John Taylor's *The Constitution Construed*. This volume, Jefferson declared, contained "the true political faith," all that anyone needed to know about the federal Constitution and how it was to be interpreted. Taylor carried strict construction to its logical conclusion and made states' rights the governing principle of the American Union. Of "life, liberty and property," he said that "the last is the chief hinge upon which social happiness depends." [15]

Taylor had always differed from the sage of Monticello on the subject of slavery. He had characterized Jefferson's strictures on slavery in the *Notes on Virginia* as "mental fermentation and bubbles" which had had the effect of obscuring from the reader the fact that slaves were more frequently the object of benevolence than anger on the part of their masters, and that the ownership of Africans usually brought out the finest instincts in white men—witness George Washington, James Madison, James Monroe, and Thomas Jefferson himself, all sterling characters and all slaveowners. Taylor regarded slavery as a misfortune to agriculture—blacks were really not intelligent enough to perform even their menial tasks satisfactorily—but it was folly to think of emancipating them: if they remained in the commonwealth they would almost certainly try to slit their former masters' throats, and if they were deported, as Jefferson advocated, the South would gratuitously strip itself of its labor force, thereby condemning itself to colonial servitude to the North. Being irreplaceable and immovable, the slaves ought to be treated kindly by the masters and their labor utilized more efficiently in the new scientific agriculture advocated by Taylor. In any event, chattel slavery, as Taylor saw it, was infinitely preferable to the brutal exploitative system of wage slavery practiced in Great Britain and the Northern states.[16]

This straightforward assessment of slavery's advantages and drawbacks was vastly more congenial to most Southerners than the caviling doomsday attitude Jefferson had adopted in the *Notes on Virginia*. In consequence, Port Royal, the estate of John Taylor, became the intellectual headquarters of Virginia republicanism, especially on the subject of slavery. At Port Royal, the ambiguities and doubts of Monticello were dispelled: Virginians could rejoice once again in the certainty that they were good people doing good work and that there was much to be said for slavery after all.

Of the books that might corrupt students at the University of Virginia, Jefferson singled out two for special censure. David Hume's *History of England* and Sir William Blackstone's *Commentaries on the Laws of England*. These books, he said, had "made Tories of all England," and he was resolved that it should not happen here. For students and others who might be seduced by the felicity of Hume's style and the importance of his subject matter, he recommended an expurgated—he called it euphemistically a "republicanized"—version of Hume's *History* which, he supposed, corrected Hume's "falsifications of Fact" by expunging his expressions of sympathy for Charles I and his preference for the prerogatives of the English monarch as opposed to the "usurpations" of Parliament.[17]

To make sure that students at the University of Virginia received a "republican" education, Jefferson recommended that the Board of Visitors be authorized to choose textbooks for the professor of law and thereby "lay down the principles of government which are to be taught." But James Madison argued that "the most effectual safeguard against heretical opinions in the School of Politics will be an orthodox Professor" who would keep anti-Missourism out of the classroom as well as out of the textbooks. Jefferson was persuaded by Madison's argument—with the result that the appointment of an "orthodox" professor of law became the touchstone of the University's credibility as a "nursery of Republican patriots." [18]

Jefferson's first choice for professor of law in the University of Virginia was Francis Walker Gilmer, a young man of unquestioned brilliance and of equally unquestioned soundness on the subject of states' rights. During the Missouri crisis, Gilmer had published several articles in which he asserted, to the gratification of his mentor at Monticello, that the unqualified admission of Missouri as a slave state and the uncontrolled expansion of slavery into the territories would further the cause of "Philanthropy and Liberty." But Gilmer was compelled to decline the appointment because of ill health and he died shortly after the University was opened. Despite this untoward event, a professor of law was found whose position on Missouri was beyond reproach.[19]

Thus Jefferson, without foreseeing and certainly not intending the consequence, by virtue of his solicitude for political "orthodoxy" fostered at the University of Virginia the climate of uniformity and conformity of thought which later came to characterize the "blockade mentality" of the South and which proved to be a formidable enemy of "the illimitable freedom of the human mind." Jefferson's primary objective was to defend the ark of true republicanism from the impious hands of Northern consolidationists and their Western allies. Yet the political "truths" he sought to establish as indubitable and self-evident—and therefore beyond the legitimate range of inquiry—proved in to be the rationale for vindicating and perpetuating the "peculiar institution." Loyalty to the South came to mean loyalty to certain constitutional principles and to a distinctive view of the proper place of people of color in a well-ordered society. Acutely conscious of the fact that the South was a minority section in a Union dominated by a Northern majority which might at any time unilaterally declare slavery unconstitutional, Southerners tended to close ranks and to concentrate their efforts upon the repression of the political "heresies" anathematized at Monticello and barred from the purlieus of the University of Virginia. Although Jefferson intended only to dispense the pure milk of Virginia republicanism at Charlottesville, he helped kill the things he loved—free speech, a free press, and the unfettered freedom of the human mind, in the sphere that really mattered to him: political theory.[20]

ᘒ 28 ᘒ

"Beyond the Reach of Mixture"

◆

FOR JEFFERSON THE MOST URGENT QUESTION RAISED by the prospect of
general emancipation was that of the removal of the freed slaves from
American soil. For many Americans, especially Virginians, the answer to
this dilemma was provided by the American Colonization Society. Organized in 1816, the American Society for Colonizing the Free People of
Color of the United States—usually abbreviated to the Colonization
Society—was dedicated to the task of removing free blacks from the
United States and placing them beyond the possibility of mixture with
whites—to Jefferson's mind a *sine qua non* of any plan of emancipation.

The paramount objective of the Colonization Society was to provide
a refuge overseas for free blacks; emancipation was viewed almost entirely
as a means to that end. Unlike the later Northern abolitionists, the
Colonization Society did not denounce slavery as a moral wrong and it
did not hold slaveowners up to execration. Although it concerned itself
only with blacks already free and with those who might be gratuitously
manumitted by their masters, it did provide an incentive to slaveowners
to free their slaves in the knowledge that they would not suffer the de-
privations and degradation that were the inevitable lot of black and
mulatto freedmen in the United States. Instead of being turned adrift in
a hostile world, the former slaves were promised a new start upon the
African continent.

Inspired by the example of the Sierra Leone Company, the Coloniza-
tio Society sent agents to Africa to find a suitable colony for the freed
slaves, and, in 1822, with the aid of a small grant of money from the
federal government, the society began sending colonists liberated from
slave ships and slaves manumitted by individual owners to Liberia, supplying them with tools, seeds, and other essentials in their new homeland.
The capital of this country (which in 1847 became an independent republic) was named Monrovia because the initial settlement was made
during the administration of President James Monroe.[1]

The Colonization Society appealed to the philanthropy, the patriotism, and the moral sense of slaveowners, but it owed much of its popularity to the fact that it afforded surcease to troubled consciences by producing the feeling, however illusory, of "doing something about slavery." It also offered another kind of relief to whites anxious to be rid of free blacks because of their putative subversive effect upon the slave population. Whatever the motives of its individual members, the Colonization Society was dedicated to the realization of the vision of an all-white America. It might have taken as its motto: Africa for blacks, and the blacks for Africa.* [2]

With the society's colonization objective, Jefferson was in hearty accord. A colony of free blacks on the west coast of Africa might, he said, "introduce among the aborigines the arts of cultivated life and the blessings of civilization and science." Moreover, since Liberia lay in the heart of the region that had supplied slaves for the American market, it could, Jefferson thought, be regarded as a small compensation for the injuries white men had inflicted upon Africans over the course of much of modern history.[3]

For many pious, churchgoing members of the Colonization Society—and the majority were of this stamp—the Christianization of Black Africa for which, hopefully, Liberia would set the stage, provided a compelling reason for resettling free American blacks on the Dark Continent. Significantly, Jefferson made no mention of the spread of Christianity in Africa as one of the reasons for supporting the work of the Colonization Society. As a deist, Jefferson found evangelical Christianity distasteful, and he had no desire to inflict it upon Africans who had, in his opinion, already suffered enough from the white man. Jefferson envisaged a civilized and enlightened, but not necessarily Christianized, Africa; indeed, considering his misgivings about the tendency of organized religion toward bigotry and persecution, he did not view the two as entirely compatible.[4]

The chartering of the Colonization Society gave Jefferson an opportunity to break his self-imposed silence upon the subject of slavery and to make Monticello the sounding board for the society's program and ideals. He ran no political risk in such a public avowal, for most of the members of the society were slaveholders. James Madison was active in its behalf, and Henry Clay, the Speaker of the House of Representatives, served as its president. At least in its early years, the Colonization Society did not seem inimical to the interests of the Upper South where the bulk

---

* Henry Clay praised the work of the Colonization Society in ridding the United States of "a useless and pernicious, if not dangerous, portion of its population. . . . Of all classes of our population, the most vicious is that of the free colored people." See Mellon 1969, pp. 154–155.

of the free blacks was concentrated and where the demand for their removal was most insistent and widespread.

Nevertheless, Jefferson attached little importance to the society's activities. In this instance, he did not cite the "torpidity" of old age or his reluctance to disturb the patriarchal placidity of life at Monticello as reasons for his singular inertia in the antislavery cause. Instead, he made clear that he wholly lacked confidence in the ability of the Colonization Society to make a significant dent in the black population of the United States. "We cannot," he said, "get rid of them this way." Statistics bore him out: during its entire history—and it has not yet wound up its affairs—the Colonization Society succeeded in transporting fewer than fifteen thousand American blacks to Liberia. As a result of the high birth rate among American blacks, the society could not keep pace with the census returns. In 1817, when it began its efforts, there were fewer than one and a half million slaves in the United States; by 1860 there were over four million. Far more blacks were smuggled into the United States during this period than were returned to Africa by the Colonization Society.*5

During Jefferson's lifetime the first rifts between the Upper and Lower South over the issue of deporting blacks began to manifest themselves. Outside of Virginia and Maryland, the work of the Colonization Society won little approval from slaveowners. In South Carolina, Georgia, and the newer cotton and sugar regions of the Southwest, planters vigorously resisted the effort to deprive them of their labor force; what was needed, they insisted, was not fewer but more black workers.6

🍁

By 1823 it seemed to Jefferson that the United States had surmounted the danger that had appeared so imminent in 1819–1821: the formation of two hostile sectional parties based on differing attitudes toward slavery and each claiming a monopoly of truth, virtue, and righteousness. Another short-lived era of good feelings succeeded the sectional bitterness engendered by the Missouri dispute. The "firebell in the night" seemed to have been a false alarm turned in by an overwrought elder statesman. For it had not tolled for the Union but for the Federalist party which, in the aftermath of the Missouri crisis, had lost control of its last state, Massachusetts. No new political alignments emerged from the Missouri controversy; on the contrary, the Jeffersonian Republican party, although bedeviled by faction, remained a powerful unifying force. Thus the Missouri crisis, the most divisive event in the early history of the American

---

* Alexis de Tocqueville reported that "in twelve years, the Colonization Society has transported 2500 Negroes to Africa; in the same space of time about 700,000 blacks were born in the United States. . . . The Negro race . . . will not disappear from the New World as long as it exists." See Tocqueville 1945, vol. 1, pp. 377–378.

Republic, appeared to have passed, leaving the Union unscathed. Jefferson credited this happy outcome to the good sense of the American people, which had saved them from falling into the "snare" laid by Senator Rufus King and his partisans. But, as later events were to demonstrate, what Jefferson took to be the final resolution of the issue proved to be no more than a reprieve: in 1819–1821 the country was not ideologically prepared for the advent of sectional parties—but that, too, came in the fullness of time.[7]

If the prospect of moralistic, self-righteous sectional political parties on the national scene had faded, the danger of a servile insurrection in the South had, in Jefferson's opinion, become more acute. After the Missouri Compromise, Jefferson again fell prey to his old fear that the Almighty's patience with Americans was running short and that condign punishment was about to descend upon a heedless, willful people ruled by the forces of greed and avarice. By 1820 the slave population of the United States stood at one and a half million, over three times larger than when Jefferson had proclaimed that all men were created equal and entitled to life, liberty, and the pursuit of happiness. Doubling every generation, the slave population of the United States was increasing at an even faster rate than Thomas Malthus had predicted for the human race under conditions most favorable to procreation.*

As early as 1796, St. George Tucker, a considerably more active opponent of slavery than was Jefferson, warned Virginians that it might already be too late to free themselves of the "incubus" of blacks. Even if twenty thousand blacks were exported annually from the state, Tucker calculated that it would take more than a century before the last Afro-American had been deposited overseas. By 1824 the wholesale removal of the black population might well have seemed a physical impossibility. But Jefferson's sanguine temperament did not permit him to despair. "It is part of the American character," he told his daughter who was having trouble with her Latin syntax, "to consider nothing as desperate—to surmount every difficulty with resolution and contrivance." [8]

Even so, Jefferson admitted that the problem could not be evaded indefinitely: the Almighty, himself no "Bungler," could not tolerate the bungling of the people whom He had chosen as the hope of mankind. Nor could the problem be palliated and endured in the hope that it would disappear of its own accord; the blacks—and they were the problem—gave every indication that they intended to remain and to replenish the American earth. What would happen, Jefferson anxiously asked himself, after the number of blacks had increased, as it inevitably must, to

---

* Malthus remarked that the people of the United States "far outstripped all others in the progress of their population," a phenomenon he attributed to cheap and abundant land, low taxes, the enjoyment of liberty and equality, and to the abolition of the laws of primogeniture and entail. See Malthus 1963, p. 248.

six million? In that event, not only would the logistical problem attendant upon their removal be almost insurmountable, but the blacks themselves, now one million fighting men strong, would almost certainly say, "We will not go!" Jefferson's fears were well founded: the blacks would not willingly leave a country which, despite the oppression they had suffered, they regarded as their homeland.[9]

The obstacles—already large and growing larger every day—in the way of effecting the repatriation of the emancipated slaves, Jefferson decided, were simply too great to be surmounted by the Colonization Society or any other organized group of private citizens. Only the resources of the state governments seemed to him to be equal to the task. He saw positive harm in private associations which insisted upon undertaking responsibilities which belonged properly to government: they might "devitalize and jeopardize the march of regular government," he warned. For this reason, while cold-shouldering the Colonization Society, he acclaimed the plan his son-in-law Thomas Mann Randolph, the governor of Virginia, proposed to the Virginia legislature in 1820–1821 requiring that "a fair proportion of slave youths" be manumitted annually and sent to Haiti by the state itself. Here, Jefferson observed, "the regular government" was addressing itself responsibly to a task that it alone could successfully perform.

But the "regular government" proved unwilling to assume its responsibility for the orderly reduction of the state's colored population. Governor Randolph's bill was laid without discussion on the table of the House of Delegates and it was never brought to the floor for debate.[10]

Dismayed by the cavalier treatment accorded his son-in-law's plan by the Virginia legislature, Jefferson found it necessary to reappraise his own approach to the problem of emancipating and deporting blacks. Although he believed that part of the cost of transporting and resettling the former slaves ought to be borne by the British government for having permitted them to be brought to America in the first place, he hardly expected that the British would admit any obligation on that score. He was driven to conclude, therefore, that the bill would have to be paid by the individual states. Taxpayers ought to consider it, he said, as a small payment for the "long course of injuries" whites had inflicted upon blacks during the centuries they had been kept in servitude.

But this was only the first installment of the bill Jefferson was prepared to demand of American taxpayers. He had always supposed that the triumph of the moral sense over greed and avarice would be so complete that enlightened slaveowners would not ask to be reimbursed for the deprivation of property to which they had no valid claim under the Laws of Nature. But during the Missouri controversy that comforting illusion was shattered. He now realized that if emancipation were to be brought about voluntarily, the slaveowners would have to be compensated

for the full value of every slave taken from them by the state. His devotion to the rights of property precluded him from entertaining the idea
of expropriating the expropriators. Yet the cost of reimbursing them for
the loss of their property and transporting and resettling the slaves was
staggering. In 1824, as a result of the insatiable demand for slave labor,
the price of a prime field hand stood at four hundred dollars at a time
when free labor was paid at the rate of one dollar a day and a good house
cost six hundred dollars. In 1819, James Madison estimated the value of
the slaves held in the South as six hundred million dollars.[11]

The cost of this combined operation—compensation, transportation,
and resettlement—would come close to one billion dollars. In 1791, Jefferson had taken the position that the national debt, swollen by Hamilton's
scheme of assuming the debts of the states to the sum of approximately
ninety million dollars, could never be paid. As president, he had made
the total extinguishment of the national debt his first financial objective,
although it was not until the administration of Andrew Jackson that this
summun bonum of Jeffersonian finance was finally, albeit temporarily,
attained.

It did not escape Jefferson's attention that if each state were made
responsible for disposing of its own slaves, Virginia, with the largest black
population of any state in the Union, would be put at a serious financial
disadvantage compared with, say, Massachusetts, which had long since
freed its slaves without compensation to slaveowners. This fact, together
with the insights into the problems of the emancipation and removal
of the blacks derived from over a half century of experience, led him to
the conclusion that the entire financial burden to be incurred by com-
pensating slaveowners and transporting and resettling the freed blacks
must devolve upon the federal government rather than upon the states
individually. Jefferson did not often admit the inability of the states to
deal with domestic problems, and even more rarely did he feel constrained
to call upon the federal government to act in lieu of the states. But the
plan of action he proposed in 1824 was based upon the premise that the
magnitude and urgency of the problem made intervention by the federal
government mandatory.[12]

As early as 1821, Jefferson indicated that he was willing to turn to
the federal government for financial aid, but it was not until 1824 that
he conceived a plan for achieving the twin goals of freeing and expatriating the slaves—a design so ambitious that it could not possibly be
implemented without massive financial support from the federal government. In that year he endorsed in his private correspondence the idea put
forward by some members of the Colonization Society that the revenue
realized from the sale of public lands be diverted by the federal government to this purpose.[13]

The execution of this plan required the expansion of the powers of the federal government and its intervention into the private affairs of American citizens far beyond anything dreamed of in the philosophy of Alexander Hamilton. True, Jefferson insisted upon an enabling constitutional amendment whereas Hamilton preferred the more expeditious route of constitutional interpretation. Even so, Jefferson's use of the powers of the federal government in the enforcement of the embargo of 1808–1809 and his willingness to thrust upon the federal government the fiscal and administrative responsibility of solving the racial problem in the United States reveals that, in practice, his aversion to "energetic" government could be conveniently suspended when great social and economic problems were involved. In this instance, he was prepared to subordinate his ideal of limited government to the higher imperative of averting the racial war he thought inevitable unless slavery were abolished.

With a million and a half blacks awaiting transportation overseas, Jefferson was inclined to prefer Haiti over Liberia because it was much closer to the United States and because he thought that the success or failure of the experiment in self-government being conducted in Haiti would go far toward proving or disproving the capacity of blacks to order their own affairs as free men. Moreover, Haiti seemed to him to be a proper laboratory for settling pragmatically the vexing question whether the apparent inferiority of blacks was innate or simply a result of servitude. Forty years after the publication of the *Notes on Virginia* this question had not been resolved to Jefferson's satisfaction.[14]

Before the stupendous sum of money involved in the cost of emancipation, compensation, and deportation, Jefferson quailed. At this time Americans calculated their national debt in the millions and even in the hundreds of thousands, not in the billions of dollars. Imperative as he deemed the removal of the black population, he recognized that it had reached a sheer numerical magnitude which effectively foreclosed the kind of mass relocation he really desired. Although he did not abandon hope of getting rid of all blacks ultimately, he was prepared in 1824 to make his immediate objective the removal of black slave children from the United States. Here, he thought, was the principal cause of the failure of the Colonization Society to effect an appreciable reduction of the black population: it confined its attention too much to adults, to the neglect of the children upon whom black posterity depended.

Accordingly, reverting to the plan he had adumbrated in the *Notes on Virginia,* Jefferson recommended that black slave children be taken from their parents at the age of five years, raised as wards of the states, and prepared for their impending expatriation by instruction in skills that would prove useful to them in their new homeland. The beauty of this plan, as Jefferson saw it, was that "it would give time for a gradual extinction of that species of labor [slavery], and substitution of another, and lessen the severity of the shock, which an operation so fundamental cannot fail to produce." From their labor, the children would pay part of the cost of their transportation and the reimbursement of their masters.* [15]

Putting his mathematical talents to work, Jefferson calculated that if sixty thousand black children were born annually, fifty vessels could carry off the annual increase, leaving the parents and grandparents to die off in the course of nature. With nature and man cooperating, long before the end of the nineteenth century the United States would enjoy the "beatitude" of having fulfilled the designs of the Author of Nature by placing whites and blacks "beyond the reach of mixture." [16]

One of the few redeeming features of American slavery was that it permitted the development of the monogamous family (without, however, sanctioning it legally). Slaveowners found it to their advantage to allow the slave family to exist; it made the slaves more tractable and it encouraged the increase of "property" by natural procreation. In another connection—he was speaking of the white family—Jefferson said that "the happiness of the domestic fireside is the first born of heaven." In line with this conviction, he had always made it a point to sell slaves as families, or at least to keep children with their mothers. Yet he now proposed to break up the black slave family by separating young children from their parents. The traumatic psychological damage resulting from rearing black children as wards of the state did not deter Jefferson; everything, he said, must be subordinated to the imperative necessity of ridding the country of blacks.

That Thomas Jefferson, by nature a kindhearted, benevolent, well-intentioned man, should have recommended such a Draconian method for attaining the "beatitude" of an all-white society reveals how urgent he deemed it to be to separate physically the two races. With, as he saw it, the future "safety and happiness" of the American people at stake, the family structure of the black community weighed hardly at all in the balance. The fear of a servile war which the proliferation of the black population in the Southern states seemed to be bringing ever nearer, together with the fact of miscegenation, the evidences of which were apparent in many Virginia households and by which he was daily confronted at Monticello, brought to the fore the vein of iron imbedded in his character: his implacable determination to dispose of an unassimilable and potentially dangerous race which, in his opinion, endangered the peace, well-being, and racial purity of the American people. [17]

---

* Jefferson's scheme for the mass impressment into forced labor of slave children should be judged in the context of eighteenth century ideas. Since that time there has occurred a truly revolutionary change in the popular view of the rights of children and their place in society. John Locke, sometimes apostrophized as the "philosopher of the American Revolution," proposed to put children of poor parents to work at three years of age, thereby relieving the parish of all charges for their upbringing. In 1724, Daniel Defoe reported with satisfaction that in Yorkshire most children above four years old appeared to be gainfully employed.

Jefferson conceded that the execution of his plan would create some formidable constitutional and humanitarian problems, but he anticipated no insuperable difficulties on either score. Of the constitutional questions raised by his scheme, he observed that "a liberal construction, justified by the object, may go far, and an amendment of the Constitution, the whole length necessary." As for humanitarian objections to the separation of infants from the parents, they must yield, he said, to the compelling necessity of relocating the blacks far from all contacts with whites. Under these circumstances, "to persist in such humanitarian scruples," he said, "would be straining at a gnat and swallowing a camel." [18]

Jefferson left the execution of his plan to those who, he said, "will live to see the accomplishment, and to enjoy a beatitude forbidden to my eye. But I leave it with the admonition, to rise and be doing." The "beatitude" which Jefferson had in mind was an all-white America; what he adjured his countrymen to be "up and doing" was emancipating and expatriating the slaves. In this way, he believed, they would close for themselves and their posterity the circle of their felicities.

Jefferson expressed the hope that his grand design of 1824—the only occasion he spelled out in detail how emancipation and deportation were to be accomplished—would be a blessing for blacks as well as whites. As he said, he was no advocate of the "misery of slaves" even though, admittedly, his main concern was always for the welfare of the white race. He felt certain that sending them to Haiti would be as beneficial to them as the colonization of America had been to Englishmen and Europeans who, fleeing oppression and discrimination in the Old World, had found peace, contentment, and happiness in the New. The forced emigration of blacks, while it seemed a hardship at the time, would later, he predicted, be accounted a blessing in disguise for it gave an enslaved and oppressed people an opportunity to make a fresh start as "a separate, free and independent people." [19]

Ironically, it was not the United States government but the government of Haiti which attempted to implement Jefferson's plan of making Haiti a refuge for free American blacks. In 1820, President Jean Pierre Boyer invited American blacks to settle in Haiti, offering them land grants and free passage to the island. Almost six thousand Afro-Americans took advantage of this opportunity, but many of them returned, discouraged and disillusioned, to the United States within a few years. In 1859 another effort was made by the Haitian government to promote immigration from the United States, but the settlers found that the Haitian government failed to live up to its promises of free homesteads and supplies. But it was the outbreak of the American Civil War that finally closed out Jefferson's utopian vision of a Caribbean sanctuary and homeland for uprooted American blacks. [20]

↬ 29 ↫

The Last Word from Monticello

———◆———

IN 1824–1825, A YEAR BEFORE JEFFERSON'S DEATH, Lafayette visited the United States for the first time since 1784. He was astonished by the changes that had occurred in the country of which he was a citizen by Act of Congress. Among these changes none was more startling that the increase in racial prejudice he observed on every hand. Lafayette, who remembered the days when black and white soldiers had messed and fraternized together during the war, now found that whites were rarely seen with blacks unless they were menials. At the time of the American Revolution, Lafayette had supposed that Americans were fighting for "a great and noble principle—the freedom of mankind." He now reluctantly came to the conclusion that white men had been concerned only with their own freedom.* [1]

Convinced by his American tour that the blacks had regressed in the last half century, Lafayette urged Jefferson to sound the summons from his mountaintop to all Americans to join in educating the slaves as a first step toward their emancipation. Jefferson, now eighty-two years old, politely excused himself; while he had no doubt that the time would come when the slaves would be emancipated, he was equally certain that that time had not yet arrived. Nevertheless, he did make a modest con-

---

* Alexis de Tocqueville, observing the United States less than a decade after Lafayette's last visit, remarked that the evidences of discrimination against blacks were far more pervasive in the free states of the North than in the Southern slave states. In the South, Tocqueville found that slaves sometimes shared the labor and the recreations of the whites. "The whites," he said, "consent to intermix with them to a certain extent, and although legislation treats them more harshly, the habits of the people are more tolerant and compassionate. In the North the white . . . shuns the Negro with more pertinacity since he fears lest they should some day be confounded together." From this circumstance, Tocqueville concluded that in the United States "the prejudice which repels the Negroes seems to increase in proportion as they are emancipated. . . . If I were called upon to predict the future, I should say that the abolition of slavery in the South will, in the common course of things, increase the repugnance of the white population to the blacks." See Tocqueville 1945, vol. 1, pp. 360, 375.

cession to Lafayette's enthusiasm for educating the slaves: he said that he favored teaching them to learn to read print but not to write; writing, he pointed out, would enable them to forge papers, thereby making it impossible to keep them in subjection.[2]

Jefferson had good reason for refusing to commit himself even to delivering a rhetorical attack upon slavery in order to please Lafayette and to enhance his fame with European liberals. With the beleaguered South engaged in a life-or-death struggle with a Northern majority imbued, as he supposed, with the centralist ideas and the "monarchical" objectives of John Marshall, he was far more concerned with the wrong done to slaveowners than with the wrongs done by them. Slavery, in Jefferson's opinion, had become such an integral part of states' rights that, until Southerners themselves could get round to abolishing the institution in their own way and on their own terms, the two—slavery and states' rights—must rise or fall together.

If, as Lafayette said, the gap between the two races had widened perceptibly in the United States since the Revolution, Jefferson attributed this in large measure to the fact that greed and avarice were becoming progressively more firmly allied with slavery. Production and still more production regardless of the human cost became the watchword of men who were amassing fortunes in cotton and sugar. Both the South and the North scented money—big money—in the breeze blowing from the Southwest, and it boded no good for the slaves who, as the chief instruments of production, were compelled to satisfy the avidity of entrepreneurs who found in the production, shipment, and manufacture of cotton and sugar the way to wealth.

As a result, in his later years Jefferson was denied the solace of reprobating "greed and avarice" as the peculiar vice of the commercial and manufacturing section of the Union and of stigmatizing businessmen as the sole enemies of American virtue. It was all too obvious that these baser passions were very much at work in the South and that the triumph of the moral sense—the prerequisite, he supposed, to the peaceful abolition of slavery and the avoidance of a servile uprising—was not likely to be celebrated in the near future.

To the end of his life Jefferson continued to believe that both the emancipation and expatriation of the black population were feasible provided that the "avarice" of the slaveowners could be overcome. He had met the enemy—greed and avarice—and he found it was the people he loved and whose background preoccupations he shared. Against such an adversary, allied as it was with a pervasive racial prejudice, the moral sense found its overmatch. For what Jefferson moralistically castigated as "greed and avarice" was to slaveowners themselves simply a prudent regard for their own economic welfare. Certainly few Northern businessmen would have consented to make the sacrifices Jefferson demanded of

Southern slaveowners in the name of an idealism that seemed to work contrary to their immediate economic interests.[3]

For the revolutionary generation, the lesson was clear and unmistakable: it was far easier to start a revolution and conduct it to a successful conclusion than to eradicate slavery. Here Jefferson and his fellow revolutionaries encountered powerful social and economic undercurrents which turned back all their efforts to bring this indispensable reform within the mainstream of the revolutionary movement. Blaming George III for the existence of slavery, while it eased the conscience of American slaveholders did nothing to remove the evil itself; and declamations against tyranny did not noticeably advance the cause of racial equality. Nor was the problem to be resolved by free intellectual inquiry: the injunction "For God's sake, let us hear both sides" did not apply to slavery. From Jefferson's point of view there simply was no rational or moral argument on the side of slavery; free discussion could lead only to the condemnation of the institution as a wrong that was offensive to the moral sense, contrary to nature, and inviting Divine retribution.

In 1825, when the English social reformer Frances Wright came to the United States to enlist support for her plan to establish an interracial community at Nashoba, Tennessee, she asked Jefferson for his public support. Jefferson, who was now eighty-two years old, answered that he was past the age of embarking on new enterprises, even though their purpose was "bettering the condition of man." Still, Jefferson gave his blessing—all he now had to give—to the proposed community. But he seems not to have understood that it was conceived by Miss Wright as a racially integrated collective: "it has succeeded with a certain portion of our white brethren, under the care of a Rapp and an Owen," he told Miss Wright, "and why may it not succeed with the man of color?" James Madison, who clearly saw the racial implications of the Nashoba community, set the lady straight about the true Jeffersonian position: an interracial community was an invitation to miscegenation, the Jeffersonian horror of horrors.[4]

With Miss Wright's cardinal objective—to train the blacks in vocations with a view to their speedy removal from the United States—Jefferson was in complete accord. It required only a brief sojourn in the United States to convince her that there was no future for free blacks in the American Republic. In 1830 most of the blacks under her care at Nashoba were removed to Haiti.[5]

Toward other social reforms and political causes in which his contemporaries urged him to take part, Jefferson invariably gave the same answer: the infirmities and lassitude of age, the exhaustion resulting from a lifetime spent in public service, ruled out any action on his part. For example, the independence of Latin America which, he believed, was as certain to occur as the abolition of slavery in the United States, must, he said, be the work of younger men to whom the achievements of the revolutionary generation ought to serve as an inspiration. "From an old man," he said, "they can receive no aid but prayers." Jefferson, of course, did not expect his prayers to work miracles, and he never suggested that prayers would be of any avail whatever against the "consolidationism" of Chief Justice John Marshall.[6]

Jefferson preserved his optimism even in his old age—perhaps the supreme test of that quality. At the age of seventy-three he could assert, "I steer my bark with Hope in the head, leaving Fear astern," and he expressed disdain for "those characters wherein fear predominates over hope"—by his definition, Tories, Federalists, monarchists, and consolidationists. He still maintained the exhilarating sense of riding the wave of the future, and, even though he had long since resigned himself to the probability that he would not live to see slavery abolished, he remained confident that the *Notes on Virginia* would serve as a testamentary legacy for the guidance of future generations who would vanquish slavery by "the generous energy" of their minds. To the end, he exemplified the characteristically American attitude that every problem, however intractable, can be solved by the exercise of reason, ingenuity, and persistence; and he remained certain in his own mind that the United States was an object of special concern to the "Creator and Benevolent Governor of the World." "The abolition of the evil [slavery] is not impossible," he said in August 1825. "It ought never therefore to be despaired of. Every plan should be adopted, every experiment tried, which may do something towards the ultimate object." [7]

In his own lifetime Jefferson had seen things accomplished which had seemed at the time even beyond his own high hopes of future felicity. The American people, he felt sure, were destined by the Author of Nature to demonstrate to makind that nothing was impossible; men could convert the world into a paradise if they but threw off, as Americans had done, the chains imposed by kings, priests, and nobles and gave reason and the moral sense free play. As he told John Adams in 1826, they had lived like Argonauts in the Heroic Age and they had successfully brought their bark into "the Halcyon calm succeeding the storm which our Argosy has so stoutly weathered." He and Adams, he continued, were about to disembark; a new crew had come aboard; and the ship could be safely entrusted to their hands. "I console myself with the reflection," Jefferson told John Adams, "that those who will come after us will be as wise as we are, and as able to take care of themselves as we have been." [8]

And, indeed, Jefferson could not abandon his faith in the eventual abolition of slavery without at the same time abandoning his country to the horrors of racial war. For he believed to the last day of his life that the stark choice facing the South lay between freeing the slaves or experiencing the "bloody process of St. Domingo." [9]

Ten days before the fiftieth anniversary of the Declaration of Independence, Jefferson set down on paper his thoughts on the Declaration's place in history. He was certain in his own mind, he said, that the Declaration would prove to be "the signal of arousing men to burst the chains . . . and to securing the blessings and security of self-government. All eyes are opened, or opening to the rights of man. The general spread of the light of science has laid open to every view the palpable truth that the mass of mankind has not been born with saddles on their backs or a favored few booted and spurred, ready to ride them legitimately, by the grace of God."

Despite the unmistakable relevance of these words to the American scene—where but in the South was the idea that masses of men were born with saddles on their backs to serve the purposes of a favored few given wider application as a fundamental law of human existence?—Jefferson had no intention of encouraging the slaves to "burst the chains." He never conceived of the Declaration of Independence as a signal for the slaves to strike for freedom; rather, it was a signal for the whites to strike the chains from the slaves. As for the "blessings of freedom and self-government," Jefferson was here referring in the first instance to the subject peoples of Europe and Latin America to whom he believed that the principles of the Declaration of Independence directly applied. If American blacks were ever to enjoy these blessings, it would be in Africa or Haiti, not in the United States. [10]

Jefferson asked to be judged by his acts rather than by his words. But on the issue of slavery in America he emerges with greater luster if he is judged by his words rather than by his acts. For here he signally failed to live up to his own precepts: "to do whatever is right, and leave the consequences to Him who has the disposal of them," and to "give up money, give up fame, give up science, give up the earth itself and all it contains, rather than do an immoral act." In the antislavery movement, except for the abolition of the slave trade in 1808, he chose—or, as he said, was constrained to choose by imperious circumstances beyond his control—to philosophize about the moral evil of slavery, to warn his countrymen of the divine chastizement they were inviting by their intransigence, and to plant ideas in his wide-ranging correspondence which he hoped others would bring to fruition. By so doing, he played a part congenial to the retiring, studious, and literary side of his character. His refusal to follow up the *Notes on Virginia* with an active assault upon slavery never ceased to occasion regret among the later abolitionists: as William Lloyd Garrison said, if Jefferson had acted upon his theories of the rights of man "what an all-conjuring influence must have attended his illustrious example." Whatever the tenor of Jefferson's words, his "illustrious example"—and nothing in that regard was more telling than the fact that he remained a slaveowner all his life—tended to countenance the institution he abhorred.[11]

Clearly, Jefferson shared the racial prejudice which compounded the problem of ridding the United States of what he called "this great political and moral evil," "this blot on our country." But he succeeded in concealing this prejudice from himself by imagining that he was acting in response to divine edicts which ordained, among other things, that while the slaves should go free they should also be expelled from the country they regarded, for better or for worse, as their homeland. "Nothing is more certainly written in the book of fate," he asserted in his *Autobiography,* "than that the two races, equally free, cannot live in the same government. Nature, habit, opinion have drawn indelible lines of distinction between them." [12]

In one of his last "peeps into futurity" Jefferson said that the American people "shall go on, puzzled and prospering beyond example in the history of man." It was not revealed to him, however, that sharing this puzzlement and, to a lesser degree, this prosperity, would be twenty million black citizens of the United States. Jefferson's failure to foresee this salient fact of American history has enormously complicated the Jeffersonian heritage of freedom and equality, majority rule and minority rights. For the ideals and aspirations to which he gave imperishable expression in the Declaration of Independence, the Statute for Religious Freedom, and the University of Virginia, have to be applied, not in the all-white society of Jefferson's vision, but in the multiracial society of the twentieth century. More prescient than Jefferson, Alexis de Tocqueville stated the real nature of the American dilemma: "These two races are fastened to each other without intermingling; and they are alike unable to separate entirely or to combine." [13] Jefferson read in the Book of Fate that slavery was doomed, but the sequel of that event was not revealed to him.

On the other hand, it was also legibly written in the Book of Fate that had Jefferson made himself conspicuous as a fervent, militant, and uncompromising abolitionist on the model of William Lloyd Garrison, or had he even gone so far as to suggest that whites and blacks ought to enjoy equal rights as citizens of the United States, he would not have succeeded in doing the things in which he took the greatest pride and by which he wished to be remembered by posterity. Nor would he have had the slightest chance of becoming president of the United States: it was not until 1860 that a man known to be hostile to the spread of slavery into the territories was elected to that high office. From the beginning of his career it was impressed upon Jefferson that he must choose between the preservation of his political "usefulness" and active opposition to slavery. In spite of his real and abiding abhorrence of the "peculiar institution," he was too much the political pragmatist, too intent upon achieving lofty but realizable goals, and too much the product of his background as a Virginia slaveowner to grapple with this particular example of man's tyranny over man with the same fervor he had displayed in contending against British tyranny.

Harriet Martineau said that the United States is a country possessed with an idea—an idea that was enunciated most eloquently by Thomas Jefferson. "There is the strongest hope of a nation that is capable of being possessed with an idea," she observed, "and this kind of possession has been the peculiarity of Americans from their first day of national existence till now." But, she reminded the American people, it is not enough merely to proclaim this idea to a candid world. It must, she said, be acted upon.[14]

Notes

◆

Chapter 1.

1. See Elkins 1963, pp. 37–52, and E. S. Morgan 1975, pp. 295–331.
2. See Isaiah Berlin 1956; Clive 1960; Gay 1964; Gay 1966; Vynerberg 1958; and Watson 1973.
3. See Davis 1970, p. 7; Hawke 1964, p. 54; Parton 1889, pp. 97–98; Robinson 1970, pp. 81–82; and *Virginia Magazine* 80, p. 146.
4. See Fogel and Engerman 1 (1974), pp. 131–133, and Macleod 1974, p. 82.
5. See P. L. Ford 1, p. 380; Hawke 1964, pp. 53–54; and Malone 1948, pp. 121–122.
6. See Cotterill 1 (1926), pp. 90–92, and Brodie 1974, pp. 90–92.
7. See Brown and Brown 1964, p. 284.
8. See *Virginia Magazine* 80, pp. 146–150.
9. See Mullin 1972, pp. 130–132, and Schachner 1953, p. 134.
10. See D. B. Davis 1975, pp. 73, 76, 80.
11. See Malone 1954, pp. 85–88.
12. See Hawke 1971, p. 160.

Chapter 2.

1. See J. R. Howe 1970, p. 67.
2. See Miller 1975, p. 149, and *Virginia Magazine* 44, p. 45.
3. See *William and Mary Quarterly*, July 1925, p. 167.
4. See Griswold 1948, pp. 36–37; R. W. Harris 1968, p. 58; Larkin 1930, pp. 74–75; Levy 1968, p. 413; Malone 1951, p. 284; and Vereker 1967, p. 58.
5. See *William and Mary Quarterly*, July 1925, p. 167.
6. See Griswold 1948, pp. 36–37.

Chapter 3.

1. See Hunt 9, pp. 257–258, and McColley 1973, pp. 90, 125.
2. See Chinard 1926, pp. 321, 324; Hunt 9, p. 25; Lipscomb and Bergh 1, pp. 62, 257; Lipscomb and Bergh 12, pp. 298–300; and Malone 1948, p. 271.
3. See Jefferson 1959, p. 62.
4. See Ira Berlin 1974, pp. 29–30, and D. B. Davis 1970, p. 8.
5. See Brown and Brown 1964, pp. 285–286; and Cotterill 1, p 72.

Chapter 4.

1. See J. C. Hamilton 1, p. 204; J. C. Hamilton 9, p. 161; and *Journal of Negro History* 46, pp. 83–88.
2. See Brodie 1974, pp. 139–140, and E. Morgan 1975, p. 385.
3. See Brodie 1974, pp. 139–140; Brown and Brown 1964, pp. 285–286; and McColley 1971, pp. 88–89.
4. See Boyd 5, April 14, 1781; Boyd 11, pp. 16, 36; Boyd 13, July 16, 1788; P. L. Ford 5, p. 248; and Sheehan 1973, pp. 209–210.
5. See Boyd 11, pp. 13, 16, 363.
6. See Amble 1910, pp. 34–44; Boyd 7, pp. 25–27, 558; *Journals of the Continental Congress* 6, p. 108; Malone 1948, pp. 218, 412; Philbrick 1965, pp. 127, 294; and Rainsford 1972, p. 33.
7. See Philbrick 1965, p. 294; and Rainsford 1972; pp. 32–33.
8. See Boyd 7, April 25, 1784; Robinson 1970, pp. 379–380; and *Selected Essays on Constitutional Law* 3, pp. 13–14n.
9. See Jordan 1974, p. 127; McColley 1971, p. 171; Peterson 1970, pp. 283; and Robinson 1970, pp. 379–380.
10. See Chastellux 1927, pp. 294–295, and Locke 1969, pp. 185–186.

Chapter 5.

1. See Boyd 9, p. 445; Boyd 11, p. 636; and Fithian 1969, pp. 266, 279.
2. See Boyd 9, p. 449.
3. See Boyd 11, pp. 633, 636, 682.
4. See Boyd 11, p. 636, and *William and Mary Quarterly*, 3rd series, 15 (1958), pp. 74–92.
5. See Boyd 11, pp. 633–634.
6. See McLean 1961, pp. 211–212.
7. See *Warren-Adams Letters* 2, p. 277.
8. See *William and Mary Quarterly* 30 (1973), pp. 136–140.
9. See Potter 1968, p. 118.

Chapter 6.

1. See Gerbi 1973, p. 261n.
2. See Boyd 12, p. 39; Chinard, ed. 1929, p. 119; Koch 1950; pp. 25–26; and Malone 1948, pp. 374–377.
3. See Lipscomb and Bergh 1, pp. 72–73, and Peterson 1970, p. 1001.
4. See *Virginia Magazine* 62, pp. 251–280.
5. See Chinard 1929, pp. 495–497; Chinard, ed. 1929, p. 390; Lipscomb and Bergh 14, pp. 49, 206; and Peterson 1960, pp. 324–325.
6. See Brown 1969, p. 106; R. B. Davis 1964, p. 415; Foster 1954, p. 307; *Pennsylvania Magazine* 48, p. 134, and Simpson 1962, p. 66.
7. See Chastellux 1927, pp. 296–297, and *Journal of Negro History* 60, pp. 325–326.
8. See P. L. Ford 7, p. 381, and Lipscomb and Bergh 14, p. 421.
9. See Johnson 1962, p. 46, and Lipscomb and Bergh 14, p. 297.

10. See Healey 1962, pp. 36–39; Lipscomb and Bergh 15, p. 130; and Santayana 1971, pp. 41–43.
11. See Bultmann 1972, pp. 35–40; Chinard 1929, p. 522; Hampson 1968, p. 99; D. W. Howe 1970, pp. 125, 134–135, 141; and Peterson 1967, pp. 253–265.
12. See Knollenberg 1975, pp. 261–263; Locke 1969, pp. 46, 59; and McManus 1966, pp. 152–153.

Chapter 7.

1. See Malone 1948, p. 267, and Martin 1952, p. 33.
2. See M. Harris 1968, pp. 87–88; Jordan 1974, pp. 9–10; and Peterson 1970, pp. 261–262.
3. See Boorstin 1948, pp. 92–93, and M. Harris 1968, pp. 87–88.
4. See Boorstin 1948, pp. 94–96; Boyd 14, January 28, 1789; and Locke 1969, p. 54.
5. See Blassingame 1972, pp. 200–201, 206, 216.
6. See Morrison 1909, pp. 99–100.
7. See Finley 1968, pp. 188–189, and Gibbon 1963, pp. 64–65.
8. See Davis 1966, pp. 62–90; Dudley 1970, pp. 80–81; Finley 1968, pp. 163–165, 168–170; and Grany 1960, pp. 100–125.
9. See Kerber 1971, p. 57.
10. See Finley 1968, p. 174; *Times Literary Supplement,* July 2, 1976; Tocqueville 1 (1945), pp. 379–380; Warville 1797, pp. 154–157.
11. See D. B. Davis 1966, p. 454; Hampson 1968, p. 153; M. Harris 1968, pp. 78–88; Jordan 1974, p. 110; and Manuel 1965, p. 122.
12. See D. B. Davis 1966, p. 440, and *Virginia Magazine* 80, p. 144.
13. See Boorstin 1948, pp. 91–94; *Journal of Modern History* 47, p. 720; and Malone 1948, pp. 267–268.
14. See Arendt 1951, pp. 56–57; Boorstin 1948, pp. 81–82; Jordan 1974, p. 115; *Pennsylvania Magazine* 80, p. 151; and Rush 1969, pp. 24–25.
15. See Boswell 1959, pp. 41, 140, 182; Boswell 1963, p. 45; Bryson 1945, pp. 71–74; Butterfield 1950, p. 226; and A. Hall 1954, pp. 297–298.
16. See D. B. Davis 1970, p. 11; Jordan 1974, pp. 10, 193–197; and Robinson 1970, p. 91.
17. See Frederickson 1973, pp. 1–2; *Journal of Negro History* 40, p. 321; Macleod 1974, p. 127; and McColley 1964, p. 127.
18. See Thorpe 1967, pp. 8–9.
19. See Boyd 9, p. 441; Locke 1969, pp. 180–181; and McLean 1961, pp. 61–66.
20. See Boyd 9, p. 441; Locke 1969, pp. 180–181; McLean 1961, pp. 63–64; and Morrison 1909, p. 101.
21. See Lipscomb and Bergh 12, p. 322.
22. See Jordan 1974, p. 172; Robinson 1970, p. 91; and Smelser 1968, p. 43.
23. See Foster 1954, pp. 155–156.
24. See D. B. Davis 1970, p. 11; M. Harris 1968, p. 98; *Journal of Negro History* 57, pp. 297–299; *Journal of Southern History* 39, p. 265; and Robinson 1970, p. 91.
25. See Frederickson 1971, p. 2n and M. Harris 1968, p. 80.

Chapter 8.

1. See D. B. Davis 1966, p. 440; Greene 1965, pp. 38–39; Jordan 1974, pp. 62–63; Locke 1969, pp. 130–184; McColley 1964, p. 162; and *Virginia Magazine* 80, pp. 66–67.
2. See Tocqueville 1 (1945), pp. 375, 381.
3. See Jordan 1974, p. 44.
4. See Jordan 1974, pp. 79–81, and Rochefaucauld-Liancourt 2 (1792), p. 357.
5. See Jordan 1968, pp. 84–87.
6. See *American Historical Review* 77, pp. 81–91; D. B. Davis 1966, pp. 468–469; *Journal of Negro History* 57, pp. 67–68; and Thorpe 1967, p. 8.
7. See Jordan 1974, pp. 207–208, and Koch 1966, pp. 142–144.
8. See Jordan 1974, p. 70.
9. See Boorstin 1948, pp. 84–85, 87, 94; Chinard 1926, p. 425; Jordan 1974, pp. 9–10; and Sheehan 1973, pp. 16, 43.
10. See Boorstin 1948, pp. 94–95; Chinard 1926, p. 425; Gay 1966, p. 55; Jordan 1968, pp. 427–428; Jordan 1974, pp. 191–192; Malone 1962, p. 355; Sheehan 1973, p. 174; and Tocqueville 1 (1945), pp. 334–335.
11. See Washburn 1975, p. 147.
12. See Janson 1935, pp. 230–231, and Jenness 1972, pp. 367–370.
13. See Handlin 1964, p. 126, and Martin 1952, p. 126.
14. See Boyd 11, p. 49; R. B. Davis 1946, p. 41; Koch 1941, p. 18; Malone 1951, p. 102; and Volney 1804, p. 466.
15. See Cappon 2 (1959), p. 305; Jordan 1974, p. 192; Malone 1970, p. 275; and Tucker 1 (1837), p. 25.
16. See Boyd 6, p. 331; P. L. Ford 6, p. 331; Jordan 1968, p. 480; Lipscomb and Bergh 12, pp. 139–140; and McColley 1969, p. 105.
17. See Bernal 1963, p. 464; Echeverria 1957, pp. 10–11, 13–14; Gerbi 1973, pp. 5–7, 167–168, 258n; Martin 1952, pp. 153–154; Persons 1958, p. 73; and Sheehan 1973, p. 66.
18. See Echeverria 1957, pp. 3, 8–10, and Martin 1952, pp. 154, 160.
19. See Dorfman 1 (1946), p. 441; P. L. Ford 5, p. 370; Lipscomb and Bergh 12, pp. 147–148; Malone 1951, p. 101; Washburn 1975, pp. 82, 93, 165, 262; and L. D. White 1951, pp. 498–499.
20. See Foster 1954, pp. 22–23; Janson 1935, p. 23; Randall 1 (1858), p. 209; and *William and Mary Quarterly* 9, p. 196.
21. See Boorstin 1948, p. 224; Chinard 1926, pp. 425–426; Lipscomb and Bergh 11, p. 344; and Sheehan 1973, pp. 10, 125, 149, 244.
22. See Boorstin 1948, pp. 218, 224; P. L. Ford 5, pp. 314, 370; Lipscomb and Bergh 8, pp. 226–227; Lipscomb and Bergh 12, pp. 139–148; Lipscomb and Bergh, 19, p. 218; McColley 1969, p. 105; Padover 1955, p. 399; and Parkes 1940, pp. 234–235.
23. See Lipscomb and Bergh 8, pp. 226–227; Lipscomb and Bergh 12, pp. 147–148, 209; and Martin 1952, p. 63.
24. See Chinard 1926, pp. 425–426; and Sheehan 1973, pp. 10, 125.
25. See Chinard 1926, p. 426; Lipscomb and Bergh 8, pp. 226–227; Lipscomb and Bergh 10, p. 395; Lipscomb and Bergh 16, p. 108; Sheehan 1973, p. 10; and *William and Mary Quarterly* 9, p. 196.

26. See Tocqueville 1 (1945), pp. 345–346.
27. See Boorstin 1948, p. 218; Jackson 1969, p. 40; Lipscomb and Bergh 11, p. 394; Lipscomb and Bergh 12, p. 75; and Tocqueville 1 (1945), pp. 352–354.
28. See Malone 1951, p. 101.

Chapter 9.

1. See P. L. Ford 5, 377–379; Koch 1941, pp. 118–119; and Lipscomb and Bergh 8, pp. 241–242.
2. See Rush 1773 (reprint 1969), pp. 2–3.
3. See Lipscomb and Bergh 16, p. 120.
4. See *Journal of Negro History* 60 (1975), pp. 393–398, and Priest 1802, p. 191.
5. See Collections of the Massachusetts Historical Society 1, *Jefferson Papers*, p. 41; Bedini, pp. 152–163.
6. See Boorstin 1948, pp. 56–57, and P. L. Ford 5, p. 379.
7. See Brodie 1974, p. 427; Foster 1954, p. 148; Lipscomb and Bergh 12, p. 233; and Todd 1884, p. 242.
8. See Robinson 1970, p. 96; Rogers 1962, pp. 292–293; and Smelser 1968, p. 43.

Chapter 10.

1. See Marx 1964, p. 129.
2. See P. L. Ford 7, p. 15; Lipscomb and Bergh 14, p. 161; Lopez 1966, p. 248; and Potter 1973, pp. 50, 324.
3. See Ginzberg 1934, pp. 156–158; Griswold 1948, pp. 19–20; Marx 1964, pp. 74–75; and A. Smith 1937, p. 347.
4. See Marx 1964, pp. 228, 283.
5. Collections of the Massachusetts Historical Society, Seventh Series, 1900, p. 113.
6. See Boyd 16, August 12, 1787; Ford 6, p. 14; Griswold 1948, p. 36; and Persons 1958, p. 33.
7. See Kerber 1973, p. 192; Lipscomb and Bergh 14, p. 384; and Persons 1958, pp. 138–139.
8. See Beard 1913, p. 432; Chinard 1926, p. 178; P. L. Ford 6, pp. 7, 15, 195; Hall 2 (1829), pp. 170–171.
9. See Greene 1965, p. 26; Marx 1964, pp. 19–21, 126, 129, 130; and Persons 1958, p. 133.
10. See Lipscomb and Bergh 13, p. 28.
11. See Persons 1973, pp. 20, 28.
12. See Marx 1964, pp. 257–258.
13. See Marx 1964, p. 126.
14. See Hartz 1958, p. 120; Hofstadter 1968, p. 30; Lehman 1947, pp. 178–180; Marx 1964, pp. 142–143; Weber 1958, pp. 40–41; and M. and L. White 1962, pp. 16–17.
15. See Hartz 1958, pp. 120, 230, and Pareks 1940, pp. 229–230.
16. See Burns 1957, p. 27; P. L. Ford 7, p. 459; *Journal of Economic History* 18, pp. 1–16; Parkes 1940, p. 230; Weber 1958, pp. 40–41; and M. and L. White 1962, pp. 16–17, 19.

17. See Lipscomb and Bergh 11, p. 66.
18. See Ira Berlin 1974, pp. 89–96, 316–319; Frederickson 1971, pp. 5–7; Jordan 1974, pp. 157–158; and M. and L. White 1962, p. 23.
19. See Cobbett 1965, pp. 209, 210; Elkins 1963, p. 210; Frederickson 1971, pp. 5–7; Kraditor 1969, p. 21; Priest 1802, p. 184; Tocqueville 1 (1945), pp. 373–374; and Volney 1804, p. 325.
20. See Ira Berlin 1974, p. 89.
21. See Ira Berlin 1974, pp. 63–64, 318.
22. See Fearon 1818, pp. 97, 167–168; Macleod 1974, p. 50; Mellon 1969, pp. 145–146; and Wright 1963, pp. 268–269.

Chapter 11.

1. See Boyd 14, p. 699; Lipscomb and Bergh 14, p. 70; and Mackenzie (no date), p. 221.
2. See Boorstin 1948, p. 197; *Journal of Negro History* 57, p. 433; and Robinson 1970, pp. 54–55, 93.
3. See P. L. Ford 6, p. 293; Healey 1962, p. 166; and D. W. Howe 1970, pp. 38, 59–60.
4. See Chinard 1926, pp. 18–19; Home 1751; Home 1762; and Lipscomb and Bergh 14, p. 143.
5. See Healey 1962, p. 163.
6. See Boorstin 1948, p. 154; Lipscomb and Bergh 12, p. 358; Lipscomb and Bergh 14, p. 490; and Watson 1973, p. 52.
7. See Berman 1947, p. 35; Hand 1960, p. 94; Koch 1941, pp. 19–20, 30–32; Lipscomb and Bergh 10, p. 3; Lipscomb and Bergh 12, p. 35; Malone 1962, p. 418; and *Proceedings of the American Philosophical Society* 87, no. 3, p. 303.
8. See Boorstin 1948, p. 154; Chinard 1926, pp. 524–527; Koch 1941, p. 40; Lipscomb and Bergh 12, p. 358; Lipscomb and Bergh 14, p. 496; and Persons 1958, p. 77.
9. See Bryson 1945, p. 28; Healey 1962, pp. 22–23, 45; Lipscomb and Bergh 14, p. 141; Nagel 1970, pp. 3–8; Persons 1958, p. 121; and Wallace 1921, pp. 45 46.
10. See Boorstin 1948, pp. 244–245; Boyd 12, August 10, 1787; Bryson 1945, pp. 48, 162–163; D. W. Howe 1970, p. 56; Koch 1941, p. 20; Lipscomb and Bergh 11, p. 104; Lipscomb and Bergh 12, p. 358; Lipscomb and Bergh 14, pp. 131, 139, 141–43; 490; Persons 1958, pp. 75–76; Randolph 1950, p. 322; and Watson 1973, pp. 52, 59.
11. See Berman 1947, p. 231, and S. Washburn 1961, pp. 38–39, 237–238.
12. See Bernard 1887, p. 238.
13. See Boyd, 10, p. 63.
14. See P. L. Ford 10, pp. 160–163, 169–173, 177–178; Healey 1962, p. 63; Lipscomb and Bergh 14, p. 330.
15. See Baillie 1951, p. 104; Brissenden 1968, p. 25; and Watson 1973, pp. 52, 59.
16. See D. B. Davis 1970, p. 11; Lipscomb and Bergh 1, pp. 72–73; and Lipscomb and Bergh 14, p. 183.
17. See Boyd 17, p. 195; Healey 1962, p. 66; and Randolph 1950, p. 32.

18. See Koch 1950, pp. 64–66, and Lipscomb and Bergh 11, p. 33.
19. See Peterson 1967, p. 38.
20. See Fogel and Engerman 1 (1974), p. 33, and Robinson 1970, p. 407.

Chapter 12.

1. See Aldridge 1957, p. 202; Lipscomb and Bergh 1, p. 160; Malone 1951, pp. 19–20; and Tansill 1964, p. 10.
2. See Boyd 12, pp. 162, 504.
3. See Brodie 1974, p. 220.
4. See Chill 1971, pp. 6–7, and D. B. Davis 1966, p. 178.
5. See Boyd 14, pp. 492–493; Fithian 1967, p. 145; and Foner 2 (1945), pp. 1463–1464.
6. See Boyd 14, p. 492, and D. B. Davis 1970, p. 13.
7. See *Journal of Negro History* 46, pp. 83–88; Mellon 1969, pp. 55–59; and *Virginia Magazine* 80, pp. 145–156.
8. See Boyd 16, p. 154.

Chapter 13.

1. See Betts and Bear 1961, p. 195; McColley 1964, p. 21; and Walton 12 (1975), p. 336.
2. See Randolph 1950, pp. 321–322.
3. See Bear 1967, p. 35, and Fithian 1967, p. 136.
4. See Randolph 1950, p. 152, and Thorpe 1967, pp. 3–4, 28.
5. See Bear 1967, pp. 51, 97, 99, 136, and Brodie 1974, p. 288.
6. See Blassingame 1972, pp. 182–183; P. L. Ford 7, p. 20; Graves 1966, pp. 73–76; Malone 1962, pp. 213–214; McColley 1964, pp. 20–21; Randolph 1950, p. 246; and Roberts and Roberts 1947, p. 305.
7. See Bernard 1887, p. 91; Corner 1948, p. 243; D. B. Davis 1966, p. 171; Fitzpatrick 32, pp. 65–66; Flexner 4 (1970), pp. 484–485; Padover 1955, p. 412; and Parkinson 2 (1805), pp. 419, 447, 454.
8. See Malone 1968, p. 207, and McColley 1964, p. 26.
9. See Ira Berlin 1974, p. 55; Boyd 17, p. 62, and Seneca 1 (1917), pp. 300–303, 305–309.
10. See Blassingame 1972, pp. 200–201.
11. See Peterson 1970, p. 536.
12. See P. L. Ford 7, p. 14, and Peterson 1970, p. 536.
13. See Boyd 17, pp. 344–345.
14. See P. L. Ford 7, pp. 35, 50; Genovese 1965, p. 51; Malone 1962, p. 219; McColley 1964, p. 20; and Peterson 1970, pp. 220, 336.

Chapter 14.

1. See Historical Manuscript Commission, *Report of the Manuscripts of Sir John Fortesque* 3 (1892–1927), p. 523; McColley 1973, p. 87; and *South Carolina Historical and Genealogical Magazine* 26, p. 79.
2. See Devine 1975, pp. 156–158; Fitzpatrick 29, p. 304; Henry 3 (1891), pp.

611, 644; *Pennsylvania Magazine* 34, p. 395; Ritcheson 1969, pp. 66–67; Rutland 2 (1970), p. 40; and Smyth 18 (1906), p. 113.

3. See Boyd 9, May 1788.
4. See S. M. Hamilton 1 (1893), p. 37; Henry 3 (1891), pp. 611, 644; Hunt 5 (1900–1910), p. 104; *Journal of Economic and Business History* 5, pp. 419–422; and Rutland 2 (1970), p. 46.
5. See Lipscomb and Bergh 16, p. 236.
6. See P. L. Ford 6, p. 468, and Syrett 18 (1973), pp. 518–519.
7. See Lipscomb and Bergh 16, pp. 183–185; Ritcheson 1969, pp. 231–236, 239; and Syrett 11 (1973), p. 455.
8. See Lipscomb and Bergh 16, p. 223.
9. See Syrett 18, p. 515.
10. See Boyd 17, pp. 114–115, and Ritcheson 1969, pp. 232–233, 242.
11. See Malone 1951, p. 419; Ritcheson 1969, pp. 135, 241; Syrett 6, p. 497; Syrett 6, p. 497; Syrett 11, pp. 410–412; and *William and Mary Quarterly*, 3rd series, no. 18, 1961, pp. 85–121.
12. See Beard 1913, p. 285, and Syrett 18, pp. 517–518.
13. See Syrett 18, p. 516.
14. See Devine 1975, pp. 156–158, 159–163; Dwight 1839, p. 145; Ritcheson 1969, p. 358; and *Virginia Magazine* 75, pp. 75–88.

Chapter 15.

1. See Jordan 1974, pp. 139–140.
2. See Locke 1969, p. 47; Padover 1955, p. 412; and Warville 1797, p. 160.
3. See Jordan 1974, pp. 141–142; La Rochefoucauld-Liancourt 2 (1792), p. 82; and McColley 1964, p. 65.
4. See Bernard 1887, p. 147.
5. See Robinson 1970, pp. 224–225.
6. See Boyd 16, p. 579; Corner 1 (1948), pp. 587–599; and Lipscomb and Bergh 9, p. 23.
7. See Ira Berlin 1974, p. 85.
8. See R. B. Davis 1964, p. 415; Locke 1969, pp. 129–130, 184; McColley 1964, pp. 134–135, 189; and Robinson 1970, p. 5.
9. See Jordan 1974, p. 208.
10. See Brown and Brown 1964, p. 77.
11. See Fogel and Engerman 1 (1974), pp. 195–197, and *Virginia Magazine* 80 (1972), p. 67.

Chapter 16.

1. See Dudley 1970, pp. 80–81, and Tocqueville 1 (1945), p. 376.
2. See *Journal of Southern History* 40 (1974), pp. 537–543.
3. See P. L. Ford 7, p. 467.
4. See P. L. Ford 7, pp. 457–458, and Mullin 1972, pp. 150, 157.
5. See Brodie 1974, p. 343; Jordan 1974, p. 210; Malone 1970, p. 253; McColley 1964, p. 107; McLean 1961, p. 180; and Walsh 1819, p. 399.
6. See *The Cambridge Modern History* 9 (1865), pp. 580–581, and McColley 1964, p. 110.

7. See Jordan 1974, pp. 219–220; McColley 1964, p. 110; McLean 1961, pp. 180–181; and *Virginia Magazine* 80 (1972), p. 379.
8. See Ira Berlin 1974; pp. 15, 52, 83–85, 101–102, 138; Catterall 1 (1968), p. 72; and McColley 1964, pp. 71–72.
9. See *Journal of Negro History* 58 (1973), p. 427.

Chapter 17.

1. See Oakes 1935, p. 75.
2. See McColley 1964, pp. 125, 130.
3. See P. L. Ford 8, p. 340
4. See Robinson 1970, p. 268.
5. See P. L. Ford 6, pp. 268, 349; Ott 1973, pp. 5, 7, 9, 34–35, 47, 64, 76; and Palmer 1964, p. 338.
6. See Betts and Bear 1961, p. 127; P. L. Ford 6, pp. 80, 349; and C. F. Jenkins 1906, p. 117.
7. See P. L. Ford 7, pp. 321–325; Lipscomb and Bergh 9, p. 418; Ott 1973, p. 54; Parry 1971, pp. 183–184; and Tansill 1938, pp. 57–60.
8. See Jordan 1974, pp. 148–150, and Lipscomb and Bergh 9, pp. 165, 418.
9. See Adams 8 (1853), p. 655; British State Papers, Robert Liston Correspondence (1799), Korngold 1945, p. 221; *Proceedings of the Massachusetts Historical Society* 44 (1911), pp. 396–397; Hamilton manuscripts (Thomas Pickering to Alexander Hamilton), Febraury 9, 1799.
10. See Korngold 1945, p. 221.
11. See P. L. Ford 7, pp. 324, 329, 338; Kaplan 1967, p. 86; and Tansill 1938, pp. 52–61.
12. See Brant 1953, pp. 62–93, and Peterson 1970, p. 749.
13. See *Annals of Congress* 9 (1852), pp. 2151, 2253, 2279.
14. See Brant 1953, pp. 63–64, 70, and Malone 1970, pp. 251–253.
15. See Brant 1953, pp. 63–64.
16. See P. L. Ford 8, pp. 162–163, and Malone 1970, pp. 252–253.
17. See Cole 1967, pp. 108–109, 117, 121–122.
18. See Ott 1973, p. 142.
19. See Peterson 1970, p. 750.
20. See W. C. Ford 2 (1913–1917), pp. 77–78; Brant 1953, p. 274; Peterson 1970, p. 823; and Plumer 1923, pp. 243–244.
21. See Hildreth 5 (1882), p. 547; McColley 1969, pp. 123–124; Ott 1973, pp. 143–144; and Plumer 1923, p. 243.
22. See Plumer 1923, pp. 540–541, 545.
23. See Lipscomb and Bergh 12, p. 186, and Lipscomb and Bergh 14, pp. 431–432.

Chapter 18.

1. See Foner 2 (1945), p. 1458, and Woodress 1958, p. 224.
2. See D. B. Davis 1970, p. 14, and Plumer 1923, pp. 113–114, 119–120, 129.

3. See Hildreth 5 (1882), pp. 500–501; Locke 1969, pp. 106, 114, 148; McColley 1964, p. 125; and Plumer 1923, pp. 114–115, 119–120, 129–130, 165–167.
4. See Taylor 1963, pp. 123, 194–196.
5. See Malone 1970, p. 180.
6. See *American Historical Review* 77 (1972), pp. 81–93.
7. See Brodie 1974, p. 424; Coupland 1923, p. 323; DuBois 1904, pp. 192–193; Koch 1966, pp. 138–142; Locke 1969, pp. 154–155; *New Cambridge Modern History* 9 (1965), p. 579; Robinson 1970, pp. 338–339, 341; and Walsh 1819, pp. 308–309, 320.
8. See *American Historical Review* 77 (1972), pp. 81–92, and Walton 12 (1975), pp. 439–457.

Chapter 19.

1. See Callender 1792, pp. 3, 5, 16–17, 32, 75–76, 80.
2. See Hildreth 5 (1882), p. 554.
3. See *New England Historical and Genealogical Register* 50 (1896), pp. 19, 52, 326–327.
4. See *Branch Historical Papers* 2, p. 283; Callender 1797, pp. 219–222; J. C. Hamilton 7, p. 411; and *Mississippi Valley Historical Review* 42 (1947), pp. 465–467.
5. See *Adams-Cunningham Correspondence* (1823), p. 129; Malone 1962, pp. 327, 332; and *New England Historical and Genealogical Register* 50 (1896), pp. 323–327.
6. See Jordan 1968, p. 477.
7. See Callendar to Hamilton, October 29, 1797 (in *Hamilton Manuscripts*) and *New England Historical and Genealogical Register* 50 (1896), pp. 55, 328–331.
8. See Adams-Cunningham Correspondence (1823), pp. 128–129; Callender 2, 2 (1801), pp. 16, 63–66, 76, 81, 86, 149; *New England Historical and Genealogical Review* 51 (1897), p. 323; and *Virginia Federalist,* June 16, 1800.
9. See Lipscomb and Bergh 11, pp. 42–43; Malone 1962, pp. 327, 332; and *New England Historical and Genealogical Register* 51 (1897), pp. 154, 326.
10. See Ammon 1971, p. 184.
11. See *Virginia Argus,* August 3 and August 6, 1799.
12. See Ammon 1971, p. 197; Fleming 1969, p. 28; Ford 8, p. 53; Malone 1970, pp. 207–208; and *New England Historical and Genealogical Register* 51 (1897), pp. 153–154.
13. See Brant 1953, p. 51; Cunningham 1957, p. 250; *New England Historical and Genealogical Register* 51 (1897), p. 19, and Stewart 1969, p. 10.
14. See Brodie 1974, p. 368, and Malone 1970, pp. 213–214.
15. See *Richmond Recorder,* September 22, 1802.
16. See Peterson 1960, pp. 183–184.
17. See Adair 1974, pp. 16, 63, 161, 163, and Brodie 1974, p. 357.
18. See Adair 1974, pp. 161, 166.
19. See Brodie 1974, pp. 291–292, 488, 493–495.
20. See Brodie 1974, pp. 427, 433, 482, 493, 495.

21. See Johnston 4 (1890–1893), p. 269, and Warren 1942, pp. 129–135.
22. See Adair 1974, p. 157, and *New England Historical and Genealogical Register* 51 (1897), pp. 326–328.
23. See Cunningham 1957, p. 255; P. L. Ford 7, p. 279; Lipscomb and Bergh 7, p. 279; Lipscomb and Bergh 8, p. 214; Malone 1970, p. 215; and Foner 11 (1945), p. 1466.
24. See Adair 1974, p. 161.
25. See Cappon 2 (1952), p. 614; Lipscomb and Bergh 9, p. 314; and Tucker 2 (1837), pp. 506–507.
26. See Adair 1974, p. 165; P. L. Ford 7, p. 279; Lipscomb and Bergh 8, p. 214; and Foner 2 (1945), p. 1466.
27. See J. C. Hamilton 8, p. 411.
28. See Brodie 1974, pp. 351, 361–362.
29. See W. C. Ford 1916, pp. 114–115.
30. See *New England Historical and Genealogical Register* 51 (1897), pp. 326–327.

Chapter 20.

1. See Ira Berlin 1974, pp. 98–99; Jordan 1968, pp. 465–467; and Malone 1970, pp. 495–496.
2. See Blassingame 1972, pp. 87–88; Boyd 9, p. 441; *Journal of Negro History* 46 (1961), p. 89; Sutcliffe 1812, p. 53; and *Virginia Magazine* 80 (1972), pp. 399–400.
3. See Bear 1947, p. 123; Brodie 1974, pp. 276, 287; *Journal of Negro History* 46 (1961), pp. 89–90; and Malone 1970, pp. 495–498.
4. See Adair 1974, pp. 173–178; Bear 1947, p. 123; and Jordan 1968, pp. 465–467.
5. See Boyd 5, pp. 620–622; Boyd 11, p. 551; and Brodie 1974, p. 216.
6. See Brodie 1974, p. 216; and Malone 1951, pp. 124–125.
7. See Adair 1974, pp. 184–185, and Brodie 1974, pp. 220, 474–476.
8. See Brodie 1974, pp. 380–381.
9. See *New England Quarterly* 33 (1960), pp. 393–394.
10. See Brodie 1974, p. 295; and Lipscomb and Bergh 11, p. 31.
11. See Brodie 1974, pp. 466–469; *Journal of Negro History* 46 (1961), p. 93; Malone 1962, p. 207; Malone 1970, p. 93; and Paulding 1 (1835), pp. 96–98.
12. See Malone 1970, p. 498, and Plumer 1923, p. 550.
13. See Boyd 7, p. 233; Malone 1962, p. 176; and Randall 1 (1858), p. 365.
14. See Adair 1974, p. 189, and Parton 1889, p. 44.
15. See Adair 1974, pp. 189–190.
16. See Adair 1974, p. 166; Malone 1970, p. 499; and Peterson 1960, pp. 182–184.
17. See Adair 1974, pp. 174–183; Brodie 1974, pp. 441, 467; and Peterson 1960, pp. 181–187.
18. See Brodie 1974, p. 473.
19. See Finley 1969, pp. 163–164; *Journal of Southern History* 41 (1975), pp. 523–528; and the *New York Times*, May 18, 1974.
20. See Adair 1974, pp. 180–181, and *Journal of Southern History* 41 (1975), pp. 523–528.

Chapter 21.

1. See Boyd 10, p. 446.
2. See Healey 1962, pp. 157–158; J. R. Howe 1970, p. 50; and Lehman 1947, pp. 137–139.
3. See Gay 1966, pp. 188–189; Harris 1968, p. 152; Lovejoy 1961, pp. 43–44; Shackleton 1961, p. 33; and Willey 1940, p. 269.
4. See Malone 1951, p. 124.
5. See Malone 1948, p. 397.
6. See Bear 1947, p. 100.
7. See Boyd 13, p. 623; Kaplan 1967, pp. 18–19; Morris 1 (1888), p. 166; and Webster 1 (1903), pp. 369–370.
8. See Tracy 1969, p. 120.
9. See Hunt 1900, pp. 75–77; Johnson 1967, pp. 232, 236; and Wexler 1976, pp. 266–291.
10. See Boyd 11, pp. 122–123; Boyd 12, p. 152; and Kaplan 1967, pp. 18–19.
11. See Hall 2 (1829), pp. 152–153, 159.
12. See Boorstin 1948, p. 224; Lipscomb and Bergh 15, pp. 161, 165; Malone 1951, p. 124; and *William and Mary Quarterly* 7 (1950), pp. 68–94.
13. See Brodie 1974, p. 447.
14. See Martineau 1 (1837), pp. 199–201.
15. See Morris 1 (1888), p. 61.
16. See Warville 1797, pp. 72–74.
17. See Albert 1969, p. 465, and Chinard 1927, pp. 91, 161.
18. See Massachusetts Historical Society Collections, 7th series, 1 (*Jefferson Papers*), p. 115; Tansill 1964, pp. 101–103; and Trumbull 1957, p. 177.
19. See Boyd 10, p. 450.
20. See Boyd 13, May 13, July 22, and July 27, 1788.
21. See Tansill 1964, p. 112.
22. See Boyd 10, November 19, 1786, pp. 442–444, 448.
23. See Boyd 11, p. 520.
24. See Boyd 10, November 29, 1786, p. 555.
25. See Boyd 11, February 15, 1787.
26. See Boyd 10, pp. 443–444, 446; Boyd 13, July 27, 1788; and Randolph 1958, p. 224.
27. See Boyd 13, April 24, 1788; Chinard 1926, p. 302; Koch 1950, p. 168; and Lopez 1966, pp. 25, 34.
28. See Boyd 10, p. 494, and Randolph 1958, p. 373.
29. See Boyd 12, November 13, 1787, and January 31, 1788; Malone 1951, p. 139; and Peterson 1970, p. 348.
30. See Tansill 1964, pp. 112–113.
31. See Boyd 12, p. 459, and Boyd 13, pp. 520–521.
32. See Boyd 12, March 6, 1788; Boyd 13, April 29 and July 15, 1788; and Boyd 14, p. 526, February 6, 1789.
33. See Boyd 12, p. 600; Boyd 13, July 27, 1788; and Malone 1951, pp. 139–140.
34. See Boyd 13, p. 634, and Boyd 14, January 14, 1789.
35. See Randolph 1958, p. 224.

36. See Schoepf 1 (1911), p. 100.
37. See Boyd 13, August 17, 1788; and Boyd 14, May 21, 1789.
38. See Brodie 1974, p. 470
39. See Boyd 10, pp. 448–451; Cappon 1 (1959), p. 614; Chinard 1926, p. 170; P. L. Ford 8, pp. 220–221; Lispcomb and Bergh 9, p. 313; and Tucker 2 (1837), pp. 505–506.

Chapter 22.

1. See Malone 1970, pp. 216–218, and Peterson 1970, pp. 109–111.
2. See Foner 2 (1945), pp. 986–988.
3. See Adair 1974, p. 161; Brodie 1974, pp. 368–370; and Malone 1948, pp. 447–449.
4. See P. L. Ford 8, p. 175; Lipscomb and Bergh 10, p. 155; Lipscomb and Bergh 12, p. 159; and Randolph 1958, p. 269.
5. See Lipscomb and Bergh 8, p. 406; Lipscomb and Bergh 10, p. 155; and Plumer 1923, pp. 545–546.
6. Plumer 1923, pp. 545–546.
7. See P. L. Ford 7, p. 328, and Mott 1943, pp. 40–41.
8. See Lipscomb and Bergh 11, p. 155; Lipscomb and Bergh 12, pp. 159, 406; and Plumer 1923, pp. 545–546.
9. See Levy 1963, pp. 1–24, and Lipscomb and Bergh 11, p. 155.
10. See Brodie 1974, pp. 162–163; Lipscomb and Bergh 13, pp. 288–289; and Lipscomb and Bergh 14, p. 116.
11. See Levy 1963, pp. 42–69.
12. See P. L. Ford 8, p. 31, and Foner 2 (1945), p. 1811.
13. See Lipscomb and Bergh 11, pp. 22, 72–73, 225–226; Lipscomb and Bergh 12, p. 8; Lipscomb and Bergh 13, pp. 46, 59; Lipscomb and Bergh 14, pp. 226, 314; Martineau 1 (1837), pp. 147–148; Mott 1943, p. 3; and Schlesinger 1973, pp. 227–228.
14. See Chinard 1929, p. 415.

Chapter 23.

1. See Massachusetts Historical Society Collections 1 (*Jefferson Papers*), p. 169, and Lipscomb and Bergh 12, pp. 405, 437.
2. See Chinard 1923, p. 411, and Lipscomb and Bergh 9, p. 313.
3. See Lipscomb and Bergh 14, p. 184.
4. See Boyd 10, p. 18; D. B. Davis 1970, pp. 10–11; Lipscomb and Bergh 1, pp. 72–73; and Lipscomb and Bergh 14, p. 70.
5. See Boyd 14, p. 699, and Mackenzie (no date), p. 22.
6. See D. B. Davis 1970, pp. 180–181.
7. See Lipscomb and Bergh 14, p. 296.
8. See Lipscomb and Bergh 14, p. 330.
9. See Koch 1966, pp. 146–151 and Wright 1963, p. 269.
10. See Frederickson 1971, pp. 2, 3n; Lipscomb and Bergh 14, pp. 296–297; and Lipscomb and Bergh 15, p. 164.

11. See Lipscomb and Bergh 15, p. 383.

12. See Konefsky 1969, pp. 198–201; Levy 1963, p. 149; Story 1 (1851), pp. 310–311; and Surrency 1955, pp. 121–160.

13. See Boorstin 1948, pp. 201–202; Cappon 2 (1959), p. 570; and Lipscomb and Bergh 1, pp. 121–122.

14. See Hammond 1957, p. 274; Lipscomb and Bergh 16, pp. 95–96; and *South Carolina Historical and Genealogical Magazine* 1 (1900), pp. 6–7.

15. See Baritz 1969, pp. xxix–xxx, and P. L. Ford 10, pp. 160–163, 169–171.

16. See Dewey 1970, pp. 158–159, and Lipscomb and Bergh 15, p. 212.

17. See Bates 1963, pp. 103–105; Jackson 1969, p. 34; Jones 1956, pp. 10, 82, 184–185; Hunt 9, pp. 65–66; and Surrency 1955, pp. 82–87, 170–171, 222.

18. See Bailey 1965, p. 31; Gunther 1969, pp. 54–55, 195; Jones 1956, p. 86; Konefsky 1969, pp. 110, 167–171; Schlesinger 1973, p. 1; and Surrency 1955, pp. 77–78, 160, 170–172.

19. See Hammond 1957, p. 26; *Harvard Law Review* 41 (1928), p. 126; Jones 1956, pp. 58–59; Koch 1950, p. 43; Konefsky 1969, pp. 127, 130, 267; Surrency 1955, pp. 99, 118–119, 168; and B. F. Wright 1942, p. 51.

20. See Dewey 1970, pp. 34–35; Faulkner 1968, pp. 18–22, 25–28, 36–37; *Harvard Law Review* 41 (1928), p. 130; and B. F. Wright 1942, pp. 47, 50–51.

21. See Bates 1963, pp. 85, 136; Jones 1956, p. 9; and Surrency 1955, p. 117.

22. See Bates 1963, p. 112, and Beveridge 4 (1919), pp. 347–357.

23. See Ambler 1910, pp. 100–103, Hartz 1955, pp. 103–104, 133; and Konefsky 1969, pp. 244–246.

24. See Faulkner 1968, p. 112; Hunt 9, pp. 65–66; D. G. Morgan 1954, p. 291; Risjord 1965, p. 225; Surrency 1955, pp. 77, 174; *University of Pennsylvania Law Review* 109 (1966), pp. 157–202; *William and Mary Quarterly*, 2nd series, 21 (1941), pp. 1–26; and Wiltse 1961, p. 63.

25. See R. B. Davis 1964, p. 410; Lipscomb and Bergh 16, pp. 24, 153; and Risjord 1965, pp. 15, 114, 224–225.

26. See Pound 1942, pp. 51–52, and Risjord 1965, pp. 224–225.

27. See Levy 1963, pp. 149–150; Lipscomb and Bergh 16, pp. 14–15, 79, 149–150; Peterson 1970, p. 1003; and Risjord 1965, p. 258.

28. See Bates 1963, p. 127; Gunther 1969, p. 214; McClellan 1971, pp. 270–271 *Proceedings of the Massachusetts Historical Society* 14 (1901), pp. 321–329; Story 1 (1851), p. 41; and *William and Mary Quarterly*, 2nd series, 21 (1941), pp. 1–26.

29. See Dewey 1970, pp. 34–35; Faulkner 1968, pp. 30, 47, 49; *Harvard Law Review* 41 (1928), p. 130; and *Proceedings of the Massachusetts Historical Society* 14 (1901), p. 321.

30. See Gunther 1969, pp. 54–55, 195; Konefsky 1969, p. 167, and Surrency 1955, pp. 76, 168–169.

31. See Beard 1913, p. 456; Lipscomb and Bergh 16, p. 79; and Macleod 1974, p. 39.

32. See Beard 1913, p. 456; Lipscomb and Bergh 16, p. 79; and Macleod 1974, p. 39.

33. See P. L. Ford 10, 1822; *Journal of Southern History* 28 (1962), pp. 422–437; Lipscomb and Bergh 16, p. 148; Nelson 1964, p. 27; Parkes 1940, p. 235; and *South Carolina Historical and Genealogical Magazine* 1 (1900), pp. 6–7.

34. See Brown 1969, pp. 98–106; Konefsky 1969, p. 206; Lipscomb and Bergh 16, p. 147; and Surrency 1955, p. 154.

Chapter 24.

1. See *The Federalist* 1892, pp. xxxvi–xxxviii, 357.
2. See *Journal of Southern History* 7 (1941), pp. 315–342; Kerber 1973, p. 36; and Turner 1962, p. 146.
3. See *Journal of Southern History* 7 (1941), pp. 315–342, and Turner 1962, p. 146.
4. See P. L. Ford 7, p. 417, and Lipscomb and Bergh 8, pp. 396–397.
5. See *Journal of Southern History* 39 (1973), p. 263.
6. See Potter 1973, pp. 107–108.
7. See Hildreth 1 (1882), p. 667, and Moore 1953, p. 316.
8. See Moore 1953, p. 179, and Robinson 1970, pp. 412–413.
9. See Lipscomb and Bergh 15, p. 152; Lipscomb and Bergh 16, pp. 19, 151–152; Parkes 1940, p. 226; and Potter 1968, p. 118.
10. See Macleod 1974, p. 80.
11. See Nash 1964, pp. 261–262.
12. See Moore 1953, pp. 252–253, and Potter 1973, pp. 107–108.
13. See Ammon 1971, pp. 454–458, and Moore 1953, pp. 183, 343.
14. See Hildreth 6 (1882), p. 667, and Moore 1953, p. 316.
15. See Lipscomb and Bergh 15, p. 238.
16. See Moore 1953, pp. 125, 308–314, and Robinson 1970, p. 409.
17. See Macleod 1974, pp. 59–60.
18. See Chevalier 1961, p. 154, and Locke 1969, pp. 131–133.
19. See D. B. Davis 1970, p. 7; Lipscomb and Bergh 16, p. 10; and Robinson 1970, p. 412.
20. See *Journal of Southern History* 28 (1962), pp. 422–437; Moore 1953, pp. 332–333; Nelson 1964, p. 27; and Parks 1940, p. 235.
21. See *Journal of Southern History* 8 (1942), pp. 3–22; Moore 1953, p. 256; and Robinson 1970, p. 97.
22. See Peterson 1960, pp. 191–193.
23. See Lipscomb and Bergh 16, p. 163.
24. See Chevalier 1961, p. 403, and Lipscomb and Bergh 15, p. 103.

Chapter 25.

1. See Lipscomb and Bergh 14, pp. 280–283.
2. See Lipscomb and Bergh 11, p. 135, and Plumer 1923, pp. 112, 130.
3. See Hunt 8, p. 428, and Mellon 1969, p. 152.
4. See R. D. Brown 1969, pp. 100–105, Hunt 9, pp. 10–12; and Moore 1953, p. 293.
5. See Brodie 1974, pp. 441–442, and Peterson 1970, p. 997.
6. See Foster 1954, p. 307; Fitzpatrick 32 (1933–1944), p. 65; and Weld 1 (1799), p. 150.
7. See R. D. Brown 1969, p. 106; Brown and Brown 1964, pp. 74–76; Fithian

1967, pp. 287–288; Sutcliffe 1812, p. 44; and *Virginia Magazine* 80 (1972), pp. 70–71.

8. See D. B. Davis 1970, p. 12 and Moore 1953, p. 292.
9. See Chinard, ed. 1929, pp. 356, 362, 407.
10. See Macleod 1974, pp. 59–69.
11. See Fogel and Engerman 2 (1974), pp. 44, 47–48; R. L. Ford 10, March 1820; Genovese 1965, pp. 23–27; and Moore 1953, p. 319.
12. See Lipscomb and Bergh 15, p. 249.
13. See Ambler 1910, pp. 108–113; *Journal of Southern History* 39 (1973), pp. 283–284; Lipscomb and Bergh 16, p. 157; and *Virginia Magazine* 80 (1972), pp. 30, 80–82.
14. See Potter 1969, p. 98, and Sutcliffe 1812, pp. 53, 92, 100, 180.

Chapter 26.

1. See Ammon 1971, p. 458; Lipscomb and Bergh 5, pp. 250, 280; Moore 1953, pp. 299–300; and Risjord 1969, pp. 132–135.
2. See Bernard 1887, p. 91; Flexner 4, pp. 484–485; and Macleod 1974, pp. 22–23.
3. See Lipscomb and Bergh 15, p. 247, and Moore 1953, p. 284.
4. See Cappon 2 (1952), pp. 549, 570.
5. See *American Historical Review* 77 (1972), pp. 81–91; Lipscomb and Bergh 15, pp. 238, 247, 256; and Peterson 1970, p. 996.
6. See F. Wright 1963, p. 270.
7. See Moore 1953, pp. 221, 232–233, 238, 243, 247, 250–251.
8. See Dangerfield 1965, p. 125; Kraditor 1969, pp. 198, 235–236; and McColley 1964, pp. 174–175.
9. See Ambler 1910, pp. 107–108, and Moore 1953, pp. 234–244, 250–251.
10. See Potter and Fehrenbacher 1976, pp. 275–276.
11. See Ammon 1971, pp. 460–461, and Moore 1953, pp. 135, 142.
12. See *American Historical Review* 77 (1972), pp. 81–91.
13. See R. D. Brown 1969, p. 106, and Nelson 1964, p. 87.
14. See Wiltse 1961, p. 67.
15. See *American Historical Review* 77 (1972), pp. 81–93; D. B. Davis 1966, pp. 183–184, 192; Konefsky 1969, pp. 108–109; and O'Conner 1968, pp. 46–47.
16. See Moore 1953, pp. 232–234.
17. See W. S. Jenkins 1935, p. 63.
18. See Lipscomb and Bergh 14, pp. 266, 346.
19. See Healcy 1962, p. 66, and Lipscomb and Bergh 14, pp. 183–184.
20. See Brodie 1974, p. 431.
21. See Ambler 1910, pp. 111–112; Koch 1966, p. 190; and Martin 1952, p. 9.

Chapter 27.

1. See Lipscomb and Bergh 14, p. 496.
2. See Cappon 2 (1952), p. 387; Cady 1949, p. 99; Conant 1962, p. 12; Ford 10, pp. 169–173, 177–178, 286–288; *Harvard Law Review* 79 (1966), p. 38; Lehman 1947, pp. 191–192, 220; Lipscomb and Bergh 13, pp. 19, 72–73;

Lipscomb and Bergh 16, p. 301; *Political Science Quarterly* 68 (1953), pp. 552–557; and Wiltse 1960, p. 40.

3. See Healey 1962, pp. 51–52.
4. See Lehman 1947, p. 206.
5. See Healey 1962, p. 70.
6. See Kraditor 1969, p. 21.
7. See Ira Berlin 1974, p. 75.
8. See *William and Mary Quarterly,* March 1973, pp. 62–63.
9. See Conant 1962, pp. 2–3; R. B. Davis 1964, p. 69; Lipscomb and Bergh 15, pp. 289–290; and Lipscomb and Bergh 19, pp. 234–238.
10. See Ambler 1910, pp. 120–121; *Journal of Southern History* 17 (1951), pp. 303–326; Levy 1963, p. 151; Lipscomb and Bergh 15, pp. 14, 317, 384; Lipscomb and Bergh 16, pp. 151–152.
11. See Levy 1963, p. 154, and Tucker 2 (1837), p. 547.
12. See Lipscomb and Bergh 15, p. 269.
13. See Lipscomb and Bergh 15, p. 315.
14. See Lehman 1947, p. 191.
15. See Levy 1963, pp. 148, 157, and *Virginia Magazine* 46 (1938), p. 236.
16. See *Virginia Magazine* 75 (1967), pp. 290–304.
17. See Koch 1941, pp. 124–126; Levy 1963, pp. 143–145; Lipscomb and Bergh 14, pp. 63, 120, 223–234; and Lipscomb and Bergh 16, pp. 104, 128, 156.
18. See *Harvard Law Review* 36 (1922–1923), pp. 39–40; Levy 1963, pp. 154–156; and Tucker 2 (1837), p. 547.
19. See R. B. Davis 1939, pp. 205, 215–217, 220, 241–242; R. B. Davis 1946, p. 106; R. B. Davis 1964, pp. 419–420; Lipscomb and Bergh 16, p. 156; and Massachusetts Historical Society Collections, 7th series (*Jefferson Papers*) 1, pp. 332–333.
20. See Potter 1968, p. 124.

Chapter 28.

1. See Hildreth 6 (1892), pp. 626–627; *Journal of Negro History* 53 (1973), pp. 409, 414, 424; Miller 1975, pp. 45–48; and Peterson 1970, p. 999.
2. See Martineau 1968, p. 226.
3. See Lipscomb and Bergh 6, p. 8, and Meyers 1973, pp. 400–401.
4. See Miller 1975, p. 53.
5. See D. B. Davis 1970, p. 6; Frederickson 1971, pp. 5–12; Jordan 1974, p. 213; Lipscomb and Bergh 6, p. 10; McColley 1964, p. 110; Miller 1975, p. 54; and *Science and Society* 25, no. 4 (December 1961), pp. 369–371.
6. See *Journal of Negro History* 60 (July 1975) p. 436, and *Journal of Southern History* 39 (1973), pp. 395–396.
7. See Lipscomb and Bergh 15, pp. 492–493, and Moore 1953, pp. 184, 217, 227, 247, 314, 339, 343.
8. See Healey 1962, p. 147; Malone, ed., 1930, p. 134; and *Virginia Magazine* 75 (1973), pp. 290–304.
9. See Lipscomb and Bergh 16, p. 13.
10. See Graves 1966, pp. 125–126.
11. See Brown 1969, pp. 93–94; Jordan 1974, pp. 125–126, 155–157; Lipscomb

and Bergh 16, p. 101; Hunt 8, pp. 443–444; Hunt 9, pp. 51–52; McColley 1964, pp. 16–18, 24–25, 141; Meyers 1973, pp. 398–400; Nash 1964, p. 272; and Robinson 1970, p. 10.

12. See Elkins 1963, p. 210.
13. See Chevalier 1961, pp. 152–153; Koch 1966, p. 144; Lipscomb and Bergh 16, pp. 8–10; and Peterson 1970, p. 1000.
14. See Lipscomb and Bergh 16, pp. 12, 120.
15. See D. B. Davis 1970, p. 16, and Peterson 1970, p. 1000.
16. See Lipscomb and Bergh 16, p. 13.
17. See Blassingame 1972, pp. 77–80, and Lipscomb and Bergh 13, p. 220.
18. See Lipscomb and Bergh 16, pp. 10, 13.
19. See Lipscomb and Bergh 16, pp. 8–9, 13.
20. See Miller 1975, pp. 75–76, 80–82, 93, 232, 246–249.

Chapter 29.

1. See Chevalier 1961, pp. 348–350, and Martineau 1 (1843), pp. 196–197.
2. See Brodie 1974, p. 481, and Tocqueville 1 (1945), p. 380.
3. See Robinson 1970, p. 97.
4. See Brodie 1974, p. 464, and Burns 1957, p. 188.
5. See F. Wright 1963, pp. xvi–xvii, 42–44.
6. See Keller 1956, pp. 231–232.
7. See Lipscomb and Bergh 16, p. 119, and *New England Quarterly* 33 (1960), pp. 390–394.
8. See Cappon 2 (1952), p. 614, and Malone, ed., 1930, p. 134.
9. See Koch 1941, p. 111; Lipscomb and Bergh 14, p. 491; and Peterson 1970, p. 1001.
10. See Lipscomb and Bergh 16, p. 182.
11. See Chinard 1929, p. 529; D. B. Davis 1970, pp. 4, 25; and Healey 1962, p. 144.
12. See Jefferson 1959, p. 62.
13. See Tocqueville 1 (1945), p. 356.
14. See Martineau 1 (1843), p. 391.

Bibliography

Manuscripts

Hamilton, Alexander. Library of Congress, Washington, D.C.

Jefferson, Thomas. Library of Congress, Washington, D.C.

Madison, James. Library of Congress, Washington, D.C.

Marshall, John. Library of Congress, Washington, D.C.

Rush, Benjamin. Library Company, Philadelphia, Pa.

Washington, George. Library of Congress, Washington, D.C.

Books

ADAIR, DOUGLASS. *Fame and the Founding Fathers*. New York, 1974.

ADAMS, CHARLES F., ed. *The Works of John Adams*, 10 vols. Boston, 1853.

ALBERT, ROBERT C. *The Golden Voyage: The Life and Times of William Bingham*. Boston, 1969.

ALDRIDGE, ALFRED O. *Franklin and His French Contemporaries*. New York, 1956.

AMBLER, CHARLES H. *Sectionalism in Virginia*. Chicago, 1910.

AMMERMAN, DAVID. *In the Common Cause*. Charlottesville, Va., 1974.

AMMON, HARRY. *James Monroe*. New York, 1971.

ARENDT, HANNAH. *Imperialism*. New York, 1951.

BAILEY, STEPHEN K., ed. *American Politics and Government*. New York, 1965.

BAILLIE, JOHN. *The Belief in Progress*. New York, 1951.

BARITZ, LOREN, ed. *John Taylor: An Enquiry into the Principles and Policy of the Government of the United States*. Indianapolis, 1969.

BATES, ERNEST SUTHERLAND. *The Story of the Supreme Court*. Indianapolis, 1963.

BEAR, JAMES A., ed. *Jefferson at Monticello*. Charlottesville, Va., 1967.

BEARD, CHARLES A. *The Economic Origins of Jeffersonian Democracy*. New York, 1913.

BEDINI, SILVIO A. *The Life of Benjamin Banneker*. New York, 1972.

BERGER, RAOUL. *Congress v. The Supreme Court*. Cambridge, Mass., 1969.

———. *Impeachment: The Constitutional Problems*. Cambridge, Mass., 1973.

BERLIN, IRA. *Slaves Without Masters*. New York, 1974.

BERLIN, SIR ISAIAH. *The Age of Enlightenment*. Boston, 1956.

BERMAN, ELEANOR D. *Jefferson Among the Arts.* New York, 1947.

BERNAL, J. D. *Science in History.* New York, 1965.

BERNARD, JOHN. *Retrospection of America.* New York, 1887.

BETTS, ERWIN, and BEAR, JAMES, JR., eds. *The Family Letters of Thomas Jefferson,* Columbus, Mo., 1961.

BEVERIDGE, ALBERT J. *The Life of John Marshall,* 4 vols. Boston, 1919.

BLASSINGAME, JOHN W. *The Slave Community.* New York, 1972.

BOORSTIN, DANIEL. *The Lost World of Thomas Jefferson.* New York, 1948.

BOSWELL, JAMES. *For the Defence.* New York, 1959.

——. *The Ominous Years.* New York, 1963.

BOYD, JULIAN, ed. *The Papers of Thomas Jefferson,* 21 vols. Princeton, N.J., 1950–1975.

BRANT, IRVING. *James Madison, Secretary of State.* Indianapolis, 1953.

BRISSENDEN, R. F., ed. *Studies in the Eighteenth Century.* Canberra, Australia, 1968.

BRODIE, FAWN. *Thomas Jefferson: An Intimate History.* New York, 1974.

BROWN, RICHARD D., ed. *Slavery in American Society.* Lexington, Mass., 1969.

BROWN, ROBERT E. and BROWN, KATHERINE. *Virginia, 1705–1786.* East Lansing, Mich., 1964.

BRYSON, GLADYS. *Man and Society: The Scottish Inquiry of the Eighteenth Century.* Princeton, N.J., 1945.

BULTMANN, RUDOLPH. *Primitive Christianity.* New York, 1972.

BURNS, EDWARD. *The American Idea of Mission: Concepts of National Purpose and Destiny.* New Brunswick, N.J., 1957.

BUTTERFIELD, HERBERT. *The Origins of Modern Science, 1300–1800.* London, 1950.

CADY, EDWARD H. *The Gentleman in America.* Syracuse, N.Y., 1949.

CALLENDER, JAMES T. *The History of the United States for 1796.* Philadelphia, Pa., 1797.

——. *The Political Progress of Britain.* Edinburgh, 1792.

——. *The Prospect Before Us,* 2 vols. Richmond, Va., 1800–1801.

CAPPON, LESTER, ed. *The Adams-Jefferson Correspondence,* 2 vols. Chapel Hill, N.C., 1959.

CATTERALL, HELEN H., ed. *Judicial Cases Concerning American Slavery and the Negro,* 5 vols. New York, 1968.

CHASTELLUX, MARQUIS DE. *Travels in North America.* New York, 1927.

CHEVALIER, MICHAEL. *Society, Manners and Politics in the United States.* Garden City, N.Y., 1961.

CHILL, EMMANUEL. *Power, Property and History.* New York, 1971.

CHINARD, GILBERT. *Thomas Jefferson: The Apostle of Americanism.* Boston, 1929.

——. *Trois Amitiés françaises de Jefferson.* Paris, 1927.

——. *Volney et l'Amérique.* Baltimore, 1925.

——, ed. *The Commonplace Book of Thomas Jefferson.* Baltimore, 1926.

————, ed. *The Letters of Lafayette and Jefferson.* Baltimore, 1929.

CLARK, W. E. LEGROS. *History of the Primates.* Chicago, 1957.

CLIVE, GEOFFREY. *The Romantic Enlightenment.* New York, 1960.

COBBETT, WILLIAM. *A Year's Residence in the United States.* Carbondale, Illinois, 1968.

COLE, HUBERT. *Christophe, King of Haiti.* New York, 1967.

CONANT, JAMES. *Thomas Jefferson and the Development of American Public Education.* Berkeley, Calif., 1962.

COON, CARLETON S. *The Living Races of Man.* New York, 1965.

CORNER, GEORGE E., ed. *The Autobiography of Benjamin Rush.* Princeton, N.J., 1948.

COUPLAND, REGINALD. *Wilberforce: A Narrative.* Oxford, 1923.

CUNNINGHAM, NOBLE E., JR. *The Jeffersonian Republicans.* Chapel Hill, 1957.

————. *The Jeffersonian Republicans in Power.* Chapel Hill, 1963.

————, ed. *The Making of the American Party System.* Englewood Cliffs, N.J., 1965.

DANGERFIELD, GEORGE. *The Awakening of American Nationalism, 1815–1825.* New York, 1969.

DAVIS, DAVID B. *The Problem of Slavery in Western Culture.* Ithaca, N.Y., 1966.

————. *Slavery in the Age of Revolution.* New York, 1975.

————. *Was Thomas Jefferson an Authentic Enemy of Slavery?* Oxford, 1970.

DAVIS, RICHARD B. *Intellectual Life in Jefferson's Virginia.* Chapel Hill, N.C., 1964.

————. *Francis Walker Gilmore.* Richmond, Va., 1939.

————, ed. *Correspondence of Thomas Jefferson and Francis Walker Gilmore, 1814–1826.* Columbia, S.C., 1946.

DEVINE, T. M. *The Tobacco Lords.* Edinburgh, 1975.

DEWEY, DONALD C. *Marshall versus Jefferson.* New York, 1970.

DORFMAN, JOSEPH. *The Economic Mind in American Civilization,* 2 vols. New York, 1946.

DUBOIS, W. E. BURGHARDT. *The Suppression of the African Slave Trade.* New York, 1904.

DUDLEY, DONALD R. *The Romans.* New York, 1970.

DWIGHT, THEODORE. *The Character of Thomas Jefferson.* Boston, 1839.

ECHEVERRIA, DURAND. *Mirage in the West.* Princeton, N.J., 1957.

ELKINS, STANLEY W. *Slavery: A Problem in American Institutional and Intellectual Life.* New York, 1963.

FAULKNER, ROBERT K. *The Jurisprudence of John Marshall.* Princeton, N.J., 1968.

FEARON, HENRY B. *Sketches of America.* London, 1818.

FINLEY, M. I. *Aspects of Antiquity.* New York, 1969.

————, ed. *Slavery in Classical Antiquity.* New York, 1968.

FITHIAN, PHILIP V. *Journal and Letters.* Freeport, N.Y., 1969.

FITZPATRICK, JOHN C., ed. *The Writings of George Washington*, 39 vols. Washington, D.C., 1933-1944.

FLEMING, THOMAS. *The Man From Monticello*. New York, 1969.

FLEXNER, JAMES T. *George Washington*. Vol. 1: *The Forge of Experience*, Boston, 1965; vol. 2: *In the American Revolution*, Boston, 1968; vol. 3: *And the New Nation*, Boston, 1970; vol. 4: *Anguish and Farewell*, Boston, 1972.

FOGEL, ROBERT W., and ENGERMAN, STANLEY L. *Time on the Cross*, 2 vols. Boston, 1974.

FONER, PHILIP, ed. *The Works of Thomas Paine*, 2 vols. New York, 1945.

FORD, PAUL L., ed. *The Federalist*. New York, 1892.

——, ed. *The Writings of Thomas Jefferson*, 10 vols. New York, 1892-1899.

FORD, WORTHINGTON, C., ed. *Thomas Jefferson's Correspondence: Printed from the Collections of William K. Bixby*. Boston, 1916.

——, ed. *The Writings of John Quincy Adams*, 7 vols. New York, 1913-1917.

FOSTER, AUGUSTUS JOHN. *Jeffersonian America: Notes on the United States of America*. San Marino, Calif., 1954.

FREDERICKSON, GEORGE M. *The Black Image in the American Mind*. New York, 1973.

GAY, PETER. *The Enlightenment: An Interpretation*. New York, 1966.

——. *The Party of Humanity*. New York, 1966.

GENOVESE, EUGENE. *The Political Economy of Slavery*. New York, 1965.

GERBI, ANTONELLO. *The Dispute of the New World*. Pittsburgh, 1973.

GINZBERG, ELI. *The House of Adam Smith*. New York, 1934.

GRANT, MICHAEL. *The World of Rome*. Cleveland, 1960.

GRAVES, WILLIAM, JR. *Thomas Mann Randolph*. Baton Rouge, La., 1966.

GREENE, JACK. *Landon Carter*. Charlottesville, Va., 1965.

GRISWOLD, A. WHITNEY. *Farming and Democracy*. New York, 1948.

GUNTHER, GERALD, ed. *John Marshall's Defense of McCulloch v. Maryland*. Stanford, Calif., 1969.

HALL, A. R. *The Scientific Revolution, 1500-1800*. New York, 1954.

HALL, CAPT. BASIL. *Travels in North America*, 3 vols. Edinburgh, 1829.

HAMILTON, JOHN C., ed. *History of the Republic of the United States as Traced in the Writings of Alexander Hamilton and his Contemporaries*. Philadelphia, Pa., 1864.

HAMILTON, S. M., ed. *The Writings of James Monroe*. New York, 1893-1901.

HAMMOND, BRAY. *Banks in Politics in America*. Princeton, N.J., 1957.

HAMPSON, NORMAN. *A Cultural History of the Enlightenment*. New York, 1968.

HAND, LEARNED. *The Spirit of Liberty*. New York, 1960.

HANDLIN, OSCAR, ed. *This Was America*. New York, 1964.

HARRIS, MARVIN. *The Rise of Anthropolitical Theory*. New York, 1968.

HARRIS, R. W. *Reason and Nature in the Eighteenth Century*. London, 1968.

HARTZ, LOUIS. *The Liberal Tradition in America*. New York, 1955.

HAWKE, DAVID F. *Benjamin Rush, Revolutionary Gadfly*. New York, 1971.

————. *A Transaction of Free Men.* New York, 1964.

HEALEY, ROBERT M. *Jefferson on Religion in Public Education.* New Haven, Conn., 1962.

HENRETTA, JAMES. *The Evolution of American Society, 1700–1815.* Lexington, Mass., 1973.

HENRY, WILLIAM W. *Patrick Henry: Life, Correspondence and Speeches.* New York, 1891.

HILDRETH, RICHARD. *The History of the United States of America,* 6 vols. New York, 1872–1882.

Historical Manuscript Commission, *Report of the Manuscript of Sir John Fortesque.* London, 1892–1927.

HOFSTADTER, RICHARD. *The American Political Tradition.* New York, 1968.

HOME, HENRY, LORD KAMES. *Elements of Criticism.* London, 1762.

————. *Principles of Morality and Natural Religion.* London, 1751.

HOWE, DAVID W. *The Unitarian Conscience.* Cambridge, Mass., 1970.

HOWE, JOHN R., ed. *The Role of Ideology in the American Revolution.* New York, 1970.

HOWELLS, WILLIAM. *Mankind in the Making.* Garden City, N.Y., 1959.

HUNT, GAILLARD. *Life in America One Hundred Years Ago.* New York, 1900.

————, ed. *The Writings of James Madison,* 9 vols. New York, 1900–1910.

JACKSON, P. E. *Dissent on the Supreme Court.* Norman, Okla., 1969.

JANSON, CHARLES W. *The Stranger in America.* New York, 1935.

JEFFERSON, THOMAS. *The Autobiography of Thomas Jefferson.* New York, 1959.

JENKINS, C. F., ed. *Jefferson's Germantown Letters.* Philadelphia, Pa., 1906.

JENKINS, WILLIAM S. *Pro-Slavery Thought in the Old South.* Chapel Hill, N.C., 1935.

JENNESS, DIAMOND, ed. *The American Aborigines.* New York, 1972.

JOHNSON, JAMES W. *The Foundation of English Neo-Classical Thought.* Princeton, N.J., 1962.

JOHNSTON, HENRY P., ed. *Correspondence and Public Papers of John Jay,* 4 vols. New York, 1890–1893.

JOHNSTON, JAMES H. *Race Relations and Miscegenation in the South, 1776–1860.* Amherst, Mass., 1970.

JONES, W. MELVILLE, ed. *Chief Justice John Marshall.* Ithaca, N.Y., 1956.

JORDAN, WINTHROP. *The White Man's Burden: Historical Origins of Racism in the United States.* New York, 1974.

————. *White Over Black.* Chapel Hill, N.C., 1968.

KAPLAN, LAWRENCE S. *Jefferson and France.* New Haven, Conn., 1967.

KELLER, WILLIAM F. *The Nation's Advocate.* Pittsburgh, Pa., 1956.

KERBER, LINDA K. *Federalists in Dissent.* Ithaca, N.Y., 1971.

KNOLLENBERG, BERNHARD. *Growth of the American Revolution, 1766–1776.* New York, 1975.

KOCH, ADRIENNE. *Jefferson and Madison: The Great Collaboration.* New York, 1950.

———. *Madison's "Advice to My Country."* Princeton, N.J., 1966.

———. *The Philosophy of Thomas Jefferson.* New York, 1941.

KONEFSKY, SAMUEL J. *Marshall and Hamilton.* New York, 1969.

KORNGOLD, RALPH. *Citizen Toussaint.* Boston, 1945.

KRADITOR, AILEEN S. *Means and Ends in American Abolitionism.* New York, 1969.

LARKIN, PASCHAL. *Property in the Eighteenth Century.* Dublin, 1930.

LEHMAN, KARL. *Thomas Jefferson, American Humanist.* New York, 1947.

LEVY, LEONARD W. *Legacy of Suppression: Freedom of Speech and Press in Early American History.* Cambridge, Mass., 1960.

———. *Freedom of the Press from Zenger to Jefferson.* Indianapolis, 1966.

———. *Jefferson and Civil Liberties: The Darker Side.* Cambridge, Mass., 1963.

———. *The Origins of the Fifth Amendment.* New York, 1968.

LIPSCOMB, A. A., and BERG, A. E., eds. *The Writings of Thomas Jefferson,* 20 vols. Washington, D.C., 1903.

LOCKE, MARY S. *Anti-Slavery in America.* Gloucester, Mass., 1959.

LODGE, HENRY C., ed. *The Works of Alexander Hamilton,* 12 vols. New York, 1904.

LOPEZ, CLAUDE-ANNE. *Mon cher Papa: Benjamin Franklin and the Ladies of Paris.* New Haven, Conn., 1966.

LOVEJOY, ARTHUR O. *Reflections on Human Nature.* Baltimore, Md., 1961.

McCLELLAN, JAMES. *Joseph Story and the American Constitution.* Norman, Okla., 1971.

McCOLLEY, ROBERT. *Slavery and Jeffersonian Virginia.* Urbana, Ill., 1964.

———, ed. *Federalists, Republicans, and Foreign Entanglements, 1789–1815.* New York, 1969.

MACKENZIE, E. *View of the United States.* Newcastle-on Tyne, no date.

McLEAN, ROBERT G. *George Tucker.* Chapel Hill, N.C., 1961.

MACLEOD, DUNCAN J. *Slavery, Race, and the American Revolution.* Cambridge, England, 1974.

McMANUS, EDGAR J. *A History of Negro Slavery in New York.* Syracuse, 1966.

MAESTRO, MARCELLO. *Cesare Beccaria and the Origin of Penal Reform.* Philadelphia, 1973.

MALONE, DUMAS. *The Declaration of Independence.* New York, 1954.

———. *Jefferson and the Ordeal of Liberty.* Boston, 1962.

———. *Jefferson the President, First Term.* Boston, 1970.

———. *Jefferson and the Rights of Man.* Boston, 1951.

———. *Jefferson the Virginian.* Boston, 1948.

———, ed. *Correspondence Between Thomas Jefferson and Pierre Samuel du Pont, 1798–1817.* Boston, 1930.

MALTHUS, THOMAS. *An Essay on the Principle of Population.* Homewood, Ill., 1963.

MANUEL, FRANK E. *Shapes of Philosophical History.* Stanford, 1965.

MARTIN, EDWIN T. *Thomas Jefferson, Scientist.* New York, 1952.

MARTINEAU, HARRIET. *Society in America*, 2 vols. London, 1837.

——. *Society in America*. Seymour Lipset, ed. Gloucester, Mass., 1968.

MARX, LEO. *The Machine and the Garden*. New York, 1964.

MELLON, M. T. *Early American Views of Negro Slavery*. New York, 1969.

MEYERS, MARVIN, ed. *The Mind of the Founder*. Indianapolis, 1973.

MILLER, FLOYD J. *The Search for a Black Nationality*. Urbana, Ill., 1975.

MILLER, HELEN HILL. *George Mason, Gentleman Revolutionary*. Chapel Hill, 1975.

MOORE, GLOVER. *The Missouri Controversy*. Lexington, Ky., 1955.

MORGAN, DONALD G. *Justice William Johnson, The First Dissenter*. Columbia, S.C., 1954.

MORGAN, EDMUND S. *American Slavery, American Freedom: The Ordeal of Colonial Virginia*. New York, 1975.

MORRIS, ANN CARY, ed. *The Diary and Letters of Gouverneur Morris*. New York, 1888.

MORRISON, A. J., ed. *Travels in the United States*. New York, 1909.

MOTT, FRANK LUTHER. *Jefferson and the Press*. Baton Rouge, La., 1943.

MULLIN, GERALD. *Flight and Rebellion*. New York, 1972.

NAGEL, THOMAS. *The Possibility of Altruism*. Oxford, 1970.

NASH, GERALD, ed. *Issues in American Economic History*. Boston, 1964.

NELSON, WILLIAM H., ed. *Theory and Practice in American Politics*. Chicago, 1964.

NEW, CHESTER. *The Life of Henry Brougham*. Oxford, 1961.

OAKES, C. G. *Sir Samuel Romilly*. London, 1935.

O'CONNOR, THOMAS H. *Lords of the Loom*. New York, 1968.

OTT, THOMAS C. *The Haitian Revolution*. Knoxville, Tenn., 1973.

PADOVER, SAUL K., ed. *The Washington Papers*. New York, 1955.

PALMER, ROBERT R. *The Age of the Democratic Revolution: The Struggle*. Princeton, N.J., 1964.

PARKES, HENRY B. *The Pragmatic Test*. San Francisco, Calif., 1940.

PARKINSON, RICHARD. *A Tour in America*. London, 1805.

PARRY, J. H. *Trade and Dominion*. New York, 1971.

PARTON, JAMES. *The Life of Thomas Jefferson*. Boston, 1889.

PAULDING, J. K. *Letters from the South*. New York, 1835.

PERSONS, STOW. *American Minds*. New York, 1958.

——. *The Decline of American Gentility*. New York, 1973.

PETERSON, MERRILL D. *The Jeffersonian Image in the American Mind*. New York, 1960.

——. *Thomas Jefferson and the New Nation*. New York, 1970.

——, ed. *Thomas Jefferson: A Profile*. New York, 1967.

PHILBRICK, FRANCIS S. *The Rise of the West*. New York, 1965.

PLUMER, WILLIAM. *William Plumer's Memorandum*. New York, 1923.

POTTER, DAVID. *The South and the Sectional Conflict*. Baton Rouge, La., 1968.

———. *History and American Society*. New York, 1973.

——— and FEHRENBACHER, DON. *The Impending Crisis*. New York, 1976.

POUND, ROSCOE, ed. *Federalism as a Democratic Process*. Rutgers, 1942.

PRIEST, WILLIAM. *Travels in the United States*. London, 1802.

RAINSFORD, GEORGE N. *Congress and Higher Education in Nineteenth Century America*. Knoxville, 1972.

RANDALL, HENRY S. *The Life of Thomas Jefferson*, 2 vols. New York, 1858.

RANDOLPH, SARAH. *The Domestic Life of Thomas Jefferson*. New York, 1958.

RISJORD, NORMAN K. *The Old Republicans: Southern Conservatism in the Age of Jefferson*. New York, 1965.

———, ed. *The Early American Party System*. New York, 1969.

RITCHESON, CHARLES. *The Aftermath of Revolution*. Dallas, Tex., 1969.

ROBERTS, KENNETH, and ROBERTS, ANNA M., eds. *Moreau de St. Mery's American Journal*. New York, 1947.

ROBINSON, DONALD L. *Slavery in the Structure of American Politics*. New York, 1970.

ROCHEFOUCAULD-LIANCOURT, DUC DE LA. *Travels through the United States of North America*, 2 vols. London, 1792.

ROGERS, GEORGE C., JR. *The Evolution of a Federalist*. Columbia, S.C., 1962.

RUSH, BENJAMIN. *An Address on the Slavery of Negroes in America*. New York, 1969.

RUTLAND, ROBERT A. *The Papers of George Mason*, 3 vols. Chapel Hill, N.C., 1970.

SANTAYANA, GEORGE. *The Genteel Tradition*. Cambridge, Mass., 1971.

SCHACHNER, NATHAN. *Thomas Jefferson: A Biography*. New York, 1953.

SCHLESINGER, ARTHUR, JR. *The Imperial Presidency*. Boston, 1973.

SCHOEPF, JOHANNES D. *Travels in the Confederation*, 2 vols. Philadelphia, Pa., 1911.

SENECA. *Epistulae Morales*. New York, 1917.

SHACKLETON, ROBERT. *Montesquieu*. Oxford, 1961.

SHEEHAN, BERNARD W. *Seeds of Extinction*. Chapel Hill, 1973.

SIMPSON, LEWIS P. *The Federalist Literary Mind*. Baton Rouge, La., 1962.

SIZER, THEODORE, ed. *The Autobiography of Colonel John Trumbull*. New Haven, 1957.

SMELSER, MARSHALL. *The Democratic Republic*. New York, 1968.

SMITH, ADAM. *The Wealth of Nations*. New York, 1937.

SMITH, PAGE. *Jefferson: A Revealing Bibliography*. New York, 1976.

SMYTH, ALBERT H., ed. *The Writings of Benjamin Franklin*, 10 vols. New York, 1905–1907.

STEWART, DONALD H. *The Opposition Press of the Federalist Period*. Albany, N.Y., 1966.

STORY, JOSEPH. *The Life and Letters of Joseph Story*. 2 vols. London, 1851.

STRICKLAND, WILLIAM. *Journal of a Tour in the United States of America, 1794–1796.* New York, 1971.

SURRENCY, ERWIN C., ed. *The Marshall Reader: The Life and Contribution of Chief Justice John Marshall.* New York, 1955.

SUTCLIFFE, ROBERT. *Travels in the United States.* Philadelphia, 1812.

SYRETT, HAROLD, ed. *The Papers of Alexander Hamilton,* 22 vols. New York, 1961–1975.

TANSILL, CHARLES C. *The Secret Loves of the Founding Fathers.* New York, 1964.

——. *The United States and Santo Domingo, 1798–1873.* Baltimore, Md., 1938.

TAYLOR, JOE GRAY. *Negro Slavery in Louisiana.* Baton Rouge, 1963.

THORPE, EARL T. *Eros and Freedom in Southern Life and Thought.* Durham, N.C., 1967.

TOCQUEVILLE, ALEXIS DE. *Democracy in America,* 2 vols. New York, 1945.

TODD, CHARLES BURR. *The Life and Letters of Joel Barlow.* New York, 1884.

TRACY, ANTOINE L. C. D. DE. *A Commentary and Review of Montesquieu's Spirit of the Laws.* New York, 1969.

TUCKER, GEORGE. *The Life of Thomas Jefferson.* Philadelphia, 1837.

TURNER, LYNN W. *William Plumer of New Hampshire.* Chapel Hill, 1962.

VEREKER, CHARLES. *Eighteenth Century Optimism: A Study of the Interrelations of Moral and Social Theory in English and French Thought between 1689 and 1789.* Liverpool, 1967.

VOLNEY, C. F. *A View of the Climate and Soil of the United States.* London, 1804.

VYNERBERG, HENRY. *Historical Pessimism in the French Enlightenment.* Cambridge, Mass., 1958.

WALLACE, GRAHAM. *Human Nature in Politics.* New York, 1921.

WALSH, ROBERT. *An Appeal from the Judgment of Great Britain.* London, 1819.

WALTON, GARY M., ed. *Explorations in Economic History.* New York, 1975.

WARREN, CHARLES. *Odd Byways in American History.* Cambridge, Mass., 1942.

Warren-Adams Letters, 2 vols. Boston, 1917–1925.

WARVILLE, BRISSOT DE. *New Travels in North America.* Boston, 1797.

WASHBURN, SHERWOOD L. *The Social Life of Early Man.* Chicago, 1961.

WASHBURN, WILCOMB E. *The Indian in America.* New York, 1975.

WATSON, GEORGE. *The English Ideology.* London, 1973.

WEBER, MAX. *The City.* New York, 1958.

WEBSTER, DANIEL. *The Writings and Speeches of Daniel Webster.* Boston, 1903.

WELD, ISAAC, JR. *Travels through the States of North America.* London, 1799.

WHITE, G. EDWARD. *The American Judicial Tradition.* New York, 1976.

WHITE, LEONARD D. *The Jeffersonians.* New York, 1951.

WHITE, MORTON and LUCIA. *The Intellectual Versus the City.* Cambridge, Mass., 1962.

WILLEY, BASIL. *The Eighteenth Century Background: Studies in the Idea of Nature in the Thought of the Period.* London, 1940.

———. *The English Moralists*. New York, 1964.

WILLIAMSON, CHILTON. *American Suffrage: From Property to Democracy*. Princeton, N.J., 1960.

WILTSE, CHARLES. *Jeffersonian Tradition in American Democracy*. New York, 1960.

———. *The New Nation*. New York, 1961.

WOODRESS, JAMES. *A Yankee's Odyssey: The Life of Joel Barlow*. Philadelphia, Pa., 1958.

WRIGHT, BENJAMIN F. *The Growth of American Constitutional Law*. Boston, 1942.

WRIGHT, FRANCES. *Views of Society and Manners in the United States*. Cambridge, Mass., 1963.

Articles

COHEN, WILLIAM. "Thomas Jefferson and the Problem of Slavery," *Journal of American History* 56 (1969): 503–526.

WEXLER, VICTOR G. "'Made for Man's Delight': Rousseau as Antifeminist." *American Historical Review* 51 (April 1976), 2:226–291.

Magazines and Journals

American Historical Review
Harvard Law Review
Journal of Economic and Business History
Journal of Economic History
Journal of Negro History
Journal of Southern History
Michigan Law Review
Mississippi Valley Historical Review
New England Quarterly
Pennsylvania Magazine of History and Biography
Political Science Quarterly
Quarterly Journal of Economics
South Carolina Historical and Genealogical Magazine
University of Pennsylvania Law Review
Virginia Argus
Virginia Magazine of History and Biography
William and Mary Quarterly

Index

Index